D1433414

TERRORISM IN IRELAND

Edited by
YONAH ALEXANDER and ALAN O'DAY

CROOM HELM
London & Canberra
ST. MARTIN'S PRESS
New York

© 1984 Yonah Alexander and Alan O'Day
Croom Helm Ltd, Provident House, Burrell Row,
Beckenham, Kent BR3 1AT
Croom Helm Australia, PO Box 391, Manuka,
ACT 2603, Australia

British Library Cataloguing in Publication Data

Terrorism in Ireland
   1. Terrorism − Ireland
   I. Alexander, Yonah   II. O'Day, Alan
   322.4'2'09415   HV6433.173
   ISBN 0-7099-0522-X

All rights reserved. For information, write:
St. Martin's Press, Inc., 175 Fifth Avenue, New York, NY 10010
First published in the United States of America in 1984

Library of Congress Cataloging in Publication Data
Main entry under title:

Terrorism in Ireland.

   1. Terrorism − Ireland − Addresses, essays, lectures.
I. Alexander, Yonah.   II. O'Day, Alan.
HV6433.173T47   1984   303.6'25'09415   83-3106
ISBN 0-312-79260-3

Printed and bound in Great Britain

CONTENTS

Notes on Contributors
Introduction. Yonah Alexander and Alan O'Day

NOTES ON CONTRIBUTORS

Yonah Alexander (co-editor) is Professor of International Studies and Director of the Institute for Studies in International Terrorism at the State University of New York at Oneonta and Research Associate at the Center for International and Strategic Studies at Georgetown University.

Paul Bew is Lecturer in Modern History at the Queen's University of Belfast.

D.G. Boyce is Reader in Political Science and Government at University College, Swansea, in the University of Wales.

Suzann Buckley is Associate Professor of History and Womens' Studies at the State University of New York at Plattsburgh.

Tom Corfe was formerly a Senior Lecturer at the Sunderland Polytechnic and is now a freelance writer.

Martha Crenshaw is Associate Professor in Political Science at Wesleyan University (Connecticut).

Tom Gallagher is Lecturer in Peace Studies at the University of Bradford.

Sheridan Gilley is Lecturer in Ecclesiastical History, Department of Theology, at the University of Durham.

Ken Heskin is Lecturer in Psychology at Trinity College, Dublin.

John Kirkaldy teaches for the Open University and has previously been Lecturer in Contemporary European Studies at the Polytechnic of North London.

Pamela Lonergan studied at the State University of New York where she was, also, a research assistant.

Michael McKinley is Lecturer in Politics at the University of Western Australia.

Alan O'Day (co-editor) is Senior Lecturer in History at the Polytechnic of North London.

Raymond J. Raymond is Assistant Professor in History at the University of Connecticut.

Philip Schlesinger is Senior Lecturer and Head of the Sociology Department at the Thames Polytechnic.

Ken Ward is Lecturer in History at the New University of Ulster.

INTRODUCTION

Yonah Alexander and Alan O'Day

Terrorism and other forms of political violence are topics of obvious importance though the ebb and flow of public interest rather depends on the presence or absence of spectacular incidents. Hence certain occasions, for instance, the Birmingham pub bombings in late 1974, explosions on Oxford Street in London, political murders, and injuries and deaths inflicted on soldiers and animals in London parks make vivid impressions on the public mind. However, the daily routine of killings and psychological terrorism in Northern Ireland now fails to attract much interest - they have become the expected and no longer seem exceptional. However, it is the regularity of violence which makes it so vital an issue. For how long can the people of Northern Ireland endure violence? What effects will years of terrorism have on the afflicted population? To what extent can a liberal democratic society like Britain co-exist with rampant terrorism activity within its legal boundaries? Just as Irish terrorism has not admitted to an easy solution, questions about the impact of violence on British and Irish society are not easily answered either. Yet there is urgency in both asking appropriate questions and attempting to supply answers or, at least, to dispel certain myths about terrorism and terrorists. The essays in this volume attempt to look at certain selected aspects of Irish terrorism and to advance the discussion of those topics. It is a modest attempt to provide building stones for what must be a large and complex structure.

The volume begins with three essays which assess some of the broader and international dimensions of Irish terrorism. Except for the Irish terrorists' dependence on foreign arms and American cash, they are not deeply involved with similar movements elsewhere. Nevertheless, the wider facets of Irish terrorism and violence remain important. Indirectly, Lord Jellicoe's report to the Government in February 1983 makes precisely this warning. He and others have seen that London may become the battle ground for warring political factions from the Middle East and elsewhere. Before 1978 international terrorism in Britain was insignificant when compared with violence generated by Irish problems but now police have to deal with as many of these acts as those of Irish provenance. London is not alone. Paris has experienced many terrorism incidents totally unrelated to French politics. Lord Jellicoe warns, 'My view is that we may be facing this threat for many years to come.' He urges the extension of police powers of arrest and detention of suspected terrorists. His recommendations are at present only freshly before the Government and public and will be a matter of intense debate. What is significant about his report, though, is that a clear recognition has emerged that terrorism in Britain is a virus with many origins which will not be eradicated easily or quickly. The dangers are clear. International terrorists working in concert with their Irish counterparts or simply conforming to a similar time scale have the potential to create havoc.

Michael McKinley's essay introduces a timely reminder that to date Irish terrorist movements have few international links. While the potential for wider contacts may be present the Irish conflict is a localized affair where the acts of Republican inspired terrorism fit the Clausewitzian definition of the practice of diplomacy by other means. Prior to rushing headlong towards visions of London in flames, it is crucial to assess, as Dr McKinley does, the likelihood of this outcome. Yet, if the international links of Irish terrorism have been exaggerated, Raymond J. Raymond provides an equally timely indication that the one area of traditional Republican sympathy, the Irish-Americans, today are still a bastion of support for political violence in Ireland. Dr Raymond sees a great deal of muddle in the United States and among American policy makers over the Northern Ireland question. He argues that a few committed Republicans in the United States have had disproportionate influence in misleading Americans over the true intentions of the I.R.A. Dr Raymond stresses the international nature of the Northern Ireland crisis when he states that the American Government has a constructive role to play in the situation but that this can only be achieved when U.S. policy makers disabuse themselves of their cherished illusions about the fundamental character of the problem in Ulster.

A further dimension of the crisis is highlighted by Tom Gallagher's consideration of the impact of the violence on people of Irish origin in Scotland. As he points out, Scotland is an appropriate region to study for there over many generations communal tensions based on religion and origins have been intense. Some of this passion manifests itself in crowd violence at the football matches of the Glasgow rivals Rangers and Celtic – the former being the traditional Scots and Protestant club and the latter representing Scots Catholics of Irish origin. Certainly the question of how the large community of people of Irish origin in Britain has been treated or thinks it has been treated is a matter of importance when assessing the impact of Irish terrorism. No doubt on certain occasions, for instance, following the Birmingham pub bombings, the Irish community has been faced with physical harrassment. Probably Irish men and women have had an additional set of informal barriers to overcome – the sort of discrimination which is difficult to document. But Dr Gallagher shows that overall even in Scotland the story is far from bleak. Contrary to what might have been anticipated, Scots of all persuasions have stayed passive in the face of communal fighting in Northern Ireland. His conclusions afford a ray of hope for the future reconstruction of Ulster and for limiting the extent and repercussions of Irish terrorism.

The second part of the volume consists of four case studies of particular aspects of the terrorism problem – the role of women, the psychological make-up of terrorists, political assassination, and a historical consideration of the attitudes of the Catholic Church. In an age when the rhetoric of female equality rings through the liberal democratic world it seems worthwhile to ask how such ideals have impinged upon terrorist movements. Suzann Buckley and Pamela Lonergan find that a 'modernized' language does not conceal the profoundly traditional and limited character of both Republicanism and Ulster Unionism. Women, in their opinion, have remained merely supportive of their menfolk and families although they may in instances, like applying pressure on hunger strikers to break their fasts, play decisive roles. To the degree that women have pushed into political action, Buckley and Lonergan assert, it has been to secure personal and traditional ends rather than to advance or deepen the general position of women. Ken Heskin sees substantial traditionalism from a quite different perspective. His investigation of terrorists suggests that the typical I.R.A. bomber is not a half-mad social misfit but a normal personality who behaves rather similarly to other ordinary people who belong to conflict-oriented groups. The terrorist is _of_ the community sharing in its perceptions. To cure terrorism requires something stronger than merely capturing a few killers or attempting to isolate them from the larger community. Tom Corfe's essay on political assassination suggests that it is an Irish technique of long standing now but one which has never been particularly effective. Curiously, the level of public horror at assassinations does not correspond to the particular relevance of a killing. Finally, Sheridan Gilley looks at the position of the Irish Catholic Church on political violence. His particular canvas is the nineteenth century which he uses to remind us that the British have long expected rather a lot from the Catholic Church in the way of assistance in curbing violence.

Yesterday, as today, the ability of the Church to fulfil its assigned role has been tempered by Irish realities. During the hunger strikes of 1980 and 1981 British leaders and the media assumed that Church leaders could exert effective influence over the prisoners and their families. As usual, the British found the clerical response disappointing. Dr Gilley demonstrates the complexity of the relationship between Church and people and notes the paradox of Protestant Britons in other respects secular and profoundly suspicious of Catholic authority seeking to employ that mythical power on an Irish secular movement.

The third section of this book looks at the problem of political communication and terrorism. Four themes are explored. George Boyce assesses the relationship between public opinion and terrorism in Northern Ireland. He makes the important observation that though violence has a long pedigree in Irish society terrorism does not. He notes that the present-day I.R.A., however, has been able to play upon the attitudes, prejudices, susceptibilities, and fears of various public opinions that exist in the British Isles and abroad. At the same time the most effective forms of counter-terrorist tactics have not been acceptable to a wider British and world opinion and thus have not been used consistently. He believes that rather than dazzling 'political solutions' or wide-ranging Anglo-Irish agreements, successful pacification calls for a sensitive appreciation of the needs and fears of very small, very clannish groups of people.

Public opinion of a different type is the subject matter of essays by John Kirkaldy and Ken Ward. The former studies the record of Fleet Street and the latter the performance of the American television news coverage. Both come to the depressing conclusion that the sort of information which has been disseminated is of a poor quality. If the press is the 'fourth estate' and information the basis of a free people making intelligent decisions, we have much to worry about for there is little to be complacent over in the reporting of the crisis in Northern Ireland. Indeed, Philip Schlesinger argues that there is also little to be complacent about in our assumption concerning the supposed links between terrorism and the media. He suggests that the media have engaged in self-regulation to such a degree as to form part of the crisis-management apparatus of the state. The media, then, has become an agent of the state and not independent or critical. He wishes to place the issue of prevention of terrorism within the broader context of the British state's inability to discipline labour and to restore the profitability of industry.

The final section, the future of terrorism, seeks to project tomorrow's prospects by understanding the sources and influences which have sustained Republican inspired violence. Paul Bew points out the inability of either the

Nationalist or Unionist communities to comprehend the other side's feelings, worries or aspirations. He, also. comments on the increasingly neglected economic roots of antagonism which continually assures the ranks of the I.R.A. are replenished. There is, Dr Bew asserts, little prospect for the eradication of terrorism until the class inequities of Northern Ireland are mitigated. Martha Crenshaw agrees with Dr Bew that we must expect the persistence of I.R.A. terrorism in the foreseeable future. She observes that such violence now has the double coupon of being right with history and has accrued remarkable prestige from its apparent successes. But, even if the British state should prove successful now in curtailing Catholic support for the I.R.A., she suggests that terrorism will continue because, from an I.R.A. perspective, history justifies its cause and methods. In this case, as in others, historical legacies make attempts at starting with a clean slate difficult and probably impossible.

In all this volume contains thirteen essays with only Philip Schlesinger's having been published previously. A range of issues are discussed by the various contributors who themselves reflect different perspectives and who are drawn from several disciplines - history, political science, psychology, sociology, theology, feminist and peace studies. The contributors live in both the North and South of Ireland, Britain, the United States and Australia. No panacea to the current problem of Northern Ireland is offered, facile solutions are eschewed. Our objective is to offer some feeling for the complexity of the problem. No-one reading this book will come away with the impression that peace will be brought to Ulster easily or quickly.

PART ONE

OVERVIEW

Essay One

THE INTERNATIONAL DIMENSIONS
OF TERRORISM IN IRELAND

by Michael McKinley

Many times since 1968 the circus of carnage which the situation in Ulster has often resembled has left observers so alienated that they were unable to explain what their senses described. In general this resulted from a confrontation with conditions which were unaccustomed to the point of being foreign, as this 1980 account illustrated.

> Anyone accustomed to wandering around the countries of the Third World would find little in Ulster that is unfamiliar. Guerrillas, suspended democracy, armies and gunmen on the streets, unthinkable behaviour in prisons, questionable and questioned frontiers, squalid housing, grinding poverty, indifferent multi-nationals, once vibrant economies in visible decline - these are the essential characteristics of much of the contemporary world. The uniqueness of Northern Ireland is that it lies, not south of the equator, but just off the shores of Britain.[1]

In particular it was a consequence of the inability to understand why the United Kingdom - its political system stable and democratic, its wealth distributed reasonably well, its society open and obsessively moderate - should include within its boundaries organisations, commonly denoted terrorist and paramilitary, which displayed an almost autistic fury across their whole range of actions. Many observers, therefore, adopted the habit of mind which Joseph Conrad so clearly manifested in The Secret Agent over seventy years ago in relation to an act of anarchist terrorism:

> a blood-stained inanity of so fatuous a kind that it was impossible to fathom its origins by any reasonable or even unreasonable process of thought.[2]

Since 1968 it is obvious that the "circus" and the concomitant refusals to countenance rational explanations for certain violent phenomena in Northern Ireland have been matched by extravagant propositions concerning the international dimensions of the conflict. And in turn these propositions have struck an answering chord in many putative strategists and others who were attracted to studies of violence which have earned the appellation "international terrorism". This is not to claim that the conflict in Northern Ireland was, or is, without its influences from outside the Six Counties - the "American dimension" refutes this - but the evidence to hand suggests a far different picture than Walter Laqueuer's multinational, corporate view of an international terrorist operation:

> ...planned in West Germany by Palestine Arabs, executed in Israel by terrorists recruited in Japan with weapons acquired in Italy but manufactured in Russia, supplied by an Algerian diplomat, and financed with Libyan money.[3]

Indeed, it is the purpose of this essay to challenge the assertions that there existed in Northern Ireland an international terrorist network as evidenced by the contacts, supply of arms and operations of the paramilitary organisations involved in the conflict, particularly the Irish Republican Army (IRA). The reality, it will be argued, supports this view only selectively and provides but a poor basis for a general proposition of this type.

I propose, therefore, to confine this essay in accordance with the following four terms of reference. First, the period under discussion is, for the most part, 1968-1980. Second, although several paramilitary organisations exist in Northern Ireland, the principal focus will be upon the Provisional IRA, as it is both the most active and the one about which the greatest number of claims are made in respect of international affiliations and operations. To this end, unless otherwise stipulated the initials IRA will denote the Provisionals. Third, the "American dimension" of the troubles is excluded. Despite the fact that groups within the United States have proved to be an important source of finance, arms, and psychological support for the Provisionals, this aspect is the subject of a separate essay. And fourth, the linkages which will be examined will be only those which relate to terrorism in Ireland per se. I stipulate this because the international contacts of the paramilitary organisations may be regarded as having existed on two levels. The lower, or less important, of these questions the sense of the term "contact" because in very many cases it denoted no more than loose association, or close proximity of (mainly) left-wing groupings which occasionally and temporarily matured into an actual meeting. It was as though the various organisations were agitated, as in Brownian motion, and that they were therefore subject to the probability of contact by virtue of existing as somewhat like particles in a common and restricted universe. When their paths, which seldom if ever obeyed the same compass, coincided, there was generally cause for concern as though it signified the conjunction of evil when in most instances a less sanguine conclusion was justified. As Peter Janke wrote of this phenomenon.

The point about these links and one could go on adducing evidence of contacts. is that it is not at all an international revolutionary conspiracy, but rather a network of tiny groups acting illegally that comes across one another in their search for arms and are prepared to help when called upon for a meal, a night's shelter an overcoat, a hair dye or a railway ticket.[4]

Furthermore, it should be appreciated that this judgment applies not only to contacts with groups (or governments) in Africa, Asia (including China), Latin America and very often, Western Europe, but also Eastern Europe and would cover even the rather erratic ventures made by the Soviet Union into the "troubles". To say that Soviet propaganda organs have consistently distorted events in Northern Ireland to conform to a pre-conceived pattern of a popular uprising by an oppressed community against "British imperialism", is an understatement. Indeed they so grossly misrepresented the situation that their pronouncements were ludicrous.[5] Notwithstanding this, and the need to develop friendly relations with Ireland (with which it established diplomatic relations in 1974), Moscow has maintained a cautious public attitude towards the Official IRA and a critical one in relation to the Provisionals.

There were, of course, exceptions, but these were of a different, higher, order of significance than those previously considered. It seems that once the situation in Northern Ireland had established its credentials as a conflict - i.e. as a shooting match - it attracted the attention and, it is alleged, the attendance of the acolytes of war. The appeal of some of these rested upon their past exploits, as with Otto Skorzeny, a former Nazi SS Colonel who was wanted for war crimes in his native Austria, and whose principal claim to notoriety was his leadership of the raid to rescue Mussolini after the fall of the Fascist Government in 1943. Twenty-eight years later he was linked with Ruairi O Bradaigh of Provisional Sinn Fein. Despite Skorzeny's apparent sympathy, however, the significance of his interest in the Northern conflict existed very largely in the collective imagination of the editorial staff of the Sunday Telegraph. All that that publication could muster to justify its article on him was an unconfirmed report of a meeting with O Bradaigh in Spain.[6]

Much later in the period under review, Protestant militants also came up with a World War II figure in support of their cause. In 1977 John McQuade, a former Chindit, claimed he had formed a secret "army" that would "seek out and destroy" the IRA in Ulster.[7] Evidently he was unsuccessful; indeed his only success may have been in securing a lengthy two-column coverage in the Daily

Telegraph. McQuade in any case was a Northerner and his enterprise was probably more notable for what it negatively emphasised - that reports of foreign interest generally related to the IRA. But they did not always concern themselves with figures from the past.

According to Father O'Neill of St Eugene's Roman Catholic Cathedral in Derry, two North Koreans and an Algerian (not to mention a number of Englishmen), were present among the Provisional gunmen of Creggan and the Bogside in 1972.[8] In 1977 a further measure of notoriety was added to the Republican cause with disclosures made in the Old Bailey of approaches made to a former member of the Parachute Regiment and Angolan mercenary recruiter, John Banks, for the supply of arms. As with so many of the instances cited in this and the following chapter it was, for the IRA, an indiscriminate move. Everybody and everything ended up in the wrong place: Banks in the service of the Special Branch; British Provisionals in the Old Bailey, and later, gaol; and the arms in (probably) Antwerp.[9]

However the IRA has not been without its "successes". According to David Barzilay, it was "known" that the organisation had attracted two "foreign" electronics experts to work upon sophisticated trigger mechanisms for a bombing campaign to be conducted in Northern Ireland. He also claimed that these experts were not to be found in the North but "in the South", an allegation which appeared to be based on unspecified information provided to him by the British Army. Nevertheless, for those who were convinced that the Republic was a "haven for terrorists" one subsequent allegation put the matter beyond doubt and confirmed Barzilay's cryptic reference to such people being "very well protected".[10]

In his machinations to avoid a United States deportation order, a former Provo "active", Peter McMullen, stated to the Boston Globe that the IRA had received training and encouragement from a regular Irish Army colonel in precisely the same type (photo-cell and radio-controlled) of explosive devices which Barzilay referred to the previous year. He also claimed that some of the electronic components were provided by an Irish television manufacturer sympathetic to the cause.[11] Naturally the Irish Army rejected these allegations out of hand, while McMullen, for his part, denied knowledge of the officer's identity. It is difficult, therefore, to draw from the evidence a conclusion of any strength. Hence the most balanced view which could be stated, of the period 1969-74 anyway, may be that of Lieutenant-Colonel George Styles, the commander of the British Army bomb disposal teams in Northern Ireland in that period:

> ...really we never could prove or disprove the
> rumours about foreign mercenaries. But, pressed to
> an opinion, I'd say it's more than likely they

existed...[12]

Notwithstanding this, one conclusion which may be drawn is that it is not always helpful to look beyond the borders of the United Kingdom, nor even the island of Ireland, for instances of external links to the "troubles". Strictly speaking, of course, the Republic of Ireland is a foreign country in relation to the United Kingdom, but given the unique relationship which exists between it, Great Britain, and Northern Ireland, it seems a contrivance to classify as international, or external, linkages from the Republic and Great Britain into Northern Ireland. Also, I would argue that, in this instance, North-South distinctions are meaningless. Provisionals on either side of the Border belong to the same organisation, and both the British and Irish Governments have recognised this. Further, that it would involve an unnecessary and meaningless division of labour to impose a North-South framework upon an analysis of the contacts between both wings of the IRA and various organisations in Britain.

This is not to claim that the role of such contacts was any greater than those excluded from this analysis under Janke's dismissal, rather that their involvement signified two aspects of the support network of the paramilitary organisations. The first was that these were often of a domestic or relatively local origin and that to ignore this fact results in a distortion of any study of the external links. Second, the more significant links are those with people or groups that have demonstrated a willingness either to supply, or engage in, sustained campaigns of violence.

According to this criterion, of the almost kaleidoscopic selection of the terrorist and separatist/nationalist spectrum which the IRA established contacts with in the early and mid-1970s, the most important appears to have been with various Basque organisations. In April 1972, the IRA, the Basque Euskadi Ta Askatasuna (ETA) - Basque People and Liberty - and the Breton FLB were reported to have signed a political agreement which was followed some two years later by a statement which embraced other, smaller national minorities such as Piedmontese. Via the auspices of the appropriate Sinn Fein, the officials and various ethnic groupings followed suit with a socialist equivalent, in September 1974, known to initiates as "The Brest Charter".[13] What this duality of contacts suggested was confirmed by a deeper study. The ETA, like the IRA in 1969-70, was subject to splits. Hence, the officials, in keeping with their 29 May 1972 unilateral declaration of a ceasefire, lined up with a "socialist revolutionary party" in which the operative term was "socialist". The Provisionals, on the other hand, by 1979 anyway, found more common ground with Euskal Izaultzarako Alderia (EIA) - the Basque Revolutionary Party - an ETA breakaway which supported "armed actions" and "refuse[d]

7

reformism".[14]

Although there were further similarities in their respective stands on national sovereignty and independence, and other areas besides,[15] it was the willingness of both the IRA and the (then) ETA to reciprocate with firearms and technical (explosives) expertise that placed this link in an altogether different category from those covered previously. Contact between the two organisations dates back at least to 1972 when Jose Echebarrieta, one of ETA's most influential members, was reported to have made two secret visits to Dublin to seek contact with both the Officials and the Provisionals. According to Maria McGuire, Basque leaders met Provisional Chief of Staff, Sean MacStiofain, and in exchange for training in the use of explosives, provided 50 revolvers.[16] For years, however, this was the sole item of substance upon which wild speculations were made of an IRA-ETA network. Yet the resemblance in the technical field, between the assassination of the Spanish Prime Minister, Admiral Luis Carrera Blanco, in December 1973, and that of the British Ambassador in Dublin, Christopher Ewart-Biggs, three years later,[17] gave further credence to the Spanish Police's 1974 claim of the existence of a secret pact between the two.[18]

Whether, as was alleged (but denied by the ETA), the IRA supplied the explosives used in the former, or as Albert Parry implies, the IRA trained the ETA on a continuing basis[19] is, like so many questions in this area, undetermined. Both were possible but neither necessarily followed. As to the former, explosives appear not to have been an overly difficult material for terrorists to obtain in the last decade, and with regard to the latter, a training in explosives was surely within the range of competence of the ETA once they had learned the first lessons. Besides, there is no record of further "quid pro quo" exchanges after that mentioned by McGuire. Since the time of Ewart-Biggs' death, the IRA-ETA-EIA link has been somewhat less substantial and confined to an exchange of visits and congratulatory statements. In all, given that this link appears to have been the most significant, there is little to justify other than the most modest claims being made as regards the paramilitary organisations in Northern Ireland and their place within an international terrorist network.

At first sight this was in sharp contrast to the supply of arms from external sources to the same groups. If the information relating to the discovery of arms - be they actually in their possession, or intended for same - is correct, the paramilitaries could have forgone few opportunities to obtain them from every quarter. By 1973, at least 282 types of weapon had been discovered[20] representing fifteen countries of origin (manufacture).[21]

Later disclosures were equally impressive. Official

figures released on the eighth anniversary of the British Army's involvement in the Northern Ireland conflict showed that it had by then recoverd 902,554 rounds of ammunition, 257,489 lb. of explosives, 297 machine-guns, 2,667 rifles, 2,962 pistols, 881 shotguns, 18 rocket launchers, 57 rockets, 427 mortar tubes and 441 mortar shells. In addition, Army personnel had defused 2,828 bombs.[22] (And this does not include the amounts recovered, etc., from paramilitary sources by the Irish and other Governments.) From a closer examination of arms recovery information it became clear that not only had the numbers of weapons increased, but also they had become both more modern and sophisticated as well.[23] From the presence in the Provisional IRA arsenal of various semi-automatic weapons, historian of the IRA, J. Bowyer Bell, concluded that:

> ...basically the Provos were better armed for their business than the British Army for theirs. Equally significant by the end of 1977, the Provos were far more elegantly armed than the loyalist paramilitaries or the militias-in-being...[24]

These figures and reports notwithstanding, it is important to treat the following discussion of the actual supply of arms to the conflict in the North with caution. First, it must be emphasised that it is concerned only with the estimated (maximum) 40-50 per cent of arms which originated from sources outside of the USA.[25] Second, in relation to these countries of origin, there is considerable merit in the repeated caveats given by British Ministers of State for Defence, to the effect that the place of manufacture of arms and explosives was not necessarily the place where the terrorists obtained them.[26]

Third, it is necessary to be sceptical of claims that some suppliers of arms, by virtue of that fact, were exerting a controlling influence over the conflict. As Richard Rose wrote:

> Probably the outsiders who have benefited most from the Troubles have been dealers and brokers in arms from Hamburg to Libya. To continue to benefit, however, they must maintain their distance. Otherwise, they too will find themselves tagged as Catholic arms dealers, whether they are actually Christian, Muslim or atheist.[27]

And finally, the scale of the operation must at all times be borne in mind. By the standards of many conflicts the above inventory of recovered weapons was modest. Nevertheless, no-one would deny the effectiveness of the IRA campaign since 1968, even if it has not been successful in its own terms. The point to be made, of course, in relation to arms, was simply but accurately expressed by Peter Janke: "very, very few suffice".[28]

From the seven Western European countries which

produce one quarter of the world's weapon supplies, came the bulk of the arms that is the concern of this essay.[29] Having stated that, it must also be repeated that it is in this part of the discussion that the cautions mentioned before are particularly apposite. Thus a common feature to be noted was that the city in which the negotiations took place, the port of loading, and the city of origin of the arms were almost invariably different within each venture. Furthermore the distinction between Eastern and Western Europe was blurred to the point of meaninglessness.

Maria McGuire, for example, wrote of accompanying Daithi O Connaill (Dave O'Connell), a member of the Provisionals' Army Council, between Dublin, Zürich and Amsterdam, for the latter to negotiate a deal in Prague with Omnipol, the sales organisation for the Czech arms factory at Brno, for a shipment ex Rotterdam.[30] It was, for all that a not unusual episode in which the elements of foreign venues, intrigue and (frequently) failure were to be repeated on numerous occasions.

Unfortunately for a work such as this most of the publicly available information has been derived from the successful interception of illegal arms intended for Northern Ireland. The reports of such operations were, therefore, subject to security considerations and devoid of virtually all mention of the politics of both purchase and apprehension. Furthermore, in many cases the arms in question appeared to be part of an independent arms dealer's stock on hand, from which information the conclusion to be drawn was that the deal was made on financial rather than political criteria.[31] And this becomes more compelling in the common knowledge that no government in Western Europe has permitted either its state or private enterprises to sell arms to the paramilitary organisations in Northern Ireland. Consequently, in those instances where only an antiseptic collection of facts were reported such that Browning pistols (and matching ammunition) had been imported from the Continent, or that French arms, ammunition, and chemicals were discovered, there are but poor grounds for deducing more than that the Provisionals (in the foregoing cases) took advantage of the international commercial availability of weapons and supplies.

Furthermore, nothing in the foregoing cases seriously challenges previous judgments in respect of communist intervention by Czechoslovakia or the Soviet Union. There remains of course, a residue of uncertainty arising from O Connaill's apparent success in, to use McGuire's words, "making an arms deal with a Communist country."[32] (emphasis added). Subsequently, further doubt was added by the recovery of Czech pistols so new that they did not appear in any standard works of reference.[33] Yet no matter how suggestive these facts were of an active and substantial Czech interest in the North, they must also be tempered by accounts which supported a contrary interpretation.

The first is that O Connaill, his negotiations with Omnipol in Prague notwithstanding, was required to work through an American intermediary and an arms dealer. As both were regarded by him as untrustworthy, and as the latter was to be contacted in Brussels,[34] there are grounds for inferring that Omnipol did not agree to supply arms direct to the Provisionals.

The second concerned O Connaill's certainty that he was shadowed in Switzerland by the "Czech or Russian secret police"[35] which, if true, and taken in conjunction with the first reason, may have indicated that the manufacturers were in some doubt as to the wisdom of supplying those he represented.

The third was Jones' (presumably) expert opinion that the Browning pistols mentioned earlier, and the Czech pistols discovered at the same time, may well have represented arms obtained by a single purchase.[36] If so, the case alleging Czech intervention would be weakened correspondingly, since the supply of arms of differing national origin would (again presumably) have been the prerogative of an independent dealer.

Finally, the absence of any further body of evidence which could implicate the Czech Government or its agencies since the time of O Connaill's 1971 approach to Omnipol, must question the resolve with which Prague was prepared to act, if at all.

The same is true of the Soviet Union, but in its case the conclusion is less equivocal. This does not mean that Soviet-made weapons have not been in evidence – they have – in the form of rifles, hand-grenades, and even rocket launchers, but the numbers involved have been small, and there was no serious suggestion that they signified Russian intervention.[37] However, the discovery of Soviet weapons in transit for the Provisionals did signify that Soviet weapons were quite widely available on the international market (see the following discussion of the Claudia affair).

The case which perhaps best illustrated this was the celebrated affair surrounding the use of Soviet-designed, but Bulgarian made RPG-7 rocket launchers in November 1972.[38] Although the Soviet Government rejected a Foreign Office request for its help in investigating the matter, and although it seems certain that it could have assisted, the opinion in Whitehall was that there was no direct connection between the Soviet Union and the Provisionals.[39] Indeed, the likeliest source of weapons was a group of Middle East states (discussed in the following), at least four of which had been Russian clients for the RPG-7.

In turn this underscored the Provisionals' logistics dilemma. Close co-operation between American, British and Irish law enforcement agencies ensured that attempts to supply arms from the United States were made at a high risk and could be successful only in odd lots.[40] Hence a reliance on that source meant that the IRA would be slow to rearm. The alternative, it appears, was to expedite this objective by recourse to sympathetic organisations and regimes, but at even greater risk. The RPG-7s, despite their successful debut, are to be seen within the latter category. It is necessary, therefore, to turn to a consideration of a small number of revolutionary regimes/movements.

With but tolerable distortions, "small number" is easily reduced to two · in descending order, the Libyan Government of Colonel Mu'ammar al-Qadhafi and the Palestine Liberation Organisation (PLO). Basically, Qadhafi's interest in the Northern Ireland situation stemmed from his perception of it as a nationalist revolution in which the IRA for the most part, represented the progressive forces. Anti-colonialism, his self-appointed role as an instrument of God, and an understanding of the whole Ulster Question which bordered on fantasy were contributing factors.[41] And even then this may not have covered them all. Robert Fisk probably captured the essence of his motivation when he wrote "The nature of the struggle seems to be of less importance than the fact it exists..."[42]

While the aforementioned disposition would not necessarily preclude it, the suggestion that Qadhafi was acting as a proxy for the Soviet Union in this period seems unlikely. Apart from the fact that his country was not receiving Soviet arms, the President was also known to have directed his displeasure towards Egyptian leaders for their over-dependence on such supplies, and to have attacked the Soviet Union during the 1973 conference of non-aligned nations in Algiers.

Notwithstanding Qadhafi's outlook it was March 1973 before it found a tangible expression. On the 28th of that month, the Claudia, a 298 ton coaster, was intercepted by the Irish Navy off Helvick Head, Co. Waterford, and was found to contain five tons of arms intended for the IRA.[43] It was an operation which not only provided an illustration of the propensity for the conflict in Northern Ireland to exceed the boundaries of the Province, but also allowed brief glimpses of the complexities which have increasingly attended it.

It was complex because the voyage of the Claudia had been the subject of another one of those international deals, initiated in Germany and negotiated in two foreign capitals, Tunis and Tripoli. The vessel itself had taken considerable pains both to conceal its route - by re-tracking - and to disguise the immediate origins of its cargo - by loading it in international waters. It was, moreover, registered in Cyprus by the German Giromar Shipping Company (for which Lloyds had no address), a company 90 per cent owned by Gunther and Marlene Leinhauser, the former of whom had been convicted in 1967 for attempting to smuggle arms from Czechoslovakia to Kurdish rebels in Iraq.[44]

The concern that the IRA had been able to negotiate such a relatively large arms purchase was only heightened by persistent reports that the Claudia had delivered between one and three arms shipments to Ireland in the previous fifteen months.[45] Furthermore, there were questions which remained unresolved, although dismissed by the Irish Government, as to whether the 5 tons of arms recovered were the entire shipment or but part of a very much larger one which had been either trans-shipped earlier or dumped overboard when the crew of the Claudia realised their predicament.[46] The belief that the Soviet Union, despite the appearance of arms of its manufacture in the cargo, was probably not involved was of little consolation to the British and Irish authorities. The evidence all too clearly pointed to the fact that Libya was.

One prior development in this general period prompted speculation that another state (or organisation) had adopted a similar role. The introduction of the Soviet-designed RPG-7 rocket launcher to the IRA's arsenal in November 1972 did much to give this suggestion currency some months before the Claudia affair. At that time, the general suspicion which attached to Qadhafi as a supplier of arms to the IRA was of a low order: Libya was not an arms client of the Soviet Union, whereas Algeria, Egypt, Iraq, and Syria were reported to have received recent shipments of RPG-7s.[47] As best as can be ascertained from available sources, however, these four client states were not directly implicated and the IRA's possession of the weapons in question is still put down to an undetected arms deal negotiated in the Near or Middle East sometime in 1972.[48]

While the Claudia incident appeared not to dampen Qadhafi's enthusiasm for the Northern Ireland conflict, his subsequent attitude towards it was somewhat erratic. From being a benefactor of the IRA in 1972-73, he became, in 1974, the willing host for supplicant parties from the other side of the province's paramilitary divide. Early that year the Libyan Government began to consider whether, in addition to the Provisionals, some extreme "Loyalist" groups which favoured an independent Ulster might not also qualify for support as "anti-imperialistic". Qadhafi himself was reported to have expressed admiration for the Ulster Workers' Council Strike of May 1974 which, according to his Irish education adviser, Eddie O'Donnell, the Libyan leader viewed as a "valid mechanism" that reminded him of his own non-violent coup in September 1969.[49]

Thus, in late 1974, the Ulster Defence Association (UDA) was invited to participate in a visit to Libya arranged for the Development of Irish Resources organisation (DIR), a previously little known group suspected of being subject to

13

"Republican" influences. However, according to DIR's chairman, Walter Hegarty, the organisation was not aligned with any political cause, and it had co-operated with the UDA's involvement because of a common interest in the development of Ireland's offshore oil and gas resources.[50]

This was a credible position as it was a motive equally attributable to those seeking a united Ireland and those contemplating an independent Northern Ireland (as the UDA were known to favour if the British link could not be maintained to its satisfaction[51]). But it was not entirely consistent with Eddie O'Donnell's claim that he secured the UDA invitation so that the Libyans could meet the men behind the Protestant strike, nor with the reports that the UDA had made representations to Qadhafi, particularly concerning his patronage of the IRA, and certainly not with the simultaneous presence of a Provisional Sinn Fein delegation at the same hotel in Tripoli at which the UDA were staying.

The reasons given were plausible, but in relation to the representations by the UDA and the presence of the Provisionals, incomplete. Whatever the truth in UDA spokesman Tony Lyttle's claim that his organisation had been invited to Libya "to enlighten [the Qadhafi regime] on the truth of the Northern Ireland situation" it was surely to be expected that every opportunity would be taken to do so in any case. In turn, the arrival of the Provisionals some five days after the loyalists was guaranteed by the anxiety on the former's part that an attempt was under way to disrupt their arrangement with Libya, and that this should be strenuously resisted.[52]

In the ensuing period it was possible, without putting too fine a point on it, to conclude that the IRA had not been successful. The first indication that Qadhafi may have undergone a change of heart was provided by a statement made in November 1974 by Glen Barr, a leading UDA figure on the visit.

> ...the Libyan Government appeared to be under the impression that the IRA were Freedom Fighters... We were able to show them the other side of the coin. They were interested in our proposal for an independent Northern Ireland and I think we were successful in putting our case across...[53]

From the time of this announcement until late 1977 there was no further evidence of arms reaching Ireland from Near or Middle East sources. Yet in the month following the UDA visit, Qadhafi was reported as having told senior Maltese Government officials that his aid to the IRA to that point was £5 million, although he did not specify whether this was in cash or in kind.[54] November 1974 also saw the report of a similar statement from Kuala Lumpur, Malaysia, made in this instance by the Libyan Prime Minister, Major Abdul Jalloud.[55]

After April 1975, however, the equivocal nature of the

Libyan attitude became more pronounced. After receiving an Irish parliamentary delegation in that month a Libyan spokesman disclaimed any further interventionary role for his government.[56] From further statements by the delegation leaders on their return this was taken to imply that Libya would no longer aid any illegal organisation in Ireland, including the IRA.[57] Yet, in so far as the supply of arms was concerned, further developments suggested that the Libyan Government, while it had come to a realisation that the Irish question was not as simple as it first believed, was not about to embrace a practice of self-denial with regard to Northern Ireland. In September 1975, two of its representatives, including Eddie O'Donnell, met with UDA leaders in Northern Ireland and, it was understood, discussed in general terms the potential for Libyan investment in the event of British withdrawal.[58] If this was true then the core of Libyan interest in Northern Ireland was still derived from, and defined in terms of, Qadhafi's Anglophobia. By extension, he was seeking, through discussions with the UDA, to manipulate the Province's tensions, if not to his advantage, then certainly to Britain's embarrassment and discomfort. Furthermore, given the strength of his hatreds, and the fact that his Government's (then) recent pronouncements eschewing support for "illegal organisations" left much to be desired in Dublin and London, some residual doubt remained whether Libya had actually desisted from supplying arms to the IRA. Indeed, Qadhafi's statements in this time were, without being too specific as to how, so strongly supportive of the IRA that its propaganda in early 1976 continued to proclaim the affinity between Libya and the Provisional cause.[59] Presumably this would not have been the case had Libyan support been withdrawn.

From then until the close of the period under review, any assessment of Libyan involvement in the affairs of Northern Ireland must be based on developments of an indeterminate and sometimes conflicting nature. Following the December 1977 arrest of Provisional Chief of Staff, Seamus Twomey, in Dublin, there were unofficial reports of IRA leaders once more visiting Tripoli. In this period the IRA received both a military and a psychological boost with the introduction of the M.60 machine gun to its arsenal, a weapon then suspected in some quarters of being supplied from the Middle East. A 1979 report by Peter McMullen, a former member of both the Parachute Regiment (from which he deserted), and the IRA (from whom he defected), tended to confirm this suspicion. McMullen claimed that in 1977-78 the Provisionals had received seven tons of arms from Libya, including "Russian surface-to-air missiles, RPG5s and RPG7s".[60] By his account the major obstacle to their use had been the prospective operators' inability to understand the Russian text of the instruction manuals![61] Finally, it was alleged that Thomas McMahon, convicted in early 1980 for the murder of Lord Mountbatten, had perfected his remote-control bomb-making skills (under Russian supervision) in Libya.[62] Against such "evidence" three contraindications should be taken into account. The first was that it was later held, with near certainty, that the origin of the M.60 machine guns brandished by the Provisionals in early 1978 was later held in a National Guard armoury in Danvers, Massachusetts, from whence they were stolen in August 1976.[63] The second was that, in the period late 1977-mid 1980, which presumably was sufficient time for a translation of instruction manuals to be effected, there was no recorded instance of an attack involving an RPG-7 or a surface-to-air missile. Both indications were therefore consistent with, and supportive of, the third, which was a report of discussions held in Libya between Qadhafi and the British Conservative Party's Shadow Foreign Secretary, John Davies. According to Davies, the Provisional IRA had ceased to be regarded as among the world's liberation movements, from which it was inferred that Libya was no longer prepared to support the Provisionals.[64]

As on previous occasions when Qadhafi had given assurances to this effect there was much unsaid that encouraged doubt as to his real intentions. Davies was not then regarded as being within the top echelon of the Tory opposition's hierarchy, even less could he have been regarded as a representative of the British Government. Thus Qadhafi's choice of messenger was curious. Davies' report moreover, suffered not only from being based on inference but also from being given ex parte. (In combination, these considerations may have accounted for the poor attention given to it in the press.) Even then its contents provided no answer to whether Libya had recently supplied the Provisionals with arms, or more importantly, whether it was absolutely committed to not supplying them in the future. Furthermore, two additional reasons to doubt Qadhafi's sincerity were afforded by the knowledge that at the time of Davies' visit, a sale of trucks, aircraft and spare parts worth more than £200 million was being held up by the United States Government in an attempt to persuade Libya from harbouring international terrorists.[65]

Given Qadhafi's outlook and record of erratic behaviour it could not be assumed that any action he took in the face of American pressure was likely to become an established feature of Libyan policy. And even if to all appearances it did, there remained a distinct possibility that one or more of the numerous Arab liberation movements he gave considerable backing to - such as the PLO - might act as his proxy with the IRA.[66] Indeed, there was evidence that this organisation had been so involved for some years, albeit in a secondary and shadowy capacity. To be precise this activity was carried out by two of the PLO's constituent groups, the Popular Front for the Liberation of Palestine (PFLP), and Al Fatah.

One commentator on Middle East affairs, Yonah Alexander, dates IRA-PFLP co-operation from as early as 1968.[67] Certainly, by May 1972, it was more widely acknowledged, even heralded, as in Radio Cairo's exultant report of the massacre at Lod Airport, near Tel Aviv, by three members of the (Japanese) Red Army specially recruited for the occasion.

The participation of three Japanese members in the suicide action at Lod proves that the PFLP succeeded in obtaining international support as a truly revolutionary movement. Strong bonds exist between the Palestinian resistance organizations and other liberation movements in Africa, the I.R.A., the Vietnamese revolutionaries.[68]

But as evidence of a substantial nexus with the IRA, this was very thin as the contacts then in evidence appeared to be at the ideological level and almost exclusively concerned Official Sinn Fein.[69] Thus there was no suggestion that Irish revolutionaries were willing to emulate the Japanese example and be sacrificed for the Palestinian cause; ironically, only the night before the above broadcast, the Official IRA had ordered an immediate cessation of all hostilities other than those of a defensive nature.

Subsequently, whether as a result of this unilaterally declared cease-fire or some other reason, the PFLP liaison with Ireland was expanded to include the Provisional IRA.[70] In May 1972, at Baddawai in the Lebanon, the PFLP and Black September hosted a meeting attended by representatives of numerous terrorist and nationalist/separatist organisations including the IRA.[71] In the same year subsequent meetings in Algeria, Japan and Dublin gave rise to reports not only of a closer liaison between such groups, but also of agreements "to supply each other with arms and information and to carry out operations on behalf of and in the name of a brother movement".[72] Furthermore, McMullen claimed in 1979 that a young Arab woman living in Dublin was the liaison officer between the PLO and the IRA.[73]

To date, the IRA-PFLP co-operation has allegedly found a tangible expression in three areas. The first concerns the provision of training facilities. If testimony given in an Old Bailey trial by mercenary-recruiter, John Banks, was to be believed, an IRA training camp had existed in Algeria, in 1973, on the edge of the Sahara Desert.[74] While doubts as to Banks' reliability as a witness were raised by his admission that he had previously lied on two counts to the London Evening Standard, the substance of his claim received confirmation the following year.

In a BBC documentary on terrorism, Abu Maher, a member of the PFLP team, which attacked an El Al aircraft at Athens airport in 1968, told of a camp run by his organisation at which people from several nations, including

Ireland, were being trained. (Neither the location of the camp nor a more detailed description of the Irish members was provided.) In the same programme an IRA presence at a training camp in Aden was reported by Israeli Colonel Elihu Lavite, who claimed that this information was forthcoming from his interrogation of terrorist Lidwina Janssen.[75] McMullen also claimed that in more recent times (after 1977), the IRA leadership was able "to attract money, arms and training from the Palestine Liberation Organisation and representatives of Libyan Leader Colonel Qadhafi".[76]

Substantially similar accounts were provided following the deployment of the United Nations Interim Force in Lebanon (UNIFIL) in 1978. While covering its activities, Irish Times correspondent, Conor O'Clery, interviewed a PLO colonel in Beirut who advised that a small number of IRA members had received instruction in explosives and guerrilla warfare techniques, in Lebanon, until just prior to that time (June 1978). O'Clery also noted that UN observers in UNIFIL were in agreement that such an arrangement had been in existence for a period of years.[77] In some quarters this was held to be a disingenuous assessment: Alexander, for example, contended that the training continued through the course of 1978 "apparently with the full knowledge of the UN officers serving in the area", and that at least 10 IRA members arrived for training in each of the following 15 months.[78] Notwithstanding the differences as to place, quantity and time which were to be found between the foregoing accounts, they were sufficiently consistent to establish the IRA's client relationship with the PFLP for the provision of services.

McMullen's 1979 claim would extend this to a second area. According to him the murder of Sir Richard Sykes, British Ambassador to the Netherlands, in the Hague in March 1979, was a combined IRA-PLO operation.[79] Unfortunately (again) for this inquiry, there were other, conflicting accounts as to who might have been responsible: in Holland, spokesmen for the IRA, and for the Italian Red Brigades on behalf of the IRA claimed the deed.[80] And further doubt must be attached to McMullen's claim as, by the time of the incident in question, he had been persona non grata with the IRA for at least a year.[81]

If either of these "arrangements" also included the provision of arms it was not readily apparent from the available information. However a case may be made that this third area was the subject of a separate understanding with another PLO constituent, Al Fatah. In the literature on terrorism, Al Fatah (Yasser Arafat's group) was cited as the source of IRA-intended arms on three separate occasions since 1972. The first appears only in Alexander and there are simply no records of a seizure of such a consignment in Antwerp in December 1972.[82] (However, he may have meant the 1977 episode, which follows.) There was also some doubt as to the second, which was John Barron's unsubstantiated claim that the Claudia's captured shipment had been supplied from Al Fatah, and not Libyan stocks.[83] The remaining instance concerned a consignment of arms which was discovered in Antwerp, but in December 1977, and which led to the trial of Seamus McCollum in Dublin in July 1978. While his testimony in no way implicated Al Fatah, the markings on several of the boxes did.[84] Of themselves they were less than conclusive evidence of its involvement, but in the context of the RPG-7s used in 1972, the Claudia interception, and Qadhafi's interest in Ireland, they were sufficient to encourage the belief that Al Fatah, or an organisation closely aligned with it, was a likely source of some of the IRA's arms shipments.

The strength of this belief varied – from numerous commentators on the right who, irrespective of the evidence, saw the Middle East suppliers as mere agents for what was fundamentally a Soviet enterprise of sowing disaffection where it could – to the official and frequently expressed view of Her Majesty's Government, which was somewhat less sanguine. During one period of Question Time in the House of Commons in 1978 a number of Members who were inclined to the former view were assured by the Northern Ireland Secretary, Roy Mason, that the IRA's contacts with "Palestinian terrorists" were neither "significant" nor even "a real link".[85] Indeed, Mason extended his assessment to cover not only organisations in the Middle East but "international terrorist" organisations in general.[86]

In support of his Government's position the Secretary relied in part upon the relative ease with which arms could be purchased in the Middle East and seemed to imply that such deals were commercially rather than politically inspired.[87] In part though, he relied upon a form of wishful thinking which was controverted by evidence cited earlier in this chapter, namely that

> The appalling record of the Provisional IRA within
> the Province and its lack of political support do not
> enable it to establish any significant international
> links.[88]

He thereby left unanswered why it was that such organisations as the Red Army and the Red Brigade were seemingly able to operate on an international scale while enjoying considerably less political support than the IRA. Equally, Mason was ignoring the substantial support which had been lent the Provisionals from the United States, and even their ability, demonstrated over some eight years, to operate in Northern Ireland in the face of the very difficulties he described. However, his position was arguably reinforced by none other than Yasser Arafat who, when asked if the PLO supplied arms to the IRA, replied, "No, I am searching for weapons myself".[89] But in the same interview

19

the Al Fatah leader was also reported to have denied that the PLO had "any links" with the IRA which, in the light of the foregoing comments, questioned his credibility.

These Middle-East sources excepted, the only other source of arms outside the United States that warrants inclusion here is Canada, because of several attempts in that country to supply arms and finance to both Loyalist and Republican paramilitary organisations in Northern Ireland. The first evidence of this supportive activity was seen in August 1969 with an announcement by some 150 Toronto Irish-Canadians that they intended sending money, which could be used to buy guns if necessary, to the women and children of the (Catholic) Bogside in Derry.[90] Thereafter the networks of the US-based Irish Northern Aid Committee (NORAID) and the Irish Republican Clubs were extended to Canada but support activities on behalf of both the Official and Provisional movements were thought by observers to be limited by the mainly Protestant complexion of the estimated two million Canadians of Irish descent. Nevertheless, in 1972 (admittedly a "high" year in relation to international interest in Northern Ireland), it was reported that "about $40,000" had been forwarded by NORAID.[91] (It has not proved possible to obtain other reliable estimates of financial aid.)

In the matter of supplying arms the available record is slightly more forthcoming. Judging by this, 1973 and 1974 were the years in which would-be gun-runners were most active. And the police most diligent. Three arms shipments intended for the Irish Republican Army (IRA) were intercepted - one on the Canadian side of the Canada/United States border,[92] and the other two as part of a combined operation involving Canadian and Irish authorities, in Toronto and Dublin, respectively.[93]

The total amount of arms involved was small, but in each case consistent with the numbers recorded in several other seizure operations originating in the United States:[94] 15 rifles and ammunition in the border case;[95] 5 sten guns, 12 hand guns, about 18,000 rounds of ammunition, and 10 hand grenades. in Toronto; and 17 rifles, 29,000 rounds of ammunition, and 60 pounds of gunpowder in Dublin.[96]

Of particular interest in the border interception was the American affiliations of Joseph Myles, a resident of Michigan, who was described by the Canadian authorities as an "executive officer of an American organization Northern Irish Aid" (sic).[97] For his pains he, and at least three accomplices, were sentenced to jail terms ranging from 17 months to two years.[98]

As regards the combined operation, two aspects were notable. The first concerned the co-operation between the Canadian and Irish authorities over a three month period, while the second was that the shipment was intended for the Official IRA. This was somewhat curious, because that organisation had unilaterally declared a cease-fire on 29 May 1972. However, it appeared not to denote a renewed campaign of violence by the Officials. According to Commissioner Edward Lysyk of the Royal Canadian Mounted Police (RCMP), investigations revealed that the man responsible for the attempt, one John Patrick Daniel Murphy, was engaged in a "lone operation".[99] His efforts, therefore, were probably to be explained by the Official IRA's need, as a paramilitary organisation, to maintain an armoury for self-defence and in case a situation arose in which it would need to reconsider engaging once more in an armed struggle. There is no evidence that it has done so since. Thus, with regard to both wings of the IRA, the influence of the Canadian connection upon their ability to operate in Northern Ireland was minimal.

The same was true in respect of the Loyalist paramilitary organisations, although official estimates do concede that "one or two" successful attempts have been undertaken to supply arms out of Canada.[100] In addition, at least two attempts were unsuccessful. Both were related and both involved consignments which were destined for the Ulster Defence Association, either for the purpose of training members on the Yorkshire moors, or for use in Northern Ireland itself.[101]

As was the case with the attempts in aid of Republican elements, these Loyalist ventures were of a small scale and included World War II-vintage arms (e.g. Sten-guns).[102] In common with the Murphy attempt they were also frustrated by international (British and Canadian) police co-operation – involving the Hampshire police at the Southampton docks and the RCMP in Toronto – which led to the arrest of two Canadians and three Britons.[103]

Subsequent to these events, there is little evidence of Canadian involvement in the affairs of Northern Ireland. In 1977 a claim was made by one Jim Kennedy that Canada was being used by Loyalist extremists as a base for gun-running with the knowledge of the Canadian authorities. However, since Kennedy was at the time in an immigration jail in Vancouver and was thought not to be Kennedy, but James McCann, an IRA fugitive, the accuracy of his statement was open to considerable scepticism.[104] Yet it, or at least not that part of it which referred to the continuing role of Canada as an arms source – could not be dismissed out of hand. In Dublin, just three months later, Donald C. Jamieson, the Canadian Secretary of State for External Affairs, made a statement in which he admitted that, because of his country's long undefended border, it was possible that illegal arms movements to Northern Ireland were taking place. As he put it, "sometimes these things do happen".[105]

Mention will be made of just one other area of external support which the IRA might have received. Although there is no reference to it in any published documents, the possibility – more the probability – that the IRA occasionally obtained the services of professional assassins from outside Ireland, for service in Northern Ireland, has been suggested.[106] Because of the sensitive nature of security operations in the North, no further information was forthcoming, and it is therefore not possible to elaborate on the matter beyond this paragraph.

At this point it is appropriate to return to the perspective of what is being discussed in this essay. It principally concerns the supply of arms to a relatively localised conflict which, between 1968 and 1978, claimed the lives of some 2,000 people. Sadly, in terms of the natural and man-made hazards to which the world is accustomed, it is frequently regarded as a small toll of a small war in the north-eastern confines of a small country. Other indices confirm this: according to a Foreign and Commonwealth Office authority on the situation in Northern Ireland, ballistic signatures indicated, that in 1978, only about 1,000 weapons were in active use in the Province. This, and the relatively small quantity described in virtually all of the IRA's attempts to acquire arms, both frustrated and successful, is a caution against taking too expensive a view of the current "troubles".

The record of paramilitary operations related to the conflict reduced its international dimensions even further. By far the greatest number of incidents were the responsibility of one organisation - the Provisional IRA - although on a few occasions its pre-eminence was challenged by the Officials,[107] some unnamed Protestant extremists,[108] and latterly the Irish National Liberation Army (INLA).[109] Even then, in the context of some of the more spectacular or news-generating activities associated with international terrorism, the IRA's could only be described as modest. It had not, for example, ever attempted to hijack an aeroplane, nor has it, the Niedermayer incident notwithstanding,[110] been noticeably drawn to kidnapping.[111] In other fields, however, such as those of ambush, assassination and bombing, the IRA demonstrated an ability to sustain a virtual urban guerrilla war which, in 1978 and in Northern Ireland alone, continued to occupy a regular British garrison of over 13,000, the part-time Ulster Defence Regiment of some 8,000, and a considerable proportion of an expanded Royal Ulster Constabulary.[112] Across the Border the comparable figure was less than 5,000.[113] As a 1978 British intelligence report concluded:

> [The IRA] has the dedication and the sinews of war
> to raise violence intermittently to at least the level
> of early 1978, certainly for the foreseeable
> future...
>   [Its] "campaign" of violence is likely to
> continue while the British remain in Northern
> Ireland.[114]

Although statistics are but poor indices of the suffering

and disruption to daily life which has been caused by the conflict in Northern Ireland, they do at least reveal that its more violent manifestations have been contained within the Six Counties (1837 dead); only secondarily and sporadically were they experienced in the Republic (73 dead); and mainland Britain (65 dead).[115] Outside these boundaries they were seen but fleetingly - in Western Europe towards the close of the period, and exclusively against targets defined as British (less than 5 dead).[116] What these statistics suggest, then, was the intention, or perhaps the inability, on the part of the antagonists not to expand the conflict beyond the borders of Northern Ireland under "normal" circumstances.

A close inspection of the records of out-of-state incidents lends considerable support to this interpretation. They appeared to have arisen out of various ulterior, as opposed to central, motives which otherwise governed the conflict in the North. And there were sound reasons for the general avoidance of foreign battlegrounds, as McGuire explained:

> ...it was our [the Provisional IRA's] definite policy then not to take the war to England. We knew we would not be able to sustain operations there: on classic guerrilla theory you fight only where the population will support you and give you refuge. Previous attempts to carry the war to England had been... disastrous and counter-productive.[117]

Thus revenge,[118] the need of a bargaining chip[119] and the desire to dramatically re-focus British attention on the Province[120] were the motivating forces behind British operations when they were undertaken. It was as though the paramilitaries had decided upon a fundamental distinction - regarding the war in Northern Ireland in the classical Clausewitzian sense of the practice of diplomacy by other means, and the terrorist operations further afield as the gruesome arm of public relations.

Developments in 1978-1981 may lead to a modification of this view, if they continue. The murder of Airey Neave (by the INLA) in March 1979, and Provisional IRA bomb attacks on the Hammersmith Territorial Barracks, the Royal Air Force base at Uxbridge, and the Bromley-by-Bow gas works in December 1980 may be indications that the principles of "classical guerrilla theory" have been put aside with regard to operations in England. At the end of 1981 it was still not possible to decide this matter unequivocally. Although targets loosely defined as "military" had been subjected to several bombing attacks in the summer and autumn, it was difficult to see them as a departure from the IRA's previous modes of conduct, particularly since they could be construed as retribution for the collapse of the Maze Prison hunger strike.

Moreover, such instances were no less noticeable in Europe. There, too, British diplomats,[121] Army establishments and military personnel[122] were the focus of attacks. There was also speculation (1976-77) that the Provisionals were connected with the incendiary attacks on British interests in Austria,[123] and the murder of a Belgian bank official (presumed to have been mistaken for a British diplomat at the North Atlantic Treaty Organisation headquarters) in March 1979.[124] This pattern (such as it was) in Europe appeared to confirm, albeit belatedly, McMullen's 1979 claim that the IRA had, in early 1974, created a new position - Director of European Operations.[125]

But neither English nor European operations were the main thrust of the campaigns conducted by any of the paramilitary organisations in Northern Ireland. In the final analysis the conflict remained, throughout the period under review, essentially within the dimensions of the questions from which it sprang. Although the antagonists garnered supplies from external parties, the fight itself never seemed likely to include, to any significant level, other than the Irish and the British in Ireland. For that reason, Sir Walter Scott's description of it all was as accurate in 1981 as it was in 1825.

> Their factions have been so long envenomed, and they have such narrow ground to do their battle in, that they are like people fighting with daggers in a hogshead.[126]

Notes

1   Richard Gott, "A Foreign Land", Guardian Weekly, 24 February 1980, p.4.
2   Joseph Conrad, The Secret Agent: A Simple Tale (London: J.M. Dent, 1947), p.x.
3   Walter Laqueur, Guerrilla: A Historical and Critical Study (London, Weidenfeld and Nicolson 1977), p.324 (hereafter cited as Laqueur, Guerrilla).
4   Peter Janke, "The Response to Terrorism", Royal United Services Institute for Defence Studies (RUSI), Ten Years of Terrorism: Collected Views (London: RUSI, 1979), p.25.
5   See Dev Murarka, "Moscow Takes A New Look At Ulster", The Observer Foreign News Service, No.30023, 24 March 1972; and "Soviet Distortions On Northern Ireland", February 1977, a paper held by the International Institute for Strategic Studies, and noted "Source Not Known". In the writer's opinion, this second paper, which juxtaposes Soviet comment with verifiable fact was produced by British Government authorities for general distribution to offices and personnel who might have a need to refute Soviet allegations.
6   Sunday Telegraph, 31 October 1971, pp.1 and 3.
7   Daily Telegraph, 8 February 1977.
8   BBC Radio 4 Programme, "Today", as cited in Clutterbuck, Protest and the Urban Guerrilla (London:

Cassell, 1973), pp.217-18.
9   Daily Telegraph, 7 April 1977, and Guardian, 7 April 1977.
10   Irish Times, 28 September 1978.
11   Boston Globe, 7 September 1979, p.2.
12   George Styles, Bombs Have No Pity: My War Against Terrorism (London: William Luscombe, 1975), p.111.
13   Galician, Breton, and Welsh groupings were represented in company with Official Sinn Fein and Herriko Alderi Socialista Iraultalea - People's Revolutionary Socialist Party - to sign a "Declaration on the struggles against colonialism in Western Europe" [Roger Faligot, "Basques, Sinn Fein and the Brest Charter", Hibernia, 20 January 1978, p.12 (hereafter cited as Faligot, "Basques, Sinn Fein and the Brest Charter")].
14   ibid.
15   ibid.
16   Maria McGuire, To Take Arms: A Year in the Provisional IRA (London: Macmillan, 1973), pp.71 and 110 (hereafter cited as McGuire, To Take Arms).
17   Both were killed by the detonation of an under-the-road explosive device as their respective motor vehicles passed over it.
18   Roger Faligot, "Basques, Sinn Fein and the Brest Charter", p.12.
19   Albert Parry, Terrorism: From Robespierre to Arafat (New York: Vanguard Press, 1976), pp.171-2.
20   Parliamentary Debates, House of Commons, Official Report, Vol.811, 15 February 1971, col.1237 (hereafter cited as House of Commons, Official Report).
21   Austria, Belgium, Czechoslovakia, Finland, France, West Germany, Hungary, Italy, Japan, New Zealand, Spain, Sweden, the United Kingdom, the USA and the USSR (House of Commons, Official Report, Vol.851, 20 February 1973, col.47). Later a sixteenth was added - Venezuela (R.D. Jones, "Terrorist Weaponry in Northern Ireland", British Army Review (April 1978): 19 (hereafter cited as Jones, "Terrorist Weaponry in Northern Ireland")).
22   Times, 15 August 1977.
23   For examples, see the reports of a mortar attack on Belfast's Aldergrove Airport using electrical ignition devices (Guardian, 8 March 1975), and the Hijacked beer train episode in which it emerged that the Provisionals had become skilled in the use of light-sensitive circuits and what are known as radio-controlled improvised explosive devices (Times, 23 November 1978).
24   J. Bowyer Bell, The Secret Army: The IRA 1916-1979, revised and updated edn. (Dublin: Academy Press, 1979), pp.439-40 (hereafter cited as Bell, The Secret Army).
25   And even this figure is subject to considerable doubt. In the 1970s there was some disagreement in Anglo-American

relations as to exactly what constituted arms of US origin, and hence, the proportion of total arms that were classified accordingly. British estimates were as high as 85 per cent - a claim that the US Government found quite unacceptable. The figure of 40-50 per cent is the writer's estimate, based on both an analysis undertaken elsewhere and recent British estimates: see my The Ulster Question in International Politics, 1968-1978, unpublished PhD thesis submitted in the Australian National University, Canberra (hereafter cited as McKinley, PhD Thesis); and International Herald Tribune, 30 July 1981.

26   House of Commons, Official Report, Vol.850, 13 February 1973, col.321; and Vol.851, 20 February 1973, col.47.

27   Richard Rose, Northern Ireland: A Time of Choice (London: Macmillan, 1976), p.68.

28   Peter Janke, "The Response to Terrorism", Royal United Services Institute for Defence Studies (RUSI), Ten Years of Terrorism: Collected Views (London: RUSI, 1979), p.25 (hereafter cited as RUSI, Ten Years of Terrorism).

29   Conor Brady, "Provisions of Violence", Irish Times, 25 March 1977. The seven countries were given as: Belgium, France, Italy, Sweden, Switzerland, the UK and West Germany.

30   McGuire, To Take Arms, pp.42-9.

31   This for example, appears to have been so in the case involving the mercenary recruiter, John Banks (Guardian, 22 February 1977 and 7 April 1977).

32   McGuire, To Take Arms, p.45.

33   Jones, "Terrorist Weaponry in Northern Ireland", p.21.

34   McGuire, To Take Arms, p.44.

35   ibid., pp.43-4.

36   Jones, "Terrorist Weaponry in Northern Ireland", p.21.

37   House of Commons, Official Report, Vol.908, 30 March 1976, col.472, and Albert Parry, Terrorism: From Robespierre to Arafat (New York: Vanguard Press, 1976), p.379.

38   Guardian, 29 November 1972; and Times, 30 November 1972. In 1981, Boris Shtern, a former Russian journalist, claimed that he was on board a Soviet trawler when it stopped off the Irish coast one night in 1971 and unloaded a secret cargo to waiting boats. Unfortunately, Shtern's certainty on the matter goes no further than reporting that the cargo was concealed in a crate and that it was received by two Irishmen from the KGB officer on board the trawler. Exactly who they were, or what they represented, was not reported; similarly it was only Shtern's (and others of the crew) opinion that the crate contained arms. (Times, 30 April 1981, p.7). If it did, the quantity involved was obviously quite small.

39   House of Commons, Official Report, Vol.848, 21 December 1972, cols.470-2; and Daily Telegraph, 11 December 1972.

40   J. Bowyer Bell, A Time of Terror: How Democratic Societies Respond to Revolutionary Violence (New York: Basic

Books, 1978), p.135.
41   This is a conclusion drawn from material which appears elsewhere - see McKinley, PhD Thesis.
42   Times, 21 April 1975.
43   Guardian, 30 March 1973. The arms recovered were 250 Russian-made (AK 47) self-loading rifles, 247 Webley .38 revolvers, more than 20,000 rounds of Belgian and Russian ammunition, 100 anti-tank mines, 100 cases of anti-personnel mines, 600 lb. of TNT, 500 lb. of gelignite, and 300 hand grenades (see also Guardian, 31 March 1973; Sunday Telegraph, 1 April 1973; and Times, 21 April 1975).
44   Leinhauser had been caught at an intermediate point, on the French-German border, with a consignment of American, German, Italian and Yugoslav pistols and revolvers (Daily Telegraph, 31 March 1973).
45   Guardian, 30 March 1973; and 6 April 1973.
46   Guardian, 3 April 1976; Financial Times, 4 April 1973; Sunday Telegraph, 1 April 1973; and Times, 3 April 1973. Similar reports were to be found in other British newspapers throughout the two weeks after the operation and were also repeated by the above at different times in this period.
47   Foreign Report, No.1277, 3 January 1973, p.5.
48   In its attempts to locate the origin of the rocket launchers, British Intelligence sent samples of the dust and sand found inside one of the weapons to scientists of all the leading petroleum companies in Britain in the hope that it could be geographically identified. But it wasn't. (Times, 21 April 1975).
49   Times, 22 April 1975; and Belfast Telegraph, 4 December 1974.
50   Irish Times, 15 November 1974, p.1.
51   In view of the unionist orientation of the UDA, this may seem a contradictory statement. Basically, it arose because although the UDA demanded that Ulster remain British, it also came to the conclusion that the British may not wish to retain Ulster. Hence, the UDA's response was to opt for an Ulster identity, independent of Britain and the Republic of Ireland, which would preserve the Protestant character of the Province. For a brief exposition of this view see Andy Tyrie (supreme commander of the UDA), "Independence is the only alternative", Guardian Weekly, 24 February 1980, p.5.
52   The late arrival of the Sinn Fein delegation might also have suggested that the DIR was either an inefficient conduit or less "Republican" than imagined.
53   Belfast Telegraph, 15 November 1977.
54   Sunday Telegraph, 22 December 1974. This claim was consistent with former IRA member Peter McMullen's 1979 claim that Libyan "arms and loans" ran to $5 million per year (emphasis added). See Boston Globe, 2 September 1979, p.12.
55   Times, 21 April 1975.
56   Financial Times, 23 April 1975.

57   Irish Times, 28 April 1975.
58   Daily Express, 26 August 1976; and Financial Times, 15 September 1975.
59   McKinley, PhD Thesis.
60   Boston Globe, 7 September 1979, p.1.
61   ibid. The abbreviation RPG stands for Rocket Propelled Grenade. Although the existence of the RPG7 has been known since 1962, there is no such weapon as the RPG5, or even a SA5 or SAM5 (both would refer to surface-to-air-missile). However, the urge to dismiss McMullen's account out of hand may be resisted in the knowledge that there is a weapon of similar appearance to the RPG7, designated SA7 (F.W.A. Hobart, ed., Janes Infantry Weapons 1975 (London: MacDonald and Jane's, 1974), pp.779-81).
62   A Daily Mail report, as cited in Encounter LIV (February 1980): 25.
63   Irish Times, 21 September 1978.
64   Times, 24 June 1978.
65   London Sunday Times, 25 June 1978.
66   Edward S. Ellenberg, "The PLO And Its Place In Violence and Terror", Livingston, Kress and Wanek, eds., International Terrorism in the Contemporary World, p.175.
67   Yonah Alexander, "Terror International: The PLO-IRA Connection", American Professors for Peace in the Middle East, Bulletin, October 1979, p.3 (hereafter cited as Alexander, "The PLO-IRA Connection").
68   As cited in Yonah Alexander, "Terrorism and the Media in the Middle East", Yonah Alexander and Maxwell Finger, eds., Terrorism: Interdisciplinary Perspectives (New York and Maidenhead, Berkshire: John Jay and McGraw-Hill, 1977), p.177.
69   Financial Times, 11 December 1972.
70   According to Dr Garret Fitzgerald, it was just possible that the PLO did not altogether understand the nature of their association with the IRA. During Ireland's Presidency of the Council of Ministers of the European Community in 1975, he toured the countries of the Maghbreb as one of his official duties, but in Algiers took the opportunity to hold discussions with a PLO spokesman. In the course of this Fitzgerald gained the impression that the PLO regarded the IRA as the "Irish Government's underground army", and hence, Dublin's condemnation of their activities as no more than pro forma statements intended to placate (say) the British Government! With some difficulty, he attempted to persuade the PLO otherwise. Among his measures were the withholding of Irish Government support for various PLO demands, which were otherwise considered just, for as long as the organisation continued to support the IRA (Interview, 1978).
71   Paul Wilkinson, Terrorism: International Dimensions, Conflict Studies No.113 (London: Institute for the Study of

Conflict, 1979), p.8.
72   ibid. Wilkinson claims that, in May 1972, the West German Embassy in Dublin was bombed by the IRA with the Baader-Meinhof gang claiming responsibility for the attack.
73   Boston Sunday Globe, 2 September 1979, p.12.
74   Guardian, 25 March 1977.
75   "Terror International", BBC 1, 30 January 1978.
76   Boston Sunday Globe, 2 September 1979, p.1.
77   Irish Times, 19 June 1978, p.1.
78   Alexander, "The PLO-IRA Connection", p.3. He also claimed that others were being trained in Libya and Syria.
79   Boston Sunday Globe, 2 September 1979, p.12.
80   International Herald Tribune, 24-25 March 1979.
81   By his own account he faced an IRA court of inquiry (for refusing an assignment) in February 1978, and flew to the US in April 1978 to escape an IRA squad charged to kill him (Boston Globe, 6 September 1979, p.2).
82   Alexander, "The PLO-IRA Connection", p.3.
83   John Barron, KGB: The Secret Work of Soviet Secret Agents (New York: Reader's Digest, 1974), p.255. Bell claims they were "donated to the anti-imperialist struggle by Colonel Qadhafi" (The Secret Army, p.398).
84   Irish Times, 19 July 1978.
85   House of Commons, Official Report, Vol.949, 11 May 1978, col.1378.
86   ibid. (See also House of Commons, Official Report, Vol.947, 13 April 1978, col.1653.)
87   ibid., col.1388.
88   ibid., col.1378.
89   Interview of Yasser Arafat by Barbara Walters for ABC Television News, 9 September 1979, as reported in the Irish Times, 10 September 1979, p.1.
90   Daily Telegraph, 20 August 1969.
91   Irish Independent, 13 May 1974.
92   Times, 7 June 1975.
93   Toronto Star, 17 July 1973, pp.1 and 2. The Dublin seizure was made at the docks, upon containers loaded from a British freighter, the Manchester Vigour.
94   See McKinley, PhD Thesis.
95   Times, 7 June 1975.
96   Toronto Star, 17 July 1973, pp.1 and 2.
97   Times, 7 June 1975.
98   ibid. According to information received from official sources, seven "Irish immigrants" went to trial in Toronto in 1975 on charges of conspiring to export, and attempting to export, a machine gun, 20 semi-automatic rifles, 10 sten-guns and more than 8,000 rounds of ammunition. Unfortunately, the writer has not been able to establish for certain whether the Myles, et al. case was part of this general attempt, or a separate attempt entirely. But in the writer's opinion, it was probably the former.

99   Toronto Star, 17 July 1973, p.1. In England, the Daily Telegraph was not impressed with Lysyk's modest assessment – it ignored his comments and carried the headline, "Canadian Arms Ring Broken" (Daily Telegraph, 18 July 1973).
100   Jones, "Terrorist Weaponry in Northern Ireland", p.21.
101   Irish Times, 19 August 1974.
102   The arms recovered in Toronto were 9 M1 rifles, 13 sten-gun housings, sten-gun ammunition clips, and 2,000 rounds of rifle ammunition (Times, 9 April 1974). The quantity of arms recovered at Southampton was not cited; however, an idea may be gained from evidence that it was found within a box and a trunk within a container which also held other items (Irish Times, 19 August 1974).
103   Daily Telegraph, 18 April 1974. Unlike the Murphy case, there was a 9-10 day delay between the Southampton and Toronto seizure operations.
104   Daily Telegraph, 11 June 1977.
105   Irish Times, 7 September 1977.
106   One source was of the opinion that certain shootings in Derry, because of the circumstances surrounding them, were either the work of a freelance operator, or hired killer who visited the city specifically for the operation and left again.
107   The bombing of an Army Officer's Mess at Aldershot, on 22 February 1972, which killed six civilians and a Roman Catholic chaplain was claimed by the Officials.
108   Persons so described were generally held to be responsible for the Dublin and Monaghan car bombings which claimed 28 lives in the space of 3 hours on 17 May 1974.
109   In March 1979, the INLA murdered the Conservative Party's principal spokesman on Northern Ireland as he was leaving the House of Commons car park. According to McMullen, Provisional IRA co-operation was provided (Boston Sunday Globe, 2 September 1979, p.12). However, David O'Connell (Daithi O Connaill), then of Provisional Sinn Fein, denied this (International Herald Tribune, 27 November 1980, p.4).
110   A fatal kidnapping undertaken by a small group of volunteers without official approval of the IRA command. See Bell, The Secret Army, pp.406-07.
111   However, the Provisionals have, on at least two occasions, hijacked a goods train on the main Belfast-Dublin railway and blown it up. See Daily Telegraph, 30 December 1975; and Times, 21 November 1978.
112   In 1978 approximately one quarter of the UDR's strength was on full-time duties.
113   In the absence of official figures in the last few years the figure of 5,000 was estimated by the writer, perhaps generously, to allow for the increase in the numbers of the security forces on Border duties since mid-1974, when it was nearly 3,000 (Dail Eireann, Parliamentary Debates, Official Report, vol.273, 26 June 1974, col.1576). Even if the

estimated figure is inflated, the order of comparability is not greatly affected.

114 Guardian, 19 October 1980, p.5. The report cited was a private assessment stolen from military intelligence by the IRA in 1979, and released by it. However, the authenticity of Document 37, as it was formerly titled, was admitted by the British Government (Canberra Times, 12 May 1979).

115 John Whale and Chris Ryder, "Ulster 1968-1978: A Decade of Despair", London Sunday Times, 18 June 1978, p.15 (hereafter cited as Whale and Ryder, "Decade of Despair").

116 The total of casualties resulting from European incidents, including the murder of Sir Richard Sykes (previously discussed) has not been published, but it would almost certainly be less than 5.

117 McGuire, To Take Arms, p.92.

118 This motive, a consequence of Bloody Sunday, was clearly behind the Aldershot bombing of 22 February 1972 (see Bell, The Secret Army, p.385).

119 The rash of bombings in London and Manchester in January 1975 was designed specifically for this purpose (Whale and Ryder, "Decade of Despair", p.15).

120 Two incidents in 1974 - the bombing of a coach on the M62 carrying servicemen and their families (12 dead), and explosions at Army barracks at Guildford and Woolwich (7 dead) were timed to coincide with the British election campaign of February and October/November of that year respectively (ibid., p.16).

121 On 3 December 1980, Mr Christopher Tugendhat, the British European Commissioner, was the subject of a shooting attack in Brussels (Guardian, 19 January 1981, p.4).

122 In August 1978, eight explosions in six British military installations on the Rhine were reported (International Herald Tribune, 21 August 1978). Another example of this expanded theatre of IRA operations concerned the bombing of a stage, in Brussels, on which a British Army band was about to play (Irish Times, 30 August 1979).

123 Times, 19 July 1977; and Times, 6 August 1977.

124 International Herald Tribune, 24-25 March 1979.

125 Boston Globe, 5 September 1979, p.1. The appointee, according to McMullen, was Martin McGuiness.

126 As cited in A.T.Q. Steward, The Narrow Ground: Aspects of Ulster, 1609-1969 (London: Faber and Faber, 1977), p.12.

Essay Two

THE UNITED STATES AND TERRORISM IN IRELAND
1969 - 1981

Raymond James Raymond

The late 1960s marked the beginning of the United States's struggle with international terrorism. Since that end of that troubled decade, there have been numerous attacks on American diplomats, airliners, and citizens travelling abroad. The initial American response to this problem was one of conciliation and negotiation.[1] Under the leadership of Henry Kissinger, however, United States policy on terrorism shifted towards what one recent author has described as "deterrence by denial"; a refusal to negotiate with or make any concessions to terrorists.[2] During the Carter Administration this policy was reversed to give greater emphasis to negotiations and the human value of hostages. With the election of Ronald Reagan as President has come a firmer response to terrorism. Indeed, when he was Secretary of State Alexander Haig announced that combating terrorism would be the top priority in the Administration's foreign policy. It is curious, therefore, that for all its emphasis on defeating international terrorism, the Reagan Administration has been blind to the danger to liberal democracy in the middle of the North Atlantic Alliance posed by the Irish Republican Army's guerrilla campaign in Northern Ireland.

Unfortunately, the Reagan Administration has not been alone in its failure to comprehend the threat to American strategic interests from the I.R.A.'s guerrilla campaign. Irish-Americans and their Congressional representatives, along with Presidents Nixon, Ford, and Carter, have all failed to grasp the danger inherent in the Ulster crisis: the danger of allowing Irish terrorists to create a dangerous Civil War on the shores of the North Atlantic approaches to Western Europe. This essay argues that the United States can play an important role in defeating terrorism and promoting reconciliation in Ireland. It will also be argued that a new departure in American policy towards the Irish crisis is needed immediately. Before this can take place, however, the Irish-American community and the United States government must shed their respective illusions about the nature of violence in Northern Ireland. For their part the Irish-American community must abandon its romantic view of the I.R.A. and learn more about the causes of the present conflict. On the other hand, before the United States government can play a meaningful role in bringing peace to Ulster, both the State Department and the White House must abandon their traditional assumption that the Irish question is simply an Anglo-Irish problem with no international ramifications. Quite the contrary; the conflict in Northern Ireland now involves crucial international issues and threatens the political stability both of the Republic of Ireland and the United Kingdom.

I
Irish-America and Terrorism in Ireland

Today there are five Irishmen in America for every Irishman in Ireland, and it is these immigrants who until recently provided the bulk of the money and arms to the I.R.A. Despite the sustained efforts of the Irish government to educate Irish-Americans to the reality of Northern Ireland, a substantial minority of Irish-Americans still cling to romantic illusions about the I.R.A. campaign in that troubled province. They still see it in simple terms of driving the British out, a job left unfinished in 1922. This is not to suggest, however, that the Irish-American response to the Ulster crisis since 1969 can be compared to that of their forbears to the Anglo-Irish war in 1921. At that time the sustained outburst of Irish-American political lobbying combined with their enormous output of money and other resources played a significant role in shaping the final outcome of the struggle. In comparison today's Irish-Americans seem curiously silent and even apathetic; there appears to be only a passive detached interest in the violence in Northern Ireland. But appearances are often deceptive and prevailing Irish-American attitudes conceal as much as they convey. The old shibboleths die hard. Irish-American anglophobia is still a force to be reckoned with. Despite the best efforts of the F.B.I. and British Intelligence, some Irish-American organizations continue to subscribe money for Northern Ireland through dubious channels. The most fruitful questions to raise seem to be, therefore: why have Irish-Americans continued to sustain the Provisional I.R.A. whose Marxist program is opposed to every moral and political principle they hold dear? And what can Irish-Americans do to help in Northern Ireland? To answer these questions and to understand the Irish-American response to terrorism in Ireland since 1969, we must first review the changing history of Irish-American involvement in Irish affairs generally over the past 200 years.

Irish-Americans are Americans of Roman Catholic Irish descent, but not all are imbued with Irish-American nationalism nor have they all retained their Catholic heritage.

Many of those whose forbears moved to states with few Roman Catholic clergy have adopted Protestant religions. Many more have long been assimilated into the mainstream of American society. The first records of Irish settlement in what is now the United States date back to 1621, but the modern Irish-American community was founded largely by the influx of emigrants following the Great Famine of 1846-1849.[3] In the wake of this catastrophe thousands of stricken victims emigrated to the United States carrying with them a hatred of Britain which they bequeathed to their descendants as a potent legacy of anglophobia. Consequently, since the middle of the nineteenth century Irish history has been inextricably bound up with the action of the Irish in America.

It was not simply a matter of carrying a preformed hatred of the English to the United States and transmitting it unchanged to their children. In every American city Irish-American emigrants experienced profound hostility from anglophile elites who found Irish culture, race, religion and poverty repulsive to their established values.[4] A vicious circle developed. Anglo-Saxon hostility heightened the Irish-American ethnic consciousness and tended to accentuate the ghetto mentality. Ethnic inmarriage and communal assertiveness deepened this hostility towards the prevailing culture.

Although bitterly hostile towards Britain, the Irish emigrants to the United States were at first politically impotent. They were socially disoriented and economically disadvantaged in an Anglo-Saxon culture which despised them. But the Irish-Americans' struggle against nativist hostility and socio-economic discrimination strengthened their identification with Ireland's difficulties and provided the incentive to organize. Their genius for organization led the Irish-Americans naturally enough into political life and by the third quarter of the nineteenth century they had become a potent force not only within the Democratic Party, but also within the political system as a whole with a vast network of ethnic organizations. Throughout the period from the Fenian rising of 1867 through the Anglo-Irish war of 1919-1921, this vast network of organizations worked dilligently to keep guns and money flowing into Ireland.[5]

Although the influence of Irish-Americans on the Anglo-Irish conflict has been exaggerated, Irish-America was important in the vital years of the Anglo-Irish war. At the height of this struggle, chapters of the Ancient Order of Hibernians, the secret Clan na Gael, sympathetic labor unions with Irish leaders, and Catholic school alumni groups were mobilized to exert intense pressure on Congress, the newspapers, and the Wilson Administration. Millions of dollars were collected to sustain the Irish struggle, while American public opinion was persuaded to sympathize with Irish aspirations for self-determination and deplore British repression. It should be emphasized, however, that the Irish-Americans failed to compel either the British or United States governments to take decisive action on the Irish question; Irish-American efforts failed to have Irish independence placed on the Versailles peace conference agenda, for example. Indeed, Irish-Americans ended up being cynically manipulated by traditional isolationists who found it expedient to support the Irish cause so as to enlist Irish-American support to defeat Wilson's peace settlement.[6] Once this was achieved the Irish cause was forgotten. The only real contribution which Irish-America made to the solution of Anglo-Irish conflict was to help shape world opinion. They played no role in influencing British attitudes towards British policy in Ireland - the decisive factor in ending the Anglo-Irish war.

In retrospect, the intense Irish-American agitation from 1919 through 1921 represented the apex of Irish-American nationalism. In the 1920s and 1930s Irish-America declined rapidly in significance. Its influence on Irish affairs was reduced; as a distinct entity it even began to disintegrate. There were two main reasons for this new development. The first was the achievement of Irish independence; the second, a major Irish-American identity crisis.[7]

The Anglo-Irish Treaty signed on 6 December 1921 gave Ireland a substantial measure of independence, and after this many Irish-Americans not only lost interest in Ireland, but also disassociated themselves from Irish affairs. To a large proportion of Irish-Americans the treaty offered a real opportunity for the continued development of Irish independence. The conflict was over; Ireland was substantially free. The brutal civil war which followed the signing of the Anglo-Irish treaty between the defenders of the treaty and the die-hard republicans horrified and alienated many Irish-Americans. The agonies of this fratricidal conflict only intensified the desire of most Irish-Americans to disengage from Irish affairs. The reason was simple. Up until 1921, Irish-Americans identified with the national struggle for independence; the degree of their involvement depended on the fortunes of the Irish nationalist movement. When success seemed near, the involvement and assistance rose; when hope for independence fell away, Irish-American assistance fell away. It was not surprising, therefore, that when the Treaty was signed, Irish-Americans began to lose interest.

Irish-American anglophobia was also weakened because the American-Irish experienced a serious identity crisis and in the process lost their psychological dependence on Irish nationalism. Throughout most of the nineteenth century the Irish-Americans blamed their low social status in the United States on the continued British "oppression" in Ireland. They insisted that Irish independence would somehow free them from the humiliation of Anglo-Saxon contempt. After World

War I, however, many Irish-Americans began to lose their dependance on Irish nationalism as they acquired a higher social and economic status.

Already the best established of the immigrant groups by 1920, a large number of the Irish had moved into the lower middle class, and a small but highly visible group of businessmen and professionals had penetrated the upper middle class. Sociological research conducted during the 1920s by Lloyd W. Warner and Leo Srole in New Port, Massachusetts, for example, demonstrated that the social class distribution for the Irish as an ethnic group included 13 per cent in the "lower-lower" class, 54 per cent in the working class (or "upper-lower" class), 28 per cent in the lower middle, and 6 per cent in the upper middle class.[8] When Warner and Srole examined the third generation of native born Irish separately, however, only 2 per cent remained in the "lower lower" class. 39 per cent were in the "upper lower class", 42 per cent were lower middle, and 17 per cent were in the upper middle class. Even in this Protestant yankee community, each successive generation of Irish immigrants rose higher and higher in the stratification order. For Irish-Americans like these the crutch of Irish nationalism no longer seemed relevant. By the late 1920s, many Irish-Americans were much too preoccupied with their flight to the suburbs and their loyalty to their new found professions, suburban neighborhoods, and economic groups to worry about Ireland. As a result, there was a sharp decline in the level of Irish-American anglophobia.

Irish neutrality during World War II dealt a further devastating blow to Irish-American nationalism.[9] It appears that anti-British and anti-war sentiments did remain in some of the older Irish-American communities up until Pearl Harbor, but the Japanese attack and the hostilities that followed it destroyed the credibility of isolationists and in particular those Irish-Americans who had been prominent among them. The mobilization of the entire nation in the cause of total war further shifted attitudes. The United States now found itself at war not only with Japan, but also with Italy and Germany. Both the Roosevelt Administration and American public opinion would have welcomed with enthusiasm a declaration by the Irish government that the attack on the United States had changed the conditions in which they had decided to assert their neutrality. Prime Minister de Valera's refusal to abandon neutrality was a shock to American public opinion, even to the most anglophobic Irish-Americans. American opinion was quite ready to admit that the Irish might have good cause to feel no gratitude to the British and to remain out of their quarrels. But even Irish-Americans whose sons and husbands were being conscripted for war against Germany, were finding it difficult to understand why Ireland should endanger the sea lanes on which their loved ones were being transported to Great Britain. The widely held belief that the use of Irish naval bases and airfields would have given greater protection to Allied convoys brought home to Irish-Americans that Irish neutrality was a handicap to the successful prosecution of the war against Germany. This, along with the discrediting of Irish-American isolationists decisively weakened Irish-American anglophobia. By 1945 the winds of change were blowing through the Irish-American community as never before; thousands of young Irish-Americans returned to their homes with their vision broadened and their expectations heightened. John F. Kennedy was their leader not Eamon de Valera.[10]

Kennedy's election as President in 1960 not only marked the belated fulfillment of the wartime generation's political aspirations, but also begat an emotional Irish-American resurgence. Nevertheless, John Kennedy was more Brahmin than "paddy" and the Irish-America of 1960 was not that of 1920. The unprecedented economic boom of the 1950s had brought further social mobility and economic prosperity to Irish-Americans dulling their ethnic consciousness even further.

Throughout the 1960s two major forces conspired to intensify this disruption of the traditional mores of Irish-America: the religious reforms of the second Vatican Council and the emergence of the hippy "counterculture". The Catholic church had always been a bastion of emotional and cultural stability for Irish-Americans. As an ethnic and cultural institution of vital importance it decisively shaped the thinking of the Irish-American community. The second Vatican Council introduced sweeping changes not only in the Roman liturgy, but also in the whole role of the Church in society.[11] These changes had very disturbing effects on Irish-American families already under strain from the developing pop culture of the 1960s. This "counterculture" with its emphasis on individual identity, self awareness, and the new sexual morality struck a devastating blow at the social and psychological base of the traditional Irish-American family.[12] By 1969, the old sense of ethnic community seemed to be finally disintegrating.

At the same time, however, there were a number of countervailing forces which served both to sustain Irish-American traditions and to heighten their awareness of social injustice in Ireland. For one thing, in the 1960s some members of the new generation of Irish-Americans now secure in society became interested in reestablishing ties with Ireland. The 1960s also saw the beginning of scheduled international jet travel between the United States and Ireland. Tens of thousands of Irish-Americans returned to their homeland for vacations thus reawakening their interest in Ireland and Irish affairs. This new Irish-American concern was decisively influenced by their experience of religious pluralism in the United States and of the black civil rights movement. This concern found its tangible manifestation in the founding of the Friends of the Northern Ireland Civil Rights Association in the winter of 1968-69, a non-denominational committee concerned to focus American opinion on social and economic injustice in Northern Ireland.[13]

When violence erupted in Northern Ireland in 1969, however, the Irish-American response was both timid and uncoordinated. In contrast to 1921 when Irish born Americans numbered nearly 4 million, there were only 290,000 Irish born emigrants living in the United States in 1969. Despite the influence of the civil rights movement, Irish-American attachment to the old country was now much weaker. The old ethnic organizations were pale shadows of their former selves. The Roman Catholic church, that most important of ethnic institutions, was now espousing the rhetoric of ecumenism and was reluctant to get involved in what appeared to them an age-old Protestant-Catholic vendetta. In any event, the Church was much too preoccupied with its own crisis of institutional self-confidence caused by its younger militant clergy. Politically, the Irish-Americans no longer held sway in the Democratic party and had no influence in the shaping of public policy, foreign or domestic. There was even a sizeable body of Irish-American opinion which saw the Ulster riots arising not from British imperialism but from economic malaise and social inertia. By 1970, therefore, the newly formed Provisional I.R.A. had their work cut out for them to persuade Irish-America to bankroll another effort to drive the British out of Ireland.

Although their apparent resources were meager, the supporters of the Provisional I.R.A. knew that the Irish-American community still had a number of psychological predispositions which could be manipulated. First, there was a latent anglophobia particularly among those who had recently emigrated from Northern Ireland. Second, the inherent sociability of Irish-Americans could be counted on to provide numerous opportunities for fund raising. Third, there was the legacy of the old I.R.A.; what Dennis Clark has described as the "viable tradition of the patriot patriarch". Finally, there were a small number of old I.R.A. men still living. These men had great symbolic significance for the Irish-American community and they still believed in the power of the desperate deed, the terrible act that would strike fear into beholders.[14] The key to understanding Irish-American support since 1969 lies in understanding how the Provisional I.R.A. have manipulated these predispositions for their own ends, and how American television has unwittingly helped them.

The degree to which Irish-Americans have become involved in Irish affairs has always been a function of how they have perceived Ireland. Since 1969 Irish-Americans have been confronted by two obstacles in understanding what has transpired in Northern Ireland. First, their vision has been clouded by a curious romantic mist concerning the Provisional I.R.A. Normally, such a terrorist organization would be universally detested and condemned in the United States, but to many Irish-Americans they are noble freedom fighters. Second, American television has unwittingly fostered this misconception by acting as a channel through which the Provisionals have presented themselves in the compelling role of opponents of British imperialism and the champions of a united Ireland.

Although most Irish-Americans share to some degree a common perception of Ireland and the I.R.A., it is important to distinguish between two distinct layers in the Irish-American perception of and response to terrorism since 1969. First, there is the general Irish-American response weakened by fifty years of assimilation, economic progress, and social mobility. Their vision is clouded by a romantic haze, but while supporting the concept of Irish unity many of them do not support the Provisional I.R.A. These people are sincere and well-intentioned, but their romanticism leaves them vulnerable to manipulation by the second layer of Irish-Americans; the recent emigrants from Northern Ireland whose commitment to the Provisionals is complete. The first layer of Irish-Americans is likely to have held aloof from direct involvement with the I.R.A., yet they deeply sympathize with friends who are directly involved. They attend Irish Northern Aid functions but do not support violence as such; they would like to see a political solution to the Ulster question, but they have been to Ireland often enough to believe that Northern Protestants will not willingly make a pact with Ulster Catholics. The militant supporters of the Provisionals, however, are really not very different from Provisional supporters in Ireland in the roots of their argument and the depth of their feelings. They are sustained by a warped nostalgia for a past which never existed. The chief assumption underpinning their support for terrorism is that British government in Ireland has been a disaster, that the Irish people have consistently expressed a deep desire for unity, and that the state of Northern Ireland is a contrived English fixture, an instrument of British imperialism. The Provisionals, therefore, are seen as the heroic opponents of British oppression and the champions of a united Ireland. This small minority of Irish-Americans is driven by a blind elemental malevolence and has no faith in power-sharing or any rational political compromise. They want no guarantee of minority rights from the United Kingdom, the United States, or the United Nations. They believe that their claim to full sovereignty over Northern Ireland is historically justified, but must be enforced by force of arms. Their perception of Ireland is simplistic, intolerant, and unhistoric.

The ignorance and blind hatred of this minority of Irish-Americans has caused hundreds of violent deaths in Northern Ireland, for it was they who supplied a large proportion of the money and weapons that caused the deaths. It is impossible to know how many illegal arms the I.R.A. have smuggled in from the United States. It is equally impossible to determine how they are brought in. Some estimates would suggest that at least six and perhaps as many as eight out of ten illegal weapons smuggled into Ireland come from the United States. Most of them were bought with funds donated by the first layer of naive Irish-Americans in the belief that the money was being used to relieve the sufferings of innocent victims in Northern Ireland.

Unfortunately, American television has helped the Provisional I.R.A. and its Irish-American allies to increase their support among the Irish-American community.[15] In the first place, covering terrorism in Ireland is a task for which American television reporters are hopelessly unprepared. They have neither the sources in Northern Ireland nor the necessary knowledge of Irish history. Their methods of operation make it even more difficult for them to understand the extraordinary complexity of forces which have shaped the Ulster crisis. Based in London, American television newsmen fly to Belfast on the shuttle flight whenever a hunger striker dies or it appears likely that there will be another outburst of rioting. They stand around street corners at 3 a.m. in the morning waiting for something to happen. Frequently, the very presence of American newsmen causes a riot especially orchestrated for American television viewers.

It should be emphasized, however, that no American television crew has ever been charged with inciting violence or starting a riot. It should also be noted that their British and Irish counterparts give them high marks for courage, energy, and perseverance. But it is also clear that the quality of their coverage leaves much to be desired. Terrorism in Ireland is being conveyed to the United States in the most superficial, romanticized, and simple-minded terms of a battle between Irish natives and British colonizers with the I.R.A. as the dashing defenders of the natives. In a recent interview with an American popular magazine, Jeremy Sands, a veteran British journalist in Ulster, said: "There's a level of naivete among them. Most have never learned the nuances. I've covered Northern Ireland more than anybody else at ITN, and I don't always get the story right. If I don't, their chances of getting it right are nil."[16]

Still more serious is the attention which the Provisional I.R.A. lavish upon visiting newsmen from the United States. At the recent funeral of hunger striker Bobby Sands, American television crews were given fully equipped scaffolding on which to mount their cameras so as to get the best possible pictures. Thus, American television viewers were treated to the dramatic spectacle of hooded figures at the grave site firing volleys of salute towards an overcast sky. American sympathy is the prize the Provisionals want most in their propaganda war with the British government, and they are prepared to go to inordinate lengths to get it. The I.R.A. puts its case in colorful and romantic terms designed to appeal to the psychological predispositions of Irish-Americans. By contrast, the British government's case is couched in such humorless rational terms as to be completely ineffective.[17]

The Provisionals have reinforced their campaign by sending carefully chosen emissaries and relatives of I.R.A. prisoners to the United States to speak to Irish-American organizations and to appear on local American television. The sending of emissaries began in 1970. The vast majority were carefully trained to deceive the Irish-American community by playing on their traditional hatred of England. As Maria McGuire noted in her book To Take Arms, Provisional I.R.A. fund raisers were instructed "to make copious references to the martyrs of 1916 and 1920-22 the period most of the audience would be living in".[18] It was also recommended that anti-British sentiment recalling the potato famine and the Black and Tans could be profitably exploited, but that on no account should anything be said against the Catholic church or about socialism. Thus Irish-Americans were conned into believing that the I.R.A. campaign was a simple effort to free the Catholics of Northern Ireland from the yoke of British imperialism, instead of a singleminded effort to destroy the existing order north and south of the border.

More recently the Provisionals have begun to export relatives of hunger strikers and other prisoners to the United States to appear on talk shows where they have been welcomed as celebrities. Local stations in cities like Boston, New York, Chicago, and Philadelphia have shown a particular willingness to welcome these agents of disinformation, and as a result, these local stations become the mouthpiece of the Provisionals. The perception has thus been created that the essence of the Ulster crisis - and the major cause of terrorism - is the struggle of the downtrodden Catholics of Northern Ireland to free themselves from the tyranny of British rule, the same enemy the United States defeated in 1781.

Given the psychological predispositions of Irish-Americans, and the success with which the Provisional I.R.A. has developed their propaganda campaign, it is not surprising that an extensive support network has developed across the United States since 1970. Its components warrant serious attention not only in an Irish-American context, but also as part of the international terrorist network. The core of the Provisional I.R.A. network developed around recent emigrants from Northern Ireland and others with ties of blood and kinship to the North of Ireland. It was and is a small network, but it functions with the full cooperation of an ancillary network of Irish-American organizations many of which have no overt connection with terrorism. As Dennis Clark has put it:

> The network was militant with a gut motivation, but it was not a rigidly organised system. The Irish characteristic of sociability and traditional antagonism towards England were its great resources. The affluence of the United States made sufficient money available so that even hard-working immigrants could spare enough for contributions to the movement. The work to aid the minority in Northern Ireland was both clandestine and open, but the terror bombing in Ulster and the limitations of the support network's influence precluded capturing the very broad and complex opinion bloc of the mass of Irish-Americans. Nor could the network affect American government policy toward Northern Ireland or England. Deprived of broad support from the Catholic church, American politicians, or wealthy Irish-Americans, the network did what it could do best, maintain its immigrant followers and their close allies, and raise money through a steady but limited cycle of events in cities across the country.[19]

To sum up, Irish-America has bankrolled the Provisional I.R.A. because they have been led to believe that the Provisionals are the only true opponents of British rule in Ulster and the only champions of a united Ireland. Irish-Americans still see the Provisional I.R.A. campaign as a holy war, the continuation of the Anglo-Irish war and the age-old struggle between the Celt and the Anglo-Saxon. The curious romantic mist that obscures Irish-America's vision has been assiduously fostered by the Provisionals in one of the most remarkably successful disinformation campaigns in recent history.[20] The fact that the Provisional I.R.A. have turned from killing for a cause to killing for their own vested interests has been lost on Irish-America.

Given this appalling situation, what can Irish-Americans do to help in Northern Ireland? First, they could try to reappraise their basic assumptions concerning the origins of the present Ulster crisis. One welcome result of the violence in Northern Ireland has been the way in which many people in the Republic of Ireland have been forced to rethink their position on Northern Ireland. Many have also begun the healthy but painful process of rethinking their attitudes towards the Provisional I.R.A. Irish-Americans have the capacity of mind to do the same, and there are already the beginnings of a more sophisticated understanding of the Northern Ireland problem.

Second, having reappraised their basic assumptions, Irish-Americans can stop funding the Provisionals. Nobody's freedom but their own now inspires the I.R.A.; their political platform calls for a Marxist system - nationalization of banks, insurance, mining, and all major industries North and South of the border. No one can imagine that these radical objectives hold any appeal for Irish-Americans. The Provisionals have carefully disguised their objectives behind the traditional symbols of Irish nationalism. Irish-America has been cruelly deceived. It really deserves better.

II
The United States Government and Terrorism in Ireland

Traditionally, the United States is the country for which Irish people have the warmest affection and the greatest admiration. The most important diplomatic relations between the United States and Ireland have usually been informal and spontaneous. The relationship between the two countries has traditionally been one of mutual friendship and goodwill brought about in part by American support for Ireland in her struggle for independence from Great Britain, and in part by the ties of family and kinship resulting from successive waves of Irish immigration to the United States before 1900.[21]

In contrast to the widespread sympathy for Ireland so evident throughout all branches of the Federal government during Ireland's struggle for independence between 1914 and 1921, Eire's neutral stand during World War II evoked little or no support from any important groups within the Administration or in Congress.[22] On the contrary, there was widespread criticism of Ireland's insistence on its full rights as a neutral.[23] There was also a growing awareness of the still more serious problems which would be raised for North Atlantic security if Ireland remained neutral in any future war with the Soviet Union.

In the tense early decades of the Cold War following the defeat of the Axis, United States-Irish relations were often turbulent.[24] The recurring collisions between Dublin and Washington in this period did not reflect any real ideological difference between successive Irish governments and the Truman and Eisenhower Administrations. If anything, the Irish were more anti-communist than the Americans. The main source of contention was the bipartisan determination of Irish leaders to secure American assistance to make partition an international issue and to safeguard Irish neutrality, and the equally firm resolve of American policymakers not to do any such thing. Ireland wanted to preserve her neutrality and bring an end to partition; the United States wanted military cooperation as part of its Cold War grand strategy. Neither got what it wanted.[25]

The Kennedy era reawakened the traditional friendship between the two governments, but after the President's assassination, relations cooled to the point where, by 1969, Henry Kissinger could describe Ireland coldly as a potentially useful neutral.[26] The eruption of violence in Northern Ireland did not cause the Nixon White House any undue concern. Preoccupied with the war in Vietnam and the development of detente with the Soviet Union, the Nixon Administration saw the Ulster crisis as an internal British problem best left in the experienced hands of Whitehall. This view was shared to a greater or lesser degree by Presidents Ford and Carter.

Nevertheless, the United States did take some constructive steps in the war against terrorism.[27] At the request of the British and Irish governments agencies of the Federal Government began to disrupt the Provisional I.R.A.'s network in the United States. Over the past 10 years successive Irish governments have made it clear to Washington that the Republic is very nervous about the I.R.A. and anything the United States could do to hinder the Provisional campaign and its American network would be very much appreciated. Since 1970, therefore, the Immigration and Naturalization Service has been busy stopping I.R.A. activists entering the United States. The United States Customs Bureau has been active in stopping arms smuggling; the Internal Revenue Service has sought to prosecute illegal fund raising. In 1977, President Jimmy Carter offered a pledge of economic assistance for Northern Ireland, but his call for reconciliation and his offer of assistance was followed by three years of silence and inaction.

Unfortunately, Congress has been equally unable to come up with any constructive suggestions for a positive American role in Ulster. This is largely a result of the unwillingness or inability of Irish-American Congressmen to break free of their traditional Irish Catholic heritage and its assumptions. In order to keep their Congressional representatives from ignoring Ulster, the Irish-American network has organized sustained letter-writing campaigns and other forms of political pressure. Unfortunately, this pressure has produced an all too predictable response: demands for a British withdrawal and ritual denunciations of British policy on the floor of the House and Senate. Senator Edward Kennedy, in particular, took a strong if simplistic stance throughout the early 1970s.[28] In October 1971, for example, he and representative Hugh Carey of New York, jointly submitted a resolution to Congress. This resolution advocated an immediate British withdrawal from Northern Ireland, and charged that British rule was maintained in the province only by bayonet and bloodshed. This simplistic view of the Northern problems was shared by other leading Irish-American Congressmen including speaker Thomas P. O'Neill, and Senator Daniel Patrick Moynahan. Their understanding of Northern Ireland was an inherited one, derived from long standing Irish-American anglophobia. The underpinning assumption of their numerous public statements during this period was that Ulster Protestants were simply instruments of Britain's will, and the British (if sufficiently pressured) could force the Protestants to reverse their position and enter a united Ireland. Consequently, Irish American Congressional representatives argued that the United States should put pressure on Britain to put pressure on the Ulster Unionists to concede Irish unity. This policy was seriously misconceived for it was grounded in assumptions that were both unhistoric and false.

In 1978, the so-called "big four" of Irish-American politics, Senator Edward Kennedy, House Speaker, Thomas P. O'Neill, Governor Hugh Carey of New York, and Senator Daniel Patrick Moynahan of New York finally began to realise the danger which the Provisional I.R.A. posed to the political stability of the Republic of Ireland. On Saint Patrick's Day of that year they issued a joint statement deploring Irish-American financial aid to the Provisional I.R.A. without criticizing British policy in Northern Ireland.[29] They came under such heavy attack from the Irish-American network, however, that they quickly repaired this omission. Their 1979 statement noted that a solution in Northern Ireland was no closer than it had been in 1978. The "four horsemen" charged Britain with either negligence or acquiescence in the torture of Irish prisoners by the Northern Ireland police. They further charged that Protestant leaders in the North were blocking negotiations by "intransigence" and that Britain was encouraging them in this course.

This kind of inflammatory response only intensified the pressure on all parties in Northern Ireland. It inflamed the general climate of opinion and made a solution even more difficult to come by. This is not to suggest, however, that there have been no serious Congressional efforts to understand the Ulster crisis and suggest a way in which the United States could promote peace. In July 1977, for example, Senator George McGovern visited Ireland and met with government officials on both sides of the border. In a thoughtful report presented to the Senate Foreign Relations Committee, McGovern recommended that the United States government should make every effort to discourage support for the Provisional I.R.A.; that United States diplomats should encourage British and Irish officials to pursue constructive solutions; and that the United States should indicate its willingness to join with other countries in offering reasonable financial aid to Northern Ireland to help a new government address the province's pressing economic problems.[30]

In August and September 1978, Congressmen Joshua Elberg and Hamilton Fish, Jr, visited Northern Ireland, the Republic, and the United Kingdom. At the conclusion of a lengthy report entitled "Northern Ireland: A Role for the United States", the two Congressmen recommended that the

Carter Administration reassess its noninterventionist position on Northern Ireland and seek to assist in a political solution. They also suggested that the United States assume the role of guarantor for any solution arrived at by the elected representatives of both communities in Northern Ireland.[31]

While valuable, these two reports had a number of serious flaws. First, they ignored the fact that there are now two distinct but related problems in Northern Ireland; that of reconciling the two conflicting traditions of nationalism and unionism, and that of defeating terrorism without which reconciliation can not be effected. Consequently, the United States must do more than simply "discourage" Irish-American support for terrorism; it must take firm action to eradicate it. Second, American financial aid must be given <u>before</u> Anglo-Irish negotiations begin <u>not</u> afterwards. The economic stagnation of Northern Ireland (where in some areas male unemployment has reached 40 per cent) provides a breeding ground for resentment and violence. Until this breeding ground of hatred is destroyed there can be no meaningful solution to terrorism in Northern Ireland. Third, the notion that the United States would act as guarantor of any agreed political solution is useful, but must be accompanied by a recognition that the United States has a role to play in bringing that political solution about. The Provisional I.R.A. will seek to destroy any compromise agreement which does not meet their demands. In order to safeguard the possibility of a negotiated agreement, the United States must supply the military assistance needed to defeat the terrorists. To do this, however, means that the United States must recognize that its strategic interests are involved in Ulster.

It is now clear that the United States will only respond substantively to the Ulster crisis when it becomes aware of the threat to its security posed by the Provisional I.R.A.'s campaign of terror: the pressure of continued political violence on the development of the European Community; the violations of human rights both by the I.R.A. and the British army, and the threat of a European Vietnam created by the unchecked terrorism of the Provisional I.R.A. This final threat is the most serious, for the Provisionals have been politicized by the European terrorist international and their Marxist objectives now pose a serious threat to liberal democracy in Northern Ireland, the Republic, and the United Kingdom.

The politicization of the Provisional I.R.A. began in 1972 under the influence of representatives of the Trotskyite IV International who visited Belfast frequently during that year.[32] The "Official" I.R.A. of course had always been hard line Stalinists before 1969, and Soviet Intelligence had quickly established contacts with them when the troubles broke out. But after the "Officials" declared a unilateral cease fire in 1972, the K.G.B. switched its attention to the Provisionals.[33]

From May 1972 onwards Provisional I.R.A. members began to travel to South Yemen for training by Cuban and East German instructors.[34] Colonel Qadafi of Libya took up the Provisionals' cause that same year, and early in 1973 the Provisionals' former Belfast Commander, Joe Cahill arrived in Tripoli to negotiate a large shipment of 250 Kalishnikov rifles and other weapons supplied to Qadafi by the Soviet Union.[35] By 1976, Qadafi had supplied the Provisionals with over $2.3 million, and between 1977 and 1980 this figure had risen to almost $5 million a year.[36]

Indeed, throughout the 1970s massive terrorist aid flowed in to the Provisional I.R.A. from a number of sources other than Qadafi: from George Habash's Marxist Palestinian Front, from Czechoslovakia, and from the Soviet Union.[37] Lest any doubts remain, the Provisionals are on record in several interviews with European newspapers and through their own political organ, An Phoblacht. In An Phoblacht on 12 April 1977, the Provisionals declared: "Both the Quisling regime in the Free State and the colonial regime in the Northern war zone have failed to produce a lasting solution. The war will continue until these structures are demolished."[38] As Claire Sterling has written, "They are still peddling it to the broader public as a war of national ethnic, and religious liberation, a wonderfully profitable way of putting it. The war they are really fighting, though, is hardly distinguishable from the one waged by Armed Parties everywhere." In November 1978, the Provisionals told the Red Brigade's own Control Informazione:

> The Nationalist factor has won vast popular support for our armed struggle to destabilize capitalism in Ireland... but it absolutely does not diminish the legitimacy of urban guerilla bands like the Red Brigades, the German Red Army Fraction and the Spanish GRAPO. We recognize their motivation, based on social injustice. Our cooperation with international groups is certainly not based on narrow national considerations, but on the common struggle against colonial and imperialist domination.[40]

It is clear, therefore, that the Provisional I.R.A. and their Irish-American network pose a threat to the stability of the Western Alliance and that the United States cannot stand idly by.[41] The question remains what the United States can do to help. First, the Federal Government can intensify its campaign against the Provisional I.R.A.'s support network. Although Irish-American money now is but a part of the Provisional I.R.A.'s funding, if it could be cut significantly this would be a substantial contribution. Second, the Reagan Administration could offer a military and economic aid program to the Republic of Ireland. The government of the Irish Republic lacks the military capability and financial resources to effectively combat the Provisional I.R.A., and is particularly short of helicopters and armoured vehicles. Third, the Reagan Administration must resist all pressure from Irish-American groups or their Congressional allies to demand an immediate British withdrawal from Northern Ireland. As Conor Cruise O'Brien has recently argued, pressure from the United States could produce in the British population such war weariness and disgust with Ulster that Britain could decide to withdraw even with the knowledge of the disastrous consequences which would inevitably follow.[42] Fourth, the Reagan Administration should seek to promote a full political dialogue both in the United States and in Northern Ireland. This could be accomplished in the United States through increased funding for Irish studies through the National Endowment for the Humanities and the Department of Education's Ethnic Heritage Grants Program. A major cultural exchange program through the International Communications Agency could bring central figures in Northern Ireland such as political and labor leaders, scholars, students, and clergymen to the United States to expose them to broader perspectives and reduce the sense of paranoia that feeds terrorism on both sides of the sectarian divide. Fifth, the United States should strengthen Britain's hand by financial aid channeled through the European Community's Fund for depressed areas. The appaling economic conditions of Northern Ireland have promoted recruitment for Protestant and Catholic terrorist organizations, and there will never be a meaningful solution to Ulster's problems until this terrible economic distress is removed. Moreover, as Kevin Cahill has recently argued, technical assistance funds for mass transit and the reconstruction of Belfast's working class ghettoes would also go a long way towards helping alleviate tensions in Northern Ireland. A matching fund could also be established through the Organization for Economic Development to finance cross-border projects, while Export-Import Bank credits could help promote American investment in Ulster.

It must be emphasized, however, that this entire program must be offered without political preconditions. To insist on Irish unity as the price of American economic aid or diplomatic assistance would be disastrous for it would simply afford the Provisional I.R.A. more political encouragement. It should also be emphasized that this program is not designed to be merely a reinforcement of the status quo. The United States must encourage both the United Kingdom and the Republic of Ireland to reconcile the aspirations of both communities in Northern Ireland by continuing to search for mutually acceptable institutions of government.

III

Conclusions

This paper has argued that the United States can and must help in decreasing the pressures on all parties concerned in Northern Ireland. To do this, Irish-Americans must abandon their most cherished assumptions and rethink their position on the Provisional I.R.A. The Provisionals are not the noble freedom fighters that some Irish-Americans perceive; they kill for their own vested interests and for a Marxist political platform that is not only anathema to Irish-American values, but is also a threat to the strategic interests of the Western Alliance. The Reagan Administration should recognize this and act accordingly. It must act before the pressure of events pushes Ireland - all of it - over the abyss into civil war.

Notes

1 See: Ernest Evans, "American Policy Response to International Terrorism: Problems of Deterrence", in Yonah Alexander and Seymour Maxwell Finger (eds.), Terrorism: Interdisciplinary Perspectives (New York, 1977), pp.106-17. See also: Alex George and Richard Smoke, Deterrence in American Foreign Policy: Theory and Practice (New York, 1974), pp.48-60.

2 For Kissinger's view, see: Department of State Bulletin, 15 September 1975, p.408. The author referred to in the text was Ernest Evans. See his contribution above.

3 See Terry Coleman, Going to America (New York, 1973); W.F. Adams, Ireland and Irish Immigration to the New World from 1815 to the Great Famine (New York, 1967); Arnold Schrier, Ireland and the American Emigration (New York, 1967).

4 See: H.M. Gitelman, "No Irish Need Apply: Patterns of and Response to Ethnic Discrimination in the Labor Market", Labor History 14 (Winter 1973), pp.56-68; Stanley Feldsten and L. Costello, A Documentary History of the White Working Classes 1830-1970 (Garden City, 1974), pp.344-48.

5 See: Charles Tansill, America and the Fight for Irish Freedom (New York, 1957); Brian Jenkins, Fenians in Anglo-American Relations During Reconstruction (New York, 1969); Alan J. Ward, Ireland and Anglo-American Relations 1899-1921 (London, 1969) and Francis M. Carroll, American Opinion and the Irish Question 1910-1921 (Dublin, 1978). See also: Marjorie Fallowes, Irish-Americans: Identity and Assimilation (Englewood Cliffs, 1979), p.54; William Shannon, The American Irish (New York, 1963), p.113.

6 See Raymond James Raymond, "Irish-Americans and Isolationism 1920-1944", paper written for The Historian's Project, 1981.

7 See Lawrence J. McCaffrey, The Irish Diaspora in

America (Bloomington, 1976), pp.152-78 on which this section of the paper draws heavily. See also: Marjorie Fallowes, Irish-Americans: Identity and Assimilation (Englewood Cliffs, 1979), pp.69-81 (hereafter cited as Fallowes, Irish-Americans).

8   W. Lloyd Warner and Leo Srole, The Social Systems of American Ethnic Groups (New Haven, 1945), pp.71-72. See also: M. Barron, "Intermediary: Conceptualizing Irish Status in America", Social Forces 27 (March 1949), pp.256-63; Fallowes, Irish-Americans, pp.60-80.

9   See Raymond James Raymond, "Irish-Americans and Isolationism 1920-1944", paper written for The Historian's Project, 1981. See also my paper, "American Public Opinion and Irish Neutrality 1939-1945", paper presented to the Southwestern Social Science Conference, Dallas, Texas, 25 March 1981. A fascinating glimpse of Irish-American attitudes towards the war can be gleaned from the reports of British Consuls in the United States to their superiors in London. The bulk of the reports have been gathered on Dominions Office file D.O. 130/55, file 158/45. See also John Stack, International Conflict in an American City: Boston's Irish, Italians and Jews 1935-1944 (Westport, 1978), pp.118-23 and 124-60, and Ronald Bayor, Neighbors in Conflict: The Irish, Germans, Italians, and Jews of New York City 1929-1941 (Baltimore, 1978), pp.110-12.

10   See John Stack, International Conflict in an American City: Boston's Irish, Italians, and Jews 1935-1944 (Westport, 1978), pp.158-60.

11   See Fallowes, Irish-Americans, pp.138-41.

12   In an article in the January 1975 issues of The Critic, Fr. Andrew Greeley reported a National Opinion Research Center survey of Catholic opinion which revealed a sharp fall in regular attendance at mass and the sacraments between 1965 and 1975. Only 32 per cent of those surveyed said they believed that the Pope was infallible on questions of faith and morals, while 83 per cent approved artificial contraception. These data, although based on a survey of American Catholic opinion as a whole, are probably representative of Irish-American opinion also.

13   See: Denis Clark, Irish Blood: Northern Ireland and the American Conscience (London, 1977), pp.23-25 (hereafter cited as Clark, Irish Blood).

14   Ibid., pp.29-41 and 51-61.

15   For a general theoretical perspective on the influence of the media, see: Frederic Wertham, "The Scientific Study of Mass Media effects", American Journal of Psychiatry 119, No.4, October 1962. See also: Hilde Mosse, "The Media and Terrorism", in M.H. Livingstone (ed.), International Terrorism in the Contemporary World (Westport, 1976); Bernard Johnpoll, "Terrorism and the Media in the United States", in Yonah Alexander and Seymour Maxwell Finger

(eds.), Terrorism: Interdisciplinary Perspectives (New York, 1977), pp.157-66; Yonah Alexander, "Terrorism and the Media: Some Considerations", in Yonah Alexander, David Carlton and Paul Wilkinson, Terrorism: Theory and Practice (Boulder, 1979), pp.159-74. This section of the paper draws heavily on Neil Hickey, "The Battle for Northern Ireland", in TV Guide 29, No.39, 26 September 1981, pp.8-28 (hereafter cited as Hickey, "Northern Ireland").

16   Hickey, "Northern Ireland", p.24.
17   Ibid., pp.9-27.
18   Maria McGuire, To Take Arms (London, 1973), p.110.
19   Clark, Irish Blood, p.40.
20   Hickey, "Northern Ireland", p.26.
21   See: D.H. Akenson, The United States and Ireland (Cambridge, Mass., 1972).
22   See: Raymond James Raymond, "American Public Opinion and Irish Neutrality 1939-1945", paper presented at the Southwestern Social Science Conference, Dallas, Texas, 25 March 1981.
23   Ibid.
24   Harry S. Truman, for example, loathed de Valera. See: Eben Ayers Diary, 1 April 1947, Harry S. Truman Library, Independence, Missouri.
25   See: Raymond James Raymond, "The United States, Ireland and the Cold War: NATO, Mutual Security and the end of Marshall Aid", unpublished paper, University of Connecticut, October 1981.
26   In the briefing book for President Nixon drafted prior to his arrival in Ireland in 1969.
27   See: Clark, Irish Blood, pp.60-72.
28   See: Richard W. Manshack (ed.), Northern Ireland, Half a Century of Partition (New York, 1973), pp.88-89, 144-45, 147 and 160. See also: Edward M. Kennedy, "Ulster is an International Issue", Foreign Policy 11 (Summer 1973), pp.57-73. The New York Times between 1969 and 1973 contains major stories on Senator Kennedy's views on Ireland on no fewer than 11 occasions.
29   The New York Times, 18 March 1978; The Washington Post, 18 March 1978.
30   "Ireland in 1977", 95th Congress, 1st Session, Committee Print for the Senate Committee on Foreign Relations.
31   "Report to the Committee on the Judiciary", 95th Congress, 2nd Session, Committee Print No.23.
32   Confidential Government Source; Claire Sterling, The Terror Network: The Secret War of International Terrorism (New York, 1981), p.158 (hereafter cited as Sterling, Terror Network).
33   Confidential Government Source. Other sources on the KGB in Ireland include: John Barron, KGB (New York, 1974), pp.254-55; Brian Crozier, Strategy for Survival (New York, 1978), p.137. See also: Stefan Bossony and Francis

Bouchey, International Terrorism: The Communist Connection (Washington D.C., 1978), p.35.
34   Sterling, Terror Network, p.159.
35   Ibid., p.160.
36   Ibid., p.161.
37   The evidence of the I.R.A.'s links with international terrorism is now overwhelming.
38   An Poblacht, 12 April 1977.
39   Sterling, Terror Network, p.169.
40   Ibid.
41   Some of these suggestions have already been offered in a valuable essay entitled "Healing Hands" by Kevin Cahill in Foreign Policy 37 (Winter 1979-80), pp.87-100.
42   Conor Cruise O'Brien, "Hand Off", Foreign Policy 37 (Winter 1979-80), pp.101-11.

Essay Three

SCOTLAND, BRITAIN AND CONFLICT IN IRELAND[1]

Tom Gallagher

It is not often that the smaller partners in the United Kingdom take precedence over England in any matter affecting their common destinies. This is the case in relation to the Irish conflict which, down the generations, has influenced the character of Scottish politics and life in a far more obvious way than it has done for England. So in an article discussing the impact of successive waves of Irish conflict on the neighbouring island, it is perhaps appropriate to concentrate on the Scottish dimension, while concluding the discussion with a briefer overview of how Britain as a whole (and particularly its Irish community) has withstood the stresses and strains imposed by the long-running Northern Irish conflict in the 1970s and early 1980s.

Ireland and (more especially) the Irish became a controversial subject in Scotland after the mass emigration of Catholic peasants in the wake of the disastrous 1846-49 famine. Over the next century, Irish people, mainly from the province of Ulster continued to migrate and settle in Scotland, though in decreasing numbers. Large-scale migration to Scotland had begun as early as the 1820s at a time when the west and centre of the country were in the throes of industrial revolution. Over time the newcomers would make up a greater percentage of the resident population in Scotland than did their counterparts in England. So through weight of numbers the Irish were more visible in Scotland where their reception was often a cold one. Although Ireland and Scotland are two Celtic countries (whose inhabitants share a similar ethnic background along with the language of Gaelic which was spoken widely in large areas of each country up to the 19th century), religion has caused their paths to diverge sharply. While Ireland remained a lonely north European oupost of Catholicism after the 16th century, Scotland quickly became one of the European strongholds of the new Protestant faith. The Reformation there was not merely imposed by royal fiat but had some of the overtones of popular revolution. Anti-Catholicism became a

53

pronounced feature of national culture when several attempts were made to restore the Roman Catholic faith in England with which Scotland was united in 1603 in a union of crowns. After 1707, the year in which the Scottish and English parliaments were combined, there were more anti-Catholic societies in the growing city of Glasgow than actual resident Catholics.[2] So religion was a barrier which, in the next century, prevented easy assimilation with the host community on the part of the newcomers. By now, the Scottish Protestant Church was losing its hold over much of the indigenous working class but Irish incomers and resident Scottish workers did not form a united proletarian class. Class solidarity developed rather later than in England because native Scots workers often bitterly resented the fact that the newcomers in their midst tended to depress real wages by being prepared to work for lower rates. A minority were also under the influence of the 'Orange' anti-Catholic wing of the Tory Party, which was stronger in Scotland than in other parts of the island.[3]

By the end of the 19th century, the Catholic community taking root in mainly Protestant Scotland was ceasing to be directly Irish. But until quite recently, several commentators persisted in referring to the Scottish Catholic communities as the 'Irish' as if they were total newcomers and unwelcome ones at that. The Catholicism of the immigrants and the belief that even among second and third generations, their primary loyalty was not to Scotland (or Great Britain) but to Ireland made many Scots unwilling to extend a welcoming hand. The attitude of some newcomers to their hosts could be reciprocal and, initially, the Irish preferred to establish their own communities in exile rather than assimilate with the general population. The west of Scotland industrial belt in general and the city of Glasgow in particular was where most immigrants preferred to settle down. On the south-side of Glasgow and in a number of towns and villages in neighbouring Lanarkshire, strong Irish communities emerged which managed to retain a separate identity even after the heirs of the original settlers had, to all intents and purposes, adopted the speech and ways of west-central Scotland.

Today over three-quarters of Scotland's 823,000 Catholics are still to be found in the west-central region.[4] In 1977, they made up 30.6 per cent of the population of Glasgow, the largest city in Scotland. Today Scotland has proportionately one-and-a-half times as many Catholics as does England (15.9 per cent of Scots were Catholic in 1977). But the evolution of the community was not without its dramas.

Community relations in Scotland between Protestants and Catholics underwent their stiffest test during the 1920s and 1930s. During the Anglo-Irish war (1919-21) sectarian tensions were high at a time when the struggle for independence in Ireland was receiving a massive endorsement from the Irish in Scotland and their heirs. Pro-IRA activity was extensive in several areas and one source reckons that "Glasgow had 4,000 IRA volunteers in 1920, including some 150 ex-servicemen".[5] Irish republican newspapers were printed in Glasgow, weapons were smuggled from there to Ireland and according to Eamon de Valera:

The financial contribution to the Irish struggle from among the Scottish communities was in excess of funds from any other country, including Ireland.[6]

The 1919-21 period was perhaps the only time when any section of the resident Scottish population played a substantial role in modern Irish politics. Once the main portion of the island received a large measure of freedom, the Irish 'movement' died away although interest in the progress of the young Irish state would remain high for many years as perusal of The Glasgow Observer (the main Catholic newspaper in Scotland) would attest. If Ulster had been involved in the more violent events of the 1916-23 period, then it is likely that partisans of 'Orange' and 'Green' causes in Scotland would have locked horns in more violent ways than they did. The fact that most of the fighting took place away from the already seething province of Ulster probably had a vital and salutary effect on community relations in Scotland. However, the unenviable position of the Catholic nationalist minority in Unionist Ulster still attracted sympathy and concern in Scotland. In 1935, after Orange rioters attacked Nationalist areas of Belfast in an onslaught which resulted in over ten deaths, a key pressure group of middle-class Glasgow Catholics known as the Catholic Union made the Belfast 'pogrom' an electoral issue in that city. It pressed for a British government enquiry into the riots and sought the views of parliamentary candidates for the main parties in the 1935 general election. Readers in The Glasgow Observer were given the results in the eve-of-poll issue with none-too-subtle hints about how to vote accordingly.[7]

In the event, it was not supporters of Irish freedom but pro-Unionist and anti-Catholic activists who were most in evidence between the wars. Their raison d'etre, the 'fifth column of almost one million followers of the Church of Rome' had not gone away but was increasing in numbers. In 1920, a Protestant party appeared with the formation of the Scottish Protestant League (SPL) led by Alexander Ratcliffe.[8] For most of its existence, the SPL engaged in stunts such as anti-Catholic plays or in disrupting Catholic functions and ceremonies of a public character. Its rowdyism reached serious proportions in Edinburgh during 1935 when three major sectarian outbreaks occurred between April and June.[9] On separate occasions, violent demonstrations occurred: when Joseph Lyons (1879-1939), the Catholic Prime Minister of Australia was awarded the freedom of the city; when a Eucharistic Congress was held in the city; and when the Catholic Young Men's Association of Great Britain was given a civic reception by the city council. On the last occasion. Archbishop Macdonald (1871-1950) of St Andrews and Edinburgh came under attack from a large crowd outside the city hall and it was only with difficulty that he was rescued by the police.[10]

Similar outbursts, though not of the same velocity, have taken place in Scotland before and since whenever Protestant zealots have felt that Catholics are receiving undue recognition from local or national authorities. The Pope's visit to Scotland in 1982 was a potential source of discord.The Grand Orange Lodge of Scotland (which has fraternal links with the Orange Order in Ireland) issued a pamphlet protesting against Pope John Paul II's visit and a Scottish-based anti-Catholic journal called The Bulwark has been in publication for many years.[11] Yet, the visit went off peacefully. Still there is a small but not insignificant market for anti-Catholic rodomontades. Some years in Glasgow, it is the Orange Order which holds Scotland's largest demonstration when on the first Saturday in July, thousands parade through the streets to hear speeches from local Orange leaders and Ulster politicians imported for the occasion. But it was only in the 1930s that Orange anti-Catholicism seemed poised to become a major political force.

During the early 1930s, the Scottish Protestant League (SPL) made spectacular progress in Glasgow politics, winning seven seats in 1932-33 with a campaign directed against the 'twin' evils of municipal corruption and the Catholic Church. For a time, the SPL seemed on the verge of becoming a dangerous third force in local politics but it was poorly led and had no real programme 'beyond ranting against popes and nuns'.[12] Within a few years, it had lost all the seats previously acquired in Glasgow, and in Edinburgh, its leaders A. Ratcliffe and John Cormack quarreled, and much ridicule greeted the formation of a Scottish Ku Klux Klan in 1938. Some time before, one of the stalwarts of the SPL had travelled to Belfast, where he slashed a picture hanging in an art gallery of the Pope blessing King William of Orange at the Battle of the Boyne in 1690.[13]

One aspect of Scottish life providing fertile soil for sectarianism is the rivalry that has grown up between two Glasgow football clubs: Rangers and Celtic. The respective fortunes of both teams attracts great interest and much traffic from the other side of the Irish Sea. Rangers, an all-Protestant team, has more than thirty supporters clubs in N Ireland while Celtic, their main rival, has fourteen there and many more in the Irish Republic. Rivalry between the two clubs became really fierce after World War I. Since the 1940s Rangers has not signed a single Catholic player while Celtic fields mixed sides but continues to enjoy most appeal among the Catholic population of Scotland.[14] Today Rangers-Celtic confrontations are synonymous with hooliganism and disorders which sometimes reach serious proportions. Disturbed by the adverse publicity Scotland was receiving as a result of this long-running feud, the Church of Scotland (the leading Protestant denomination) passed a resolution in 1980 at its annual assembly which stated:

> We feel that tensions would be eased if all clubs, and Rangers FC in particular would publicly disclaim sectarian bias.[15]

The Church of Scotland was not always so sensitive about sectarian problems. Catholic-Protestant relations were often fraught at the ecclesiastical, as well as community, level during the inter-war years. The age of ecumenism had yet to dawn and the temper of the times might be guaged by the fact that in 1923 the General Assembly of the Church of Scotland formally approved a report entitled <u>The Menace of the Irish Race to Our Scottish Nationality</u>.[16] Published in pamphlet form and appearing when the St Vitus dance of extreme European nationalism was shortly to reach its climax, the pamphlet demanded that means be devised to "preserve Scotland the Scottish race" and "to secure for future generations the traditions, ideals and faith of a great people unspoiled and inviolate".[17] Many Protestant clergymen were antagonised by the fact that the 1918 Education (Scotland) Act allowed Catholic schools to be subsidised by the state. 'Rome on the rates' was their cry and although relations between Protestant and RC religious leaders have improved almost out of all recognition, education still remains a vexed topic. RC clergy are still adamant that Catholic children should be taught in single religion schools. One fairly progressive bishop is quite prepared to admit that "Roman Catholic schools divide society" but he would not apparently have it any other way since there is much in contemporary society from which he and his colleagues would like to shield young and impressionable Catholics.[18]

The existence of separate RC schools has undoubtedly kept the community solidified while inviting claims that they were a bridge-head in a renewed attempt to 'Romanise' Scotland. Nationally-minded Scots expressed this view between the wars. In a colourful essay in futurology published in 1927, the writer George Thomas looked far into the future to 1981 when "the Irish population had passed the one million mark and in that year slowly deepening irritation between the races flashed into open war".[19] By 2027, he depicts the public libraries in many towns under the Roman Index but fortunately he was a poor prophet (unless his mind had momentarily wandered into an alternative universe).

A fellow Scottish separatist, Andrew Dewar Gibb (1893-1974), professor of law at Glasgow University and chairman of the Scottish National Party in the 1930s, was scathing about the 'Irish' in Scotland. In a book published in 1930, he described them as "riff-raff... responsible for most of the crime committed in Scotland which otherwise would be the most law-abiding country in the world".[20] This view never caught on in a party which is obsessive about minimising internal Scottish differences. Anti-Irish elements in the other parties were also fairly isolated. In the Conservative or Tory Party, the second largest force in Scottish politics after the Labour Party, only two really prejudiced MPs spring to mind after 1918: Lord Mungo Scone (1900-1971), Tory MP for Perth (1931-35) who fulminated in parliament against "a separate race of alien origin" in the west of Scotland "bitterly resented by tens of thousands of the working class";[21] and Hugh Ferguson, Tory MP for Motherwell in 1923-24 who was a member of the Orange Order and one of the few Tories of humble background chosen to repre nt the party in parliament at that time.

Why in the end was inter-ethnic conflict unable to assume greater significance and shape the contours of politics in the way that occurred in N Ireland? A number of possible reasons can be advanced. First of all, the scope for Scottish-based political movements (whether progressive or reactionary) has always been limited owing to the fact that most political decision-making takes place outside the country; it is interesting to reflect that hard-core sectarianism did not become an absolutely dominant element of N Ireland society until it was given a large measure of self-government. And even before the Ulster conflict demonstrated to shocked neighbouring societies what the full horror of mindless sectarianism could lead to, there always was 'a profound distaste of sectarian conflict co-existing with an equally profound sense of Orange-Green identity among many people'.[22] Of crucial importance was the fact that the industrial bourgeoisie did not use the sectarian card to divide-and-rule the working class. At no tome did any Scottish equivalent of Sir James Craig (1871-1940), the Ulster whisky millionaire and first premier of N Ireland, ever loom on the Scottish horizon. In general, the industrial bourgeoisie preferred to remain aloof from politics.[23] Their corporate mouthpiece, the staid mercantilist Glasgow Herald avoided controversy and in 1929 the paper did community relations a service by publishing a series of six articles which disproved some of the more fantastic stories then circulating about the Irish in Scotland and their descendants.[24]

Another important point when seeking to explain why sectarianism remained under control in an environment not totally dissimilar from that of N Ireland is the unwillingness of the political parties to capitalise on the issue for partisan ends. The only possible exception was the Glasgow Moderate Party (the name Conservatives adopted in municipal politics) who made a brief and costly pact with the extremist SPL in the early 1930s which resulted in Labour taking power in Glasgow in 1933.

The Scottish National Party (founded in 1934) was always reluctant to play upon Scottish ethnocentrism at the expense of RCs of Irish descent with the exception of a few individual members, some of whom later mellowed. As for the Conservative Party, its record is more ambivalent. Before 1966, it held on to a number of constituencies in Scotland with a sizeable working-class population by beating the Orange drum. For many years, it was known in Scotland as the Unionist Part without there being any close links with the N Ireland party of that name. Although the Tory Party's aristocratic managers kept the unruly Orange element out of the higher echelons of the party, Freemasons and Orangemen were sufficiently strong to prevent the election of a Catholic Tory MP until the 1970s. In 1945, a sitting Tory MP, Sir John McEwen (1894-1962) lost the hitherto safe seat of Berwick and Haddington, having become a Catholic convert in 1940. Today a significant change has taken place in the composition of the Tory Party in Scotland which makes it even less likely that it will provide an impetus for inter-ethnic conflict. In slowly increasing numbers, Catholics from professional and middle-class backgrounds are being nominated as Tory parliamentary candidates. Four RCs were selected in 1979 (three more than in 1970) and one was elected: Michael Ancram (1945-   ), an RC aristocrat of liberal tendencies (for Edinburgh South) who later became chairman of the Scottish Conservative Party (though not without opposition in some quarters).[25]

The Liberals, in Scotland as elsewhere, grew less and less relevant after the year 1918 but it is interesting to reflect that before then, they had been the dominant party in Scotland where they fulfilled a role not dissimilar to that of the Democratic Party in the USA.

Before 1918, the Liberals were simultaneously the party of a majority of the lower middle-class, the indigenous working class, and the 'Irish'. Many, though certainly not all, Church of Scotland ministers backed the Liberals and there was never any great danger of the informal alliance between the Kirk (as the Church of Scotland is often termed) and the Conservative and Unionist Party which Ulster witnessed after the 1880s. The Orange Order likewise remained a marginal force in Kirk affairs and was usually more of a social than politico-religious movement in Scotland. Confirmation of this was perhaps provided in the 1970s on Orange Day in Glasgow when the numbers drinking cans of beer or eating ice-cream on the grass verges away from the rally exceeded those listening to speeches by top Unionist politicians from Ulster.

Catholics and Protestants tend to live side by side in Glasgow and elsewhere thanks to the housing policies of municipal authorities. These discouraged the likelihood of rival working-class ghettoes emerging. Discrimination in employment was common between the wars but no rigid patterns were established perhaps because Scotland ceased to be a heavily industrial nation after mid-century and instead became rather post-industrial in appearance with service industries very much to the fore. The state became far and away the largest employer of skilled labour and merit or availability took precedence over religion in the job market.

Emigration was another factor which defused communal tension. Always of a high order in Scotland, it provided an escape-hatch for individuals whose counterparts in central Europe after 1918 stayed at home and immersed themselves in extremist politics of one sort or another. But perhaps the overriding reason why sectarianism failed to shape Scottish society in a Northern Irish mould was the success of the Labour Party in politics from the 1920s down to the present-day. Labour has kept the working-class movement politically united and has proved too formidable a force for proponents of sectarianism to take on.

From 1906 onwards, the Catholic/Irish community in Scotland went over to the emergent Labour Party in ever increasing numbers so that by 1919 an attempt in Glasgow to form a separate ethnic Irish party was doomed to failure even though solidarity with the Irish struggle was shortly to reach a crescendo. For the background to this convergence one ought to look back to 1906 when an Irish-born former miner John Wheatley (1869-1930) had founded the Catholic Socialist Society in Glasgow. The CSS emerged at a time when one of the distinguishing marks of European socialism was its anti-clericalism.[26] It was a truly pioneering initiative, especially since, until the very end of his life, Wheatley would be on the left of the Labour movement. Local priestly opposition was at first fierce towards what many clerics viewed as the subversive Trojan horse methods of the Catholic Socialists. Some priests urged Archbishop John Maguire (1851-1920) of Glasgow to excommunicate Wheatley but this prelate (who was radical for his day) refused. Wheatley then got elected to Glasgow town council and, after 1910, enjoyed increasing success poaching Irish votes from the Liberals.

Since no general election took place between 1910 and 1918, the swing towards Labour showed itself only in local elections. On the eve of the 1918 election, an important development occurred when Charles Diamond (1858-1934), owner of The Glasgow Observer and a chain of Catholic papers published throughout Britain, urged his readers to abandon Liberalism and vote Labour. The Irish issue was his main pretext but Diamond himself stood as a Labour candidate, having been an Irish Home Rule MP from 1892 to 1895.[27]

Wheatley failed to win Glasgow Shettleston by less than one thousand votes in 1918 but four years later he was returned (one of the first three Catholic MPs in Scotland) along with 28 other Scottish Labour members. Labour received

32.2 per cent of the vote in Scotland in 1922 compared with 28 per cent in England and its good showing was undoubtedly due to strong endorsement from the Catholic working class.[28] Two other RCs, Hugh Murnin (1865-1932) and Joseph Sullivan (1866-1935) were returned for Stirling & Falkirk and N Lanarkshire respectively. In 1924, Wheatley became minister of housing in the first British Labour government and was widely regarded as the one ministerial success of that shortlived administration. Writing in the 1960s, Sir Oswald Mosley (1896-1980), the former British Fascist leader), described Wheatley as "the only man of Lenin quality the English (sic) Left ever produced".[29] He died in 1930, a radical figure to the end although also a prosperous businessman and a practising Catholic. However, other Catholics of Irish descent like John McGovern (1887-1968) and Patrick Dollan (circa 1880-1963) who were prominent in Scottish politics, moderated their previously radical views, both men returning to the faith before their deaths. The career of McGovern, in particular, illustrates how the Labour Party became conformist and staid, having once been a far more dynamic and radical force in Scotland than elsewhere in the United Kingdom. The son of Catholic Irish parents, McGovern as a young man considered being a priest but quickly renounced the RC faith first for anarchism and then socialism. In 1930, he was sufficiently radical for the Catholic Church to urge its members to vote for the Tory candidate in Glasgow Shettleston, when he was the Labour candidate following Wheatley's death.[30] As a member of parliament, he was expelled from the House of Commons and arrested at demonstrations. However, in the 1950s his fate was to become a convert to Dr Frank Buchman's Moral Re-Armament after paying a visit to the MRA's alpine headquarters at Caux in 1954. Moving steadily to the Right. he retired from parliament in 1959 and in 1964 was campaigning for the Tories in Glasgow under the banner 'Give Harold Wilson power and you will live to regret it'.[31] Earlier, he had penned a testimonial for the Shah of Iran finding 'the young monarch a very impressive person who is clearly aware of what is necessary as an alternative to communism'.[32]

Wherever they have settled and become politically active, the Irish have tended to show greater interest in the building of political organisations than in ideology and policies. Evidence for this claim comes from Scotland as well as other centres of the Irish diaspora. In the absence of a national parliament in Scotland, local politics has turned out to be an area of more intense party competition than parliamentary politics and it is in the former area that RCs have channelled their energies. For many years after 1931, very few local RCs were returned for Scottish Labour seats. There was only one in 1935, two in 1945, and three in 1955. At local level, Catholic politicians who were often bar-owners, trade-union officials or bookmakers helped turn Labour into an orthodox and careerist party in which grassroots involvement steadily waned. Only in the 1970s have radical Catholic MPs once again been elected to Scottish seats. However, RCs still support the Labour Party in massive numbers; two political scientists in the 1960s estimated that the Catholic vote for Labour was more solid than that of the working-class and the same remains true today.[33]

Its massive and repeated endorsement for Labour makes the RC community more visible in politics than it might otherwise be, perhaps a not altogether healthy situation but at least the party has reciprocated by protecting the interests of the RC community, which might not have happened if the Catholic vote had been split more equally among all the parties.

One is more readily prepared to use the term 'Catholic' rather than 'Irish' for the Irish emigrants and their descendants since they retained a strong religious identity long after losing most (though not all) of their Irish heritage. This is understandable. It was the clergy who often provided the leadership within the Catholic community and it was the schools, churches, and halls built under religious auspices which, after the 1880s, became the chief focal-points of the Catholic community. Many priests were authoritarian and traditionalist but through their work in the parishes, the RC community acquired a cohesion and unity which made it stand up well to the rigours and challenges to be encountered in what often could be a hostile environment. A whole host of lay organisations, often sponsored by the church, emerged in the early twentieth-century designed to protect Irish Catholic interests or provide an outlet for the energies of assertive Catholics. These included the Catholic Young Men's Society, the Catholic Truth Society, the Knights of St Columbus, the Ancient Order of Hibernians, the St Vincent de Paul Society, recreational and social groups, pious societies, sodality associations, and Catholic societies grouping together doctors, lawyers, teachers, nurses and transport workers. This rich framework of groups and societies gave Catholic Scotland an identity and confidence which it had previously lacked but their success perhaps ironically militated against the interests of the RC community by cutting them off from the rest of the population. So the role of the institutional church and lay offshoots was a dual one: on the one hand they steeled the community against the threat of internal disintegration, or attack from without; on the other, the omnipotence of the Church and RC organisations tended to cut much of the community off from those groups in Scottish society willing to cooperate with the RC population for the 'common good'.

Perhaps the main force which could have acted as an integrative one for the Catholic community was the Labour Party. At first, like most Catholic churches, the Scottish one was hostile to the claims of socialism. But by the end of World War I, clerical opposition to the Labour Party was much reduced and the Scottish RC Church was on its way towards becoming one of the first national churches in the world to reach a modus vivendi with socialism. What lay behind this accommodation with the left? First of all, it seems clear that many priests feared the revolutionary alternative to the Labour Party. With the emergence of Communist Russia in 1917, marxism was no longer a distant theoretical spectre. Soon the west of Scotland, the stronghold of Catholicism in Scotland, would itself become internationally famous as Red Clydeside and it does seem that an increasing number of priests concluded that all-out resistance to socialism of any kind might result in the repudiation of the church by increasing numbers of Catholics.

Where RCs were urged to join the Labour movement, it was less as an attempt to work out a Catholic road to socialism than to tone down its radicalism and frustrate red agitators.[34] The fact that the 'Irish' vote had been a disciplined one which before 1918 had supported the candidates or party recommended by the United Irish League, caused the church's power to be feared in some Labour circles. But its power to sway the masses in the polling booths grew increasingly limited and McGovern's victory in the 1930 Shettleston by-election in the teeth of clerical opposition was a sign of the way the wind was blowing.

Without a strong church to guide it, the RC community would have been far less parochial in its outlook but it would probably also have fared less well in its dealings with the host Scottish community.

Scots RCs of Irish descent have family and cultural ties with the historic nine-county province of Ulster to a greater extent than any other section of the British RC population of Irish descent. It is often forgotten that Ulster Protestants, as well as Catholics, also emigrated to Scotland from the 1820s onwards, though in much smaller numbers. After World War I, it was the arrival of Protestant engineering workers from Belfast to work in the Harland and Wolf shipyards on Clydeside which is said to have given the Rangers-Celtic conflict a virulence which it previously lacked. In 1981, interest in their ancestral homelands was still considerable among rival supporters of the two Glasgow football clubs. 'The Pope's Coming Over, The Pope's Coming Over' was the triumphant cry of thousands of Celtic fans before the football season ended in April 1981. Rangers supporters in reply would roar, 'Two Popes Have Died, Two Popes Have Died, But the Queen Lives On.' It has even been suggested only half-jokingly that the success of the Pope's 1982 visit to Scotland could have been marred if Rangers had had a bad soccer season and her fans had been particularly dispirited.

Such almost trivial displays of animosity disturb the

outsider but communal friction rarely breaks out over Irish political matters. It is usually native issues like religion, education, or football which, in the past, have led to open friction between partisans of Orange or Green views.

Significantly, the Ulster Unionist mobilisation against Irish Home Rule was not emulated in Scotland although the Orange Order was then very strong. Irish separatist leaders like Padraig Pearse (1879-1916) and Arthur Griffith (1871-1922) addressed a number of Glasgow meetings before 1914 but it was in Liverpool not Glasgow that the moderate Irish Home Rule Party was able to capture and hold a British parliamentary seat.[35] Perhaps if Parnell, the Irish nationalist leader, had stood Home Rule candidates in Scotland after 1885, the chances are that one seat might have been captured, the most likely one being Glasgow Blackfriars. In the 1880s, and for long afterwards, the Irish in Scotland would concern themselves with events in Ireland to a greater extent than any other section of the Irish diaspora. This is the view of the historian Owen Dudley Edwards of Edinburgh University who has compared the Irish in Scotland with the Chinese in America, two groups who resided in, but were not really part of their respective new homelands.[36] There is evidence for and against this viewpoint. In the 1970s, the 'Irish' in Scotland were paying far less attention to the N Ireland conflict than the 'Irish' in the United States. But in the late 1920s, interest was still sufficiently strong for six branches of the new Irish political party, Fianna Fail, to be founded in Scotland (as against only one in England and none in N Ireland). But thereafter, Scotland influenced the fractured political situation in the remaining British-ruled part of Ireland only indirectly, as in the 1960s when the Coatbridge-born Eddie McAteer (1914-) became leader of the Nationalist Party in N Ireland.[37] At first, some Glasgow Labour MPs such as Neil Maclean (1875-1953) and the turbulent John McGovern were vocal spokesmen on behalf of Irish unity. These two addressed a large indoor anti-partition rally in Glasgow during 1939 shortly after the foundation of the Anti-Partition League in N Ireland. (A later Labour MP, James Carmichael (1894-1966) regularly attended the annual commemoration of the 1916 Easter Rising, in Dublin even although his constituency, Glasgow Bridgeton, had perhaps the strongest Orange vote of any Scottish seat.)[38]

But Scottish Labour MPs were largely conspicuous by their absence in 'The Friends of Ireland' and Campaign for Democracy in Ulster, two pressure groups organized in the Labour Party in the late 1940s and mid-1960s respectively. John Wheatley played down his Irish associations after being elected to parliament in 1922 and, had he lived, he would probably not have been too happy at de Valera's proposal for an exchange of populations as a means of solving the Ulster question. In 1934, the Irish leader suggested that Irish people and their descendants living in Scotland could take the place of hardline Unionists unwilling to remain in Ulster in the event of a united Ireland.[39] Among the community in Scotland, there was little conspicuous enthusiasm for this plan which, anyway, did not receive much publicity. Later in the 1940s and 1950s, interest in Ireland diminished and would not be greatly revived by the Ulster troubles of the late 1960s and the 1970s. In the early 1950s, the Catholic novelist Evelyn Waugh spoke at a 4,000 strong Glasgow Catholic meeting called in protest at President Tito of Yugoslavia's state visit to Britain but Irish republicans could not muster such numbers. By the 1970s, Billy Connolly, the popular entertainer, was much better known than his namesake James Connolly (1868-1916), the Edinburgh-born Irish revolutionary, described in 1979 as "the most original left-wing political thinker produced by the British Isles since Engels".[40] At the end of 1980, pro-IRA slogans could be seen in Glasgow housing estates but it is to London and Birmingham that the conflict has spilled over (in terms at least of blood and death) not Scotland.[41] In the last thirty years, emigration from Ireland to the economically-depressed west of Scotland has died down almost to a trickle, thereby slowly killing off the phenomenon of exile politics. As the RC population becomes less ethnically distinct and more Caledonian in its world-view, assimilation has been stepped up. Nevertheless, links between Unionist Orangemen in Scotland and N Ireland continue to be important, as RC interest in what seems increasingly to them as an ancestral quarrel dies away.

With the exception of the ephemeral Ancient Order of Hibernians, there is no Irish nationalist equivalent to the mass membership Orange Order. Its trans-class membership, sophisticated infrastructure, and vote-gathering power give Ulster Unionism a formidable extra dimension which Irish Republicanism has always lacked. In Scotland alone, the Orange Order was alleged to have had 80,000 members in 1976.[42] During the same year, one former British army sergeant claimed that there were three divisions of the paramilitary Ulster Defence Association (UDA) in Scotland with a total strength of at least 2,000 men.[43] Writing then, Brian Wilson, an observer of the Loyalist scene in Scotland, declared that:

> It seems clear that the Loyalist paramilitary activity around Glasgow, like its Republican counterpart, is geared towards intervention in Northern Ireland rather than to bringing the conflict into Scottish streets.[44]

Nevertheless, during the first half of 1981, Glasgow witnessed several violent clashes between Orange supporters and pro-H-Block demonstrators marching in solidarity with IRA prisoners on hunger-strike in Northern Ireland.[45] But these incidents were not communal disorders since the RC population have little backing to them: the main impetus for these demonstrations came from the far-Left, often in the shape of English political activists resident in Scotland, who were often painfully unaware of the residual importance of sectarianism. After one clash in Glasgow, BBC Radio's World Service declared on February 15 1981 that Glasgow was "a city notorious for its bigotry".[46] However, this is not (and should not be thought) the case and it is doubtful if, in the past, the facts of the situation ever justified such notoriety. Scotland in the 1970s was absorbed with its own domestic politics while Ulster burned. In that decade, the impact of economic decline on community relations was as minimal as that of the Irish question. Unemployment and the resurgence of social distress has not triggered off intra-working-class strife. 'No Irish Wanted Here' or 'No Catholics Need Apply' are slogans of the 1930s which have not been resurrected in the 1970s, although some trades and factories in Glasgow are still the preserve of one distinct religious grouping.

Why did predictions of doom and gloom expressed in the late 1960s about Scotland becoming a mini-version of N Ireland fail to come to pass? One important reason must be the growth of exogamy (inter-marriage). Biology has frustrated the bigots to an increasing extent: in 1966, only 28 per cent of marriages involving a Catholic were with a non-RC but by 1977 this figure had leapt to 44 per cent. Orange and Green pre-occupations cannot last indefinitely if such integration continues apace. Another important consideration is Scotland's geographical proximity to N Ireland. Possibly more than any other people, the Scots are aware of what horrors sectarianism can lead to thanks to the grandstand view of the N Ireland conflict their geographical and cultural proximity affords them. Even among stalwarts of Orange and Green views, there is a reluctance to 'push it' because very few people wish to see the tragedy across the water repeated in their own midst. However, the stagnation and relative conservatism of Scottish society has meant that no concerted effort has been made to eradicate the remaining vestiges of sectarianism in Scottish life be they in the worlds of soccer or employment.

Another reason why the Irish conflict has not spread may be the fact that Scottish political culture is relatively non-violent. The main radical force in politics, the separatist National Party (SNP) has not been tempted by extra-parliamentary methods, although it may have been severely pressed in 1979 over the failure of the British government to grant a parliament for Scotland even though a majority of Scots voted in a referendum for this measure.

In England, the only place where the Irish issue had serious overtones was the city of Liverpool which, up to the Second World War, was wracked by major sectarian conflict.[47] The bitterness between Irish incomers and local Protestant workers of English or Ulster descent seems to have been even more intense than in the west of Scotland since it prevented the rise of the left in this proletarian city until well into the twentieth century. The Working Men's Conservative Association (whose membership was firmly closed to Catholics) led by the Tammany politician Archibald Salvidge (1863-1928) dominated city politics from the 1890s to the 1930s. Labour did not capture the city council until the 1950s and as late as 1958, the Catholic archbishop of Liverpool was stoned, while paying a visit to a parishioner who lived in a Protestant stronghold. Fifty years before, the Labour politician Ramsay Macdonald had declared to Salvidge at an election count that:

> It is astounding how in Liverpool, whatever the issue appears to be at the start, you always manage to mobilise the full force of Orangeism. We will never do any good here until that power is broken.[48]

As a force, Orangeism was not really broken until housing renewal got underway in Liverpool after 1945. Massive slum-clearance programmes played havoc with the traditional religious geography of the city and it is significant that the riots which erupted in Liverpool in mid-1981 seem to have owed nothing to residual sectarian feeling but were motivated by the twin issues of race and unemployment.[49]

No new Liverpools emerged in the 1950s when Britain witnessed the most concentrated wave of Irish immigration since the late 19th century. Upwards of 400,000 people settled mainly in England, having found that there were few prospects of material advancement in the stagnant Ireland of the 1950s. The 1950s exodus may have been the last major influx of Irish people who will come to Britain. The new exiles settled not in the traditional centres of Manchester, Liverpool, and Glasgow but in Birmingham, London and the generally more prosperous south. The 1950s generation and their offspring have blended in with the host community far more rapidly and completely than previous emigrants and they have also been more socially mobile.[50] Because of the presence of large numbers of Irish people in different walks of life, British public opinion refuses to regard Ireland or the Irish as completely alien entities even after the eruption of the Ulster conflict in 1969. Ulster Loyalists may have Catholic southern Irish people domiciled in England to thank for the fact that the English still refuse to regard Ireland as a totally foreign land. Anybody with an Irish accent is taken for a 'Paddy' or a 'Mick' (familiar English terms for the Irish) which can be infuriating for Ulster Unionists who sometimes like to insist that they are the most loyal Britons of them all.

English reluctance to acknowledge Irish political or ethnic distinctions may be part of a deep-seated reluctance to become involved in the politics of the place. Boredom with the Irish conflict has even survived the IRA bombing campaign in

British cities which reached a peak during the mid-1970s. No anti-Irish backlash occurred although Birmingham came very close to one in November 1974 after the bombing of several bars resulted in over a dozen people killed and many more horribly mutilated. The killing in April 1979 of British Conservative politician Airey Neave (1916-1979) and the assassination in the west of Ireland of Lord Mountbatten (1900-1979) in August of that year produced no violent reaction against the Irish in Britain although outrage was virtually universal. The Irish community was generally saddened by these killings, especially that of Lord Mountbatten, a friend of the Irish people who was on record as supporting a united Ireland.

The IRA does have sympathisers among the Irish in Britain and their numbers have undoubtedly been enlarged during the H-Block hunger-strike of 1981 (and more especially by Mrs Thatcher's intransigence). But the Irish in Britain have usually kept their distance from the Ulster conflict and are reluctant to get involved. The Troops Out Movement which campaigns for British withdrawal from Ireland, has few Irish activitists and is mainly supported by the English Left. Nevertheless, the Irish in Britain have been singled out by the authorities as a potentially subversive element in British society. The Prevention of Terrorism Act (PTA) passed by a Labour government in 1974 in the wake of the Birmingham bombings, gives the state the power to deport Irish people to Ireland even if they have been living in mainland Britain for decades and have not set foot in Ireland since their arrival. Citizens of Northern Ireland can be, and are, refused entry into mainland Britain. These and other draconian clauses of the PTA have been used against Irish people who have no proven involvement in Irish republicanism but who may have been active in trade-unionism or in left politics. It has also been conceded by the authorities that the 1974 act has been a failure in regard to trying to curtail IRA activity.[51] Yet there is no sign that it will be removed from the statute books even though its architect Home Secretary Roy Jenkins, conceived it as a short-term emergency measure.

The PTA and the 1974-79 Labour government's backing for Ulster Unionism produced growing disillusionment among Irish voters in Britain with the party they have traditionally supported: Labour. One of the anomalies of British politics is the fact that the large Irish-born community still enjoys voting rights at election time even though few Irish people have taken out British citizenship. Tory MPs have been angered by this state of affairs and, after 1979, pressure was put on Prime Minister Margaret Thatcher to take the vote away from the Irish. She has so far refused and the controversial 1981 Nationality Act has no provisions concerning the Irish even though their disenfranchisement would be bound to benefit the Tories considerably. Mrs Thatcher has perhaps been dissuaded by the fact that it would be too complicated to alter the electoral register, especially where individuals have married British people as well as by the fact that the Irish in Britain would be able to vote in Irish Republic elections if disenfranchised in Britain.

British governments have always been concerned that the Irish Republic remains a stable entity and the fear has been expressed by John Biggs-Davison MP (Tory: Epping Forest) that to allow the Irish in Britain to vote back home might have a disruptive effect on Irish politics since the community in Britain is so vast compared to the voting population in the Republic.

Recently, the political allegiances of the Irish in Britain have begun to alter. Since 1970, their voting habits have been closely scrutinised by The Irish Post, the large circulation weekly newspaper of the Irish community. On the eve of each election in the 1970s, the paper commissioned a leading opinion research company to sample the voting intentions of the Irish.[52] In 1970, over 75 per cent who intended to vote supported the Labour Party. In the two 1974 elections, pro-Labour sentiments were seen to be in decline but over 60 per cent were still prepared to vote Labour according to The Irish Post: Irish peeople were still apparently voting for the Socialist Party in a higher proportion than the British working class. But when the April 26 1979 issue of the paper published the results of its survey, it was found that less than 30 per cent of those canvassed were going to vote Labour on May 3 1979.[53] This was an incredible decline of more than half and even if the survey was out by ten per cent, it still represented a huge desertion by a traditionally solid Labour support group.

Ironically, some of Labour's leading figures were men of Irish descent such as Denis Healey, Don Concannon, and the leader from 1976 to 1980, James Callaghan. None of them took a particularly pro-Irish line on the Ulster question unlike American counterparts Edward Kennedy and 'Tip' O'Neil. Indeed it is the former coalminer Don Concannon who in recent times has been the most vilified of Labour politicians for his strongly pro-Unionist line on Ireland. Some of the British Army casualties in N Ireland have had distinctly Irish names, another clue indicating that the slow integration of the Irish in Britain has continued apace.

Finally, it would do no harm to remind readers that the last twelve years have demonstrated that Irish and Anglo-Saxons can co-exist more easily than the rival Irish communities in Northern Ireland. This is an achievement that is often overlooked but really ought not to be.

Notes

1   I would like to thank the British Academy for a grant in 1981 for research on this article.

2   Interview with Bishop Joseph Devine, Auxiliary Bishop of Glasgow: August 26 1981.

3   Scotland was the only area in mainland Britain where a trans-class alliance of the Ulster type seemed remotely feasible. If one had developed in 19th century Scotland, the Ulster's political and economic elite might have been able with more success to play the Prussian Junker role which they seemed to be adopting in the United Kingdom as a whole during the years before 1914.

4   See James Darragh, 'The Catholic Population of Scotland 1878-1977', in David McRoberts, ed., Modern Scottish Catholicism 1878-1978 (Glasgow: John Burns, 1977), p.230. This collection is hereafter cited as McRoberts.

5   James E. Handley, The Irish in Modern Scotland (Cork: Cork University Press, 1947), p.299.

6   See Kevin O'Connor, The Irish in Britain (Dublin: Torc Books, 1974), pp.41-42.

7   The Glasgow Observer. November 16 1935, p.3.

8   Information about the foundation of the SPL is contained in The Glasgow Observer, December 20 1930.

9   Glasgow, where the bulk of 'alien Irish' resided, would never witness such scenes, at least in the 1900-81 period, perhaps because of their numerical strength. The Edinburgh incidents may be due to the fact that the Protestant faith was much stronger among the non-Catholic population of the city than in leftist Glasgow.

10   The Glasgow Observer of August 17 1935 reported that The Times of London had played down the Edinburgh riots and had expressed surprise that so much attention was given to them in the European press, especially in Nazi Germany. It also reported that Archbishop Macdonald had written to The Times on August 12 criticising the newspaper for its low-key coverage and pointing out just how violent the incidents earlier in the summer had been.

11   The Pope Cannot Be Welcomed to Britain, Grand Orange Lodge of Scotland, Glasgow, 1980.

12   See Harry McShane and Joan Smith, Harry McShane: No Mean Fighter (London: Pluto Press, 1978), p.206.

13   Ibid.

14   Henceforth Catholics will frequently be referred to as 'RCs' in order to avoid undue repetition.

15   This quote appeared in 'Credo', a programme on the Rangers-Celtic football conflict broadcast on London Weekend Television, November 23 1980.

16   The Menace of the Irish Race to Our Scottish Nationality (Edinburgh: William Bishop, 1923).

17   Ibid.

18   Interview with Bishop Joseph Devine, August 26 1981.

19   George Thomson. Caledonia or the Future of the Scots
(London: Kegan. Paul. Trench, 1927), p.76.
20   Andrew Dewar Gibb, Scotland In Eclipse (London:
Toulmin, 1930), p.54. Statistics for the first half of the
century do clearly prove that the Irish were responsible for
more crime in Scotland than their numbers might warrant.
However, most of them were located at the bottom end of the
social ladder and the great majority were engaged in the often
difficult process of family advancement. If Professor Dewar
Gibb was trying to make a radical point about the Irish in
general he would have derived little comfort from looking at
the Irish in Ireland. Until the onset of rapid modernisation in
the 1970s, they were one of the most law-abiding communities
in the entire western world.
21   See Hansard, Vol.32-33, p.329, November 24 1932.
22   I am grateful to Graham Walker for this insight.
23   Sydney Checkland, The Upas Tree: Glasgow 1875-1975,
A Study In Growth and Contraction (Glasgow: Glasgow
University Press, 1976), p.14.
24   See The Glasgow Herald, March 20, 21, 22, 23 and 25
1929.
25   The British Conservative leader Mrs Thatcher was
adamant that it was right and proper for Michael Ancram to
be party chairman in Scotland.
26   Several worthwhile studies of Wheatley and his novel
political departure have appeared. See Sheridan Gilley, 'Irish
Catholics and Socialists in Glasgow 1906-1912' in K. Lunn
(ed.), Hosts, Immigrants and Minorities (Folkestone: Dawson,
1980); Samuel Cooper, John Wheatley: A Study in Labour
History (University of Glasgow PhD, 1973); Ian S. Wood,
'John Wheatley, the Irish, and the Labour Movement in
Scotland', The Innes Review vol.21, Autumn 1981, pp.71-85;
and Bob Purdie, Outside The Chapel Door, The Glasgow
Catholic Socialist Society (Ruskin History Diploma, 1976).
27   For a study of Diamond's career, see Owen Dudley
Edwards, 'The Catholic Press in Scotland Since The
Restoration of The Hierarchy', in McRoberts, pp.156-83,
especially pp.169-74.
28   See Tom Gallagher, 'Catholics in Scottish Politics', The
Bulletin of Scottish Politics No.2, Spring 1981, p.31.
29   See Robert Skidelsky, Oswald Mosley (London:
Macmillan, 1980), p.169.
30   See The Glasgow Observer, June 21 1930 and especially
the article 'Shettleston Election. Irish Voters Vote Tory!'
31   Obituary, The Times, February 15 1968.
32   John McGovern, Neither Fear Nor Favour (London: The
Blandford Press, 1960), p.197.
33   Ian Budge and Derek Urwin, Scottish Political
Behaviour: A Case Study In Political Homogeneity (London:
Longmans, 1969).
34   See John McCaffrey, 'Politics and the Catholic Community

Since 1878' in McRoberts, p.151.

35   T.P. O'Connor was MP for Liverpool Scotland, 1885-1929.

36   He made this point when delivering a paper on 'The Irish in 19th Century Scotland' at the 8th Annual Symposium of the Irish Labour History Society in Belfast on September 6 1981.

37   McAteer's personal evolution indicates that Irish RCs who migrated to Scotland sometimes returned to Ireland or else used Scotland as a jumping off point for England, North America or the Antipodes. Undoubtedly, if all emigrants had remained in Scotland, the RC percentage of the population would today be much higher than it actually is.

38   Interview with Neil Carmichael MP, Glasgow, August 25 1981.

39   T. Ryle Dwyer, De Valera (Dublin: Gill and Macmillan, 1980), p.111.

40   Owen Dudley Edwards, 'The Catholic Press in Scotland Since the Restoration of the Hierarchy' in McRoberts, p.165.

41   The IRA has refrained from offensive action in the Celtic nations of Scotland and Wales since bombings started in England during the early 1970s.

42   Brian Wilson, 'Scots stoke the Orange Fire', The Observer, January 18 1976.

43   Ibid.

44   Ibid.

45   For a recent discussion of Scottish loyalism, see Ian Sutherland, 'Doing the Orange walk', New Society, July 9 1981, pp.49-50.

46   News About Britain, BBC World Service, February 15 1981.

47   See P.J. Waller's massive Democracy and Sectarianism: A political and social history of Liverpool 1868-1939 (Liverpool: Liverpool University Press, 1981) as well as articles by R.S.W. Davies and A. Shallice in North West Labour History Society Bulletin No.6, Manchester 1979-80.

48   Stanley Salvidge, Salvidge of Liverpool (London: Hodder and Stoughton, 1934), p.80.

49   For a description of Liverpool in the 1970s see Kevin Sim, 'Mersey's Non-Sectarian Sound', The New Statesman, July 21 1972, pp.80-81.

50   Several monographs about the Irish in Britain exist. See John A. Jackson, The Irish in Britain (London: Routledge Kegan and Paul, 1965) and Kevin O'Connor, The Irish in Britain (Dublin: Torc Books, 1974).

51   The British police have been generally successful in their drive against the IRA but few terrorists have been apprehended through the use of the PTA.

52   See Tom Gallagher, 'Casting Votes', The Irish Times, March 26 1980.

53   The survey found that the great majority of former Labour voters preferred to abstain than vote for any of the more conservative parties.

PART TWO

SOCIOLOGICAL, PSYCHOLOGICAL
AND OPERATIONAL ASPECTS:
CASE STUDIES

Essay four

WOMEN AND THE TROUBLES, 1969-1980

Suzann Buckley and Pamela Lonergan

Female participation in struggle for freedom can begin in support of activities defined by males. As the struggles develop, some women perceive their lack of freedom within a patriarchal society. Aware of their limited power not only in the public sphere but also in the domestic one, they act on this feminist consciousness by creating their own movement which focuses on women's liberation. In the yet unresolved political troubles in Northern Ireland, Catholic women have participated actively. What is the nature of that activity and what impact has it had upon feminism in Northern Ireland? Does the recent experience of the Irish Catholic women correspond to the model of support efforts in political activity leading to feminism?

Before analyzing the Catholic females politically active in Northern Ireland, one must first understand the status of these women. We may then analyze their motivations in the political arena. Specially, we will determine if political action resulted in the development of a feminist consciousness.

In the times and struggles before the present troubles, males were responsible for the gun-carrying and breadwinning. The women promoted the republican movement by being mothers to the family and supporters of the soldiers. Any political activity for the equality of women had to be subordinated to the republican cause.

Prior to the 1970s, IRA women worked chiefly through its female auxiliary, Cumann na mBan, which dates from shortly before the Easter Rising. According to their recent organizational handbook, the Cumann na mBan is organized into areas corresponding to IRA battalion areas, with a branch or squad attached to each IRA company. Suggested activities include such military features as drills, scouting, signalling, intelligence, first aid classes and cleaning and unloading of guns, "where practible". The emphasis is on the more domestic aspect of first aid skills. Branch officers are to select three safe houses in their area which must remain stocked with splints, sulphur ointments, clean shirts and socks. The women are also expected to pursue such traditionally female activities as making their branch financially solid through sales, displays and concerts and by organizing Dail Eirann Loan Clubs and Gaelic social gatherings. Women fare only slightly better in the election procedures. The auxiliary assists "in the election of the Republican candidates, keeping before the Public the fact that under the Republican Proclamation women are entitled to the same rights of citizenship as men". The auxiliary is also urged to "press forth women candidates". But these assumedly will espouse republican rather than specifically feminist causes.[2]

The political activity of women might have continued in this vein had it not been for the burgeoning Civil Rights movement which kindled a violent new phase of the troubles in 1969. The Civil Rights movement began in 1967 when middle-class Catholics organized the Northern Ireland Civil Rights Association (NICRA). Although the movement considered itself nonsectarian, its demands for equality were largely Catholic demands. By means of nonviolent demonstration and civil disobedience the movement aimed to secure "one-man-one-vote", an end to gerrymandering, fair allocation of jobs and housing, the repeal of the Special Powers Act and disbandment of the B-Specials. Women had much to gain in fair allocation of housing and in a reformed voting system, which would no longer limit the franchise to heads of households.

The Civil Rights movement had a wide basis for support among the minority population because it sought to redress institutionalized Catholic oppression. With every march and demonstration, support for the Civil Rights movement grew. Queen's University, Belfast, became a focal point for the movement as students organized the left-wing faction of the People's Democracy. It was out of this organization that the social activist Bernadette Devlin emerged.

In 1968, Devlin was a third year student majoring in psychology. Throughout her schooling she had excelled in Gaelic, her original major at Queen's. During her first two years at the university she had felt the need of some ideology. Off she went "on [her] round of the parties in search of one". Disenchanted with the "self importance" of Queen's politics she had "moved to the do-good organizations", but had decided that they were "just perpetuating aspects of the system [she] didn't like".[3]

According to Devlin, People's Democracy started out without political affiliation, "with very little political awareness even, the majority attitude could then be summed up as a sort of liberal belief in the necessity for justice". The movement turned to the left "due to the simple fact that the most effective solutions to the problems we discussed always turned out to be the solutions offered by the Left. We educated ourselves into Socialism."[4]

In April of 1969 Devlin agreed to stand for a seat in Westminster as the Republican unity candidate in a by-election for mid-Ulster. She agreed because of popular demand and to block Austin Currie who, according to Devlin, "was speaking most refined Nationalism".[5] Although she saw her campaign as a political gesture without much hope of success, she won.

Unionist claims of the People's Democracy being a disguised IRA were not totally unfounded. The IRA had moved to the left since the failure of its 1956-62 border campaign. Most of their arms had been sold to the Free Welsh Army, and the IRA had turned to instigating social revolution to achieve a united socialist republic. Many nationalist republicans, alienated by the shift, either receded into the background or left the movement for other groups.

On August 12, 1969, when revelling Protestants in Derry threw their traditional insults and pennies into the Bogside below, defiant Catholic youths retaliated with stones and curses. Protestants swarmed out of the old walled city and descended on the Bogside to beat up and burn the Catholic ghetto. The RUC arrived to stop the fighting but began rioting themselves when attacked by Catholics. Hundreds of families were driven or burned out of their homes. Civilian rioting continued for a week despite the arrival of the British Army on the 14th.

In earlier times the Catholics in Derry and elsewhere would have turned to the IRA for protection. Because the Officials were unprepared, their prestige plummeted. Newly-fired dissenters and deserters formed a "Provisional" IRA, Sinn Fein and Cumann na mBan. Behind Belfast's "peace line" Provos and vigilantes built their own barricades, establishing areas of "no go" such as Free Andersonstown and Free Derry. Within Free Derry, the Women's Action Committee organized systems of garbage-can-cover alarms to warn residents about the arrival of potentially dangerous non-residents into their neighbourhood. Unionists charged that the no-go areas were becoming secure bases for the growing Provisionals and demanded that the Army open them up. Barricades would be dismantled, often with internal cooperation, but only temporarily.

Protestants built their own neighbourhood barricades and established some secure bases for defence. Confirmation of the validity of their actions came when Britain ordered the disarmament of the RUC and disbandment of the B-Specials. A siege mentality settled over the cities of Belfast and Derry. Violence escalated and became partially offensive as Provisionals began to strike back at any Army action they perceived as aggressive.

Catholic sympathy and support for the Provos grew when internment without trial was implemented under the Special Powers Act. The initial pre-dawn sweep on August 9, 1971

77

picked up over three hundred men suspected to be in the IRA. Most of the Provisional leaders had got to hear of the dragnet and spent the night in hiding or across the border in the Republic. Introduction of internment immediately provoked the worst wave of violence the North had recently experienced. From August to September, 2,500 Belfast families fled from their homes, most of them from borderline or mixed neighbourhoods. From August to December, 1576 men were interned, 934 of whom were released by the end of the year.

Internment was used almost exclusively against Catholics (as it was meant to be) and the resentment of family, friends and relatives increased support for the IRA. Complaints of abuse and torture of prisoners caused Westminster to order an investigation of the charges. The Compton Commission, which was ordered to investigate only the initial sweep, reported beatings and the use of sensory deprivation in interrogations, but concluded that no torture had occurred. People protested across the province. In Derry, for example, women organized into a group against internment.

Whatever Catholic sympathy remained with the British disappeared after Bloody Sunday, January 20, 1972, when Army troops fired on a Derry crowd protesting against internment. The Army claimed that the thirteen men killed had been armed, but witnesses and TV cameras saw no weapons. Catholics rioted, the Provos swore revenge, and the British once again became the unequivocal enemy.

On March 18th, William Craig MP addressed an Ulster Vanguard rally in Belfast. In his speech he said: "We must build up a dossier of the men and women who are a menace to their country because if and when the politicians fail us, it may be our job to liquidate the enemy."[6] The politicians did in fact fail them when Britain suspended Stormont and reestablished direct rule. What followed was more violence. Many of the civilian deaths were eye-for-an-eye sectarian killings. The authors of Political Murder in Northern Ireland claim that when the killing escalated and continued unabated in 1972 it was a Protestant campaign "made with a vengeance only the righteous can inflict".[7] In a report on intimidation compiled by the Northern Ireland Community Relations Commission it was reported that over 60,000 persons (48,000 Catholics) had been intimidated and, as a result, had fled from their homes from August 1969 to January 1973.[8]

Meanwhile, other citizens, mostly women, organized to maintain or regain some semblance of normal life. Women Together, a non-sectarian group founded in 1970 by Monica Patterson, an English Catholic, organized projects in individual neighbourhoods - setting up credit unions, youth clubs, playgrounds, children's outings and dinners for the elderly. On December 1, 1971, they launched an unsuccessful "Peace for Christmas" campaign.

Another women's group, Women for Peace, was organized in 1972 by Margaret Dougherty, a Derry mother of seven. Spurred by the death of an innocent woman who had been killed in the crossfire of an IRA-Army shootout in April, the group met to plan a meeting with Sean MacStiofain, the Provisional Chief of Staff. But this political meeting was chiefly for the same goals as those of Women Together. They wanted MacStiofain to effect a cease-fire in order to make the environment safe for women and children.

Republican women actively objected to these attempts to have the objectives and safety for children and other such concerns take precedence over the national struggle. The aforementioned meeting was disrupted by about one hundred republican women who attempted to intimidate Women for Peace into abandoning their peace proposal. Led by Maire Drumm, they had little sympathy for women who did not heartily endorse all measures aimed at driving the English from the island.

Unlike the peace women, whose entry into the public arena seems to have stemmed from a desire to protect their children, Drumm's views had been shaped by a long history of political activity that had begun in the 1940s. Frequently, she served as Sinn Fein's temporary president. while other leaders were in jail. Her status was such that in October 1976, after she had been assassinated in her hospital bed by three Protestant gunmen, the Provisionals gave her a military funeral with full honors in tribute to her death for a political cause.

Evidently Drumm's attempted intimidation of the peace women had limited impact insofar as two months later five representatives of the peace women met with MacStiofain at his request. The women made it clear that they wanted a cease-fire. Eleven days later, it began. Pressure from the peace women was not the only reason for the cease-fire because many people had been appalled at the extensive, bloody and poorly targeted violence of the Provos' revenge for Bloody Sunday. The Provos called the truce to appease these persons and demonstrate their discipline to everyone. Yet, apparently some women interpreted the cease-fire as recognition of the legitimacy of the pursuit of their peace goal.

The day the truce began (August 26), the Loyalist Women's Association sent off a 90,000-signature petition to Westminster which called for an end to the violence and the restoration of Stormont. But the truce lasted only thirteen days, despite the petition and efforts by Women Together to prolong it by offering to meet with various groups.

No one responded. From then on peace women became personae non grata, obstacles to the paramilitaries and suspected collaborators with the British. Many peace groups accepted funding from Whitelaw on behalf of the British government, thereby leaving themselves open to charges of treason. In the ensuing years they increasingly became objectives of intimidation. Dougherty's home was attacked several times. She sent her children away and eventually she herself had to move out of the Creggan.

Bernadette Devlin McAliskey (married in April 1973) and the Civil Rights movement were also on the way out. By 1973 the CRA had lost most of its membership and had been thoroughly infiltrated by the Official IRA, which had used it for propaganda. Devlin believed that the movement "had misjudged the people", been poorly organized and had been "rendered irrelevant by paramilitaries".[9] Devlin herself was to be so rendered when influential SDLP co-founder Gerry Fitt called her "totally irrelevant"[10] some months before her 1974 re-election bid. She lost to the Unionist Council candidate in a three-way race that also included Ivan Cooper (SDLP), whom she had once called her "best friend in Stormont".[11]

These groups and individuals failed to exert any more political pressure on the paramilitaries or Britain and returned to the personal sphere. But by no means were women out of the political arena. The Official Sinn Fein/IRA formally accepted women as equals within the organizations at their annual congress, Ard Fais (1972). Also, loss of men to death and internment forced the Provisionals to make increasing use of Fianna Scouts and women. According to Sean MacStiofain, in his autobiography, Revolutionary in Ireland:

> In the early 70s a selected number of suitable women were taken into the IRA and trained. Some of the best shots I ever knew were women. So were the best intelligence officers in Belfast. From that time women were admitted on a basis of full equality with men, as in the Israeli. Chinese and certain other armed forces.[12]

He also noted that British strategists of counterinsurgency failed to appreciate the "significant part" played by women in the struggles because they came from "a society in which women's contributions are usually underrated".[13]

But by 1972, British strategists must have had trouble overlooking the terrorist activities of women. On June 26 (the same day the truce began) three women dressed as nuns robbed the Irish Allied Bank, Belfast. In August, a 24-year-old man and a 17-year-old girl were killed when the bomb they unsuccessfully tried to plant in a supermarket exploded in their van. Also in that month an 18-year-old Belfast girl was detained for a week under the Special Powers Act.

The new year for female terrorists was rung in on January 1, 1973, when Elizabeth McKee, 19, became the first woman picked up under the Detention of Terrorists Order that had been introduced the previous November. Five hundred women in Andersonstown marched to protest against the action. Maire Drumm was the main speaker.

Every week of February and March, terrorist women popped up somewhere:

11/2: Girl, 17, man, 24, killed in explosion of 50 lb. bomb they were handling. Both identified as Provos.

16/2: Girl, 17, held in interim custody.

20/2: Gang of six men, one woman rob train of 600 in Canadian dollars.

4/3: Five women attempt escape from Armagh prison.

8/3: Three women, seven men detained at Heathrow Airport after two car bombs explode in London; one dead, 180 injured.

23/3: Girls lure three soldiers to house on pretext of party where they are ambushed and killed.

27/3: Two teenaged girls charged with possession of a 150 lb. gelignite bomb in a baby carriage.[14]

On the same day that the girls were caught with the loaded pram, Northern Ireland Secretary Whitelaw told the Westminster House of Commons that "women are active in the IRA campaign" and that thirteen of these women were in prison for terrorist offences, eleven were awaiting trial, two were detained and two had been served with interim custody orders. Almost as Whitelaw spoke, Bernadette Devlin McAliskey, Vanessa Redgrave and Edna O'Brien unsuccessfully tried to post bail for the ten persons charged with the March 8th London car bombs. Meanwhile, women, especially young ones, continued their terrorism:

12/6: Two teenaged girls charged with the attempted murder of a soldier.

22/6: Two young women charged with explosion murder of six in Coleraine.

31/7: Young woman arrested with loaded, telescopic lens-fitted .303 rifle in her pants.

1/9: Woman dies while making bombs in apartment.

14/10: Woman involved in rocket attack on Army post.

21/10: Three women, one man involved in shooting attack on Army post.

Some, for example, UDA leader Harding Smith (later assassinated by unknown persons) even claimed that as a result of a decline in Provisional ranks by August 1973 "girls of 16 and 17 were in command positions".[15] (One year later, an Army raid netted 28 persons believed to be the Belfast commanders - two of whom were women.)

Failure to deal with women except possibly for the recruitment of the younger generation had serious repercussions for the terrorists' activities when in 1976 the personal once again spilled into the political picture. On August 10, the random death of three young children killed in IRA-Army action sparked an uprising of protest to end the violence. This movement was more serious than previous peace movements because of the great publicity, international funding and honor it received. The Peace People movement of 1976 was a large personal movement which was meant to be molded into an influential political movement by one of its leaders, Ciaran McKeown. As it was organized, the movement moved through a period of demonstrative mass marches to small scale neighborhood service and government.

The movement's most visible leaders were Anne Corrigan and Betty Williams. Corrigan had been raised in Ballymurphy and left school at 14 because there was no money for further education. Trained as a secretary, at 18 she had moved to Andersonstown and taken a job at the Guinness Brewery. She had led a small cell of the Legion of Mary which grew to over one hundred members. In the troubles of '69, she had helped to evacuate children from dangerous areas. When a close friend and co-leader was killed in the violence, she had taken over his Legion group. As a member of the Legion, the only lay organization allowed to visit Long Kesh, she spent every Sunday there, listening to prisoners and their families, talking, "trying to change opinions".[16] Despite all her activity, she still felt she was not doing enough to stop the violence, even though her priest assured her she could do no more, With the death of the children, her nieces and nephew, she became determined to end the bloodshed.

Betty Williams was a Belfast housewife with her two children and a Protestant husband who was often away working as an engineer in the merchant marine. Like Corrigan, there had been no republican tradition in her family; yet when the troubles re-erupted, she supported the Provos. She almost took up arms but didn't because, after much agonizing, she realized that she could not kill people. Instead, she sheltered IRA members and smuggled them over the border. She eventually became disillusioned with the Provos because of the intimidation and harrassment their activities brought down on the innocents of the neighbourhood. Outside of a mild participation in the Belfast Reverend Parker's peace group, she had remained quiet until swept up in the Peace People.

After witnessing the death of three children, and watching the television coverage of it, Williams began a peace petition in her Andersonstown neighbourhood. Corrigan heard of the petition, which was signed by over 6,000 women, and invited Williams to the children's funeral. After the funeral, Corrigan went on the evening news to announce a demonstration for peace on the following day and to declare that "this must be a movement that must not disappear".[17] Ten thousand women came to the demonstration held in the republican stronghold of Andersonstown.

The following morning, the women met with McKeown, a Belfast journalist who had earned his degree in philosophy at Queen's. He had been active in the CRA and bitterly blamed the like of Bernadette Devlin and Michael Farrell for the movement' downfall. The women were eager for help in continuing the movement's momentum and accepted him as their mentor. McKeown preferred to remain in the background but was forced to come forward because, in Corrigan's words, "everyone thought that Betty and I were puppets and that he was pulling the strings".[18] The three leaders considered themselves to be a complementary trio with McKeown as the intellectual, Williams as the pragmatist and Corrigan as the conscience.

In the beginning, as the press tried to distinguish between the two women, Corrigan was always referred to as "the pretty one". In response to the tag, Corrigan said, "I'm not at all interested in clothes or fashion... however, since the movement began, I've made an effort to look as good as I can. I feel that I'm representing my country and that I should look very feminine, that I should set an example."[19]

Peace People marches were held every weekend in different cities (picked by McKeown) of Ulster and England from August to the end of December 1976. The marchers were mostly middle-aged working-class women. Many of them lacked much political awareness and merely considered the festive, friendly, songfest atmosphere of the buses a pleasant holiday from household tension and drudgery.

Calling for an end to IRA activity, the movement's leaders consistently avoided condemnation of the British Army and encouraged people to inform. As a result, they provoked intimidation. Soon after Margaret Dougherty and her husband led the local contingent in the Londonderry march (they left quickly over the stand on informing) their 17-year-old son was twice beaten up - first by members of the UDA, the second time by persons who carved "IRA" on his leg and on the back of his hand. Corrigan was attacked by people who had belonged to her units in the Legion of Mary.

Devlin McAliskey called the Peace movement dangerous because it had the potential of dulling women's political consciousness. She said:

We were stupid to never organize the women, we never did and the inevitable happened. There was an explosion of female rage, only there was no political analysis to back it up. They are being used and will be discarded as I was. The British will use them for information, the opportunistic politicans for personal glory.[20]

From its beginning in the dog days of August, the Peace movement had been covered by the international press. When its leaders, Corrigan and Williams, were declared ineligible for the 1976 Nobel Peace Prize because the movement had begun after the February deadline for nominations for the prize, newspapers in Scandinavia and West Germany raised over $340,000 for the movement.

In 1977, the women were awarded the prize

retroactively, but by that time the movement began to totter because of internal dissent and external criticism. Most of the marchers wanted to continue with the marches and were unwilling to move into community politics. Protestant members felt left out of policy-making. Catholics could not agree on the policy towards informing. Outside pressures came from the IRA and its supporters. The IRA launched a London bomb campaign when the movement met for its first annual convention and also mounted a propaganda campaign against the "furcoat brigade", as the Peace women were mockingly labelled by the IRA. Paddy Devlin, leader of the SDLP, denounced them for fear they would attract members of his party. Social workers accused the Peace People of offering "miracle cures" and resented what they saw as duplication of services. Members of the movement and the opposition both disapproved of the peace women's international travel and the fact that the two women had split the Nobel Prize money, $340,000, between themselves.

The movement lingered on until 1980, its donations dried up. The IRA suffered limited damage from the movement's encouragement and protection of informers. Membership in 1980 was down to 23 chapters from a high of 136. Williams quit in 1980, blaming the Peace Prize for taking them away from the people. She came to consider the organization too bureaucratic and preferred to "be a peace person by myself".[21] Corrigan remained to lead, McKeown stayed on as a close advisor and continues to write and print the movement's publication, Peace by Peace. Anne McGuire, mother of the three children whose deaths sparked the mass movement, killed herself in February of 1980 after having suffered continued breakdowns and depressions. Their personal goal and political efforts to eradicate violence had come to naught.[22]

The IRA continued its elusive campaign of guerrilla warfare but became more involved in its well publicized campaign to regain special status for its prisoners of war and to draw international attention to the injustices of life under domination. At least 400 male and 30 female prisoners took part in the "dirty protest" to smash H-Block, wearing blankets, refusing prison clothing, covering their cell walls with urine and faeces. At the women's prison in Armagh, menstrual blood was added to the mess. Demonstration also went on outside. Bernadette Devlin McAliskey, who returned to the headlines after she and her husband had been shot by protestant paramilitaries, and Rose Dugdale Gallagher, a Provo who had been released from prison after serving time for robbery actively publicized the protest for political status.

The Provos conducted a well disciplined campaign of hunger striking to death from December 1980 to October 1981. Several of the male hunger strikers ran for and won political offices, thus bringing them more into the public eye. Nine men died before the strike was brought to an end by pressure from the strikers' families and the Catholic Church. Three women were also in the hunger strike but none fasted to the death. The women who were singled out in the strike were sisters, wives and mothers. Initially, these women were once again important only in support roles, embodying a mixture of Mother Ireland and the Virgin Mother in their willingness to sacrifice their males. This pattern was broken by Patrick Quinn's family and Laurence McKeown's mother. In the eleventh hour they allowed hospital officials to intervene to save the unconscious prisoners. In this respect they acted similarly to those in the Women for Peace, entering the political arena for the personal goal of saving their children.

The IRA ignored any political implications of the women's intervention. The collapse of the hunger strike was attributed to the influence of the Catholic Church, which suggests that the IRA perceived the women's intervention merely as female acquiescence to religious authority.

One outcome of the hunger strike was permission for prisoners to wear their own clothes, thereby bringing an end to the "dirty protests". On the surface, not much else changed. The IRA returned to targeted bombing by men and women and the economic situation continued to get worse. Inflation still ran over 20%. Under the surface, a great deal of change had begun. More people were unemployed than ever before, particularly women. Many of the textile factories have closed or moved because of domestic trouble and foreign competition. For those women pushed back into the role of solely wife and mother, the traditional neighborhood kinship or cooperative networks for child care had been eroded by the increasing trend of isolated-unit high-rise public estates. Children are less easy to supervise because they now play in segregated areas away from the home or roam the streets in gangs. Those women still employed, but having an unemployed spouse, labor under other burdens. Where only the wife works, no substantive role reversal results. Her husband assumes no domestic responsibilites. There are few outlets for women to vent this frustration. Unemployed Protestant men can vent their emasculation on the less esteemed Catholic worker; the Catholic man, if unrelieved through republican activity, can only turn on himself or his family. A total population of 1.5 million has eaten 35 million tranquilizers in one year.[23]

Positions and perceptions of their roles within the home may have changed for some women but the mass consciousness remains traditional. The feminist movement has met with little success among Catholic women in Northern Ireland. The Belfast Women's Collective, founded in 1977, argued:

> All of the women in the group agreed on their opposition to British imperialism, but we made

criticisms of the republican movement, particularly of its position on women. We showed how women had been used and forgotten in the previous struggles for Ireland. This stand led to an increasing political isolation. Because we protested against the British presence, we were labelled as Republicans; at the same time, because we were highly critical of the republican movement, we were labelled as a bourgeois women's group. We couldn't win either way.[24]

In conclusion, it appears that women's political participation either for or against terrorist activities had made little contribution to their equality. Feminist criticisms have been largely ignored and most women remain faithful to an increasingly difficult or unrealizable domestic role. Female guerrillas or those like Bernadette Devlin McAliskey seem to remain preoccupied with the national struggle that has yet to go far beyond male norms and dictates. The various women and women's groups for peace appear to have little feminist awareness. Even in the case of intervention to save the sons in the hunger strike, the woman was simply choosing between the opinions of the IRA and the clergy.

Participation in political awareness for Irish Catholic women in the North has not led to a feminist consciousness. It seems unlikely that such activity will be the catalyst for change. If any change occurs, it may stem from the stresses upon the traditional family and from a decline in clerical influence upon women. These factors could cause women to realize the nature of a patriarchal society. Such a realization might cause them to question their relationship to present political activities.

Notes

1   Margaret MacCurtain, ed., Women in Irish Society: The Historical Dimension (Westport, Conn.: Greenwood Press, 1979), p.54.
2   Rona Fields, A Society on the Run (London: Penguin Press, 1976), p.149.
3   Bernadette Devlin, Price of My Soul (New York: Pan Books, 1969), p.77.
4   Devlin, p.122.
5   Devlin, p.156.
6   Richard Deutsch and Vivian Magowen, Northern Ireland: A Chronology of Events, vol.2 (Belfast: Blackstaff Press, 1974), cite 3/18/72.
7   Martin Dillon and Dennis Lehane, Political Murder in Northern Ireland (London: Penguin Books, 1973), p.26.
8   Deutsch and Magowen, vol.2, cite 5/31/73.
9   "We want Peace. Just Peace", New York Times Magazine, December 19, 1976, p.29.

10   Deutsch and Magowen. vol.2, cite 11/23/73.
11   Devlin, p.209.
12   Sean MacStiofain, Revolutionary in Ireland (London: G. Cremonesi, 1975), p.218.
13   MacStiofain, p.217.
14   Deutsch and Magowen, vol.2, cite 6/26/73.
15   Dillon and Lehane, p.177.
16   Richard Deutsch, Mairead Corrigan/Betty Williams (Woodbury, New York: Barron's Educational Series, 1977), p.34.
17   Deutsch, p.8.
18   Deutsch, p.64.
19   Deutsch. p.48.
20   "Peace. Just Peace", p.30.
21   "Peace Movement Falters in Ulster", Newsweek, March 17, 1980, p.16.
22   In September of 1981 Corrigan married Jack McGuire, her brother-in-law, the widower of Anne.
23   "Of Many Things", America, February 9, 1980, inside cover.
24   William Borders, "The Women of Ulster Are Surviving To Mourn", New York Times, May 31, 1981, Sec.4, p.3.

Essay Five

THE PSYCHOLOGY OF TERRORISM IN NORTHERN IRELAND

Ken Heskin

This chapter will address itself mainly to a consideration of the psychology of Republican paramilitary involvement. There are two main reasons for this focus. First. the Provisional IRA has proved to be the most consistently active paramilitary group in Northern Ireland throughout the present troubles. Second, what little information is available on the members of paramilitary groups tends mainly to concern the Provisional IRA. It is therefore for these pragmatic reasons only that this limited focus is adopted. The chapter will concentrate on four key areas of the problem, namely the behavioural domain in question, possible personality characteristics predisposing the individual to this sort of behaviour, sources of motivation towards paramilitary involvement in the Irish context and, finally, proximate situational determinants of the behaviour.

THE BEHAVIOURAL DOMAIN: WHAT IS TERRORISM?

What exactly is terrorism and what distinguishes it from other forms of violent behaviour not called terrorism? This is the key question of this section. At first glance, the question appears naive since the word 'terrorism' has such currency that one might feel that the answer is obvious and the whole topic is so emotionally charged that merely posing the question might seem to many to be a threatening gesture. However, from the psychologist's point of view, it is necessary to delineate exactly the kind of behaviour involved in order to proceed with a perusal of its possible causes.

A necessary defining condition of terrorism is that it involved atrocious behaviour and a lack of normal regard for human life and property in the pursuit of some objective. Thus the Birmingham (England) public house bombings in November, 1974, perpetrated by the Provisional IRA, in which twenty-one people were killed and 162 injured, clearly satisfied this condition and was universally condemned as an act of terrorism. A key feature of this and similar incidents is that property whose existence posed no direct threat to the perpetrators were killed and maimed.

So far so good. However the question immediately arises as to whether in our knowledge this sort of behaviour occurs on other occasions perpetrated by people whom we would not describe as terrorists. Unfortunately it does.

Let us take as an example the behaviour of the British government and the Royal Air Force under its command during World War 2. Let us consider specifically as an example the activities of the RAF Bomber Command between July 24th and August 3rd 1943 when Bomber Command turned its attentions to the city of Hamburg in Germany. During this period four major air raids were carried out on Hamburg with massive amounts of both explosive and liquid incendiary bombs.

In the ensuing holocaust, the bodies of 22,500 women, 17,100 men and 5,400 children were consumed and 6,200 acres of the city were gutted. The total of dead and maimed from the four raids was 82,214 (Middlebrook, 1981). This was merely one of the more than one hundred cities and towns in Germany which suffered a similar fate at the hands of the RAF culminating in the notorious Dresden bombings of February, 1945.

In terms of the consequences of these acts, leaving aside for the moment the respective scales involved, there is therefore a distinct similarity. This leads naturally to the question of intention. If we consider again the Birmingham bombings. we know that a telephone warning, albeit too late, was given to the authorities and at least one of the perpetrators, filled with horror and regret at the consequences of his actions, broke down under interrogation and made a full confession (Clutterbuck, 1978).

The picture is rather different when we turn to the Hamburg bombings because the intention of the bombing was not merely the destruction of property but, in fact, the death and mutilation of large numbers of the civilian population. What was involved was not "merely" the inaccurate bombing of military and industrial targets but the accurate bombing of civilian targets. Indeed, as Sir Basil Lydell noted, 'Terrorism became, without reservation, the definite policy of the British Government.'

Nor can it be said that the particular examples chosen are unrepresentative despite the fact that both are spectacular examples of their type. The norm in the bombing of civilian targets by the Provisional IRA has been to issue warnings to enable target areas to be cleared. Of course, this is not true of all terrorist attacks in Northern Ireland and Great Britain, even against civilian targets and it is not true at all of attacks by the Provisional IRA on targets which they regard as 'legitimate'. Nonetheless, it must be said that there does seem to be a distinction between the two representative examples given in that. compared to the activities of the British Government and the RAF in the Second World War, the Provisional IRA seems to be reluctant in general to engage in all-out and wanton attacks on 'non-legitimate' targets.

The question of the respective scales of the two activities also arises here because if it is valid to argue that in the examples given there is a difference in intention, then the relative levels of disregard for human life and property cannot simply be accounted for in terms of the relative destructive capacities involved. In other words, having accepted the policy of terror-bombing, the British Government maximised its effectiveness whereas the Provisional IRA in the past eleven or twelve years has not done so. As Bowyer Bell has commented, 'Terrorists have neither the capacity nor the desire to kill great masses; only rulers have had both.'

So why is the image of the RAF in World War 2 so vastly different to the image of the Provisional IRA in Ireland today? One obvious difference between the two situations is that Britain was at war with Germany whereas no official state of war exists between Britain and Ireland today. However, the Provisional IRA does see itself as at war with the British Government and has frequently made that view explicit even though its most fanatical members have expressed a lack of hostility towards the British public (e.g., MacStiofain, 1975).

Equally, the presence and activites of the British Army in Northern Ireland render it impossible to sustain a view of the conflict as being one-sided with Britain as innocent victim. Nor is it tenable to argue that in the intervening years since World War 2 the West has become much more conscious of the humanitarian evils of conflict. At no time in history has the potential for such all-consuming devastation been so great nor its increase so assiduously sought. The American experience in Vietnam also tells us that the will to inflict hideous and obscene devastation still exists, even in the most apparently civilised countries.

And yet, despite all of this, the tendency is to perceive as heinous the activities of the perpetrators of the Birmingham bombings while the activities of the perpetrators of objectively more terrible acts are seen as heroic or at least understandable. It would appear that the distinction has something to do with the institutional mantle of some atrocious behaviour and with the scale and overtness with which it is carried out.

However, even this distinction does not fully turn the key in the lock. As Clutterbuck (1975) has pointed out, we glamourise, even to this day, the activities of the French Resistance in World War 2 who were brutally cruel to their victims whom they killed by stealth. Equally, the British Government's bloodthirsty glee and favourable British public reaction to the questionable manner in which the SAS ended the recent Embassy Siege in London illustrates the fact that in some circumstances we are not too fussy about the manner in which our heroes achieve their objectives; overtness is not always crucial.

Again, institutional sanctions do not always appear to be crucial either. It is, for example, difficult to counter the Provisionals' argument that the British Government's attitude to terrorism has been hypocritical in view of tacit British support for the Patriotic Front in Rhodesia (Sunday Times, 25 June, 1978). One would imagine also that there would be some public sympathy in the West for black terrorist groups in South Africa or for similar groups in Afghanistan. In some sense, therefore, attitudes to terrorism are affected by one's perception of the cause involved and by one's distance from the action. In fact, it is difficult to avoid Clutterbuck's argument that the distinction ultimately boils down to a question of 'good guys' and 'bad guys' in the light of the apparently inescapable conclusion that atrocious behaviour is the norm in conflict situations, whoever is involved.

In summary, therefore, the behavioural domain of terrorism involves atrocious behaviour but it is difficult to draw a rational psychological distinction between terrorist behaviour and what appears to be 'normal' behaviour in conflict situations. Indeed, if anything, the terrorist behaviour of the Provisional IRA appears, in some aspects at least, to be a more restrained use of terror than one perceives in the conflict activities of responsible democratic governments. It therefore follows that much of the rest of the chapter, although addressing itself to the specific issue of involvement in Republican paramilitary organisations in Ireland, provides a conceptual basis for looking at the functioning and personnel of conflict-oriented groups generally, including non-conscripted national armed forces.

PERSONALITY CHARACTERISTICS: WHAT SORT OF PERSON BECOMES A TERRORIST?

A popular view of terrorists in Northern Ireland is that they are evil, sick and psychopathic. The first of these terms is largely abusive and has no specific psychological meaning The second epithet 'sick' is somewhat diffuse as it stands but can be linked to the third, 'psychopathic', which has a more precise psychological meaning and which we can therefore usefully consider.

The typical train of thought here is that since terrorists are psychopathic, then they are predisposed to activities such as those which terrorism involved and these activities afford them some form of outlet for their anti-social tendencies which would, in normal circumstances, result in their running foul of the law. Terrorists, in this view, are simply criminals in an unusual setting. This line of thought essentially no more than garden-fence speculation, has been institutionalised in the British Government's latter-day policy of 'criminalisation'.

In fact there is no psychological evidence that terrorists are diagnosably psychopathic or otherwise clinically disturbed. Indeed, what little evidence there is on this topic tends to point in the opposite direction. Elliott and Lockhart (1980) have shown that, despite remarkably similar socio-economic backgrounds, juvenile scheduled offenders (broadly, those found guilty of terrorist-related offences) in their particular study were more intelligent, had higher educational attainments, showed less evidence of early developmental problems and had fewer previous court appearances than 'ordinary' juvenile delinquents.

The argument is also embarrassed by the fact that we have been unable to draw a rational distinction, at least in the necessary direction, between the behaviour of terrorist groups and other conflict-oriented groups. Since the very behaviour which elicits the charge of psychopathy in the Irish situation appears to be very widespread indeed in situations of conflict anywhere, then its use in this imprecise way is not justified.

However, clinical studies of psychopaths do reveal distinct features. The most detailed and extensive clinical accounts of psychopathy have been given by Cleckley (1964) but other researchers have tried to pinpoint the most crucial features and these include: 'lovelessness' and 'guiltlessness' (McCord and McCord, 1964); lack of feeling for others and a tendency to act on impulse (Craft, 1965); egocentricity and lack of empathy (Foulds, 1965; Buss, 1966).

How well does this picture fit our knowledge of terrorists in Northern Ireland, particularly those belonging to Republican paramilitary organisations? Heskin (1980) has noted some of the main sources of information and it is fair to say that these are motley indeed and vary considerably in focus, breadth and perspective. In particular, Heskin noted the lack of information on the rank and file membership of the Provisional IRA with the notable exception of Burton's (1978) study of a Belfast Catholic community in the 1972-73 period. Since Heskin's (1980) analysis was written, media coverage of the H-Blocks hunger strikes has added a new and important ingredient in that we now have more information on rank and file Republican terrorists and, in particular the families to which they belong.

A group of prominent Protestant clergymen met with several Provisional IRA leaders in Feakle, County Clare in December, 1974 in a bid for peace. As the Sunday Times of London reported on 18 June, 1978, the clergymen found their expectations of the sort of people they would encounter at odds with the reality of those they met; 'Their dedication verged on the puritanical. "We thought," said one of the clerics, "they'd be hard-living, hard-drinking morons " In fact, whereas all the ministers drank alcohol except one, only one Provisional did. and none smoked except O'Connell.'

Also, in Sean MacStiofain's (1975) autobiography, dedication to a cause at the expense of great personal hardship and difficulty is a clear feature of the life history of the former Chief of Staff of the Provisional IRA. Such characteristics are clearly not psychopathic. Psychopaths are dedicated only to themselves and would tend to favour the line of least personal resistance in their dealings with the world.

Burton (1978) makes the point that when it comes to judging the actions of terrorists, the judgement of outsiders is often made at a somewhat naive level. Thus, much of the sort of behaviour which is taken as indicative of the evil and psychopathic nature of the Provisional IRA members, such as the summary and harsh punishment meted out to local offenders of Provisional norms. is viewed differently within the community. The judgement of outsiders is made in the context of the notional standards of a perfect, liberal, democratic society. The judgement of insiders is made in the context of repressive British laws, brutal and illegal enforcement by British troops and differential treatment of the two communities in Northern Ireland.

Burton also makes the point that while a proportion of Provisional volunteers could be described as young 'yahoo' or 'hood' elements of the sort which most nearly matches the British public image, even these were not of a uniform type. While some were still 'wild men', others had become 'politicised by the IRA and straightened out of their non-political violence' (p.117). Burton claims that bouts of depression, self-doubt and guilt were common among active IRA men.

All of the evidence points to the incredibility of the notion that the Provisional IRA is an organisation of psychopaths. Sacrifice, dedication, guilt and self-doubt are not psychopathic characteristics. Nor, indeed, is the very concept of an organisation of psychopaths viable. Psychopaths have severe difficulty in maintaining trusting and lasting relationships and so would be poor material for an organisation in which such relationships are so important. More recently, the apparent willingness of Republican prisoners in the Maze Prison to make the ultimate sacrifice in the pursuit of demands which they themselves would probably not enjoy puts this issue beyond reasonable doubt.

However, while the particular idea of psychopathic characteristics predisposing individuals to involvement in Republican terrorist groups is not viable, the general proposition that some individuals will be more likely to become involved than others is one which has psychological merit. In general, conflict-oriented groups, it seems reasonable to assume, will attract certain types of individual. One finds it difficult to imagine a young man tossing a coin to decide whether to join the SAS or the clergy; such choices are not usually random.

On a priori grounds, the personality characteristic which suggests itself most readily as being relevant to such a choice is that of authoritarianism. Authoritarianism is a personality characteristic which predisposes the individual to a coherent cluster of conservative, right-wing attitudes and beliefs, the specifics varying between cultures according to social, religious and political norms. Authoritarian individuals are likely to be attracted to conflict-oriented groups by the formal and delineated structures which such organisations usually possess (and the Provisional IRA is no exception). The environment which such organisations provide is compatible with the authoritarian individual's need for order, certainty and formality in interpersonal relations.

Ireland, both North and South, is a traditionalist and conservative country both politically and religiously. One might, therefore, expect to find a somewhat higher incidence of authoritarianism in Ireland than in England, for example. What evidence is there that authoritarianism is a feature common among those involved in paramilitary activities in Northern Ireland? We have already noted the comments of the clergymen at Feakle about puritanical dedication and we should note that puritanical and authoritarian outlooks are closely related. We also know that MacStiofain as a young man in England chose to join one of the armed services and in his autobiography much of his own self-description as a young man suggests a very authoritarian outlook.

There is also evidence that this outlook remained with him and became even more pronounced in his later life. For example, Sweetman (1972) interviewed him during his days as Chief of Staff of the Provisional IRA and quotes him as saying 'I can't see any place for Craig and his type in a United Ireland. There would be no place for those who say they want their British heritage. They've got to accept their Irish heritage, and the Irish way of life, no matter who they are, otherwise there would be no place for them' (p.157). This is a classic example of an authoritarian statement.

Finally, although Burton (1978) was reluctant to typify the rank and file IRA member in his study, he did record a common and pervasive authoritarianism among them. To this we might add the evidence of recent months in the Maze Prison where, in the face of death, the unyielding and uncompromising attitude of the Republican prisoners, so typical of an authoritarian outlook, have come across clearly in the struggle for the five demands.

On the basis of the evidence, it is argued that the single most likely personality characteristic predisposing an individual to paramilitary activity in Northern Ireland is authoritarianism, although one is not arguing that all terrorists are authoritarian any more than one would argue that no psychopath is a terrorist.

MOTIVATION: WHY DO PEOPLE JOIN TERRORIST GROUPS?

In general, the leaders of terrorist organisations throughout the world, both past and present, appear to have had above average education and have come from the more prosperous end of society (Calvert, 1973). Also, the rank and file of many current or recent terrorist groups, such as the Baader Meinhof gang, the American Weathermen and the Japanese Red Army are largely intellectuals (Clutterbuck. 1975). The Provisional IRA stands in stark contrast to the general rule in having no apparent intellectual elements and being contemptuous of what little intellectual support has been offered (Clutterbuck, 1975; Lacqueur, 1977). Protestant paramilitary organisations appear to be in much the same position. The lack of intellectual support for the IRA is perhaps all the more surprising in view of the heavy involvement of politically minded students of Queen's University. Belfast in the early civil rights demonstrations from which the present conflict erupted.

One potential source of motivation for paramilitary involvement in Northern Ireland lies in the high levels of unemployment, poor standard of housing, high prices and low incomes characteristic of the province in comparison to other areas of the United Kingdom. The British government at the time of writing is beginning to discover from the civil disturbances in disadvantaged areas throughout England that the sorts of personal and community pressures which severe economic and social disadvantage generate can only be contained for so long by police activity before people start behaving in ways which are not considered cricket at Westminster.

Northern Ireland has suffered such pressures at higher levels and for longer than the areas of England now erupting in frustration. Add to that the particular local problem of 'relative deprivation' (Birrell, 1972), namely the perception by Catholics in Northern Ireland that they were disadvantaged relative to Protestants in the province, and clearly a major source of motivation to strike at the system which produces such conditions is evident. (Relative deprivation may also be a factor in some of the riots in England, particularly in areas with a large immigrant population.)

This, of course, is a very general source of motivation although it should not be underestimated on that account. In the Irish context in particular, however, there is a historical legitimacy attributed to taking up arms in the defence of one's heritage and, explicitly in the Republican tradition, a cultural exaltation of armed conflict of the guerrilla type. The IRA's history of nationalist struggle against British occupation is long and honourable and one would expect to find in the Catholic population of Northern Ireland a not inconsiderable proportion of people brought up to respect the general ideals of Irish nationalism and sympathetic to the traditional, guerilla means of attaining it. It is, in fact, not quite so absurd to imagine a young Irishman tossing up a coin to decide whether to join the priesthood or the IRA. It is interesting to note that the brother of one of the hunger-strikers who died recently, Raymond McCreesh, is a priest.

Recent months of media coverage of the hunger-strike have yielded some valuable information on Republican paramilitaries, their families and backgrounds. The fact that the media, particularly the British media, have produced information on any aspect of the conflict in Northern Ireland which can be described as 'valuable' is remarkable in view of the history of media coverage of events in Northern Ireland which have predominantly taken the form of a political ritual (Elliott, 1980) in the pursuit of systematic pro-establishment distortion and at the expense of objective and meaningful analysis (Heskin, 1980).

In one sense, media coverage followed the usual propaganda ritual with pro-establishment issues being assiduously analysed (is a hunger-strike to the death equivalent to suicide and hence a mortal sin in the eyes of the Roman Catholic church?; what rights do the victims of terrorists have?; to what extent is the Catholic population being intimidated to support the hunger-strike?, and so forth). Other issues which had at least the same claim to attention and analysis were quietly ignored. Hence there was little or no mention of such issues as: the existence and operation of the juryless Diplock courts; the fact that the hunger-strikers were asking for conditions to which others convicted of similar offences before March 1st, 1976 were entitled or the apparent double-cross of the prisoners after the end of the last hunger-strike.

However, coverage of the hunger-strike differed fundamentally from previous coverage of events in Northern Ireland. For once, despite the reluctance to tackle the issues involved, the focus was not on nameless terrorists engaged in inexplicable acts, but rather on real people with real backgrounds and real families. Despite themselves, the media simply could not resist the drama involved, particularly the pictures of and interviews with members of the families of the hunger-strikers as they made their daily visits, harrowed by the events in which they were caught up and harrowed further still by the media covering these events. Hence personal details about the men involved of a sort not usually given in media reports were made available and we were given an opportunity to study the attitudes, demeanour and bearing of the relatives of the hunger-strikers, enabling us to make some assessment of the background and upbringing they had experienced.

Perhaps the most remarkable feature is the diversity of backgrounds from which the hunger-strikers appear to have come. Sean McKenna, who came close to death during the Christmas hunger-strike, comes from a staunchly Republican family. His father had been interned for IRA activities in the 1950s, was interned again during the first swoop following the introduction of internment in 1971, interrogated by sensory deprivation techniques, released after ten months on medical grounds and died a few years later of a heart attack, allegedly brought on by his ordeal. In truth, Sean McKenna was involved in Republican struggle the day he was born.

For others. however, there appears to have been no such inevitability, but rather life events provided the motivation. Patsy O'Hara, for example, was helped by his father to the top of a hill in Derry to watch the march on Bloody Sunday from the Creggan. He was fourteen years old and on crutches, having been wounded in the leg by a British soldier. The British Army claimed he had been caught in crossfire, the locals that soldiers had simply opened fire indiscriminately. If he had had any doubts on that score, they would surely have been erased on Bloody Sunday.

O'Hara had a very normal adolescence in many respects. He was apprenticed as a mechanical engineer in a local textile firm, attended dances, played football, was rather good at chess, but found himself in a situation where normality was not possible. A matrix of personal and family harrassment, personal injury and community murder at the hands of the British Army produced a situation with inevitable consequences.

Similar in some respects is the case of Raymond McCreesh. There was no particular family history of Republicanism, the family was very respectable and the sons well brought up. One of the McCreesh boys, Brian, became a priest. Again, life situations appeared to be critical, Bloody Sunday in particular but also the spate of random assassinations of Catholics which forced young Raymond McCreesh to give up the job he travelled to each day as an apprentice sheetmetal worker in Lisburn, Co. Antrim.

A somewhat different story obtains in the case of Bobby Sands. Raised in a mixed Catholic/Protestant area of Belfast, the family was intimidated into a safer, Catholic area. He was a good athlete and belonged to a mixed athletic club in Belfast. He, too, was eventually forced from his employment by intimidation. No one who observed the quiet dignity and the deep sorrow, untinged by bitterness, of his mother on her daily visits to the Maze Prison as her son's life slipped away could doubt the goodness of her nature nor the benign influence she must have wielded on her family. But the cruel torsion of events in Northern Ireland distorted the natural

97

product of that benign influence.

All of the evidence tends to suggest the diversity of backgrounds from which members of Republican terrorist groups come, and the importance of life-events in motivating young people to join these organisations. Clearly, it is perfectly possible in Northern Ireland for a young man to have a good upbringing in a good family, with or without Republican traditions, to have normal interests and pursuits, to be hard-working and still to perceive, in the light of his experience, that paramilitary activity is the only solution to his problems. In the light of this, the Thatcher philosophy that 'a crime is a crime is a crime' is not only mere sophistry, but a pig-headed evasion of British responsibility in creating the very situation from which paramilitarism springs.

PROXIMATE SITUATIONAL DETERMINANTS: HOW CAN PEOPLE COMMIT TERRORIST ACTS?

If an individual has a personality suited to the demands of a conflict-oriented group, and if his background, for one reason or another, has provided a motivation to engage in paramilitary activity, there still remains a formidable hurdle to cross to arrive at the sorts of behaviour mentioned in the first section of this chapter. How can normal, everyday people cross this hurdle? The key to this puzzle, I believe, can be found in experimental social psychology.

Research by Stanly Milgram (1974) in the United States has shown very clearly that ordinary individuals are quite capable of very cruel behaviour in the right circumstances. Milgram set up a situation in which people were paid to participate in what they believed was an experimental investigation of the effects of punishment on learning. Each subject was introduced to his partner who, in fact, was a 'stooge' or confederate of the experimenter, and they drew lots to determine who was going to be the teacher and who the learner in the experimental situation. This procedure was rigged so that the confederate always became the learner.

The task of the teacher was to punish incorrect responses by the learner in a learning task. The learner was strapped into a chair with an electrode on his wrist. Punishment was to be administered by an impressive apparatus which sent electric shocks to the learner. The apparatus contained thirty switches which enabled the teacher to administer shocks of increasing severity to the learner each time he made an error on the learning task. The switches were marked at 15 volt intervals up to 450 volts and were clearly labelled at levels from 'Slight Shock' up to 'Danger: Extreme Shock' and finally an ominous 'XXX'.

The experimenter informed the subject that 'although the shocks can be extremely painful, they cause no permanent tissue damage' and to give the subject or teacher an idea of what a single shock felt like, he was given a sample of 45 volts. This was the only shock actually administered in the entire procedure. The learner received no shocks at all, although the teacher did not know this.

The situation was arranged so that the learner made many errors in the learning task, so requiring the teacher to move progressively up the voltage scale of punishment shocks. If the teacher questioned the wisdom or desirability of the procedure at any point, the experimenter, who was standing nearby, simply replied that 'The experiment requires that you continue' or 'You have no other choice; you must go on'.

The experiment was conducted under a variety of conditions. In one condition, the learner was in a separate room from the teacher (the learner responded by pressing one of four switches which lit corresponding lights on the teacher's control panel). At 150 volts the learner showed his pain by shouting 'Experimenter, get me out of here! I refuse to go on!' At 180 volts he shouted that he found the pain unbearable and at 270 volts gave an agonised scream. At 300 he pounded on the wall separating his room from the teacher's and thereafter made no further response. Under these conditions 62.5 per cent of subjects carried on shocking the learner right up to 450 volts.

In another condition, the learner (who gave an absolutely convincing performance, as film of the experiment shows) was actually in the same room as the teacher and in these circumstances 40 per cent of subjects carried on to the highest level of shock despite the visible and audible evidence of the learner's distress. In yet another condition, the teacher was obliged after the 150 volt level to physically force the learner's unwilling hand on to a shock plate in order to deliver punishment. Even under these circumstances, 30 per cent of subjects carried on to 450 volts.

It should be stressed that Milgram's subjects were ordinary people and not sadists. To check the behaviour of subjects would not be so callous and cruel without the authority of the experimenter, Milgram set up a control experiment in which subjects could choose their own levels of shock. These were selected almost entirely from the lower ranges of the shock control board.

Milgram himself was astounded at the results of his experiments. The most cynical estimate he obtained prior to his study was that about 3 per cent of subjects would obey throughout whereas, in the event, up to 65 per cent delivered the maximum shock and all subjects obeyed up to 300 volts. In one of the many variations of the experimental situation where subjects were only required to perform a subsidiary role (reading the words the learner was required to learn), 90 per cent stayed with the experiment right through to the 450 volts level. Kilham and Mann (1974) confirmed this tendency in a replication of Milgram's experiment, finding that subjects only required to give the order to someone else to shock the learner were more compliant.

So here we have a startling demonstration of the degree to which ordinary people will behave callously, harshly and cruelly against an innocent victim who has done them no harm simply on the say-so of an experimenter in a psychological experiment. It should be noted that at no time did the experimenter threaten the subject with any consequences of his disobedience but merely asserted his authority in the vaguest possible terms ('The experiment requires that you continue.'). The subjects ascribed to the experimenter an authority which he did not, in fact, possess.

Milgram's findings are regarded by many psychologists, myself included, as among the most important in the entire field of social psychology. They have also been replicated with similar results in other countries (Mantell, 1971; Kilham and Mann, 1974; Shanab and Yahya, 1977) and hence represent a particularly strong body of knowledge in social psychology.

A revealing experiment by Zimbardo and his associates (1973) also gives us pause to reflect from a somewhat different angle. on the stability of the standards of behaviour to which most of us would lay claim. Zimbardo, who was investigating the effects of roles on behaviour, set up a situation in which a group of university students were to live for a short period as prison guards and prisoners. As the situation developed, a very dramatic change in the behaviour and outlook of both 'prisoner' and 'guards' began to take place. 'Prisoners' became more withdrawn and emotionally distressed and 'guards' became more punitive and authoritarian. In fact, the situation reached such a pitch that Zimbardo and his co-workers had to call off the experiment before its scheduled finish to avoid any possible harm or distress to his subjects, who had become so involved in their roles that the roles had begun to take over from the reality. Of particular interest, from the perspective of this chapter, is the behaviour of the 'prison guards' whose roles occasioned them to behave harshly and callously even though they were normal young men.

It is in the light of such experimental evidence that one can begin to understand the behaviour which typifies conflict-oriented groups in general and terrorist organisations such as the Provisional IRA in particular. Storr (1978) has made the point that aggression is a human characteristic and that, uniquely among the species, cruelty is within all human beings. We should also note that conflict-oriented groups, such as the Provisional IRA or the British Army, are organisations based on the premise that force or violence, or at the very least the threat of force or violence, is instrumental in obtaining certain objectives. Fine sociological distinctions between force (legitimate) and violence (illegitimate) make little psychological sense since legitimacy is in the eye of the beholder and a corpse is a corpse. Violence is what you use on me, force what I use on you.

Conflict-oriented groups, therefore, are organisations designed to elicit from men (and women) the potential for aggression and cruelty which they clearly possess and to supply them with the means for maximising the effect of that aggression and cruelty. This aggression and cruelty is normally kept in check by society's norms of appropriate behaviour and the system of formal and informal sanctions on those who transgress such norms. So how do people break the grip of those norms and the effects of years of social training inculcating such values as kindness and consideration for others? Milgram (1974) has suggested some interesting reasons why his subjects behaved as they did.

First, Milgram proposes that the experimental situation had inherent 'binding factors' such as politeness to the experimenter, the obligation to fulfil a promise to participate and the awkwardness and embarrassment of withdrawal. Ironically, the very social norms that would usually prevent one from harming someone, Milgram suggests, actually prevent one from not harming someone.

Second, Milgram proposes that there were 'adjustment factors' which served to distance the subject from the effects of his behaviour on his victim. Subjects became involved in the technical aspects of their task, tried to be competent at it, attributed the responsibility for the proceedings to the experimenter and hence their moral concern correspondingly diminished. Moreover, in a process fearsomely titled 'counter-anthropomorphism', they tended to deny the human element in what was an institutionalised procedure; they suppressed their normal reactions to distress in others in the name of experimentation or scientific enquiry. The quintessential example of counteranthropomorphism in everyday life would be the attitude of the public executioner or, in these more 'enlightened' times, the attitude of the judge in sentencing a convicted man to prolonged imprisonment.

Milgram's findings and suggested explanations of them give us pause to think about our current conceptions of 'evil' and 'evil men'. Clearly, in situations where men perceive themselves to be under authority, even if that authority is vague, a remarkable proportion will obey the command to hurt and distress others. Hannah Arendt (1963), writing of the Eichmann trials in Jerusalem, has questioned the validity of the prosecution's effort to depict Eichmann as a sadistic fiend. Rather, she saw him as a desk-bound bureaucrat doing a job and commented upon the 'banality of evil'. Certainly, Milgram's analysis tends to support that conceptualisation.

If one looks at conflict-oriented groups, it is clear that they are unique in the degree to which they are structured and the emphasis which they place on authority and pecking order. While other sorts of organisations, for example in industry, have tended to move away from an authority-bound approach towards a more co-operative ambience, military organisations continue to stress authority and formality. That fact is not just a reflection of the love of military organisations for tradition, but rather a recognition that authority and organised violence are inextricably linked.

Milgram's research has brought to light and subjected to theoretical analysis a phenomenon of human behaviour with which military practitioners have been familiar for centuries. All the square-bashing, saluting, kit-cleaning and endless, apparently pointless regimentation and authority is geared towards the day when vile acts and atrocious behaviour will be called for and received.

We usually tend to think that death and destruction are the business of armies other than our own and particularly the business of our enemies. But death and destruction, or the threat of death and destruction (which can only be a real threat if one can actually kill and destroy) is the very stuff of any conflict-oriented group. And the ability to deliver these goods effectively in any sizeable organisation is dependent upon the clear and unequivocal establishment of authority and obedience. Only in these circumstances will otherwise normal men truncheon, rifle-butt, shoot, stab and bomb complete strangers and ransack and destroy their property. Milgram's analysis has suggested to us the psychological means by which men can do these things and live with themselves during and after the event.

Transplanting this argument to the IRA, it is not by accident that the command structure of the IRA is so formalised. David Blundy has described the extremely stiff and formalised meetings of the Provisional Army Council in which military discipline is the norm. Christian names are banned and members are addressed by their full paramilitary titles despite long acquaintance and close friendship within the group (Sunday Times, 3 July 1977). New recruits to the IRA enter a formalised structure in which orders are given, obedience demanded and disobedience punished harshly.

Within this relationship of obedient member to authoritarian structure, it begins to come clear how the terrorist can cope with the awesome responsibility of his deeds. He too will be subject to binding factors even if the reality of his membership proves less palatable than the expectation. For example, he will feel obliged to fulfil the commitment of his membership. It would be awkward and embarrassing (not to mention possibly dangerous) for him to get out. Equally, he will have technical and practical aspects of his activites on which to focus and so diminish his moral concern. For example, he may be called upon to gather explosive substances, construct explosive devices, avoid the attentions of the security forces and so on. And he too will be prone to engage in counteranthropomorphism in the name of Irish liberation, freedom from British rule and so on.

Not only will the new recruit have entered a formal structure, he will also have entered a role which will make specific demands on his attitudes and behaviour. The role is one of 'guerilla', 'freedom fighter', 'revolutionary' or the role favoured and promoted by the Republican movement, 'soldier-politician' (Burton, 1978). This promotion is deliberately undertaken to counter the imputation of the more current label which I have used throughout this chapter, namely 'terrorist'. The requirements of the role of Provisional IRA member are many and varied - toughness, courage, ruthlessness, daring, planter of bombs, killer of soldiers and so forth. And, as Zimbardo's work has demonstrated, roles can powerfully affect how we behave and how we perceive ourselves.

Above all, perhaps, the Provisional IRA man's role is that of perpetrator of deeds, especially deeds of violence and destruction. The political element of the role is very much the poor relation and, as Burton (1978) notes, the experiences undergone by Provisionals during a protracted and ugly conflict tend to make them mistake political compromise for treachery, an insult to their dead and to the suffering of their communities. Having accepted the role of freedom fighter or soldier-politican, and thus measuring one's role success in terms of violent and certainly visible action, the difficulty arises of getting off what has become a self- propelled roundabout. Action equals strength, strength equals success and success equals action. As Laqueur (1977) notes, 'Terrorism in any case is not a philosophical school - it is always the action that counts.'

In summary, therefore, this analysis has shown that the behaviour of terrorists in Northern Ireland does not differ substantially from the behaviour of men in conflict-oriented groups generally. That behaviour is explicable to some extent in terms of the personality characteristics which predispose individuals to join such organisations, in terms of the particular motivations to engage in paramilitary activity in the Northern Ireland context, and in terms of the formalistic and authoritarian structures of conflict-oriented groups and the role-requirements of members of such groups.

It is no part of my intention to condone in any way the activities of paramilitary organisations, for that I could not do. However, there is little point at this stage in continuing blindly on the mud-slinging, propaganda bandwagon which media commentators and politicans alike have hid behind in dealing with, or rather failing to deal with the problems of Northern Ireland. It is only by trying to understand the people involved in terrorist organisations that one can realistically begin to tackle the problem which they and the situation they are in represent.

References

Arendt, H. (1963), Eichmann in Jerusalem: A Report on the Banality of Evil, New York: Viking Press.

Birrell, D. (1972), 'Relative deprivation as a factor in conflict in Northern Ireland', Sociological Review, 20, 317-43.

Burton, F. (1978), The Politics of Legitimacy, London: Routledge & Kegan Paul.

Buss, A.H. (1966), Psychopathology, New York: Wiley.

Calvert, M. (1973), 'The characteristics of guerilla leaders and their rank and file', The Practitioner, London, December 1973, n.p.

Cleckley, H. (1964), The Mask of Sanity, St Louis, Mo.: Mosby.

Clutterbuck, R. (1975), Living with Terrorism, London: Faber and Faber.

Clutterbuck, R. (1978), Britain in Agony: The Growth of Political Violence, London: Faber and Faber.

Craft, M.J. (1965), Ten Studies into Psychopathic Personality, Bristol: John Wright.

Elliott, P. (1980), 'Press performance as political ritual', The Sociological Review Monograph, No.29, 141-177.

Elliott, R. and Lockhart, W.H. (1980), 'Characteristics of scheduled offenders and juvenile delinquents', in J.I. Harbison and J.J.M. Harbison (eds.), Children and Young People in Northern Ireland, London: Open Books.

Foulds, G.A. (1965), Personality and Personal Illness, London: Tavistock Publications.

Heskin, K. (1980), Northern Ireland: A Psychological Analysis, Dublin: Gill & Macmillan; New York: Columbia University Press.

Kilham, W. and Mann, L. (1974), 'Level of destructive obedience as a function of the transmitter and executant roles in the Milgram obedience paradigm', Journal of Personality and Social Psychology, 29, 696-702.

Laqueur, W. (1977), Terrorism. London: Weidenfeld and Nicolson.

McCord, W. and McCord, J. (1964), The Psychopath: An Essay on the Criminal Mind, Princeton, N.J.: Van Nostrand.

MacStiofain, S. (1975), Revolutionary in Ireland, London: Gordon Cremonesi.

Mantell, D.M. (1971), 'The potential for violence in Germany', Journal of Social Issues, 27, 101-12.

Middlebrook, M. (1981), The Battle of Hamburg, London:

Allen Lane.

Milgram, S. (1974), Obedience to Authority, London: Tavistock.

Shanab, M.E. and Yahya, K.A. (1977), 'A behavioural study of obedience in children', Journal of Personality and Social Psychology, 35, 530-36.

Storr, A. (1978), 'Sadism and Paranoia', in M.H. Livingston (ed.), International Terrorism in the Contemporary World, London: Greenwood Press.

Sweetman, R. (1972), On Our Knees - Ireland 1972, London: Pan Books.

Zimbardo, P.G., Haney, C., Banks, W.C. and Jaffe, D. (1973), 'The Psychology of Imprisonment: Privation, Power and Pathology', unpublished manuscript, Stanford, Calif.: Stanford University.

Essay six

POLITICAL ASSASSINATION IN THE IRISH TRADITION

Tom Corfe

Assassination was long held to be the vilest of crimes, the
most sinister form of attack upon established religion, state
or society. The hysterical fears engendered by the Jesuits'
notorious advocacy of tyrannicide lingered long after the
decline of personal monarchy had rendered them irrelevant.
Victorians, confident and convinced, saw as blasphemy any
such cowardly threat to natural order and social propriety.
But as religion, establishment and social order have become
less sacrosanct in the later Twentieth Century, so
assassination has acquired some sort of political respectability
as the most incisive form of political criticism. This growing
acceptance of assassination as a regular if deplorable feature
of modern political life is reflected in a semantic change. The
word itself has lost some of its overtones of reprehensibility.
It has become the neutral's term for what one side would
regard as execution (righteous justice) and the other as
murder (inexcusable, sordid, mercenary, criminal).
Assassination implies political purpose and dedicated idealism,
and in an understanding age such motives are acceptable as
justification for almost any misdeed. The change is apparent
in any comparison of modern with Nineteenth-century
comment.

The most spectacular assassination of recent years was
the blowing up of Lord Mountbatten, with members of his
family and friends, off Mullaghmore in County Sligo, in
August 1979. It was the climax of a campaign whose victims
had included over the previous five years Airey Neave (at
the hands of a different organization), Sir Richard Sykes,
Christopher Ewart-Biggs, Ross McWhirter, and (by mistake)
Gordon Hamilton Fairley. To these might be added several
prominent business men and judges in Northern Ireland, and
some scores of lesser figures; there is no clearcut definition
to suggest just how distinguished a victim must be for his
death to rank as assassination rather than plain political
killing.

The world's press reported Mountbatten's death as a

simple if sensational case of murder. The political motivation was obvious, though the press generally implied irrational viciousness rather than calculated and deliberate policy. An Poblacht however, heading its own account "Execution of Soldier Mountbatten", showed no qualms in accepting responsibility on behalf of the Provisional IRA.[1] Others, who deplored the deed yet sympathised with or understood the motives, preferred to describe it as an assassination.

Similar language was applied a century earlier to the one comparable crime in Irish history, the killing of Cavendish and Burke in Phoenix Park; but in that case the connotations were somewhat different. The small group of Fenians who published a manifesto dated 8th May 1882 in defiant approval of "the late executions in Dublin" declared that "the men who have carried out this execution... deserve well of their country".[2] The forceful if wordy statement earlier issued by the horrified Irish Party members in London and largely drafted by Davitt deplored "a horrible deed", an "atrocity" committed by "the murderers of Lord Frederick Cavendish and Mr Burke". The action they denounced so unequivocally they defined repeatedly as an assassination. More recently this term has been annexed by those who would argue that no "murders" took place, by sympathisers with the Invincibles such as the enthusiasts of the Kilmainham Jail Restoration Society. Their 1963 booklet takes melancholy pride in the fact that "the policy of the Invincibles was to assassinate English officials in Ireland, so as to force the English government to withdraw from the country".[3] Assassination is thus a justifiable act of war, not a "horrible crime".

The last two decades have made assassination a familiar tragedy, and familiarity has duly bred contempt. As a local phenomenon this is the product of persistent Anglo-Irish conflict, but it was the series of assassinations and attempts in the USA during the '60s that established the international pattern: the Kennedys, Martin Luther King, George Wallace, Malcolm X and Lincoln Rockwell in turn captured world headlines. As violence and irrational fanaticism have become familiar features of the political scene, so too has increasingly sophisticated technology solved many of the assassin's personal problems; pressing a remote, impersonal button requires a different kind of courage from that demanded for messy close-quarters involvement with knife or pistol.

Assassination tends to be the work of a minority within the terrorist minority, often acting without explicit authority or approval. Mixed motives and purposes are common, and there may well be uncertainty, confusion or disagreement over these as between the leaders initiating the action and those who must execute their orders. But some discussion of the motives inspiring assassins over the past century of Anglo-Irish relations can be attempted.

In the arsenal of terrorist weaponry the killing of

opponents in cold blood and without public trial is regarded as effective and necessary, justified in a state of one-sided warfare because open judicial proceedings are impracticable in an "occupied" territory. Tyrannicide here implies the elimination of the state's servants in order to destroy its effectiveness. The assassination weapon was used in this sense to greatest effect during the Anglo-Irish war, when Michael Collins' "Execution Squad" of dedicated gunmen disposed of potentially dangerous enemies. As a compact private army responsible to Collins alone, the Squad interpreted one man's understanding of tactical necessity with notable single-mindedness. Their most notorious exploit was the killing of twelve British officers on "Bloody Sunday" (21 November 1920) who were identified (for the most part correctly) as agents of the Castle's intelligence service. This action effectively paralysed for the time being Special Branch activites against the IRA.[4] Press and public opinion at the time interpreted the action as an indiscriminate terrorist massacre, directed against officers and gentlemen who had chosen to live peaceful, semi-civilian lives in Dublin homes and hotels. It was seen as an act of desperation, as the last attempt of "cornered rats against the fate which they may delay but cannot avert".[5] The murderers were denounced for their scheming brutality, taking their victims by surprise while some were still abed, and killing ruthlessly and messily in the presence of screaming wives and bystanders. Yet however shocking and unreasonable the violence appeared, however great the public revulsion, its perpetrators could fairly regard their deed as justified by its political and military results.

In the event the impact of the assassinations was to some extent offset by the news of the equally horrifying Croke Park "massacre", which followed so speedily that it has generally been regarded as a spontaneous reprisal, though this has been questioned.[6] It seems unlikely that Collins deliberately intended to provoke the Crown forces into retaliation, but such ill-disciplined response was of course a common by-product of IRA activity generally during the War, and offered a useful bonus in its alienation of public support from the forces of law and order.

A few months before Bloody Sunday the Squad had carried out an equally effective assassination with the same kind of purpose, that of the Resident Magistrate Alan Bell. To the watching world this was the cold-blooded murder of an inoffensive civilian, a civil servant of impeccable record, "ruffians dragging a helpless old man to his death" as the Daily News, forgetting its normal sympathy for the Irish viewpoint, put it.[7] Taken from a Dublin tram on his way to work, Bell was shot in the gutter while those around appeared too intimidated to protest. Only gradually did the assassins' purpose become clear, as it emerged that the innocuous Bell had been appointed to enquire into the funds held in various banks on behalf of the IRA. His investigations posed a threat to funds that Michael Collins had so industriously accumulated to finance his campaign. Again, the responsibility was one man's, and the method, though ruthless, and counter-productive in showing the IRA in a singularly unattractive guise, could be justified as an act of war. It was of course a war whose existence was denied by the government against which it was directed and the press supporting that government.

In such cases the IRA could claim that assassination was both military necessity and judicial execution, adapted to the circumstances of "enemy occupation". It involved also elements of intimidation. No one dared take Alan Bell's place. After Bloody Sunday Castle agents and their families abandoned their civilian quarters and fled into military protection.[8]

This element of intimidation, sometimes indistinguishable from that of reprisal, has played an increasingly prominent part in the sectarian and political killings of recent years in Northern Ireland. The killing of judges, prison officers, policemen and business leaders has been defended as part of a campaign to frighten those who serve an alien administration or bolster an unacceptable economy. Sectarian para-military groups have used and misused the assassination weapon to a further degree of frightfulness, carrying it to the scale of massacre. The most notorious examples (from opposite political sides) were the killing of the Dublin-based Miami Showband in August, 1975, and the Bessbrook machine-gunning in January 1976 of ten Protestant workmen. The latter outrage, at least, was claimed as a successful move in putting an end to the murders of local Catholics.[9]

Such mass killings can hardly be effective without a degree of popular sympathy, or at least complaisance. They throw into sharp relief the inability of government to act forcefully in a situation where public apathy or sympathy permits small, determined groups to move and strike freely. Normally fear of public opinion deters governments from overt retaliatory violence. Only once has official ruthlessness effectively stopped an assassination campaign, in 1922 during the Civil War. Liam Lynch, as IRA Chief of Staff, issued his "Orders of Frightfulness" in November, threatening all Dail deputies who had voted for the Provisional Government's Emergency Powers measures, under which captured rebels might be tried by military courts and shot for carrying arms, and under which Erskine Childers and others had already been executed. Soon afterwards one deputy, Sean Hales, was shot dead and another seriously wounded. The government's immediate execution without trial of four of its principal prisoners seems to have been effective in reducing the IRA's campaign to one of lesser frightfulness. But such willingness to create potential martyrs was a course no present-day

British or Irish government dare copy in the face of domestic and world opinion.

Such assassinations of lesser folk, more or less closely involved with one side or the other in the conflict, were a natural outgrowth of terrorist insurgency and the product of local initiative, rather than part of any carefully planned campaign. The hit-and-run casualness even of Collins' murderous activities on Bloody Sunday has recently been stressed; there was perhaps less cool efficiency than enthusiastic biographers have suggested.[10] Rather less spontaneously, assassination has with increasing frequency been aimed at spectacular targets, at prestigious and exceptional individuals who might be considered by outsiders as above the struggle. This is symbolic tyrannicide, the identification of the target as personifying the national enemy. There is a strong element of "propaganda by deed" as the assassin demonstrates in unmistakable fashion the underlying determination behind his cause and the ability of its supporters to strike at the enemy's most eminent representatives. Dan Breen, writing of the unsuccessful attempt on Lord French in December 1919, stressed that

> he was a corporate symbol, British Rule in Ireland... not merely a man but an institution, the evil institution of England's dominance in our land. He was the figure-head which represented British tyranny in Ireland and as such we wished to destroy him... We believed, too, that in shooting Lord French we would help to focus the eyes of the entire world upon Ireland's unhappy lot, upon her gallant fight against the might of a great empire, upon the truth that though a bloody war had been fought in Europe "that small nations might be free", Ireland, one of the smallest and weakest nations of them all, was still captive in the spider-web of Britain's empire.[11]

At the head of the list of assassinations of this type, Cavendish and Mountbatten stand in a class of their own. One degree closer to the battlefront, because each was more intimately involved in Irish politics and more obviously in danger, were Sir Henry Wilson (1922), Kevin O'Higgins (1927), Ross McWhirter (1975), Christopher Ewart-Biggs (1976), Sir Richard Sykes and Airey Neave (both 1979). One corollary of the increasing commonness of this kind of assassination is the blunting of susceptibilities and loss of shock effect, so that even the horror of the Mountbatten murder was received with some degree of resignation as tragically inevitable. Nothing the terrorist can do now could possibly have the overwhelming impact that the Phoenix Park Murders, "the Crime of the Century", had in their own day.

As an attack on major political figures the Phoenix Park Murders were unprecedented in Irish history. There was indeed a long tradition of agrarian murder, directed against landowners, their agents, or co-operative tenants. Of recent years the activities of the Land League had coincided with an upsurge, of which Lord Mountmorres in 1880 was perhaps the most distinguished victim. In a sense, it has been suggested, the Phoenix Park Murders were simply agrarian crime translated to the city.[12] Such casual violence had been endemic in troubled rural areas at least since the 1760s, and might be regarded as a natural hazard of Irish country life. On the other hand the Irish Republican Brotherhood, representing the main stream of revolutionary nationalism, specifically rejected such tactics, except in so far as they might be necessary to deal with the problems of disloyalty and informing within its own ranks. James Stephens, John O'Leary and John Devoy were all emphatic that assassination was an unacceptable weapon, abhorrent to the honest soldiers of the Republic.[13] C.J. Kickham, President of the IRB Supreme Council, was prompt to denounce the Park Murders and to suggest that only Land Leaguers could have been responsible. This attitude on the part of Fenian leaders did not, however, prevent individuals or enthusiastic groups from sometimes acting independently. Such enterprise had led to the murder in 1868 of Thomas Darcy McGee, the former Young Irelander turned Canadian politician, who had vigorously denounced the Fenian invasion of his adopted country. The man duly hanged for his murder, Patrick Whelan, may or may not have been a Fenian, but he was certainly influenced by Fenian attitudes and propaganda. Some transatlantic Fenians at least, in their frustration after the failures of the mid-sixties, were looking with sympathy towards assassination tactics.[14]

If the squalid occasional shootings of rural ribbonism helped in establishing a climate where murder seemed only too natural, the international atmosphere served to direct attention towards more exalted targets. Those who, so far as we know, were responsible for setting up the Invincible conspiracy in 1881 were international in background and outlook. Patrick Egan, Treasurer of the Land League, was a Dublin master baker; but he had moved into a wider world and was currently self-exiled - with the League's funds - in Paris. He already had interests in American and European politics; and it is worth remembering that his international activities were, within eight years, to make him a somewhat controversial United States Minister to Chile. Frank Byrne, the Liverpool Irishman who was the Westminster-based Secretary of the Land League of Great Britain, had served in the French army and knew Europe well. John Walsh of Middlesbrough and John McCafferty, the restless former Confederate guerilla, were both well travelled men. They were familiar with the current sinister role of assassination in the politics of such troubled countries as Spain and Italy and, most significantly, Russia. It was in March 1881 that the murderous campaign of the "People's Will" (Narodnaya Volya) reached the climax of three years of bloodshed in the destruction of Alexander II with many of his entourage. Despite the sickening violence of their action, and the effective suppression of all revolutionary movements that followed it, these youthful idealist opponents of an autocratic regime attracted sympathetic comment in the radical press of western Europe. In that the People's Will was an extremist group turning towards more spectacular methods after the frustration of earlier Narodnik efforts to inspire a revolution based on popular agitation among the peasant masses, the parallel with the Invincibles and the Land League is obvious. The assassins set a fashion; but their example had little relevance in the year's second major assassination, for there were no political principles at stake in the killing of President Garfield three months later.

Egan Byrne and McCafferty played significant if shadowy parts in organizing the Dublin Invincibles, with Walsh as their first go-between. Their aim was defined as the "suppression" of "the chiefs of Ireland's ravagers", the "illegal and alien administration" of Chief Secretary and Under-Secretary, and the "removal" of "every satrap of Britain... in any part of Ireland". Their method they regarded as "a species of guerilla warfare",[15] but in plain terms suppression and removal meant simply assassination; so much was made clear when Byrne early arranged the purchase and transfer to Dublin of the formidable surgical knives eventually used in Phoenix Park, weapons clearly suited to warfare of a very limited kind. At the same time they were well aware of the symbolic significance and publicity value of their deed, claiming that "it was at once understood by European statesmen; it conveyed to them the immortal truth that Irish nationality still lived".[16]

The Invincibles' highly original approach to solving the Irish problem was largely a result of frustration over alternative methods. The principals and most of the rank-and-file recruits were former Fenians, and the history of Fenianism since 1865 had been a pathetic record of futility, of internecine bickerings and betrayal. The movement's bold challenge to a Britain at the height of its economic and imperial strength had got nowhere. The long-anticipated moment of England's difficulty and Ireland's opportunity seemed farther off than ever. The Fenian leadership lay dormant under the respected but ineffectual chairmanship of Kickham, its American backers were afflicted by petty squabbles and treachery, and the membership dwindled.

But the alternatives to which so many Fenian enthusiasts turned in the 70s succeeded only in raising hopes to dash them subsequently. Many members of the Brotherhood lent their support to the revived Parliamentary Party though it meant nominal abandonment of their revolutionary principles. Some were expelled from the IRB, or left it in disgust like Egan. Many joined the Land League, as the most promising revolutionary development at the end of the decade. The tactics of these two movements severely shook Westminster in the winter of 1880-81, so that by December Michael Davitt was able to claim in a letter to Devoy that the Land League "now virtually rules the country".[17] But disillusion followed. The government's tactics of stick and carrot effectively undermined the revolutionaries. The possibilities of generous concessions arising from the Land Act reduced many farmers' enthusiasm for the League, while local leaders were detained under the Coercion Act and Davitt himself was re-imprisoned. At the same time the introduction of Parliamentary guillotine, coinciding with the apparent ebbing of Parnell's revolutionary enthusiasm as he sought to walk his delicate tightrope between convincing defiance of the government and responsible party leadership, meant that the Irish performance at Westminster was a disappointment to the activists. The revolutionary ambitions that lay behind the New Departure were not after all to be realised.

What seemed a final blow to the revolutionaries' hopes came in October, 1881, when Parnell himself, with other national and local leaders, was detained in Kilmainham; at the same time the Land League was suppressed. Parnell, so Barry O'Brien tells us, had remarked that if he were imprisoned 'Captain Moonlight' would take his place. But Egan and Byrne resolved that the violence implied should be more formidable than everyday agrarian outrage. The excess of energy among frustrated nationalists was to be channelled into spectacular action.

The Fenian attempts at open warfare and widespread conspiracy in 1865 and 1867 had collapsed ignominiously, betrayed by incompetents and informers. The new efforts, therefore, must be small-scale and secretive. In one sense it was, as Tynan remarked with some prophetic insight, "the Future making its appearance on the scene",[18] for a similar transition from open to underground tactics characterised the 1916-21 period. Since it was impossible for either Egan or Byrne to actually visit Ireland without attracting attention and possible arrest, they had to guide and influence from a distance, using busy go-betweens. The outcome was a group that numbered at most thirty-seven[19] and suffered from uncertain and inadequate lines of communication with its overseas leadership. At one crucial moment those communications failed; at another, the secrecy even of that compact group broke down.

It is not clear how much consideration the Invincibles gave to the possible consequences of their action, nor precisely what their objectives were. Tynan's melodramatic version suggests that they hoped to make British administration impossible by destroying its representatives and symbols one by one. Simultaneously they would assert their determination to the world. The danger that public opinion might react against such murderous methods in Britain and Ireland counted for little with the rank-and-file Invincibles, who were concerned simply to strike a blow for their country. But Egan and Byrne, using simple activists as part of a political strategy as Parnell had used the League, may have had more complex motives. It is possible that they hoped through their spectacular gesture to force the government into fresh negotiations with Parnell; if so they were overtaken by events, for the Kilmainham 'Treaty' had been agreed before the Invincibles struck. More likely they intended the opposite, to strike a blow that would check any possibility of a compromise settlement being reached by sharpening the conflict. As good Fenians (even if they had formally left the Brotherhood) their struggle must go on until a republic was achieved, and any danger of a reconciliation between nationalists and government must be avoided. In this sense their action was aimed against Parnell, whose immediate reaction on hearing of the murders was indeed to call it a stab in the back, "a deadly blow to his party".[20]

Perhaps Parnell was unduly alarmed. Professor Lyons has argued that he recovered his equanimity and control of the situation speedily[21] and suggested that the renewal of co-operation with the Liberals in 1886 in the 'union of hearts' meant that the assassinations were "in the broad political context... a gigantic irrelevance".[22] This seems to ignore the significant developments in the Irish (especially Ulster) and British political scene over the four wasted years after the Murders. Certainly Parnell's immediate interpretation of the assassinations was that they represented a direct attempt to undermine his new-found policy of conciliation, and he offered to resign and retire. He may well have been justified in his suspicions.

For the rank-and-file Invincibles in Dublin, mostly drawn from the working or small tradesmen classes, any kind of blow at the enemy was an end in itself. The leaders of the group included James Mullett whose bar was notoriously a centre of Republican talk; Dan Curley, a carpenter, emotional but inarticulate; Joe Brady, a tough young corporation paviour; and James Carey, a small builder with political ambitions and patriotic enthusiasm. All had been either members of the IRB or closely associated with the movement; indeed most of the Dublin Invincibles were drawn from the Fenian circle that Dan Curley headed. They included some, such as the pathetic Patrick Delaney, best described as petty criminals and habitual drunkards. Their politics were unsophisticated, though undoubtedly most were more or less sincerely devoted to the national cause. It seems hardly relevant to discuss whether their inspiration derived from their Fenianism or from their seduction by the Land League, as Kickham suggested. They were impatient men who had tried both institutions and failed to find the simple satisfaction of visibly effective action.[23]

Whatever motives inspired the Invincibles, their conspiracy suffered from the obvious organizational problems that have afflicted others since. Obsessive secrecy, mutual suspicions, a preference for circumlocutory and ambiguous language, complex channels of communication: these make it only too easy for orders to go astray or to be misinterpreted. There are too many opportunities for the enthusiastic individual to act on his own initiative, expecting and claiming the implicit approval of his leaders. It is not clear, for example, how far the death of Henry Wilson in 1922 or that of Kevin O'Higgins in 1927 were the result of independent and irresponsible action. It has been suggested that Wilson's death was the result of an order that Michael Collins issued and then forgot to countermand when circumstances changed. The two members of the London battalion IRA who killed him were relying on outdated instructions; angered by the upsurge of sectarian violence in Belfast they took it upon themselves to act at a moment when in fact the Provisional Government of which Collins was a leading member was desperately anxious not to antagonise Britain further. Their action helped to precipitate the developing Civil War. Others have suggested, however, that Collins may have fully intended his order to be carried out; he was perhaps so carried away by the efficacy of the weapon he had used so frequently at grass-roots level that he hoped it might effectively stem anti-Catholic terrorism in the North.[24] At whatever level the mistakes were made, there seems to have been an element of irresponsibility and breakdown of communication in the Wilson killing.

Some such weakness in communications may have played a major part in the tragedy of Phoenix Park. Egan and Byrne were forced to rely on a succession of rather dubious emissaries to convey instructions to Dublin. The last of these was P.J.P. Tynan, whose foolishly bombastic book is, despite its defects, a major source of information about the Invincible conspiracy. As a London-based, Irish-born commercial traveller of almost ludicrous respectability, Tynan was in some ways an ideal secret messenger. But the innocuous and dowdy appearance concealed not only a romantic devotion to the national cause but a vigorous imagination and an intense, exhibitionist ambition. So it was that at a moment when the Dublin Invincibles urgently sought fresh instructions from London Tynan was in a position to interpret the little vague guidance available in his own peculiar way. It may well be, too, that his excitable immediate reaction to news of the Ballina "massacre" (where the police had fired on a riotous crowd, killing one and injuring others), affected his judgement, just as Dunne and O'Sullivan in 1922 may have reacted to the latest tidings from Belfast. These were tense, angry men, responding to the 'last straw' and only too ready to seize any opportunity of expressing their feelings in violent form. It seems that Tynan (and we have only his own untrustworthy account to go on) had received on the 5th May some message of encouragement from London, couched in very general terms and probably despatched by Frank Byrne before the nature and implications of the revolution in Gladstone's and Parnell's relationship had become apparent. In some such circumstances Tynan, the go-between, enjoyed his moment of glory and took his fateful decision.[25]

In conditions like these secret underground activity is only too likely to go astray. Further, even if the executants actually succeeded in carrying out as intended their leaders' plans, outside opinion is very ready to assume that the wrong thing has been done at the wrong time. Here what has been called the 'Paddy Factor' comes into operation,[26] the common British assumption that, given the least opportunity, any Irishman can be trusted to make a disastrous mistake. Explosives and guns can go wrong in any hands, and assassins tend to be callously fatalistic about unfortunate bystanders who get in the way. Amateur bombers and bomb-makers apparently destroy themselves in a distinctly happy-go-lucky way, while the tragic error that cost Professor Hamilton Fairley his life in place of Hugh Fraser MP has been repeated often enough at a less exalted level. Perhaps the blackest comedy has attended the efforts of the Official IRA, whose bid to enter the assassination game included the attack on Aldershot Barracks that killed cleaning women and a Roman Catholic padre. Ominously the farce has become more lethal in recent years; growing frustration increases the tendency to take forceful action regardless of consequences and think about it later. In 1919 they were less impatient; Dan Breen recorded "at least a dozen abortive attempts to ambush Lord French and his escort", though the Lord Lieutenant never learnt of his danger. When finally "luck seemed to be with us" and the long-planned ambush actually materialised, it transpired that French was in the wrong car and his attackers got more than they bargained for.[27] Luck and chance seem to play a significant part in determining whether assassination attempts are to be ludicrous failures or disastrous successes.

The frequent failures, and the psychological mechanism that prevents our taking too seriously those who actively dislike us, have produced a contemptuous attitude towards Irish capabilities. All too often, though, this assumption has rebounded upon those making it. The Easter Rising of 1916 might have been nipped in the bud had the Castle authorities taken more seriously the militaristic activities of the Volunteers and the flamboyant language of their leaders.

The Paddy Factor played a key part in the events of 1882, and in the public response to them. Its precise significance, however, depends on dubious interpretations of obscure events. It is uncertain whether Lord Frederick Cavendish was killed accidentally or by intent. What is significant is the almost universal assumption, both immediately after the event and ever since, that he was unknown to his murderers and was assassinated only because he happened to be present and bravely leapt to defend his companion. This assumption helped salve the consciences of the Irish people and of the Gladstone administration that had sent him to his post, as well as that of the police who had failed so signally to protect him. It was duly reinforced when James Carey dutifully confirmed all that the authorities already knew or believed.

In fact the weight of evidence would seem to support Tynan's assertion that Cavendish was from the start the intended victim. In one sense he was a more suitable target than either Burke or his own predecessor, Forster, whom the Invincibles had many times failed to assassinate; Cavendish's death would make clear to the world that they sought not personal revenge against a known enemy and notorious tyrant, but that "it was British rule in any manner which these men protested against".[28] The precise manner of his death, stabbed from behind at the same moment as his companion rather than subsequently while trying to defend him, fits the Tynan version rather than the popular legend. A Castle servant, it was subsequently revealed, had been brought along by the Invincibles specifically to identify their victim; yet Burke was already a familiar figure to them and they had previously lain in wait for him without any such help. Finally, the Invincibles seemed to be anticipating their victims' arrival on foot, whereas Burke's normal practice when alone was to take a car. Yet long before any of this evidence appeared police, government and public opinion leapt to the gratifying conclusion that Cavendish's murder was simply a gigantic blunder for which no one and nothing but traditional Irish incompetence could be held responsible.

The subsequent inquiry and trial evidence confirmed this view. There was the long, ludicrous tale of the twenty odd attempts to assassinate Cavendish's predecessor, all of which had failed so completely that Forster knew nothing of them. Clearly the killing of Cavendish was the climax to a black farce, the biggest blunder of all. Further, James Carey, as approver, virtually repeated the police view of what had happened. This, it might be suggested, merely demonstrates how successful Carey was in protecting his fellow-conspirators by offering the police just enough information to satisfy them. It is ironic that in seeking a scapegoat both enemies and sympathisers of the Invincibles fastened on Carey, who could and did claim, fairly enough, that he had betrayed no one

117

whose life was not already forfeit, and who had concealed from the police much that they would have liked to know, much that the less sophisticated Curley, for example, might have been induced to reveal.

The operation of the Paddy Factor in this context illustrates a general weakness of assassination as a weapon in the Anglo-Irish conflict: the British refusal to take it seriously. Public opinion is too complacent or too tolerant to acknowledge any such action as a deliberate and purposeful expression of a very real Irish point of view. Terrorist assassination, the argument runs, is not an aspect of warfare waged by a substantial and respected enemy but rather the aberration of a few vicious, muddle-headed, isolated fanatics, who flourish so regrettably because of the unfortunate inability of the Irish to control their own fools, criminals and 'wild men'. Cavendish and Mountbatten, friendly and universally respected establishment figures, noblemen far above the daily struggle, can have nothing in common with the sordid nastiness of Irish faction and violence, or the habitual unpleasant behaviour of one Irishman to another. Those who seek to strike at such exalted beings simply reveal their own ignorance and petty viciousness; they are making a characteristic Irish mistake on a monstrous scale. It follows that all Britain need do is find some means of stopping this criminally lunatic group from making similar mistakes in future. There is no need to think in terms of some fundamental malaise for which a cure must be sought. Thus assassinations have been singularly ineffective both as a means of forcing governments into changing their policies towards ameliorative action and also in provoking indiscriminate retaliatory measures that might reinforce anti-government support.

But if this attitude reduces the value of assassination as a weapon of terror, the cumulative effect of violence remains. The continuing tale of assassinations has confirmed the general British impression of Irish viciousness and incompetence so highlighted by the deaths of Cavendish and Burke. In passing, it should perhaps be noted that the similarly distorted Irish view of the British may also derive from the actions and attitudes of a minority. Attitudes harden; conflict sharpens. Conduct of their own affairs can hardly be entrusted to those who allow crimes and blunders of such magnitude. After 1882 widespread hostility fatally undermined the Gladstone-Parnell understanding both at cabinet level, where his colleagues firmly resisted the prime minister's desire for a compromise, and at popular level, where suspicion of any kind of deal with violence played a major part in the rejection of Home Rule. Similarly after 1979 the sub-human characteristics apparently revealed by Irish actions brought a stiffening of response at government and popular levels. Prime Minister Lynch was humiliated and undermined much as Parnell had been a century earlier. Parnell was treated as something of a pariah in Parliament, and remained so in tne eyes of the British public until his vindication in 1889. Public opinion and most politicians had made up their minds about Parnellism and the crime so patently associated with it; Gladstone, shattered by private and political tragedy, was in no position to resist hawkish colleagues or to win over a hostile electorate. Nowadays a comparable suspicion persists that in some way all Catholic Irish actively sympathise with and, by negligence or design, actually assist terrorist activities. This bedevils Anglo-Irish and inter-Irish relations.

Assassination is a clumsy, ineffective and double-edged weapon. This is most apparent when the victim is a prestigious figure selected as a symbol. The weapon may indeed be more effective when used tactically and locally, under firm control, to disrupt the working of the state or to intimidate its servants. When grandiose aims are alleged, or when high-minded idealists attempt to use it, then the results hardly satisfy expectations. Striking a symbolic blow may win publicity, but it will rarely be of a sympathetic or understanding nature unless from those already heavily committed. Assassins seek to assert the validity and vitality of their cause, but they are more likely to be received with revulsion and puzzlement. Their motives will be misinterpreted, their integrity and efficiency doubted. Their only gains are likely to be purely personal: the satisfaction of self-indulgent exhibitionism or the release of pent-up frustrations in a spectacular demonstration of hatred. Assassination conspiracies are particularly vulnerable to the vagaries of chance and misunderstanding; their success or failure depends rather on such factors as luck and individual whim than on careful planning and sincerity of ideals. Even if the assassins do not make silly and tragic mistakes, public opinion may well assume that they have.

Assassination is the least effective as well as the ugliest form of warfare. It is also that most likely to intensify hatred and to polarise communities within Ireland and within the British Isles. But those so strongly afflicted by patriotic idealism as to believe that assassination is morally and politically justified are likely to be blind to its practical consequences.

Notes
1   Coogan, T.P. The IRA, part II, Collins Fontana, London/Glasgow, 1980, p.589.
2   Tynan, P.J.P. The Irish National Invincibles and their Times, Chatham & Co., London, 1894, pp.272-4; and note significant addendum to the American edition on this point.
3   Kilmainham Jail Restoration Society. Ghosts of

Kilmainham, Dublin, 1963, p.32.
4   Townshend. C. The British Campaign in Ireland, 1919-1921, Oxford University Press, 1975, pp.129-30; Gleeson, J. Bloody Sunday, Peter Davies, London, 1962, esp. ch.8.
5   "I.O." (C.J.C. Street). The Administration of Ireland, 1920, Philip Allan, London, 1921, p.149.
6   Townshend, op.cit., pp.130-1.
7   Boyce, D.G. Englishmen and Irish Troubles, Jonathan Cape, London, 1972, p.94.
8   Hogan, D. The Four Glorious Years, Irish Press, Dublin, 1953, p.243.
9   Coogan, op.cit., p.551.
10   Townshend, C. "The IRA and Guerilla Warfare", in E.H.R. vol.XCIV, April, 1979, pp.326-7.
11   Breen, D. "Lord French was not destined to die by an Irish bullet", in With the IRA in the Fight for Freedom, Kerryman, Tralee, n.d. (1955?), p.44.
12   O Broin, L. "The Invincibles", in Williams, T.D., ed. Secret Societies in Ireland, Gill & Macmillan, Dublin, 1973, p.122.
13   Sullivan, T.D. Recollections of Troubled Times in Irish Politics. Sealy, Bryers & Walker/M.H. Gill, Dublin, 1905, pp.108-9.
14   Senior, H. The Fenians and Canada, Macmillan, Toronto, 1978, pp.121-31.
15   Tynan, op.cit., p.430.
16   Ibid., p.481.
17   O'Brien, W. and Ryan, D., eds. Devoy's Postbag, 1871-1928, vol.II, C.J. Fallon, Dublin, 1953, pp.22-3.
18   Tynan, op.cit., p.430.
19   O Broin, op.cit., pp.121-2.
20   O'Brien, R.E. The Life of Charles Stewart Parnell, Smith, Elder & Co., London, 1898, vol.I pp.357-9.
21   Lyons, F.S.L. Charles Stewart Parnell, Collins, London, 1977, pp.209-11.
22   Lyons, F.S.L. in The Irish Times, 27.2.1968, p.14.
23   O Broin, op.cit., p.122.
24   Kee, R. The Green Flag, Weidenfeld & Nicolson, London, 1972, p.739; Taylor, R. Assassination, Hutchinson, London, 1961, pp.203-19.
25   Corfe, T. The Phoenix Park Murders, Hodder & Stoughton, London, 1968, pp.179-80, 194-6.
26   Coogan, op.cit., p.472.
27   Breen, op.cit., p.44.
28   Tynan, op.cit., p.264.

THE CATHOLIC CHURCH AND REVOLUTION IN NINETEENTH CENTURY IRELAND

Sheridan Gilley

After the death of Daniel O'Connell in 1847, his heart was sent to Rome, where a number of requiems were sung, the most important in the great church of Sant'Andrea della Valle, and there a packed congregation heard a two hour sermon from Father Gioacchino Ventura di Raulica, one of the finest orators of the age.[1] For Ventura, O'Connell had united what the French revolutionaries had divided 'true religion and true liberty': for 'being at once a great Christian and a great citizen, he called religion to his aid in the sublime enterprise of giving liberty to the people'. The time seemed propitious for this reconciliation of ideals: Ventura, disgraced for a time under the rule of the conservative Gregori XVI, was now high in the counsels of the Liberal Pio Nono, who was unwittingly to precipitate the revolutions of 1848, when the priests of Paris would all be in the streets blessing trees of liberty. But the mood did not last: the trees of liberty died – poisoned, anticlericals claimed by the holy water. The pope, an exile from the Roman Republic, was to return to his city as the century's greatest scourge of Liberalism, while Ventura himself fled to France and found a new career as a preacher before the ex-Carbonaro Emperor Napoleon III. Not that Ventura's Liberalism was revolutionary. He praised O'Connell for finding just the right combination of 'passive resistance' and 'active obedience' to oppression, avoiding the 'heretical' and 'Mussulman' extremes of 'active resistance' and 'passive obedience'.[2] To Ventura, the one blot on O'Connell's escutcheon was a youthful duel with an enemy of the Faith. O'Connell's supreme virtue was to have opposed heretical England not by physical force, but by the courage and virtue of the mind, by arms spiritual and invisible more powerful than guns, the religion of a Catholic people.

O'Connell and Ventura represented the close interaction between religious idealism and the nationalist revivals of the nineteenth century.[3] In much of Europe, the movements for religious and national renewal had a single origin in opposition to French invasion. In Belgium, Catholic

121

Switzerland, the Tyrol, above all in Spain, Napoleon learned the error of thinking that a people led by monks was easily conquered, as priests and even bishops raised armies against him.[4] Their resistance often took the form of a White Terror on the friends of the Revolution as in France itself in Nimes and the Vendee, and in southern Italy where Cardinal Ruffo at the head of a pious bandit band slaughtered his way through the Parthenopean Republic. But though these were movements of the political right. they were populist and still had to show their longer-term character. It is certainly easy to find clerics who preached defiance of kings. Under the standard of Our Lady of Guadalupe, Father Miguel Hidalgo y Costilla raised the Mexican revolt against Spain.[5] In much of Sicily and southern Italy, a large number, in some places a majority of the clergy, joined the Carbonari to attack the Bourbons, and the Neapolitan revolution of 1830 was led by Father Luigi Menichini.[6] Menichini, however, became a Protestant, as did a number of later Italian Nationalist priests, the most famous of them being the Barnabite friar Alessandro Gavazzi, Garibaldi's chaplain.[7] So too the most celebrated of French Liberal Catholics, the Abbe Felicite de Lamennais, was driven from the Church into pantheism by papal condemnations of his defence of a right to revolution.[8] Thus generally speaking, the Church expelled its rebels, and defended the Papal States against Liberal Italian Nationalists, and throughout the Latin world, sought to protect the Faith by alliances with conservative governments. Liberal Catholicism survived, most notably in France, but the Catholic position was increasingly one of opposition to Liberalism, especially at headquarters in Rome.

The political settlement after 1815, however, placed more Catholics than ever under non-Catholic princes, so that the Church had to strive for Catholic liberties against heretical governments. Millions of Catholic Rhinelanders and Poles were ruled by Protestant Prussia, which was twice forced to seek an accommodation with the Church after conflicts in the 1830s and 1870s. In Belgium, Catholics and Liberals threw off the rule of Protestant Holland in 1830, while Russia repressed risings of its Polish subjects in 1830 and 1863-64. Neither Belgians nor Poles had any support from the Pope,[9] but it can be seen that Catholics in Ireland were not alone in demanding their freedom as 'Liberal Catholics' from a non-Catholic power. Through O'Connell, they found a mean between the hopeless revolutionary violence of the Poles, and that obedience to authority enjoined by Rome.

This was a difficult mediating position for the Church, which was given its political role by O'Connell, as the sole surviving native institution with the authority to counter the coercion of Anglo-Irish landlords, and carry his campaign to the furthest parts of Ireland. That made the clergy O'Connell's recruiting agents in the 'jihad'[10] for Catholic

Emancipation, and the most important local leaders in the movement to repeal the Union, so that the issue of the 'priest in politics' became a matter of endemic controversy. Some ecclesiastics used spiritual sanctions against parishioners who chose a different course to theirs in a dreary round of politics from the pulpit and anathemas from the altar. But 'spiritual intimidation' was the least of the clergy's manifold political functions, for usually they 'could lead their people only in the direction that they wanted to go'.[11] Sacerdotal influence on elections may have peaked in 1852. It was eroded after 1875 by the new Dublin caucus politics and school of professional politicians, and the clergy were less prominent in the campaign for Home Rule, but were still strong enough in rural areas in the 1892 election to resolve the Parnellite split in favour of the anti- Parnellites.[12] The difficulty was then an old one. As guardians of the national tradition, the priesthood wished to preserve it from perversion, so that whenever political nationalism divided, they had to decide which politicians represented the nation.[13] But the clergy reflected the nation's divisions. A minority opposed Repeal, the Land League and Home Rule, and there was never a time when Irish ecclesiastics spoke with a single voice.

Here a major problem was the challenge posed to O'Connellite constitutionalism by the physical force school. Ireland, like Poland, bred a Catholic revolutionary tradition, out of poverty and hatred of a foreign Church and landlords. The Irish priesthood could hardly ignore their own disabilities or the sufferings of their people, and with a few exceptions, were men of no enthusiastic loyalty to the English Crown. As even an anticlerical put it, the parish priest was 'the embodiment of hostility to England'.[14] It would be difficult to state precisely where the clergy's dislike of Protestantism ended and their loathing for England began, and usually they did not need to distinguish the heretic from the stranger. Yet mere realism told them that the Empire was the strongest power on earth, and revolution in Ireland was even more hopeless than in Poland. Nor did they escape continental influences of a conservative kind. Before 1790 most priests were educated in France, and in the nineteenth century, an increasingly influential minority received their training in Rome. In the 1790s, the clergy were conscious of the French Church's martyrdom by the Revolution, and so the great majority of priests opposed the Irish rising of 1798 as Jacobin-inspired, though the revolt was at least in part a Catholic one.

Nor was there much sympathy among the faithful for Italian Nationalist designs on Rome between 1848 and 1870, and when Paul Cullen, formerly Rector of the Irish College in Rome, imposed Roman models of discipline and devotion on Ireland after 1850, he also condemned the revolutionary Irish, Young Ireland and the Fenians, as disciples of Young Italy and bad Catholics, the Irish equivalent of such anti-Roman 'secret societies' as the Freemasons and Carbonari. Cullen's insistence on seeing Ireland through Italian spectacles and his rigorous 'Liberal Catholic' constitutionalism gave rise to a black legend about the Church among the radicals and revolutionaries, who also long remembered Bishop Moriarty of Kerry's thundering in 1867 that hell was not hot enough nor eternity long enough for the Fenians.[15] Yet Cullen disapproved of Moriarty's vehemence.[16] Moriarty was an untypically extreme representative of the 'West British'[17] or 'Dublin Castle' Bishop, who wanted close co-operation with the English authorities, though according to Cullen, even Moriarty had been guilty of a youthful sympathy for Young Ireland. Cullen himself was in quite a different category. He discontinued his predecessor Murray's attendance at Castle receptions, and as an Irishman with an uncle hung in '98, he hated the English as heartily as anyone. But Cullen's politics were more religious than nationalist. and he did not represent nationalist feeling in the manner of his archrival in the hierarchy, John MacHale of Tuam. Cullen's rift with radical nationalism was only healed by the recovery of Irish constitutional politics in the two final decades of the nineteenth century, as Archbishop Walsh of Dublin and Croke of Cashel achieved good working relations with the Irish party in the Commons, and undid the damage done by Rome's attempt at England's behest to suppress the land reform agitation of the 1880s. Despite the divisions caused by Parnell's fall, the long alliance between the Church and the Westminster politicians to secure Home Rule within the Empire undergirded Irish politics from 1884 until 1916 and laid the foundations for a modern Catholic nation.[18]

That conclusion was put in doubt when constitutionalism was overthrown in the Easter Rising, for as the Church had been on the constitutional side, so her long labour for Ireland might have seemed discredited. In fact, the events of 1916 confirmed more completely than ever that Irish nationalism was Catholic. Of the four leaders of the Rising, three, Pearse, MacDonagh and Plunkett were 'Catholics with a strong inclination towards religious, or quasi-religious mysticism',[19] in Pearse's case, of a distinctly bloody kind. The fourth, James Connolly, was a peculiar Catholic Marxist, who wrote 'that of us, as of mankind before Calvary, it may truly be said "without the shedding of blood there is no redemption"'.[20] Despite their appeals to the Jacobin idealism of 1798, and the tincture of Connolly's Socialism analysis of the rhetoric of the revolutionaries indicates that the Rising was the outcome of a militant Catholic revival in association with a Gaelic nationalism which though partly Protestant in inspiration, in the event rang the knell of Protestant nationalism in Ireland.[21] The clergy's initial hostility to the Rising disappeared with the initial hostility of the Irish laity, and for the first time in modern Irish history, the bishops gave their blessing to armed rebellion. The outcome was the most Catholic state in Europe.

The paradox of this final victory of a violent Catholic nationalism was that the Church's role had been to preserve both Faith and Fatherland through a non-violent nationalism which held revolutionary nationalism in check. Not that the Church alone could be held responsible for the failures of '98 and '48 and '67; these owed as much to Irish incompetence and to English power. Yet something must also be allowed to the opposition of the clergy, which can be illustrated in detail from the story of the Young Irelander Terence Bellew McManus. In 1848, the chapel bells were rung at Ballingarry for McManus's rebel muster, but the acting parish priest Father Fitzgerald told McManus 'that violent means would not be successful under the present circumstances'. When the 160 volunteers reached Mullinahone, another priest persuaded a third of the men to disperse, and in the end only twenty remained. Their numbers had grown again when they fought with police for possession of the Widow McCormack's house in Boulagh Commons village, but there again Fitzgerald and a colleague were at work, coaxing away the peasant warriors. Eleven days later in the Keeper mountains, wrote McManus, 'an evil spirit in the form of a Father Moloney crossed our path, ... and by threats of advancing troops and friendly hints induced us to turn back'.[22] McManus never forgave the clergy for discouraging the rising, though his venture had no chance of success, and the priests can hardly be condemned for courageously intervening to save lives which he was throwing away. After his arrest, the Bishop and clergy of the diocese of Clogher petitioned the government for mercy, among them McManus's kinsman Canon Tierney, a hero of the decade of Repeal. McManus was transported to Van Dieman's land but escaped to California, where he died in 1861, and from there the Fenians returned his body to Ireland to be the focus of huge public demonstrations. The body was received en route in New York by Archbishop Hughes, and in Ireland by the Bishop of Cloyne, but was turned away by the Bishop of Cork. The Maynooth students chanted a requiem office,[23] and Cullen would have allowed a Mass for McManus in his Dublin pro-cathedral if he had been promised that there would be no political demonstration. As this was the whole point of the exercise, the Fenians buried McManus without the Church's official blessing, even turning down the Young Ireland Father Kenyon's graveside sermon as insufficiently Fenian. Kenyon's place was taken by the wild Mayo priest Father Patrick Lavelle, who placarded Dublin with a denunciation of Cullen;[24] for Lavelle was the foremost exponent of the physical force tradition which never quite died out among the clergy.

It is easy to compile a list of such ecclesiastics, from the 'croppy priests' of Wexford led by Father John Murphy, who raised their flocks against the English in 1798, though not all the clergy executed in the aftermath of the rebellion had been guilty of opposing foreign rule.[25] There were 'Young Ireland' priests like Kenyon,[26] and Devoy's famous post-bag contains references to Father Patrick McCabe, who helped John Boyle O'Reilly escape from Western Australia, the Fenian organizer Father Eugene Sheehy, and the merely well-disposed, like the Father McCartie who gave asylum to O'Donovan Rossa.[27] The Church's refusal of the sacraments to the Fenians was ineffectively enforced by reluctant priests, a distinguished historian of the Fenian movement declaring that

> the Jesuit Order turned a blind eye to the ecclesiastical ban on members of the Fenian organisation, and admitted them to the sacraments without awkward questions. And this was remembered to their credit when the hated names of Cullen and MacCabe [sic] had grown dim, and Cardinal Manning had eventually admitted these Irish imitators of the Carbonari, (and) had brought the Mass into English prisons.[28]

The Land League agitations also produced clergymen not too scrupulous of the means which they employed. Father John O'Malley of the Neale was known

> to have very friendly feelings even towards the physical force section,... His brother-in-law, Mr. J.F.X. O'Brien, was an old Fenian and a Member of Parliament in Parnell's Party, and to the home of Father John, as he was affectionately called, Mr. Davitt and the chief Land League leaders were frequent visitors.[29]

Father O'Malley's contribution to the League was the term 'boycott' to describe tenant ostracism and intimidation of unpopular or evicting landlords, in the local campaign against the notorious land agent Captain Boycott. Nothing, however, in Ireland is quite what it seems, and a recent historian of the land war declared that O'Malley's device was 'a pre-emptive intervention... against a Fenian outbreak'.[30] Certainly boycotting was a less important anti-landlord measure than withholding rent, and as a comparatively peaceful alternative to agrarian outrage, goes back to Father O'Shea's Tenant Protection Society of 1849.[31] But the line between boycotting and violence was difficult to draw. It was Father O'Connor in Kerry, claimed an Anglophile Irish Catholic conservative, who

> took such (an) active part in the scandalous Curtin case in his parish. Curtin the father of the family, was murdered in his house, & his daughters were so boycotted and insulted by the people that the late Bishop put the Church under an interdict & would not allow Father O'Connor to officiate in it.

Father O'C. took the most active part in the persecution of this unhappy family.[32]
The 'late Bishop' was the notorious 'Castle' prelate Moriarty, but he can hardly be condemned for disciplining a priest who publicly approved of murder.

The line of radical priests is only a partial refutation of the black legend of a reactionary Church. Few Fenians remembered Cullen's successful intervention to save the Fenian Burke from the scaffold,[33] or Croke's granting the sacraments to Charles Kickham and subscribing to Kickham's testimonial fund with warm compliments,[34] though Kickham, a devout Catholic denied communion by his priest at Mullinahone, had been the author of some of the most bitter Fenian attacks upon the clergy.[35] The more comprehensive reply to such attacks must take account of the fact that the Church's politics were of considerable complexity and mired in a Hibernian bog in which Rome had one interest, while bishops and priests were often divided into factions fighting one another. Under these circumstances there was little consistency of principle or practice about the Church's role among Catholics who supported violence or deplored it. Thus the Fenians in fact welcomed clerical support though claiming to dislike priests in politics. Even a radical priest, they thought, was of limited use as he would find himself torn between his Fenianism and his duty to a conservative superior.[36] In their repudiation of the political priest, the Fenians were superficially in agreement with their arch-enemy Cullen, who had tried in the 1850s to limit priestly political activity. Cullen, however, was then opposed by moderate nationalists on the grounds that the withdrawal of sacerdotal guidance left the field wide open to the landlords or revolutionaries. In fact Cullen's decrees of 1854 on clerical politicking, though supported by Rome, had only a limited effect, and were less about ends than means. Cullen wanted the priesthood to play a political role but of a moderate and circumspect kind. 'The real issue was not, therefore, whether the clergy should have political power and influence, but how they might best preserve that power and influence which was their legitimate right under a constitutional system and in a Catholic country.'[37] When confronted by the Fenians, Cullen became less cautious, and the anti-Fenian condemnations of the 1860s were as explicit a political intervention by the Church as any on the radical side.

One result of divisions among the clergy was to increase the power of lay politicians, whether 'Castle', constitutional or revolutionary. Priestly authority in politics was enhanced whenever churchmen presented a more united front, as under Croke and Walsh towards the end of the century. In mid-century, unity was best achieved at diocesan level by John MacHale of Tuam, a terrifying figure christened by O'Connell 'the lion of the fold of Judah', who imposed a single radical

127

nationalist line upon his clergy.[38] After 1850, MacHale was resoundingly defeated in his struggle to prevent Rome and Cullen from gaining complete ecclesiastical control of the Irish Church. His revenge was to frustrate the Church's attacks on the Fenians by pretending that there were none in his archdiocese, and to protect their sympathizers among the clergy from Cullen and from Rome.[39]

It was this conflict between Cullen and MacHale which made possible the career of Father Patrick Lavelle, and the case of Lavelle shows how much more was involved in the revolutionary tradition than revolutionary mythology suggests. Born near Croagh Patrick in 1825, Lavelle had been educated at MacHale's St Jarlath's College in Tuam, and after a brilliant student career at Maynooth he became in 1854 professor of philosophy at the Irish College in Paris, then governed by an enemy of MacHale, the Rector John Miley. MacHale's nephew Thomas MacHale was also a professor at the College, which Cullen wanted to control and reform, at first by strengthening Miley's hand. The denouement has been recently described by Professor Emmet Larkin. Miley, a hopeless disciplinarian, was opposed by Lavelle and John Rice, the professor of moral theology, with violence, 'using railroad whistles, shouting, kicking doors, breaking bolts, throwing the large vessel for the eaux salles des eleves - a great urinoir or bacquet...'.[40] Miley expelled Lavelle and Rice in March 1859, and locked them out of the College, which they re-entered by climbing a wall, to rouse the students against the Rector. The controversy involved the papal nuncio, the archbishop of Paris and the French Minister of instruction, who upheld Miley against Lavelle and Rice, and when the professors appealed to Napoleon III they were 'ordered out of France'. Cullen had won, but in the embarrassment of getting rid of Miley, he had to fear 'the usual letters in the newspapers justifying the late conduct of Fathers Rice and Lavelle...'.[41] There was, however, one diocese in Ireland beyond Cullen's reach, MacHale's. The lion of Judah knew his man, and sent Lavelle as Administrator to the remote Mayo parish of Partry, where his genius for a fight soon found vigorous expression in battle with Lord Plunket, Protestant Bishop of Tuam.

Partry was a large country parish, eighteen miles long, with some three thousand Irish-speaking pauper souls scattered through a number of settlements,[42] and Lavelle's career at Partry involved all the major Irish questions, peasant violence, religion, education and the land. The Protestant Bishop of Tuam, the second Baron, Thomas Plunket, 'began his episcopate by trying to live on the continent',[43] but then expanded his private Tourmakeady estate, and from 1847, supported Evangelical efforts to convert Irish Catholics to Protestantism. Plunket imposed Protestant teaching on the Tourmakeady schools, which were conducted by the Society for Irish Church Missions to Roman Catholics, established in 1849 in the aftermath of the Famine by an ex-soldier English clergyman, Lord Byron's cousin, A.R.C. Dallas, to proselytise among starving Catholics (Catholics claimed, by bribing them with food).[44] The poverty of MacHale's archdiocese and his dislike of the National School system left his people vulnerable to Protestant educational attack, and the occasional conversions to Protestantism gave a weapon to MacHale's Catholic enemies like Cullen.[45] The National School, supported by Plunket's maiden sister, Catherine, was also transferred to the Irish Church Missions after her showdown with the Partry curate, and the helpless tenants were caught between the Plunket family, their bailiffs, clergy, scripture readers and teachers, and the Partry priests and their Franciscan schoolmasters. The priests alleged that Catholic tenants were evicted for withholding their children from the mission schools, and were driven from their lands to the Franciscan farm or the Ballinrobe workhouse or America.[46] The Partry incumbent begged MacHale for a quieter parish, and on his arrival in Partry in October 1958,[47] Lavelle exhorted his flock to shun the Protestant schools and the district was at war.

Lavelle claimed that Plunket resorted to intimidation, impounding cattle, imposing fines and threatening his tenants with a general notice to quit. The editor of Plunket's mouthpiece, the Mayo Constitution, resurrected the story of Lavelle's Paris escapade, and in the ensuing libel case, which Lavelle failed to prove, the priest produced sixty-seven witnesses in a six-day trial in Galway, eighteen of whom gave evidence of children hidden or left naked to escape the Bishop's clergy and female relations.[48] From May 1859, sixty-eight tenants lived under an eviction order which Plunket appeared to withdraw in March 1860, after negotiations with a former Partry curate, and Lavelle also waived his case against the Tourmakeady parson for threatening him with a pistol. On the 20th of November, 1860, however, soldiers and policemen arrived in the district and during the three days following evicted sixty-eight people. The scene at the mountainside village of Derrivina lost nothing in Lavelle's retelling, in a public letter to E.W. Cardwell, the Chief Secretary for Ireland:

> I saw a woman, Mrs. Tom Lally, dragged by the head and shoulders out of her house, her bosom thus exposed, and her hair dishevelled. I saw her husband in the gripe of four men, dragged out like a butchered calf, and flung on the dunghill. I saw an old man, 80 years of age, and his wife, 74, tottering out of a house which had seen their great grandparents, and standing by with streaming eyes, amid torrents of sleet and rain, as the venerable roof and walls crumbled to the ground. I

saw the young mother, and the babe at her bosom,
linger on the threshold they were never to cross
again. I saw the cradle, in which slept the happily
unconscious child, carried out by the father, the
rain beating with fury on the innocent brow.[49]

Lavelle achieved enormous newspaper publicity for his
indelible image of the Lord Bishop preaching his Gospel with
the crowbar, and receiving rent from the evicting force of
police paid for by a levy on his pauper tenants. Even the
Times thought the incident a 'hideous scandal' with a 'very
bad smell, sufficient to give a nausea', which was as
detrimental to episcopal propriety as the Pope at the head of
his army.[50] The Thunderer's indignation was not shared by
the English recipient of Lavelle's eloquence, Cardwell, whose
recent Land Bill had made evictions more likely, and who
insisted in the Commons that the Bishop and similar landlords
had 'done nothing illegal'.[51] Meanwhile Lavelle had revived his
French connections, and through a brace of duchesses
secured a charity sermon for his tenants in a Parisian church
from the famous Bishop Dupanloup of Orleans. On the advice
of A.R.C. Dallas, who also wrote to Napoleon III about
Lavelle,[52] Lord Plunket sent a public letter to the English
ambassador in France, Earl Cowley, denying that he had
evicted any Catholics for keeping children from his schools.[53]
The families evicted had all disobeyed estate rules or been
violent or otherwise defied his authority. He claimed credit
for postponing the evictions till November, after the harvest.
The full truth is difficult to discover, and Plunket's nephew
and fellow-worker, later Protestant Archbishop of Dublin,
claimed that Lavelle had boasted of cursing a Scripture reader
dead, and that the tenants would have accepted the schools
but for fear of their priest's supernatural powers.[54] But
though the Plunket estate was now largely clear of Catholics,
the last word was Lavelle's. 'In the midst of an unfriendly
population the Protestant planters were not happy, and after
one such planter had been shot there was an exodus of his
co-religionists from the district.'[55] Plunket died in 1866. The
influence of his Missions did not long survive him and by
1868, their superintendant was declaring that Protestant
converts could not remain in the domain of Lavelle, 'the
cleverest and most unscrupulous priest in Ireland'.[56]

The land issue led Lavelle straight into Fenianism, which
inherited the clerical opporbrium of older societies for
committing agrarian outrage, the Ribbonmen.[57] Thus
Archdeacon John O'Sullivan anathematized the Fenian-
influenced Ribbonmen or 'Phoenix men' at the crowded third
mass in his parish in Kenmare:

Well, I was doubted, laughed at, sneered at, when
in October, early in October, I denounced the
Phoenix boys. In the middle of the December
following, when the lads were seized by police in

the dead of the night, and when, on the following day, they were, in the height of the rain, carried off to the County Jail, on the long car, handcuffed, with their parents and their friends rending the air with their shrieks, and the lads who escaped the informer with their knees knocking with fear, looking on; then, only then, they said Father John was right... Will our poor country ever have sense?[58]

The Archdeacon reminded his flock that he had saved many among them from starvation with English charity, and his act of defiance was not without courage. The authority of the priest ultimately rested on popular consent, and the priest who simply took an unpopular political line might lose them to a rival Catholic chapel, or even be burned in effigy, like the anti-Fenian Father Collins of Skibbereen.[59] Yet there was a mean for the lower clergy of passive sympathy for the Fenians, between active encouragement and active opposition, and most Irish priests would have agreed on at least one point in Dallas's letter to Napoleon III, the undesirability of their 'stirring the minds of an ignorant peasantry against the legitimate influence of law and government'. It was as just such a priestly stirrer of peasant minds that Lavelle emerged from the McManus funeral. Henceforth he was the vice president and principal moving spirit of the shadowy 'National Brotherhood of Saint Patrick' established in 1861, which 'was little more than a front-organisation for Fenianism',[60] and so Lavelle became 'the strong unyielding champion of Fenianism, and the most formidable single opponent Cullen ever had'.[61]

The two men had some things in common: both were hard-working pastors, who cared deeply about their Irish poor. But where Cullen's Catholicism was a religion of control, Lavelle's rhetoric breathed into the symbols of faith the spirit of revolutionary violence, as in his denunciation of Cullen's treatment of McManus:

St. Malachy, whom we this day commemorate - St. Laurence O'Toole - patriotic Oliver Plunkett, martyr to thy patriotism! were you to-day alive would you deny Terence Bellew M'Manus [sic] a night's rest before the lamp of your sanctuaries? Oh! Ireland! Ireland! how art thou fallen! When shalt thou rise? Is this thy act? If not, speak out! Dare to speak it, Ireland!

Lavelle invoked the example of the current Polish rebellion:

And in Poland, there the strong hand of the Czar closes the Church against the patriotic priest and people alive; here the Church closes herself against the Patriot Dead. Dear M'Manus! honoured by thy memory in every land where freedom still dares to breathe. Thou art to-day ostracised in the heart of thy native land; but thy living countrymen have no

part in the deed. Nay, thou art still dearer to
them, far and far, from the attempt to dishonour
thy name and thy grave, and the principles for
which thou hast died, than thou ever wouldst have
been had the dim lamp of the sanctuary been
permitted to cast its faint and melancholy light on
thy precious remains. But thou art enshrined in
our hearts a thousand times more than ever; and I,
for one, vow never to enter the city in which thou
art thus proclaimed on thy bier almost as I am in
my parish, without pouring out my soul at thy
grave and vowing a new vow each time of hate and
hostility to thy enemy and mine. the enemy of our
Creed, our Country, and our Holy Father.[62]

Lavelle believed that Creed and Country if not the Holy
Father, justified revolution, and this was the theme of his
lecture on the 4th February 1862, under Cullen's nose in the
Rotunda in Dublin on 'The Catholic Doctrine of the Right of
Revolution', claiming 'that Ireland is so misgoverned that she
has a right to revolt against the Queen, and in doing so she
would have the sanction of the Church'.[63] Lavelle afterwards
summed up the lecture for a mostly English audience in the
Catholic Tablet.[64] He cited a long line of Catholic theologians,
St Thomas, Bellarmine, Suarez, as all justifying a people's
right to overthrow a tyrant. 'In order to claim our heart-felt
fealty "Caesar" must be a minister in bonum. It is only as
such that "every soul is to be subject" to him; while, when
he forgets his Mission, and either neglects or cruelly
oppresses his people, that "loyalty" which was yesterday a
duty in the subject, becomes now a right for self-
protection...' Here Lavelle was correct on the point of fact,
that the divines of his Church had defended a right to
rebellion, normally on papal authorization, indeed the twelfth
century John of Salisbury and the Jesuit Mariana had justified
tyrannicide. The papal ban on the 'impetus lamentabilis
rebellionis' was an innovation arising from the special
circumstances of the nineteenth century, and in older
textbooks, the stress lay on the need for sufficient pretext
for rebellion, often determined by the norms of a just war.[65]

Was there, then, a good argument that "Caesar" had
forfeited the people's loyalty in Ireland? Lavelle thought so:

is not Ireland one of the worst governed countries
on the face of the earth? In what other country is
the deliberate and systematic effort made to
extirpate the image of God from the soil, and
replace it with the beasts of the field for the
benefit of the mistress nation?... Is it so in
Poland?... Was it so in Belgium?... Yet have the
revolts of all those countries either our silence or
our sympathy?... where else in the world could a
Bishop... employ his unlimited power of landlord to

drive the Catholic tenantry into the profession of his own faith under penalty of ruin and extermination... Were I a Polish Priest I would, like the patriotic Polish Priests that are, be on the side of the people - Cross, or if need be, sword in hand. Why, then, censure me, as an Irish Priest, for taking the side of the Irish people against the foreign government and the foe that oppress them?.. I maintain it to be our right - the right of the Irish people to make every preparation within our power to terminate that hideous misrule... This may be considered bold, nay, "disloyal" language. Let me hang or pine in exile for it. Sir, it is the sentiment of my heart. It is the sentiment of the Polish Priest in his own down-trodden land... Sir, I am no traitor. I am faithful to the first instincts of human nature faithful to the inalienable birthright of my country, the life and liberty of her people.

Lavelle summed his position up thus:

1. According to all Catholic Divines (Bossuet alone, perhaps, excepted) oppressive rulers may be deposed by their subjects.

2. No subjects in the world are more refinedly oppressed than the Irish people of the present day.

3. Therefore we have the general and indisputable right to set aside our tyrannical rulers.

4. However, at this moment it would be madness or wickedness to make the attempt because resistance would be useless.

5. Still we have not alone the right but we are bound by the duty of making all the preparations in our power against the day when our oppressor will herself be battling for her existence, and when our efforts would be morally certain of success.

Is this treason? I am then a traitor. Is this "disloyal"? So am I.

The caution against the 'madness' of taking up arms until the time was ripe - when England's difficulty would prove Ireland's opportunity suggests to Dr Norman that such sentiments 'had very little meaning... whilst indicating disaffection. .'.[66] As Norman indicates, however, this did not seem so to Cullen, who was now to dedicate a decade of hard work to getting a Roman condemnation of Lavelle.

A full account of Cullen's relations with Lavelle awaits a book-length analysis of the ample Roman materials and Irish newspapers, and a further volume, on the 1860s from Professor Larkin, but the outlines are clear from Dr Norman's researches, and from Peadar Mac Suibhne's invaluable magpie edition of Cullen's correspondence.[67] Cullen complained to MacHale about Lavelle's proclamation on McManus, and sent

MacHale's 'discourteous' reply and the proclamation to the Cardinal Secretary of Propaganda, Barnabo, while writing to his Roman agent Tobias Kirby to get Rome to force MacHale to discipline Lavelle.[68] In November 1861 and March and June 1862, Cullen wrote pastoral letters condemning oath-bound secret societies, and his example was followed by most of the Irish bishops, but not MacHale.[69] In May 1863, Cullen complained of a 'treasonable' speech by Lavelle in Dublin, and of his electioneering in Tralee.[70] In June 1863, he sent Kirby part of another published Lavelle letter 'with scandalous assertions, tending to encourage people to join the Brotherhood of St. Patrick and priests to despise diocesan reservations'.[71] In August 1863, 'all bishops condemned the Brotherhood of St. Patrick and all except Drs. MacHale and Derry passed censure on Fr. Lavelle. MacHale could not defend Lavelle, but refused to say a word against him. Several bishops told his Grace he was answerable to God for the evil done by Lavelle and the Brotherhood.'[72] 'The Pope or Propaganda must stop Fr. Lavelle,' wrote Cullen. 'Dr. MacHale supports him and will do nothing without an express command.'[73] In September Cullen asked Kirby for a copy of a 'most affectionate' letter from the Pope to MacHale, requiring Lavelle's submission. but Lavelle had 'got so much encouragement and money from his violence, it is hard to calculate what he will do',[74] especially as he had received 'great sums from Fenians in America'.[75]

The difficulty was getting the dilatory Propaganda 'to prevent the little priest trampling on them'.[76] In fact, reported Cullen. the Pope's letter 'only made things worse: it has been ridiculed by Fr. Lavelle. His letter in the (Fenian) Irishman... shows he has changed or withdrawn nothing. After stating that the archbishop of Dublin is a new Judas, he adds he submits all his important writings to the Holy See.'[77] This was a formal submission to MacHale of sorts, not good enough for Rome. which ordered the archbishop to suspend Lavelle 'ab officio et beneficio'.[78] Lavelle published a reply from 'An Irish Priest', calling for 'Gallican' resistance to Rome,[79] while MacHale did nothing to enforce the papal directive. Who paid for all Lavelle's travelling to England and Scotland to organize the Brotherhood? asked Cullen. Lavelle's parish 'is very poor' and the Irish poor were easily duped, and if roused to rebel, 'the savage of England will treat them as Mouravieff treats the Poles'.[80] In January 1864, Lavelle was travelling to Rome, to present to Propaganda a self-justifying memorial the length of six newspaper columns.[81] MacHale accepted alms from the Chicago Fenians in February and in March, Lavelle had returned to Ireland, and was quoting MacHale in the nationalist press on 'the benevolent' Fenian Brotherhood'.[82] MacHale compounded his offence for Cullen by sending three autographed portraits to the Chicago Fenian fair, while one of MacHale's Franciscans, of the order which taught in Partry, came to Cullen's notice by asking the Chicago Fenians for alms.[83] 'Fr. Lavelle will probably be suspended,'[84] wrote Cullen in April, but he reckoned without MacHale's powers of obstruction and in July, Cullen told Kirby that 'it is a great scandal that the archbishop does not carry out the Pope's instructions'.[85] In August, Cullen pleasantly speculated that 'Lavelle has letters in his hands which he would publish were he suspended, and their publication might not be agreeable to Dr. MacHale...'.[86] At a gathering of the Bishops in October, they vainly 'lectured' MacHale for four and a half hours, and passed a censure on his contumacious priest at the behest of Propaganda,[87] but the measure swung the Tuam clergy behind their archbishop, and in a fulsome address to MacHale, they expressed regret at the papal censure on 'a clergyman who has certainly done good service in extirpating heresy and proselytism... all Lavelle wrote of a political nature cannot be justified, but might well be tolerated...'.[88]

The matter was now at stalemate, and it is remarkable that so much of Cullen's energy should be lavished on a single priest though he obviously found Lavelle a convenient stick with which to beat MacHale in Rome. Lavelle was also objectionable as an old-style Gallican cleric resistant to Cullen's ideal of Roman authority, and it is likely, though difficult to prove, that he represented a growing body of anti-Cullenite opinion which silently preferred MacHale. Certainly the church after 1865 became progressively less directly opposed to the Fenians, and that was partly Lavelle's achievement as he gave the lie to Cullen's rather simple minded view of Fenianism as a Mazzinian lay anticlerical movement opposed to orthodox Catholicism. Lavelle's ideas and experience, his very violence, were like his Gallicanism rooted in an Irish Catholic culture, as his further family and parochial controversies were to show.

Like many Irish priests, Lavelle came from small-farming stock. The Lavelles had lived for four generations on a holding belonging to Sir Roger Palmer, 'one of the most extensive (absentee) proprietors' in Mayo. They had been conscientious improving tenants, and had always paid their rent; and in March 1864, Lavelle asked Palmer's agent for permission for his sister to live with his mother, after the sudden deaths within the short space of six months of his father and another sister and brother. The agent allowed the request for an unmarried daughter, but this daughter was married, thereby breaking the agreement. Though she left the house after the mother was served with a notice to quit in May 1865, Lavelle wrote that his mother's eviction was carried out, 'her house and out-offices built by my father torn down, the boarding, mantel-pieces, window-frames, and sashes carried off, and her very growing crops handed over to a favourite of the "office", neither kith nor kin to her'.[89]

Lavelle's appeals for restitution were unavailing, and the case reflected the lack of tenure of a tenancy for whom violence was the only weapon.

Lavelle secured national publicity for another case of tenant right, following the setting up of the National Land and Building Investment Company in 1865 by a Dublin wine-merchant, Andrew M'Cullagh. The company set out to improve the Port Royal estate bordering Plunket's, depriving these tenants of some of their common mountain grazing, redividing or 'striping' their holdings, putting up rents, and enforcing payment by impounding cattle and by lightning-quick notices of eviction. Lavelle denounced M'Cullagh's company and his agents from the altar, and describing M'Cullagh in letters to the Irish Times as the grasping rich man in the prophet Nathan's story condemned by David as 'a child of death' deserving to die.[90] In 1869 M'Cullagh brought an action for libel against the editor of the Irish Times for publishing Lavelle's letters, but the case was dismissed when the jury failed to agree, one juryman, Lavelle claimed, holding out for M'Cullagh. This was to be Lavelle's last controversy in Partry; for as Cullen put it, Dr MacHale by promoting Lavelle 'to the best parish in the diocese... sanctioned all the acts of that firebrand'.[91] Lavelle's progress to his new parish, Cong, on the 16th of October 1868, was a great popular occasion, 'a grand procesion [sic]', compared by an anonymous semi-literate balladeer to Christ's entry into Jerusalem.[92] It took place just two months before a final effort to complete the Lavelle case in Rome, by the Irish Bishops of the Vatican Council.

Lavelle had continued to plague his superiors, publishing an insurrectionary letter to Archbishop Manning of Westminster on the eve of the Fenian rising of 1867, and both MacHale and Lavelle sang Masses for the 'Manchester Martyrs' executed by the British.[93] The Irish Bishops in Rome in December 1869 had to consider a letter addressed by Lavelle to them collectively, Cullen declaring that he would bring the offending document 'before the Pope, my only judge. If his Holiness approved of it I would be satisfied and never write a line again on the subject of Fenianism.' MacHale opposed the presentation of the letter to Propaganda, but 'got a little frightened' and then gave in, having 'heard more truth at the meeting than ever was told to him in Ireland'.[94] In fact, the initiative in the affair came not from Cullen but from an intrigue by Earl Clarendon and the English Government, who persuaded Moriarty and two other Irish Bishops to intervene with Propaganda, the British envoy Odo Russell complaining that 'neither Cardinal Cullen nor Dr MacHale appear to notice the sermons and writings of Fathers Lavelle and Ryan in Ireland, and none of the Irish bishops appear to reprove them'.[95] Ryan was a parish priest accused of inciting tenants to assassinate their landlords. The English incomprehension of

Catholic Ireland, however, is shown by the bracketing of Cullen with MacHale, and in the end it was Cullen and the Bishops rather than Clarendon and Russell who were directly instrumental in securing a papal condemnation of the 'societas Fenianorum' by name in January 1870.[96]

Rome had spoken, but the cause was not quite finished. 'The 1870 Decree was largely without effect,' writes Edward Norman just because Fenianism was a spent political force.[97] True, there was uproar among the disaffected in Ireland, and not all the parish priests (even in Dublin) would read the anti-Fenian pastorals of their Bishops. Cullen was scandalized in March, when Lavelle was received as 'the idol of the students' in Maynooth,[98] and in 1871, he successfully helped adjudicate for a Captain Nolan the case of Nolan's evicted tenants in Galway. His friendship with Nolan led him to support this Catholic landlord in the notorious Galway election in 1872, when Lavelle called the opposing Catholic candidate a liar, but the limelight was stolen by his episcopal superiors, MacHale and the Bishops of Galway and Clonfert, who were accused in a report to the Commons of exercising undue influence, for which His Lordship of Clonfert was put on trial. The trial closed the ranks of the Irish Catholic clergy in a common resistance to lawyer and Anglo-Protestant persecution, and in the Mayo election of 1874, MacHale and Lavelle were again in trouble for supporting a moderate Home Ruler, though on the occasion they were hissed from the Fenian side.[99]

The truth was that the priest of Cong was less militant than the priest of Partry. It was said 'that he had come too much under the influence of Lord Ardilaun'[100] of Cong, and he no longer had proselytism, or in his own eyes at least, bad landlordism, to fight. His great manifesto against Irish landlordism, more than five hundred pages long, The Irish Landlord since the Revolution, arising out of the M'Cullagh affair, was published in 1870, and roamed from Connemara to Cathay in its attack on large estates and its defence of small peasant proprietorship as the source of every social blessing. The book, a moderate enough work at least in its proposals, also goes over the old battles with Plunket and Palmer, and was dedicated to Lavelle's 'dear friend' George Henry Moore, M.P., a famous nationalist leader who had given refuge to some of the victims of the Partry evictions. Lavelle was now gentle enough to offer a measure of approval to a draft which Moore had shown him of Gladstone's very moderate Land Bill of 1870.[101] Though Lavelle had some contact with Michael Davitt and the Land League after 1878,[102] he had by that date ceased to be a national figure, and at his death in 1886, was buried in an oblivion in which most Irish historians have been happy to leave him.

It is obvious that Lavelle was not a typical priest, but a man marked as a violent opponent of authority by his

youthful bad behaviour in Paris. Yet his experience, like
MacHale's, was also founded in the distinctiveness of the
West, where the provocation of Protestant proselytism was at
its most intense, where the post-Famine improvements in the
Irish economy had been felt less than in any other areas, and
where, from the landlord point of view, the smallholders
clung with an 'unreasoning fatuity'[103] to their tiny farms
against all efforts to recombine them. Thus after Cullen's
death in 1878, it was in Mayo and Galway that the clergy
were forced to show exemplary patience before the neo-Fenian
provocations of the Land League,[104] and even MacHale, who
had so long suffered for his people from Rome, had to bear
with hostile demonstrations.[105] By 1880, however, the clerical
initiative had passed to Archbishop Croke in Cashel, as Croke
gave the decisive impetus to the spread of the League beyond
Connaught. and brought about a new 'alliance of religious and
national fervour'[106] which made the Cullenite position a
minority one even among the Irish bishops.

That circumstance suggests that the years 1850-1880
were untypical in the modern history of the relations between
religion and nationalism, though Roman conservatism remained
a constant factor which even patriot Irish bishops could only
contain, not overcome. But Fenian anticlericalism failed to
produce a widespread anticlerical movement,[107] for as the
decades before 1850 had belonged to O'Connell and MacHale,
so the decades after 1880 belonged to Croke and Walsh, as
men adept at turning a possible violence of deeds into a
violence of words, and from there into constitutional
channels. In that they were at one with Cullen and Moriarty
in seeking a constructive expression for the rude passions of
their people, and only disagreed about the means. Lavelle's
reminder of a Catholic right to revolution was, therefore, in
opposition to the general clerical strategy of using English
weapons of political agitation for an Irish purpose, and among
those weapons, rebellion had no place. Yet the very Irish
methods by which the clergy tried to control their flocks,
through a violence of words, by damnatory pastorals,
intrigues with Rome, altar denunciations, denial of the
sacraments (methods largely abandoned in modern Ulster),
could not wholly contain the strain of violence in Irish
Catholicism itself. The Lavelle case is not just a refutation of
the black legend of a reactionary Church, by showing up the
Church as no monolith, but a body deeply divided, and by
pointing up the complexity and subtlety of 'churchianity', of
the ecclesiastical politics which took a decade to subdue just
one turbulent priest, and which historians of Ireland will
ignore at their peril. It also points to the inner dilemma of
violence in a religious culture wearied by too long a sacrifice,
as the Church in modern Ireland tried to provide for
nationalism a radical expression, but one with safe, non-
violent controls. The lasting consequences in violence of a

too-long-suffering Catholicism the Easter Rising and Ulster were to show.

Notes
1   On Ventura, see the New Catholic Encyclopedia, 15 vols (New York, 1967), vol.14, pp.605-06.
2   The Funeral Oration of Father Ventura on the death of the Liberator, preached at Rome on June 28 and 30, 1847. Translated in full (Dublin, 1847), pp.7, 17-18. Ventura took a further hour at another requiem to finish the sermon. I am grateful to Mr David Hall of the Cambridge University Library for a copy of this work, which belonged to Ann Jerningham, of the East Anglian Catholic family. I also wish to thank for assistance with this paper Dr Christopher Wright of the British Library, the National Library of Ireland and the Library of University College, Galway.
3   On this general theme of religious and national renewal, see Timothy L. Smith, 'Religion and Ethnicity in America', The American Historical Review (December 1978), vol.83, pp.1155-85. See also Hall in footnote 7.
4   Owen Chadwick, The Popes and European Revolution (Oxford, 1981), pp.471-81.
5   New Catholic Encyclopedia, vol.6, p.1096.
6   Chadwick, p.559.
7   Basil Hall, 'Alessandro Gavazzi: a barnabite friar and the risorgimento', in D. Baker (ed.), Church, Society and Politics: Studies in Church History (Oxford, 1975), vol.12, pp.303-56.
8   Alec Vidler, Prophecy and Papacy: A Study of Lamennais, the Church and the Revolution (London, 1954).
9   J. Derek Holmes, The Triumph of the Holy See (London and Sheperdstown, 1978), pp.87-88.
10   Oliver MacDonagh's phrase on the Clare election of 1828: 'The politicization of the Irish Catholic Bishops, 1800-1850', The Historical Journal (March 1975), vol.18, p.37. McDonagh defines the 'jihad' as 'conflating the racial, tribal and religious appeals', but he stresses the temporary character of 'such powdery stuff' in the context of Catholic emancipationist grievance politics. Yet he has surely defined the underlying emotional current of Irish politics throughout the country.
11   J.H. Whyte, 'The influence of the Catholic clergy on elections in nineteenth-century Ireland', The English Historical Review (April 1960) vo.75, p.248. This article is the source for much of what follows.
12   C.J. Woods, 'The general election of 1892: the catholic clergy and the defeat of the Parnellites', in F.S.L. Lyons and R.A.J. Hawkins (eds.), Ireland under the Union: Varieties of tension. Essays in Honour of T.W. Moody (Oxford, 1980), pp.289-320. On the eclipse of the parish priest as politician, see J. Lee, The Modernisation of Irish Society 1848-1918

(Dublin, 1973), pp.90-92.

13   Emmet Larkin argues that the Church in 1921 'threw the weight of its power and influence on the side of the constitutional majority... As long as the party in the (Irish) State fulfilled its part in the agreement and was the legitimate party sanctioned by the nation, the Church could in fact do no less.' Larkin, 'Church, State and Nation in Modern Ireland', The American Historical Review (December 1975) vol.80, p.1273.

14   Cited by Hugh McLeod, Religion and the People of Western Europe (Oxford, 1981), p.20.

15   E.R. Norman, The Catholic Church and Ireland in the Age of Rebellion 1859-1873 (London, 1965), p.117. Norman notes (footnote 4) the long memory of Moriarty represented by Brendan Behan's Borstal Boy (1961), p.254.

16   Norman, p.118.

17   Thus the Fenian John O'Leary, Recollections of Fenians and Fenianism, 2 vols. (London, 1896), vol.1, p.63.

18   This is the argument of Emmet Larkin's two volumes, The Roman Catholic Church and the Creation of the Modern Irish State 1878-1886 (Philadelphia and Dublin, 1975); and The Roman Catholic Church and the Plan of Campaign in Ireland 1886-1888 (Cork, 1978). See especially the latter volume, pp.xiii-xvi. Also Mark Tierney, Croke of Cashel: The Life of Archbishop Thomas William Croke, 1823-1902 (Dublin, 1976).

19   F.S.L. Lyons, Culture and Anarchy in Ireland 1890-1939 (Oxford, 1979), p.86.

20   Ibid., p.90. There is some debate about the genuineness of Connolly's Catholicism. I incline to the view of Bernard Ransom and Owen Dudley Edwards. Ransom suggests that for Connolly 'marxism was itself a standpoint committed to the realisation of values long embodied in the christian conscience', and that 'Connolly attempted to bridge the same conceptual gap between scientific determinism and the christian intellectual heritage', this last remaining with romantic Gaeldom a source 'of spiritual and ethical values which determinist science could not logically comprehend...' Bernard Ransom, Connolly's Marxism (London, 1980), pp.29, 94. For Owen Dudley Edwards, the Socialist denial of Connolly's Catholicism is as 'sectarian' as the Catholic denial of his Socialism: in fact, his Socialism was an outgrowth and extension of his Catholicism. Owen Dudley Edwards, The Mind of an Activist - James Connolly (Dublin, 1971), pp.28-64. Connolly's anticlericalism is of course not anti-Catholicism, and it is certainly of great symbolic significance that he died with the last rites of the Church.

21   The agreement about the relationship of Catholicism and nationalism is best stated, if sometimes overstated, in Patrick O'Farrell's ingenious Ireland's English Question: Anglo-Irish relations, 1534-1970 (London, 1971).

22   Thomas G McAllister, Terence Bellew McManus (1811(?)-

1861): A Short Biography (Maynooth, 1972), pp.15, 21, for much of what follows.
23 Norman, p.98.
24 'A most remarkable and exciting letter from the Rev. Patrick Lavelle, Adm., on the non-reception of the remains of the martyr, T.B. McManus...', Battersby's Catholic Register (Dublin, 1862), entry for 6 November, p.269.
25 The Right Rev Monsignor E.A. D'Alton, History of the Archdiocese of Tuam, 2 vols. (Dublin, 1928), vol.1, p.332.
26 On Kenyon, see the numerous indexed references in O'Leary. Also the numerous references in Norman's index under 'Young Ireland priests'.
27 William O'Brien and Desmond Ryan (eds.), Devoy's Post Bag 1871-1928, 2 vols. (Dublin, 1948), vol.1, pp.14, 97-98, 280-81, 353.
28 Desmond Ryan, The Phoenix Flame: A Study of Fenianism and John Devoy (London, 1937), pp.137-38. Cf. the Jesuits mentioned in Leon O Broin, Revolutionary Underground: The Story of the Irish Republican Brotherhood (Dublin, 1976), p.149.
29 D'Alton, vol.2, p.121.
30 Paul Bew, Land and the National Question in Ireland (Dublin, 1978), p.133.
31 Ibid., pp.39-40.
32 Emmet Larkin, The Roman Catholic Church in Ireland and the Fall of Parnell 1888-1891 (Liverpool, 1979), p.73. For the case of another priest involved in a murder, Father McFadden, see Proinnsias O Galcchobhair, The History of Landlordism in Donegal (Ballyshannon, 1975).
33 Norman, pp.25-26.
34 O'Brien and Ryan, vol.1, pp.342, 377-79.
35 O'Leary, vol.2, pp.31-54.
36 Ibid., vol.2, p.53; cf. vol.1, pp.218-19, on the Fenian Father O'Flaherty.
37 Emmet Larkin, The Making of the Roman Catholic Church in Ireland, 1850-1860 (Chapel Hill, North Carolina, 1980), p.306.
38 Ibid., p.296; cf. Whyte, p.251: 'In each diocese of Ireland the priests had a definite esprit de corps, and where several dioceses shared a constituency, rivalry between them was not unknown.'
39 Bernard O'Reilly, John Mac Hale, Archbishop of Tuam. His Life, Times and Correspondence, 2 vols. (New York and Cincinnati, 1890), vol.2, pp.532-33, 545.
40 Larkin, The Making of the Roman Catholic Church, p.424. See also the account of the incident in Tomas O Fiaich, '"The Patriot Priest of Partry" Patrick Lavelle: 1825-1886', Journal of the Galway Archaeological and Historical Society vol.35 (1976), pp.129-48.
41 Larkin, The Making of the Roman Catholic Church, pp.411, 459.

42   Patrick Lavelle, 'Court of Queen's Bench... Andrew M'Cullagh v Major Knox' in Lavelle, The Irish Landlord since the Revolution (Dublin, 1870), p.445.

43   Desmond Brown, The Protestant Crusade in Ireland, 1800-70 (Dublin, 1978), p.216. The Protestant Crusade in Tuam goes back to 1823, after the Evangelical conversion of the last Church of Ireland archbishop of the see: Bowen, p.72.

44   Incidents in the Life and Ministry of the Rev. Alex. R.C. Dallas, A.M.... By his widow (London, 1870), p.459 (henceforth cited as Dallas).

45   O'Reilly, vol.2, pp.442-60; cf. Norman, p.24; Bowen, p.237.

46   D'Alton, vol.2, p.69.

47   He had just passed a brief curacy elsewhere in Mayo. Ibid., p.70.

48   Lavelle, 'The War in Partry. To the Irish People. Octave of the Feast of the Immaculate Conception 1860', in The Irish Landlord, pp.506-15. The libels were uttered in The Mayo Constitution between 3 May 1859 and 14 June 1859. The proceedings of the court case were reported in full in The Mayo Constitution, 31 July 1860 and 7 August 1860.

49   Lavelle, 'Letter to the Right Hon. E.W. Cardwell', (Dublin, 22 April 1861), in The Irish Landlord, pp.497-98.

50   The Times, 27 November 1860.

51   Arvel B. Erickson, 'Edward T. Cardwell, Peelite', Transactions of the American Philosophical Society N.S. vol.49 pt.2 (Philadelphia, 1959), pp.29-30.

52   Dallas claimed the credit for his letter that it deterred Dupanloup's sermon, but he did not seem to know that Lavelle had already incurred Imperial displeasure over the incident at the Irish College. Dallas, pp.468-69.

53   Letter... to the Earl Cowley, Her Majesty's Ambassador at Paris, by Lord Plunket, the Bishop of Tuam, Ireland (March 1861). See also the rather contradictory letter from the Bishop's agent, The Times, 4 December 1860, which the agent subsequently withdrew (The Tablet, 21 February 1863), and The Times's crushing reply.

54   F.D. How, William Conyngham Fourth Baron Plunket and Sixty-First Archbishop of Dublin: A Memoir (London, 1900), pp.40-42. Cf. Plunket in The Mayo Constitution, 8 March 1859.

55   D'Alton, vol.2, p.73. Dallas also refers to an unpublished murder; Dallas, pp.468-69.

56   Quoted in Bowen, pp.244-45; cf. D'Alton, loc.cit.

57   On the Ribbonmen and other secret societies in Ireland, see Charles William Heckethorn, The Secret Societies of all Ages and Countries, 2 vols. (London, 1897), vol.2, pp.270-87.

58   The Tablet, 11 January 1862; also The Irishman, 11 January 1862.

59   Norman, p.90. Also Donal McCartney 'The Church and
the Fenians', University Review (Winter 1967), vol.iv, p.206:
'At Christmas and Easter the men of the Fenian circles in
Skibbereen in the diocese of Ross crossed over to the diocese
of Cloyne where the bishop, Dr Keane, had not insisted on
withholding the sacraments from Fenians.'
60   F.S.L. Lyons, Ireland since the Famine (London, 1971),
p.121. For the public aims of the Brotherhood, see The
Irishman, 15 February 1862.
61   The judgment of Peadar Mac Suibhne, Paul Cullen and
his contemporaries (Nass, 1974), vol.iv, p.425. Five volumes
of this work have so far appeared (1961-1977). See also on
Lavelle D.J. Hickey and J.E. Doherty, A Dictionary of Irish
History since 1800 (Dublin, 1980), pp.298-99. See also O
Fiaich, footnote 40.
62   The Irishman, 9 November 1861.
63   The Times, 6 February 1862. The lecture is published in
full in The Irishman, 8 February 1862.
64   The Tablet, 18 April 1863. The letter is partly quoted in
Norman, p.112. On the influence of the Polish rebellion of
1863-64 on Ireland see Norman, p.40.
65   See 'Revolution', in the New Catholic Encyclopedia,
vol.12, pp.450-51. The nineteenth-century eclipse of the
subject is indicated by the lack of an entry on 'Revolution' in
the Catholic Encyclopedia of 1907-1914.
66   Norman, p.113.
67   See footnote 61. Many of the letters in these volumes are
obviously extracts, translations, summaries, or paraphrases of
the originals rather than verbatim transcripts, so that the
quotations in the text are not precise.
68   Cullen to Barnabo, 16 November 1861; Cullen to Kirby,
27 November 1861, Mac Suibhne, vol.iv, pp.107-08.
69   Norman, p.94; The Tablet, 8 February 1982, 15 March
1862, 7 June 1862. For further episcopal censures, see
Norman, p.98.
70   Cullen to Major O'Reilly, 12 May 1863, Mac Suibhne,
vol.v, p.10.
71   Cullen to Kirby, 21 June 1863, Mac Suibhne, vol.iv,
p.147.
72   Cullen to Kirby, 11 August 1863, ibid., p.150. Dr Derry
was Bishop of Clonfert.
73   Cullen to Kirby, 4 September 1863, ibid., p.151.
74   Cullen to Kirby, 11 September 1863, 9 October 1863,
ibid., pp.152, 154.
75   Cullen to Kirby, 20 October 1863, ibid., p.155.
76   Cullen to Kirby, 3 November 1863, ibid., p.156.
77   Cullen to Kirby, 17 November 1863, ibid., p.157. For
the context of Lavelle's remarks about Cullen as a 'political
Judas', and claiming to quote from The Tablet, see The
Irishman, 31 October 1863. For his willingness to submit this
publication to Rome, see The Irishman, 7 November 1863.

78   Cullen to Kirby, 11 December 1863, ibid., p.159.
79   Cullen to Dr Gillooly, 18 December 1863, ibid., p.161.
80   Cullen to Kirby, 18 December 1863, ibid., p.162.
81   Cullen to Gillooly, 29 December 1863; to Kirby, 13 March 1864, ibid., pp.165-66.
82   Cullen to Kirby, 19 February 1864, cited Norman, p.101; Cullen to Kirby, 15 March 1864, Mac Suibhane, vol.iv, p.166.
83   Cullen to Kirby, 15 April 1864, cited Norman, p.102; Cullen to Gillooly, 28 May 1864, Mac Suibhne, vol.iv, p.168.
84   Cullen to Gillooly, 9 April 1874, ibid., p.167.
85   Cullen to Kirby, 19 July 1864, ibid., p.169.
86   Cullen to Kirby, 21 August 1864, cited Norman, p.102.
87   Ibid., p.103.
88   Cullen to Kirby, 9 December 1864, Mac Suibhne, vol.iv, p.172.
89   Lavelle, 'Mrs Lavelle and the late Sir Roger Palmer', in The Irish Landlord, p.394.
90   'Court of Queen's Bench' in The Irish Landlord, p.408.
91   Cullen to Dr Conroy, 23 December 1869, Mac Suibhne, vol.iv, p.268.
92   'A new song on the grand procesion (sic) of Father Lavell (sic) on his removal from Partry to Cong on the 16 of October 1868' (Dublin, 1868?).
93   Norman, pp.103, 123.
94   Cullen to Dr Conroy, 23 December 1869, Mac Suibhne, vol.iv, pp.267-68.
95   Norman, p.130.
96   Ibid., p.131. Cullen said on 7 January that all the Bishops except MacHale and Derry had 'signed a memorial to get the Fenians condemned nominatim': Cullen to Conroy, 7 January 1870, Mac Suibhne, vol.v, p.28. For the history of past Roman condemnations of 'secret societies', see McCartney, p.205.
97   Norman, p.133.
98   Cullen to Conroy, 3 March 1870, Mac Suibhne, vol.v, pp.69-70.
99   Norman, pp.423-25, 457.
100   D'Alton, vol.2, pp.118-19. Lavelle in this period had a part in the discovery of the celebrated 'Cross of Cong'. On Sir Arthur Guinness (later Lord Ardilaun) as a landlord see Gerard P. Moran, The Land Question in Mayo, 1868-1890 (M.A. thesis, University College, Galway, 1981), p.81. Moran demonstrates that in fact the misery of Mayo through the 1870s remained as desperate as ever.
101   Norman, p.397.
102   Devoy, vol.1, p.427. Lavelle defended Sir Arthur Guinness against the criticisms of the landlord by the Connaught Telegraph in June 1879. O Fiaich (p.148) reports the suggestion that Lavelle's earlier career had brought him into debt, and 'that the Guinness family helped to make his last years financially easier, but at their own price'.

103   Bew, p.10.
104   Ibid., p.68.
105   Lee, p.120: MacHale had got into 'bad company'.
106   Ibid., p.115.
107   MacDonagh, p.53.

PART THREE

POLITICAL COMMUNICATION
AND TERRORISM

Essay eight

WATER FOR THE FISH:
TERRORISM AND PUBLIC OPINION

D.G. Boyce

The power of the British state in the nineteenth century, and particularly its monopoly of overwhelming military resources,[1] frustrated the efforts of 'physical force' nationalists in Ireland to throw off British rule by what James Meagher called the 'sacred weapon',[2] the sword. This did not prevent the planning and outbreak of rebellions in 1848 and 1867; but it ensured that such plans and such rebellions, against a determined and powerful enemy, were short-lived affairs. The Smith O'Brien rising of 1848 is scarcely worthy of the name; and although the Fenian rebellion of 1867 might, with better preparation and luck, have posed a far greater threat to the British authorities, there can be little doubt that the government was possessed of the necessary military strength to suppress it, and enjoyed sufficient support from the British public to carry that suppression through to a conclusion.

It is perhaps surprising, therefore, that the physical force nationalists of the Irish Confederation of 1848, and the Fenian Brotherhood of 1867, should have thought of the battle between 'Saxon' and 'Celt' in heroic, formal military terms. There was, admittedly, little contemporary example of any other kind of military action. Historical precedents existed, and the Confederation and the Fenians were steeped in a certain kind of 'history'; there were the running fights (hardly worthy of the name of battles) between Irish troops and those of Queen Elizabeth in the sixteenth century;[3] but such tactics were not to the liking of romantic nationalists or would-be revolutionaries; and the men of 1848 and 1867 were anxious to use the experience of the 1848 Paris, Berlin, Vienna and Milan revolutions,[4] or the American civil war,[5] in order to defeat their foe. They were denied any possibility of resorting to guerrilla tactics after their defeat in the 'field' because these defeats were so crushingly final, and because there were simply not the means nor the necessary public support for an alternative military campaign to be launched. Fenianism was the most popular of the revolutionary

nationalist movements of nineteenth century Ireland, and the
commander in chief of the forces in Ireland, Lord
Strathnairn, believed that 'however much military and
constabulary movements have checked outrages and disorders,
I regret to say that there is no diminution of the general
disaffection, or elements of anarchy. They only wait a better
opportunity.'6 But there were powerful elements in Irish
society critical of Fenian methods (though not necessarily of
Fenian objectives), especially the Roman Catholic church; and
in any event the rise of a parliamentary party which seemed
to hold out hope of realizing Irish nationalist ambitions by
other means than force deprived Fenianism of the initiative in
nationalist politics. The home ruler with a parliament within
his reach cut a much less ridiculous figure than the physical
force nationalist without a gun in his hand.

If Irish military history had failed to teach the men of
1848 and 1867 any lessons about the most appropriate way in
which to engage the enemy, then contemporary social
developments might have been expected to prove more
enlightening. The Land War in Ireland after 1879, when
leaguers boycotted, threatened, and frequently attacked those
they deemed to be opposing the Land League's objectives,
with the widespread support, or at least acquiescence, of
large sections of the rural population, amounted to a form of
terrorism: of the kind of popular terrorism that the
authorities had found so difficult to eradicate in the
eighteenth and early nineteenth centuries. By 1881 law and
order had deteriorated to such an extent over much of
Ireland that the constabulary was incapable of dealing with it
single handed.7 Gladstone's government, which came to power
in 1880, was able to rely on public and parliamentary support
in Britain for coercion; but it was also disposed to tackle the
land problem; and it might be argued that if the agrarian
terrorism of 1879-81 had been translated into political terms,
then it might have achieved much. And, after all, Fenians did
play a prominent part in the Land League.

But this would be to misunderstand the distinction made
in Britain between concessions to Ireland and the granting of
full Irish independence. The seriousness of the Land League
threat to law and order, the difficulty of breaking through
the barrier imposed by terrorism between the law enforcing
agencies and the public, the potential threat to the peace
from innumerable centres, all revealed what a number of
determined men, able to call upon widespread social
sympathy, or at least acquiescence, could achieve. Ireland,
or parts of it at least, could be made ungovernable. And
Gladstone's government was unwilling to rely on coercion alone
to remedy their predicament. But it was one thing to modify
Irish land law and practice, and to see landlords as obstacles
in the way of peace; it was quite another to come to a point
where Britain must accept that she had to relinquish her hold

on Ireland. The former course found favour (as well as disfavour) with liberals and conservatives alike; the latter found favour with nobody; and if the agrarian terror of 1879–81 had been transformed by Fenians into a revolutionary threat to British rule in Ireland, it would undoubtedly have met with stern and unbending resistance.

The use of terror on the British mainland, in crowded British cities, was another matter. Such an attempt to carry the national struggle to the enemy's territory, to his own people, might weaken his resolve and force him to give up Ireland for the sake of safety in Great Britain. The Fenian outrages of 1867, when two policemen were killed in a rescue of Fenian prisoners in Manchester, and twenty people killed in an explosion at Clerkenwell, aroused anti-Irish fury; but they also aroused the British public from its state of indifference to affairs in Ireland, and to a recognition that there must be something amiss in Ireland which it was Britain's responsibility to cure. Such incidents, however, were not the same as a prolonged and systematic terrorist campaign; and when Clan na Gael terrorists attempted to launch such a campaign in the 1880s,[8] they achieved little except the acute embarrassment of the Irish Parliamentary Party. But perhaps unwittingly, they provided an illustration of one of the cardinal principles of terrorist activity: that such incidents achieved publicity far outweighing their intrinsic threat to the state and the public. The parliamentary newspaper, <u>United Ireland</u>, expressed its 'hearty abhorrence' of such modes of warfare, which it dubbed 'un-Irish'. But, it added,

> if there is a worse criminal than the man who explodes an infernal machine among innocent people, it is the man who preaches, as the English papers avowedly do, that there is no other way of compelling the attention and respect of England.[9]

Here was an important admission: that violence, and especially terrorism, had 'news value'; it was a means of catching press and public attention in England; it might even be a means of compelling the English state to attend to Irish affairs which it would otherwise ignore or belittle.

From 1885, however, such 'armed propaganda'[10] seemed less necessary as the Irish parliamentary party moved towards success in achieving self government for Ireland by constitutional means; and, moreover, the notion that 'Parnellism' was indeed associated with 'crime' proved a great disadvantage to the home rule party, and especially to its liberal champions in England, since the whole purpose of the party was now to convince the British public that it was a responsible body of men, fit to govern Ireland. On the other hand, this crypto-revolutionary image undoubtedly helped the party retain its following in Ireland, keep the Fenians and their successors, the Irish Republican Brotherhood, in their place, and furbish the image of a party that stood not only for home rule, but for the ancient struggle of the Irish race to free itself from Saxon tyranny. Not even the party splits and weaknesses after 1891 destroyed the view that parliamentarism could be made to work; and in any case the I.R.B. itself was committed, in its constitution of 1873, to await the favourable verdict of the Irish public before going another round with England.[11] Patriotic violence became more and more a virtue to be admired, rather than emulated; but no Irish nationalist leader who valued his seat ruled it out. if all else failed. In August 1898, at the climax of the anniversary celebrations of the '98 rebellion, John Dillon praised Wolfe Tone in terms which implied that he should not only be remembered, but his teachings followed, for they were 'a precious inheritance to the Irish people, and one which, if studied and acted upon, will, in my judgement, be the best guidance to the patriot's part'.[12] Earlier, Tim Harrington had declared that 'no one here is afraid to speak of '98', and urged young men not only to celebrate, but to organise, not only to join clubs, but to emulate the rebels 'in example of united action, in the sacrifice of liberty, and, if necessary, of life, in the vindication of the sacred cause of national freedom'.[13] The parliamentarians were playing a more dangerous game than they knew; but they believed that all else would not fail, that their methods would win the day; and after 1906, and especially 1910, they seemed on the verge of a resounding success.

The way in which the home rule party stumbled at the last - but greatest - obstacle, and the cause of their stumbling - the armed opposition of the Ulster Volunteers - naturally gave rise to the belief that force of arms was necessary for the success of the nationalist movement. But it was still unclear how arms were to be used, and against whom. The Irish Volunteers, founded in 1913 in response to the Ulster Volunteers, had as their motto 'defence not defiance'; and they were not founded to suppress the protestants nor, on the face of it, to attack the British army. The clash between a party of Volunteers carrying arms and the K.O.S.B. in July 1914 seemed to show that defence could shade into defiance; but when a section of the Irish Volunteers finally decided to assert their country's right to freedom by force of arms in 1916, their act of defiance took an essentially defensive form. They held certain key areas in Dublin, and invited the British to dislodge them if they could. The 1916 rising was no military fiasco like 1848 and 1867; the task of dislodging the rebels proved onerous and dangerous; and casualties, especially civilian casualties, were high. But in the end the superior military power of the state triumphed, as triumph it must; and within a week the fighting was over.

Once again, the defeat of the 'army of liberation' in the

'field' was not followed by any resort to different tactics by the rebels. There was no guerilla warfare, no terrorism. And when those Irish Volunteers who had survived the rising looked forward to another engagement with the British, they envisaged a war of entrenchments, base camps and even pike charges.[14] Victory or defeat would be won in the field; and calculation of the political impact of any other form of warfare does not seem to have entered their heads. In the event, however, this was to their advantage; for since Volunteer headquarters set them no tasks, the most immediate concern of the Volunteers was to seize arms; and to do so they could only engage the enemy in small, surprise attacks, as the need and occasion arose.[15] It would be misleading, therefore, to see the war of 1919-21, a war of terrorism and guerilla warfare, as the inevitable result of the defeat of the Volunteers in the field in 1916; for the politicians had asserted themselves after 1916, and the great political advances made by Sinn Fein between 1916 and 1918 seemed to render any new armed conflict of any kind unnecessary. There was no concerted plan among the Volunteers save that of 'treating the armed forces of the enemy whether soldiers or policemen, exactly as a National Army would treat the members of an invading army'.[16] There was, however, a recognition that if the Volunteers did not stir themselves, then the political wing of the revolutionary movement would subsume the military men entirely.[17] Fortunately for the Volunteers they were assisted by the British government's 'policy' of studiously ignoring Sinn Fein and its parliament, Dail Eireann. This enabled the Volunteers to seize the initiative, to claim that they were asserting Ireland's freedom in the only way possible, and to develop, in a haphazard, but effective, way the tactics that have ever since been associated with the Irish Republican Army.

The British government, faced with this military challenge, had to consider two sets of public opinion. It had to suppress Irish violence in a way that the British public would find acceptable; and it had to do so in a way that would win over, or at least not alienate further, a substantial section of the Irish public. But the choice it made to satisfy the first requirement automatically disqualified it from fulfilling the second. The government felt that the British public, while disliking the full weight of military coercion in Ireland, would tolerate a 'police war', a war that would see the R.I.C. bearing the main responsibility for defeating the I.R.A.[18] This was by no means an unsound decision, on its merits; but the problem was that the police force, under strength and with its confidence affected by the strain imposed on it as the prime target for terrorism, and by doubts about its future under home rule, doubts felt since 1910, was not capable of engaging in such a war, at least not without overhaul, rearming, and reinforcing. Overhaul and rearming took place, all too slowly; but the reinforcing of the RIC was to damage irreparably that body's standing in the eyes of the Irish people, and provide valuable propaganda to the IRA. The opening of the RIC to recruits from Great Britain, many of them unsuited for police work and discipline, lost the force any hope it had of acting as the guardians of the public, or, indeed, of law and order.[19] And the sobriquet 'Black and Tan' applied to the recruits because of their mixed military police uniform soon became a by-word for reprisals and lawlessness.

It would have taken a highly disciplined, self-controlled, and homogeneous police force to bear the attacks of the IRA with fortitude and restraint; not even the British military was free from the practice of taking reprisals on suspected 'Shinners', or anybody else, after being subjected to what they regarded as cowardly attacks. But the practice of sending what the Chief of the Imperial General Staff, Sir Henry Wilson, called 'these mobs' over to Ireland in 'lots of 25 and 50' meant that 'there would be no hope of forming and disciplining this crowd of unknown men'.[20] The same difficulty applied to that other reinforcement to the RIC, the Auxiliary Division, composed of ex-officers, and first recruited in July 1920. These men, with their courage and initiative, might, given proper training, have proved a formidable foe to the IRA; but once again they were dispatched to Ireland with no clear role assigned to them, and under police discipline which could only be applied if their local company officers were willing and able to do so.[21]

In the event, therefore, the British government found that its tools for counter-terrorism cost it not only any possibility of enlisting support amongst the nationalist population of Ireland - and such support was by no means wholly unlikely - but lost it the public backing in Britain that the decision to go for a 'police war' was founded upon. Probably most sections of the British public were apathetic about affairs in Ireland; and there is even limited evidence that among working class people the belief was held that the Irish only got what they deserved.[22] The government might have been able to deploy all the coercive powers of the modern state if it could rely on at least the indifference or acquiescence of the public; but it found itself the target of active and influential criticism from a minority of leading public figures, and pressure groups in Britain, whose influence was out of proportion to their numbers. Coercion in Ireland was by no means a new experience for the British public; but the spectacle of the forces of law and order themselves breaking the law was a development that shocked many people in Britain. IRA activities - especially the more brutal and atrocious of them - were condemned; but it was argued that 'you cannot justifiably punish wrongdoing by lawlessly doing the like... if it is by wrongdoing that you produce peace, you have not really won a peace which is worth having'.[23] And lurking in the back of the minds of some critics was the recognition that, as Harold Laski put it,

I deplore the Sinn Fein [sic] murders, but I get driven to the admission that unless they kept up guerilla warfare the Government would say that Ireland was now peaceful, and do nothing at all.[24]

The IRA had not planned nor foreseen such consequences of its campaign. It had come to the realisation that, as Michael Collins put it, 'we organized our army and met the armed patrols and military expeditions which were sent against us in the only way possible'.[25] There was no original blueprint, no concerted plan to arouse British public opinion, for the Volunteers had, for the most part, limited military and political horizons. But they had one immensely valuable characteristic: they could make the most of their limited military resources, and they could exploit their propaganda value to the full. Every incident, every 'job', however small, and, above all, every reprisal or outbreak by the crown forces, and especially the police, helped the IRA propagandists bring home the point to the British public that governing Ireland was a costly business, and one that exposed Britain to the contempt and odium of the world. If victory could be won - and few in Britain doubted that it could be won - then the road to it would be a long and arduous one, and the price, not in men but in prestige and peace of mind, would be a high one. Thus, a particular military operation like the burning of the Dublin Customs House in May 1921, which resulted in the capture of over 100 men of the Dublin Brigade, might have little military value, or might even be militarily disastrous; but it could still make the front pages of the British press, and could be presented by the Volunteer Journal An t'Oglach as symbolising the 'final collapse of British civil administration in this country'.[26] This was hyperbolic, to say the least; very little damage was done to the civil administration beyond the destruction of income tax records, certainly an inconvenience, but nothing more. If anything was brought near 'final collapse', it was the IRA.[27] But this apparently suicidal action brought the British Cabinet to the point of declaring full martial law in June 1921,[28] and, together with a flurry of small incidents in the spring of 1921, wrung from the Lord Chancellor, Lord Birkenhead, the admission that 'the history of the last three months has been the history of the failure of our military methods to keep pace with and overcome the military methods which have been taken by our opponents'.[29] The final incident that pushed the government to the point of a truce was also a militarily insignificant one   the derailing of a troop train carrying the King's cavalry back from the opening ceremony of the Northern Ireland Parliament on 22 June,[30] - but, together with the new political atmosphere created by

155

the King's appeal for peace and reconciliation in Belfast, it was sufficient to open the way for talks and the ending of the 'Anglo-Irish war'.

It was not only the apparent setbacks of the Spring of 1921, and the public criticism of the methods of the police force, that hampered the British government's efforts in their campaign in Ireland; equally important was the government's lack of a clear or decisive objective, of some important constitutional or political aim that could rally public support to see the war through to some kind of conclusion. The government had to present the campaign as necessary and justifiable, to convince the public that the cost in prestige, blood and treasure was worthwhile. But what was the aim of the campaign? It could not be to deny Ireland home rule, for home rule (admittedly with the partition of Ireland) was the government's avowed aim since at least 1918. Lloyd George sought to draw a parallel between the United Kingdom and the United States of America at the time of the civil war; there a long and costly conflict had proved necessary to save the Union. Few in Britain were prepared to allow nationalist Ireland to secede completely from the United Kingdom. But neither were they willing to stand by the Union through thick and thin; as The Times put it on 26 March 1919, 'We are all home rulers today'. Containment of Irish nationalism, not defence of Irish unionism, was the most that the British public would support; but that containment must go beyond the government's devolution proposals of 1920, most probably in the direction of dominion home rule. This meant that when the government did opt for negotiations in July 1921, it could rely on a large measure of public approval for its terms, once they were made known; but it also meant that, in the early days of the armed struggle that preceded the truce, the government had no strong or deep resources of British Unionism on which to call. Had the Soloheadbeg ambush, which is generally (if mistakenly) taken as the 'first shots' in the Anglo-Irish war occurred in 1879 instead of 1919, the British response would have been very different. But no-one in post war Britain was enthusiastic about the use of force to suppress nationalistic movements in Ireland; and no Prime Minister could follow Sir Robert Peel in his declaration in 1843 that, much as he deplored all war, and especially civil war, he was prepared to endure it rather than to submit to the dismemberment of the Union and the empire.[31]

From the beginning the government failed to carry the British public with it in its counter-terrorist campaign; but such a war was fought on two fronts, in a propaganda sense. To enjoy any reasonable prospect of success the government's forces had to win and retain the confidence of at least a substantial section of the Irish public, not only to give their campaign a semblance of credibility, but also to ensure that the military and the police were provided with a sufficient degree of information about the activities of their adversaries. The IRA were wont to claim that their war was supported by the 'risen people', that the whole of the population (except, of course, for Unionists) were the eyes and ears of Collins's Volunteers. But, as one member of the Irish Republican Brotherhood put it, as the violence increased, the

general public liked it less and less. With a growing admiration for and support for the Volunteers, there went a growing uneasiness as to the final outcome, a growing irritation at some of the military operations. In Dublin, for instance, the public resentment against the callousness of continual ambushes in "the Dardanelles" and in other crowded streets, with heavy casualties to civilians, was deep and deepening...

But, O'Hegarty added, 'it was accompanied by no weakening of the general support'.[32] But the shaky state of civilian morale was reflected in the successes of British Intelligence in 1921, and by the admission by one I.R.A. commander that the IRA was 'steadily losing its grip on the towns and villages'.[33]

Given the pressure of such a campaign on the civilian population, and the initial hostility expressed through the press and in local councils to the terrorism of the IRA when it first embarked on its campaign in 1919,[34] it might seem that the British forces might have gained the initiative in the battle for the 'hearts and minds' of the Irish public. The practice of police reprisals dealt a severe blow to that possibility; but the army seems to have felt a sense of apathy, almost of despair, about the nature of its relationship with the civilian population. There was, of course, the difficulty noted by the historian of the South Wales Borderers in distinguishing 'the active Sinn Feiners from the more peaceful or better disposed inhabitants'.[35] But 'active Sinn Feiners' were not necessarily active supporters of I.R.A. violence, as one of them demonstrated when he resigned from the Dail in January 1921 as a protest against it. In County Meath, where the S.W.B. did its Irish service, conditions were not bad, but the troops were 'surrounded by a population most of which were sullenly hostile and only deterred by fear from more active and violent opposition'. The military seems to have been reluctant to regard the civilian population in the south with anything less than suspicion; as the Brigade Major of 17th Brigade in Cork admitted, 'I think I regarded all civilians as "Shinners", and I never had any dealings with any of them.'[36] Regimental historians describe the service in Ireland as 'monotonous', 'rather unsatisfactory', 'the most unpleasant form of exercising their functions as men at arms', 'not an easy world to live in'.[37] However, when the British prime minister could dismiss Irish nationalism as a 'sham and a fraud',[38] and the Commander in Chief in Ireland, Sir Nevil Macready, express privately his loathing for Ireland

157

'and its people with a depth deeper than the sea and more violent than that which I feel against the Boche',[39] then a positive attitude to winning the confidence and loyalty of the population was hardly likely to be forthcoming from the state's servants. It is doubtful if anyone in the Irish administration, the British government. or the military command regarded the nationalist people as full citizens of the United Kingdom, in any real sense; they accepted almost without questioning that they were operating in a 'hostile' country, among a 'hostile' people, and in what one regimental historian called a 'cloak and dagger business.. distasteful to any soldier'.[40]

This sense of hopelessness - so vividly felt and expressed by Macready when in May 1921 he warned the government that 'the present state of affairs in Ireland, so far as regards the troops serving there, must be brought to a conclusion by October, or steps must be taken to relieve practically the whole of the troops together with the great majority of the commanders and their staffs'[41] - was increased by the political and administrative advances made by Sinn Fein. When clashes between the I.R.A. and the crown forces increased in 1919-20, the Dail was in no position to act as any kind of controlling body. It met only rarely; its 'government departments' were shadowy affairs; and the I.R.A. resented any attempt by the minister of defence, Cathal Brugha, to impose an oath of allegiance to the Dail.[42] Yet without it the armed struggle would have appeared much less of a 'liberation' war, and more of a sporadic terrorist campaign. Eamon de Valera, in particular, held that once the shooting had started, Sinn Fein must not allow the British to drive a wedge between the political and physical force wings of the nationalist movement; and he kept up the fiction that the Dail was in some sense in control of the I.R.A., with the Minister of Defence 'of course, in close association with the voluntary military forces which are the foundation of a national army'.[43] In April 1921 the Dail at last accepted official responsibility for I.R.A. operations; and this shadowy and belated control of the I.R.A. by the Dail, however tenuous, gave the military struggle some semblance of association with the politicians, and prevented it from degenerating entirely into a conflict between an irresponsible armed body, the I.R.A., and the crown forces. Moreover, Sinn Fein was able to demonstrate its popularity in the country in the municipal elections of January 1920 and the rural elections of May 1921. Effective republican local government was being implemented, and local courts were set up, superseding the normal law courts, to try land cases. The Sinn Fein concept of civil resistance, first formulated by Arthur Griffith, took a real and significant form when quayside workers in Dublin were supported by the Irish Transport and General Workers' Union in refusing to handle 'British war material' in Ireland. The British cabinet had no positive response to make to any of these developments, except to increase coercion;[44] it was thus to pay dearly for its failure in 1919 to take seriously Sinn Fein's claim to represent the nationalist people of Ireland in its parliament, Dail Eireann. And when all these propaganda, military, and political failures are put together, the surprising thing is not that the British lost their 1919-21 campaign in Ireland, but that they came as close as they did to winning it.

The Irish struggle of 1919-21 seemed to demonstrate that, as one authority put it, given certain factors, certain favourable 'conditions', it was 'practicable for a relatively small party of revolutionaries to embark on a war against a professional army with a fair chance of success'.[45] Certainly the conflict. its nature and its outcome, had important implications for the physical force republican tradition in Ireland. Tactically, it had developed its own methods of warfare, a mixture of terrorist and guerilla activities, that had, apparently, proved successful and might do so again. This was not a systematic or clearly thought out affair; one I.R.A. commander, Ernie O'Malley, spoke of 'open warfare' developing in Ireland in 1921, and planned to form divisional columns that would 'close' with the British columns, anticipating that 'we would have to go into the towns to look for a fight'.[46] But the I.R.A. tradition was now very different from that of Meagher and his 'sacred sword'. Its campaign had prevented the opposing army from exerting its full strength; had been carried out on a rising scale, thus wearing down the civilian as well as military morale of the enemy country; and had taken place in a country whose topography afforded cover and relative ease of movement, and sections of whose population were prepared to give the 'fish' the necessary water in which to swim. No longer could the British army reflect that

Whatever happens, we have got
The Gatling Gun, and they have not.

From 1919 Volunteering in Ireland was no longer an affair of pipe clay (or its Irish republican equivalent, polished pikes); the new image was that of the man in the trench coat with a hand-gun, not the fully uniformed Volunteer, rifle in hand, of Easter 1916; and the I.R.A. in this form was to enjoy a longevity that made it unique among terrorist organizations in western Europe.

Yet the next fifty years after the success of 1921 demonstrated, not the success, but the failure of I.R.A. tactics. The I.R.A. failed to defeat the Free State forces in the Irish civil war of 1922-3; they failed to overthrow the newly established government of Northern Ireland in 1921-24; they failed to shake the democratic foundations of southern Ireland after 1923; and their last campaign, before the post-1969 terrorist assault in Northern Ireland, spluttered on between 1956 and 1962 before ending in ignominious collapse.

159

The reasons for these consistent failures are too complex to be treated in any detail here. But it can be safely said that they arose primarily from the I.R.A.'s failure to fulfil the 'conditions' that they met, partly by accident, in the 1919-21 campaign. There are two main reasons for this. The I.R.A. had, in a sense, been at once too successful and yet not successful enough in 1921. Many of them were wont to believe that they, and they alone, had beaten the British army; that the Irish plenipotentiaries at the treaty negotiations of 1921 had 'sold out' on the republic, and so the army - or those sections of it that would not follow Michael Collins in supporting the Anglo-Irish treaty - had to retain their arms and go another round with the enemies of the republic. This gave the sea green militant republicans an almost impossible task, for the treaty was undoubtedly popular with the mass of the people, if only because it promised to end years of terror. But a 'victorious' army like the anti-treaty I.R.A. felt that, if it could beat the British army, then it could defeat any Free State army; within a year they were proved wrong, for the kind of public support that has been maintained at a sufficient level to enable the I.R.A. to remain in business between 1919 and 1921 was not forthcoming, and the anti-treaty I.R.A. also made the tactical mistake of emerging into the open, attempting to take and hold large tracts of territory, and behaving like a guerilla army in the last stages of a successful campaign rather than a fragment of a divided and increasingly unpopular force.[47]

This lack of success was again the I.R.A.'s downfall, not only immediately, but in the future. For the I.R.A. held that, if the people did not support them, so much the worse for the people: the I.R.A.'s primary allegiance was not to the real, living population of Ireland, but to the Irish nation of the dead past or the prophetic future. The I.R.A.'s hostility to the traitorous people of Ireland was summed up in the words of Rory O'Connor, a leader of the anti-treaty faction. When asked if there was any government in Ireland to which he gave his allegiance he answered 'No,' and when his interviewer speculated, 'Do we take it you are going to have a military dictatorship?' O'Connor replied brusquely, 'You can take it that way if you like.'[48] The real fears about the consequences of such attitudes were expressed by the Dail deputy for Sligo, who declared

> Give us Dominion Home Rule, give us Repeal of the Union, give us anything that will stamp us as white men and women, but for Heaven's sake don't give us a Central American Republic.[49]

Against this was the dogma confessed by one former republican that

> I was Ireland, the guardian of her Faith, the one solitary man who would keep the Republican symbol alive, keep the last lamp glowing before the last

icon, even if everybody else denied or forgot the gospel that had inspired us all from 1916 onwards. I firmly believed in the dogma that had by now become the last redoubt of the minority's resistance to the majority; that the people have no right to be wrong.[50]

The prospects of the I.R.A. succeeding in its objective of attaining the mystical republic of 1916 became more remote after 1923, and especially with the peaceful transfer of power to de Valera's Fianna Fail (Republican) party in 1932. De Valera, while seeking to retain the support and allegiance of the militant republicans, was anxious to point out that the Fianna Fail victory at the polls had rendered the use of force to achieve the republican goal unnecessary. The democratic state, he maintained, had the right to the monopoly of the legal use of force; any other physical force element in the nation was illegitimate.[51] The I.R.A. still had a residual following in certain traditionally militant republican areas, such as Co. Kerry, and along the border with Ulster; but no longer did it have the opportunity to pose as the army of the people (nor, after 1949, of the Irish Republic). In the south of Ireland at least, the fish, while never entirely deprived of water, was finding that commodity increasingly hard to come by.

In view of the political history of the south of Ireland after 1932, this is hardly surprising; but the decline of the I.R.A. north of the border is harder to explain, given the persistent sense of grievance felt against the state by the Roman Catholic minority there, and the distaste felt in many liberal circles in Britain for the character of the Unionist government and party. Moreover, the troubles in the north in the years 1920-24 revealed the vulnerability of the Northern Ireland government to terrorist attack. For not only were I.R.A. activities a direct threat to the state; by fomenting or exacerbating communal disturbances, and by encouraging protestant extremists to use counter-terror, they placed the state under threat from two sides. And they also placed it under threat from a third side, since the British government, answerable to a public that was none too happy about the state of affairs in Belfast, and the government's use of the protestant Special Constabulary, and anxious to come to terms with Dublin, was often less than enthusiastic about defending Ulster, and especially about committing the British army in a wholehearted manner.[52] The Northern Ireland government's strong security measures, and, equally important the decline in I.R.A. activity as a result of the outbreak of civil war in the south in 1922, enabled the province to settle down to an uneasy peace; but it seemed likely that such a peace would have proved fragile.

In the event, this was not so. Between 1924 and 1962 I.R.A. activity in the north was no more successful than that in the south. And the explanation lies in the failure of the organization to create or discover a favourable environment for its activities. British public opinion was only too relieved to see the apparent disappearance of the Irish question after 1924, and was in no mood to become involved again; and when the I.R.A. sought in its terrorist campaign in Britain in 1939-40 to weaken the British resolve to 'hold' Northern Ireland, it found that it had picked the wrong time: Ulster was vital to the British war effort, and Britain could not afford to relinquish its bases in the north, even if it had wanted to. To see southern Ireland enter the war was a different matter; and the British government would have been happy to encourage Irish unification for such a commitment from Dublin. But de Valera knew better than to reopen that doubtful package; and his anxiety to maintain Irish neutrality was expressed in his firm handling of the I.R.A. south of the border. The Northern Ireland government was able to introduce internment without any protest from the British public; and the security response was carried out mainly by the Northern Ireland police forces, with little or no direct involvement by the British, and thus with no opportunity provided to the I.R.A. to 'weaken' the 'hold' of Britain on Ulster.[53]

The attitude of the Roman Catholic people of Ulster still awaits its historian; but its lack of enthusiasm for a renewed terrorist campaign in the years 1924-45 can probably be explained by two main considerations: the fact that such a campaign, of doubtful prospect, would only bring the wrath of the protestant majority down on them, as it had done in 1920; and the essentially constitutional attitudes of the Roman Catholics, reinforced by their church, which discouraged the use of force by the I.R.A. This pattern seemed likely to be broken by the I.R.A. revival after the declaration of the republic in 1949 by Dublin, and the British response in passing the Ireland Act, which laid it down that the British government would not alter the border except with the consent of the Northern Ireland parliament. The British also agreed not to intervene in Northern Ireland affairs except to control a breakdown in law and order.[54] The I.R.A., whose membership had declined to perhaps 200 active members in the whole of Ireland, rose again, as it declared itself the only true defender of the one and indivisible 32 county republic. By the mid 1950s the I.R.A. was able to conduct successful raids for arms in military depots in Northern Ireland and Great Britain; in 1955 Sinn Fein candidates won a strong vote in the general election, scoring victories in South Tyrone - Fermanagh, and Mid-Ulster;[55] and in December 1956 a concerted campaign was begun in Ulster, when targets along the border were attacked.

These incidents were the work of a splinter group; the official I.R.A. campaign began the following month; and it seemed likely to gain not only northern Catholic support, but the approval of nationalists in the south as well. County councils passed resolutions condemning sentences passed on two I.R.A. men; and the funeral of Sean South, who was killed on a raid on Brookeborough Barrracks in Co. Fermanagh, was 'virtually an event of national mourning'.[56] But the northern Catholic vote for Sinn Fein in 1955, and the 66,000 votes cast for Sinn Fein in the republic's election of 1957, were not evidence of a wholehearted support of violence, but a manifestation of nationalist resentment of partition, with the I.R.A. and its political wing representing the extreme development of attitudes which existed in less extreme forms among the Roman Catholics of Ireland. The futility of the campaign, its lack of contact with the mass of the people, its lack of political objectives of any relevance to the bulk of the Catholic minority in Northern Ireland, ensured that the fleeting public approval of 1955-57 soon collapsed. The I.R.A. were also hampered by their own military incompetence and by their naive belief that 'as we build up our forces we hope to liberate large areas, that is areas where the enemy's writ no longer runs'.[57]

There were perhaps two other possible ways in which the I.R.A. campaign of 1956-62 might have produced the kind of public opinion climate in which they would have stood a greater chance of success. If the I.R.A. had provoked protestant reprisals on the Roman Catholics of Ulster, then they might have gathered sympathy by posing as 'defenders' of the minority; but the I.R.A. itself refused to hold the Roman Catholics hostage in this way; and they deliberately avoided activities in Belfast because of the danger of provoking sectarian passions. Moreover the Stormont government handled the crisis calmly, stressing that the protestants must show restraint, must not take to the streets; and although there were moments when public order seemed in danger, the crisis passed quietly. The second possibility was that the British public might be brought into the conflict. Most people in Britain were, it is safe to say, almost totally unaware of the whole business and the background to it; but if the British army were deeply involved, perhaps taking casualties, and if British liberal and labour opinion - traditionally hostile to Ulster Unionism - were to disapprove of the firm measures taken by Stormont, including the internment of some few hundred I.R.A. suspects, then again some crack in the political mould of Northern Ireland might be engineered. The British army did play a small part in counter-terrorism, with the Northumberland Fusiliers, for example, supporting the police in the Derry area; but the soldiers were not in the front line, and 'they did not enter houses but held the ring for the police'.[58] Moreover, the Stormont government was a remote affair to the British public, and Northern Ireland internal matters were not even discussed by the British parliament. Its record on community relations was not yet subject to the scrutiny of the press and television that it endured in the new, civil rights era of the 1960s. The only reaction of the British government was to make representations to the Dublin government about the use of Irish territory by the I.R.A. as a base for attacks.[59] But the Dublin government scarcely needed such representations. With the return to power of Eamon de Valera in 1957 – a taoiseach whose republicanism was hardly in doubt – the Irish government took appropriate security measures, including internment, and by the end of 1957 the threat of violence had been largely removed in the south. In the United Kingdom general election of 1959 the Sinn Fein vote in Ulster dropped from the 152,000 figure of 1955 to 69,000, with heavy abstentionism in some constituencies.[60] Internal tensions eased, and the celebration of the 50th anniversary of the signing of the Ulster covenant of 1912 passed off quietly. But the problem frustrating the minority remained: how to improve its lot without resorting to violence, in a country where all else – including violence – seemed to lead nowhere.

The I.R.A. campaign of 1956–62 failed mainly because the I.R.A. ignored moral and psychological factors, and failed to appreciate that 'the military strategies and tactics are secondary means to an end'.[61] They were, to use Mao's phrase, 'simple minded militarists'. But the frustrations felt by the Roman Catholic community in Ulster – the kind of frustrations that produced the large Sinn Fein vote in 1955 would not go away, and were soon to result in a political crisis that gave a new, less scrupulous, I.R.A. the water that the fish needed to swim in. The political events in Northern Ireland since 1968 are too well known to need recapitulation here; but their relationship to the contemporary terrorist campaign in Ulster (and, to a much lesser extent, in Great Britain) must be assessed. The problem of protest and disorder facing the Unionist government and its police forces in the 1960s was a more complex one than ever before. Before then it was – at least to the government clear cut: there was an easily identifiable enemy whose declared aim was the overthrow of the state of Northern Ireland. The government could take measures to counteract this, and whilst it had to be aware of the need not to offend British opinion by the measures it took, it was given a fairly free hand. But the Northern Ireland Civil Rights Movement presented the Stormont government with a complex and novel problem. If the demand was for reform within the state, not the overthrow of the state, then the usual methods of security response might not work, and might prove disastrous. Moreover, the era of television news reporting 'on the spot' had arrived, and the spectacle of Stormont using severity and violence against an apparently non-violent, liberal – almost 'British style' – reform movement in 1968-9 was hardly likely to enhance the image of Unionist government, already under attack from British liberal opinion. Thus the involvement of British public opinion, the weakening of the Unionist government's hand, the dividing of protestant opinion among 'hardliners' and O'Neillite moderate reformers, the sympathy and involvement of the Dublin government on the minority side, all prepared the way - quite without intention, foresight, or planning - for the kind of political atmosphere in which the I.R.A. could revive and even thrive. Even the demoralization of the R.U.C., which proved itself unequal to a crisis that would have strained to the utmost any police force in the United Kingdom, was achieved.

It must be emphasized that preparing of the way for a dangerous terrorist campaign was not the intention of the N.I.C.R.A. or of anyone else involved in the crisis of 1968-9. The I.R.A. in August 1967 called a meeting of local leaders throughout the country to assess the strength of the movement, and 'discovered that we had no movement'.[62] When violence broke out in Belfast in 1969 the entire I.R.A. strength in the city was an estimated 150 men with hardly any weapons. The protestant attacks on Roman Catholics in August 1969 might have finally discredited the I.R.A., since it was the traditional foe of the republicans, the British army, which was called in to protect the Roman Catholic minority. But the political crisis was not yet resolved, and the years after 1969 saw Stormont gradually reassert its control over security policy, while the British government stood by, lacking either the administrative machinery or the political will to do otherwise.[63] The growing alienation of the Roman Catholics from the British army gave birth to, and was exploited by, a new I.R.A. movement, which split from the 'official' I.R.A., and which was unhampered by the official I.R.A. myth about the indivisible Irish nation embracing Roman Catholics and protestants alike. As one staunch republican put it, the movement

> turned in on itself and said 'Look, we've had enough of this Wolfe Tone United Irishmen nonsense. We're just Catholics and Protestants'. A large section of the movement went Provisional and said 'Right, it's a straight fight from here on'.[64]

This was a brutal assessment of Irish history; but it represented, in a sense, the fulfilment of Irish history, while official I.R.A. belief in a united nation represented the denial of it.

Thus the Provisional I.R.A. was able to rely on sufficient public support from Roman Catholic opinion to launch and sustain its campaign, a campaign aided unwittingly by the inability of the Northern Irish and British governments either to co-ordinate security policy, or to discover ways in which I.R.A. support might be undermined. Moreover, the remaining two relevant 'publics', those of the south of Ireland and Britain, were equally susceptible to this vigorous propaganda assault. The northern crisis did not, perhaps, affect southern Irish opinion very profoundly, but it provoked atavistic outbursts, such as the demonstration after Bloody Sunday in January 1972. And British liberal opinion, already taught to regard anything that Stormont did as unworthy, was uneasy about the role of the British army after 1969, and alarmed at the Stormont government's decision to introduce internment without trial in August 1971. Some members of the British public felt that the I.R.A. threat was not as inimicable to the state as internment, which undermined the basis of all civil liberties. To this unease among the more concerned elements among the British public was added a more general indifference about Northern Ireland, a distaste for its violent politics, a resentment that British troops should be at risk there, and a growing belief in some quarters that the counter-terrorist campaign could not be won, and, possibly, was not worth winning. As well as attending to public opinion in Britain, the British government had to show awareness of the contemporary European climate on human rights, which was critical of certain aspects of the security forces' tactics, especially its interrogation methods, and which placed both the British government and the government of the Irish republic in an embarrassing predicament.[65]

All these pressures had important consequences for British counter-terrorism in Northern Ireland. There could, of course, be no question of declaring martial law; and the government instead used special powers legislation to give the army and police the means to suppress the I.R.A. This was sufficient to contain, and then weaken, the terrorists; but the government could not forget that it was expected to reconcile its security measures with democratic traditions, and these necessarily placed constraints on its military efforts. Some have argued that these were disastrous, and saved the I.R.A. when it was on the brink of defeat; they certainly appear to have had a deleterious impact on the security forces.[67]

The state of British, international, and Roman Catholic opinion in Northern Ireland itself, therefore, prevented the post-1969 I.R.A. campaign from being handled in the way assaults on both southern and Northern Ireland were handled after 1922: some internment, some censorship, and special judicial procedures.[68] The political crisis of 1969-72 ensured that the ambivalent attitude to I.R.A. violence felt among many people in the Republic and Northern Ireland, the ambivalence that enabled people to approve of the concept of an I.R.A., and its aim of a 32 county republic, while not necessarily wishing to follow this attitude to its logical, and violent, conclusion, tended to fall sufficiently on the side of the I.R.A. to enable it to launch its campaign. And while

British public opinion has shown no sign of forcing any of the major political parties in Britain to initiate a policy of withdrawal from Northern Ireland, it gains sufficient encouragement from opinion polls, occasional statements by politicians speaking 'unofficially', and media treatment of Northern Ireland affairs, to continue its campaign indefinitely. What it has not succeeded in doing is undermining the protestant will to survive and live in Northern Ireland; for this will was strong enough to defeat even the moderate power-sharing executive of 1974. Nor has it won over the major Roman Catholic political party, the Social Democratic and Labour party, to its side, despite the frustrations experienced by that party since 1974.

It has been observed that 'a terrorist campaign is largely a battle of will between the rebels and the Government rather than a direct physical battle. To sustain their resolution, the Governments need the political strength derived from the support of public opinion'.[69] The complicating factor in the Irish context is that the governments have to keep a watchful eye on so many public opinions; British public opinion is, comparatively speaking, more easily gauged and responded to than the pluralistic public opinion of Ireland, and especially of Northern Ireland. To make a response which might win the approval of Roman Catholic opinion (talks with Dublin) can arouse and alienate sections of protestant opinion; to accept what amounts to a unionist veto on power sharing might appease many (but by no means all) protestants, but alienate Catholics, and offend British public opinion, frustrated with the intractable nature of the problem, and anxious to know why the British government's patience should be exploited by Unionists to stand firm against political compromise. To give the army a freer hand might raise its morale, and the morale of Unionists, but such activity by the security forces can be a recruiting sergeant for the I.R.A., as the 1970 curfew in Roman Catholic areas of Belfast turned out to be; according to one informed observer, 'relations with the Catholics were destroyed forever'.[70]

It is hardly surprising, therefore, that a small group of I.R.A. men, capable of inflicting (by war standards) only a limited amount of damage, has operated in Ireland since 1919, and effectively in Northern Ireland since 1969. Yet it must be emphasized that I.R.A. success is relatively new; and, like the 1919-21 campaign, such success as it has attained has been because the political environment has, for various reasons, enabled the I.R.A. to play upon the attitudes, prejudices, susceptibilities and fears of the public opinions that exist in the British Isles, and abroad. They have not been able to do so in a uniform manner; and the measures that they used in 1919-21 are in many important respects dissimilar to those used after 1969.[71]

The government since 1972 has not neglected the political

aspect of counter-terrorism; but it has perhaps hoped for too much from dazzling 'political solutions', or wide-ranging Anglo-Irish agreements. As one serving officer has pointed out, the construction of a public opinion in Northern Ireland favourable to the defeat of the I.R.A. depends on local, piecemeal, sensitive appreciation of the needs and fears of very small, very clannish, groups of people.[72] This approach, to succeed, requires patience from both British and southern Irish public opinion. Neither of these publics is noted for its long-sightedness concerning Northern Irish political and social problems. But patience and hard work at the local level holds out the only hope, albeit a slender one, in a part of the world where public opinion has, up to now, been born, not made.

Notes

1   Between 1792 and 1822 the army in Ireland increased from 11,113 to 22,331, and throughout the nineteenth century its strength fluctuated from 15,000 to 30,000 men. The Irish garrison was proportionately larger than that maintained in England and Wales. In Ireland in 1871 the ratio of troops to civilians was 1 to 194.79; in England and Wales it was 1 to 304.17. (D.N. Haire, 'In aid of the civil power, 1868-90', in F.S.L. Lyons and R.A.J. Hawkins (eds.), Ireland under the Union: varieties of tension (Oxford, 1980), p.116.)

2   P.S. O'Hegarty, History of Ireland under the Union (London, 1952), pp.245-57 explains the Irish confederates' concept of war.

3   G.A. Hayes-McCoy, 'The conduct of the Anglo-Irish war', in T.D. Williams (ed.), The Irish struggle, 1916-1926 (London, 1966), pp.59-60.

4   United Irishman, 6 May 1848.

5   P. Jones, The Irish Brigade (London, 1971), passim, esp. pp.188-92.

6   Haire, op.cit., p.118.

7   Ibid., p.127.

8   For which see K. Short, The dynamite war (Humanities Press, 1979).

9   United Ireland, 20 August 1881.

10   R. Evelegh, Peace-keeping in a democratic society - the lessons of Northern Ireland (London, 1978), p.38.

11   L. O Broin, Revolutionary Underground: the story of the I.R.B., 1858-1924 (Dublin, 1976), pp.6-7, 11.

12   United Ireland, 20 August 1898.

13   Ibid., 29 January 1898.

14   Hayes-McCoy, op.cit., p.61.

15   C. Townshend, The British campaign in Ireland, 1919-1921 (London, 1975), pp.19-20.

16   Ibid., p.19.

17   M. Forester, Michael Collins: the lost leader (London,

1971), p.104; C. Townshend, 'The I.R.A. and the development of guerilla warfare, 1916-1921', in E.H.R., Vol.94 (1979), p.320.

18   D.G. Boyce, Englishmen and Irish Troubles: British public opinion and the making of Irish policy, 1918-1922 (London, 1972), pp.47-49.

19   Townshend, British campaign, pp.41-46.

20   Boyce, op.cit., p.54.

21   Townshend, British campaign, pp.109-12.

22   Boyce, op.cit., p.71.

23   Ibid., p.76.

24   K. Martin, Harold Laski (London, 1935), p.59.

25   Hayes-McCoy, op.cit., p.61.

26   Col. J.M. MacCarthy (ed.)., Limerick's fighting story (Tralee, n.d.), p.29.

27   Townshend, British campaign, p.180.

28   K. Middlemas (ed.), Tom Jones: Whitehall diary, Vol.III, Ireland, 1918-1925 (London, 1971), pp.72-74.

29   C.J.C. Street, Ireland in 1921 (London, 1922), pp.80-81.

30   Townshend, E.H.R., Vol.94, p.342.

31   69 H.C. Debates, 3rd ser., cols.23-25, 9 May 1843.

32   P.S. O'Hegarty, The victory of Sinn Fein (Dublin, 1924), pp.61-62.

33   Townshend, E.H.R., Vol.94, pp.327-28.

34   R. Kee, The green flag: a history of Irish nationalism (London, 1972 edn.), pp.632-33, 657, 663.

35   C.T. Atkinson, The South Wales Borderers (C.U.P., 1937), pp.452-53.

36   Townshend, British campaign, p.205.

37   See Brigadier C.N. Barclay, History of the Duke of Wellington's regiment 1919-1952 (London, 1953), p.9; Col. H. Whalley-Kelly, Ich Dien: the Prince of Wales Volunteers, 1914-34 (Aldershot, 1935), pp.271-72; G. Blight, History of the Royal Berkshire regiment, 1920-47 (London, 1953), p.33.

38   D.G. Boyce, 'Lloyd George and Ireland', in A.J.P. Taylor (ed.)., Lloyd George: twelve essays (London, 1971), p.150.

39   Townshend, British campaign, p.20.

40   Blight, op.cit., p.29.

41   Boyce, Englishmen and Irish troubles, p.135.

42   J.A. Murphy, Ireland in the twentieth century (Dublin, 1975), pp.14-15.

43   T.E. Hachey, Britain and Irish separatism (Chicago, 1977), p.269.

44   Townshend, British campaign, pp.67-72; see also his 'The Irish railway strike of 1920: industrial action and civil resistance in the struggle for independence', in I.H.S., Vol.XXI (March 1979), pp.265-82.

45   K. Chorley, Armies and the art of revolution (London, 1943 edn.), p.61.

46   E. O'Malley, On another man's wound (Dublin, 1936), p.334.
47   C. Younger, Ireland's civil war (London, 1979 edn.), chs.17-19.
48   Kee, The green flag, p.733.
49   C. Desmond Greaves, Liam Mellows and the Irish revolution (London, 1971), pp.276-77.
50   Ruth Dudley Edwards, Patrick Pearse: the triumph of failure (London, 1977), pp.327-28.
51   See, e.g., his pamphlet, National discipline (1936).
52   P.J. Buckland, The factory of grievances: devolved government in Northern Ireland, 1921-39 (Dublin, 1979), ch.8.
53   G. Mac Eoin, 'The I.R.A.', in Eire/Ireland, Vol.IX, No.2 (1974), pp.16-22.
54   Ibid., p.22.
55   Annual Register (1955), pp.71-72.
56   J.A. Murphy, 'The New I.R.A., 1925-62', in T.D. Williams (ed.), Secret Societies in Ireland (Dublin, 1973), pp.162-63.
57   W. CLark, Guns in Ulster (Belfast, 1967), p.101.
58   Ibid., p.111.
59   Annual Register (1956), p.70.
60   Ibid. (1959), p.60.
61   C.W. Thayer, Guerilla (London, 1964), p.202.
62   Mac Eoin, op.cit., p.27.
63   W.D. Birrell, 'The Stormont-Westminster relationship', in Parliamentary Affairs, Vol.26 (1972-73), pp.488-90.
64   W. Van Voris, Violence in Ulster: an oral commentary (Amherst, 1975), p.190.
65   D.G. Boyce, '"Normal policing": public order in Northern Ireland since partition', in Eire/Ireland, Vol.XIV, No.4 (1979), pp.48-49.
66   P. Wilkinson, Terrorism and the liberal state (London, 1977), pp.153-58.
67   Evelegh, op.cit., pp.37-38.
68   E. Moxon-Browne, 'Terrorism in Northern Ireland: the case of the Provisional I.R.A.', in J. Lodge (ed.), Terrorism: a challenge to the state (Oxford, 1981), p.149.
69   Evelegh, op.cit., p.46.
70   Mr K. Boyle, in Van Voris, op.cit., pp.178-79.
71   For example, the I.R.A. in 1919-21 used indiscriminate terror only rarely.
72   Evelegh, op.cit., pp.48-59; for an example of the consequences of the failure to construct public opinion at a 'micro' level see Van Voris, op.cit., p.178.

Essay nine

NORTHERN IRELAND AND FLEET STREET:
MISREPORTING A CONTINUING TRAGEDY

John Kirkaldy

Northern Ireland should have been one of the most important newspaper stories of the past decade[1] - a part of Britain in virtual civil war with over two thousand deaths and many more injuries. In general, British newspapers have not lived up to this responsibility: important stories have often been superficial in content, misreported or overlooked.[2] Three periods of reporting can be discerned since the start of the present disturbances in 1968. Firstly, the years 1968-9 saw a time of general enthusiasm, based on very little knowledge of Northern Ireland, for the civil rights movement there. Secondly, from 1969 the rising level of violence began increasingly to alienate the press from both Catholics and Protestants in the province. These sentiments were accentuated by the introduction of the army in August 1969; there was now a tangible British presence, which increased the feeling of 'us' and 'them'. Thirdly, by 1973 there was a noticeable decline in press interest in Irish affairs (this has been apparent even earlier in the more popular newspapers). Increasingly, events in Northern Ireland have been perfunctorily reported or not reported at all. Stories that would have made page one ten years ago now rate a passing mention in the inside pages or are missed out completely. Unless something new or dramatic occurs, Irish news seldom receives major press coverage. Yet the tragedy of Northern Ireland remains: people continue to die; bombings and shootings still claim victims; the prisons are full to bursting point; social problems, such as unemployment, are acute; and no solution appears in sight.

Like most historical generalisations these periods oversimplify a more complex phenomenon but a general pattern does emerge. It is interesting to note that, whereas in previous Anglo-Irish disputes the Irish Question was politically divisive in Britain, the present crisis has largely seen Ireland as a bipartisan issue at Westminster with widespread consensus among politicians and the media. A few exceptions to these general strictures against the British press should be made. Mary Holland of the Observer (later the New Statesman) has generally produced articles of the highest quality and is one of the few journalists who has reported the troubles since their beginning. John Whale of the Sunday Times is another who has covered the story from the start, and with members of that newspaper's Insight Team, has been consistently informative. (The Insight Team produced one of the best 'instant' histories of the first few years of the crisis.[3]) Robert Fisk's reporting of the Protestant paramilitaries for The Times in the early 1970s, culminating in his authoritative account of the Ulster Workers' Council (UWC) strike in May 1974,[4] was an isolated example of a journalist who grasped the significance of these groups at that time. Simon Winchester of the Guardian between 1970 and 1972 was, at his best, capable of reporting of the highest calibre.[5] Most journalists and their editors came nowhere near these rare exceptions.

Two important questions need to be asked before analysing in detail Fleet Street's reporting of Northern Ireland. Is it realistic to expect anything better, given the circumstances of press reporting? How indicative is the reporting of the province of the present state of British journalism? On a comparable story – the Vietnam War – the British press in subjective terms did perform better, although still inadequately. Philip Knightley in his critical study of foreign correspondents' reporting of war commented: 'British correspondents were better placed to write about Vietnam than were their American colleagues.'[6] Despite his contention that they were 'reluctant to get deeply involved', Knightley believes that, on the whole, the British press did perform marginally better than their American counterparts. John Pilger of the Daily Mirror and Sunday Mirror, for instance, produced consistently good work over many years in S.E. Asia (he later commented in 1978: 'The coverage of Ireland has been so distorted in this country that if I am going to be forced to contribute to that distortion, I may as well not go.'[7]). Although the expose of the My Lai massacre of March 1968 was started in America by a free-lance reporter, Seymour Hersh, British, European and Japanese newspapers were initially far more ready to use the story than the American press. When famous war correspondent, Martha Gellhorn, was unable in 1966-7 to publish in the United States many of her critical articles on the Vietnam war, they were printed in Britain. More important, the reporting of Northern Ireland is indicative of how the British press has been unable to come to terms with the new circumstances that now face it.[8] In 1970, 95 per cent of British households had a television set[9] and this medium was considered the most important by the Government, the army and the paramilitaries in the province. It is inconceivable to imagine British newspapers exposing Watergate, the journalistic scoop of the last decade, limited as they are by conservative attitudes and legal restrictions. The results of this failure to adjust have been depressing - falling circulations (with the major exception of the Sun), prolonged industrial troubles (particularly on The Times and Observer), numerous take-over bids and the demise of one major national newspaper, the Daily Sketch in 1971, and the threatened closure of several others.

Fleet Street's coverage of Ireland prior to 1968 was desultory and was confined mainly to the reporting of election results and other routine matters. Occasional stories were mainly in the stage Irish vein. Brian Inglis, a journalist with experience of both Ireland and England, relates of this period: 'the kind of stories that Wilson Harris (Editor of the Spectator) most enjoyed hearing about were those which were in the Punch-Oirish tradition, in which the Irish were simply figures of fun.'[10] This lack of coverage is yet another example of the continuing English bias of Britain's national newspapers: events at the fringes appear to diminish in proportion to their distance from London and the south of England. When journalists did venture into the relative unknown, their views were optimistic and uncritical. Roy Perrot of the Observer could report only a few months before the crisis broke: 'Catholics and Protestants have begun to mix with each other with less suspicion and more cordiality than they can remember.'[11] At a very superficial level this may have appeared true but the studies of Richard Rose and Rosemary Harris of society in Northern Ireland demonstrate how fundamentally divided the two communities still were in the 1960s.[12]

There was certainly enough potential for investigatory journalism in Northern Ireland prior to 1968. In many instances the province reflected what Lord Craigavon, its Prime Minister between 1921 and 1940, had called 'a Protestant Parliament and a Protestant State'. The Unionist Party has controlled Stormont since its inception without any break and there had never been a Catholic Cabinet Minister. If there were Catholic members of the Unionist Party, they could only have been a handful and voting patterns were almost entirely on religious lines. Membership of the Orange Order, a society founded specifically as an anti-Catholic body, was virtually an essential prerequisite for any Unionist MP or important Party executive. The Cameron Report gave many examples of discrimination against Catholics in terms of employment and housing.[13] In 1961, only 12 per cent of the Royal Ulster Constabulary (RUC) were Catholics and the 'B' Specials, their emergency auxiliaries, were almost entirely Protestant. In particular, discrimination was widely underpinned by multiple voting in local government elections and blatant gerrymandering of constituency boundaries, particularly in Londonderry.[14] The Special Powers Act placed large reserves of authority in the hands of the Minister of Home Affairs, and this had been used almost exclusively against the Catholic section of the community. Many Catholics in Northern Ireland had never accepted the legitimacy of the province's creation and Nationalist MPs had even refused to attend meetings of Stormont, the Northern Ireland Parliament, until 1925. In areas where Catholics predominated, such as Newry, discrimination was also practised against Protestants. The Catholic stance on separate education and mixed marriages was used by Protestants as evidence of Catholic unwillingness to integrate and events in the South, where the Catholic position on divorce, contraception, adoption and censorship were enacted as law, gave many Protestants in the North enough ammunition to revive the old slogan 'Home Rule Means Rome Rule'. Social problems in Northern Ireland were also completely ignored by the media. In 1967, the unemployment rate for the entire province was 7.7 per cent but with heavy regional concentrations - in Strabane it was 25 per cent and in Londonderry, 20 per cent (these figures were far higher than the British national average). When the lid blew off this pressure cooker of unrest it came as a complete surprise to British newspapers and their readers.

In 1968, Northern Ireland for the first time in a generation was news. The civil rights marches attracted widespread coverage and journalists poured into the province, eager to report on what looked like a major story. (The first major civil rights march was held on August 24 but the first to attract wide publicity was on October 5.) The troubles appeared to have all the 'right' ingredients; for 1968 was the high point of opposition in America and elsewhere to the Vietnam War and the year of the Russian invasion of Czechoslovakia. In France an alliance of workers and students nearly toppled the Fifth Republic and student activism was at a peak in most western democracies. Civil rights with its slogan 'One Man - One Vote' evoked memories of similar campaigns in America and the Third World. The latent violence that lay within Northern Ireland was also something that attracted media attention - press coverage between the first and second civil rights marches increased by 500 per cent as the potential for violence became apparent.[15] Northern Ireland, although part of Britain, might have been the other side of the world for all the average journalist knew about it. Max Hastings, who was to cover the early years of the disturbances for the Evening Standard, later commented: 'I not only knew nothing about the province, I had no sympathies or loyalties of any description - only, possibly, a strong dislike of the principles of the Catholic religion.'[16]

The makeshift nature of early reporting of the situation also meant that some newspaper coverage was erratic and often inadequate. Reacting to parallel events in Europe and America, many of the popular and tabloid newspapers searched in vain for a Northern Irish version of 'Danny the Red'.[17] Efforts to find such a figure, particularly among members of the People's Democracy (PD) movement, turned out to be fruitless. Gaps in knowledge were on occasion filled by stage Irishmen or dimly remembered facts about Ireland. Walter Terry of the Daily Mail, for example, started an article about the Northern Irish General Election (February, 1969) in the following fashion:

> Now, come on, don't pretend you have forgotten. Years ago, in a super film called Odd Man Out, James Mason staggered into the Belfast pub called The Crown, demanded a final drink, then quietly but passionately died in the cause of Ireland, while the rest of the customers boozed themselves away.[18]

Here and in other similar articles, long held images of the Irish, which had nothing to do with the subject under discussion, padded out stories short on fact and analysis.

Initial press reaction to a new Irish crisis was virtually unanimous - strong support, albeit of varying degree., for the Catholics' demand for civil rights. Hastings wrote:

> ...as the weeks went by and personal experience broadened, a detectable feeling for the Catholics crept more and more prominently into everything I wrote, coupled with a dislike for the Protestants, the Unionists and much of what they stood for.[19]

The following editorial from the conservative Daily Mail could have come in the first few months from almost any English newspaper:

> It is nearly 25 years since the rest of Britain decided that everyone over 21, not just householders and businessmen, should be entitled to vote for his local council... It is intolerable that council houses should be allotted for reasons of religion and not of poverty. It is intolerable that Catholics should be denied an equal chance of a job.[20]

There were a number of reasons for this broad-based support: the members of the civil rights movement had justifiable grounds for complaint; evidence to support their claims was readily available; the Catholics, nationalists and the civil rights movement generally proved adept at handling the media (contrasting with the Protestants' scarcely concealed hostility); and Catholic demands for equality and justice were seen to accord with what were considered British standards. Fleet Street's dislike of the Protestants, in contrast. grew in the early stages of the disturbances. The frequent Protestant use of the term 'loyalist' caused embarrassment, as John Chertres, one of The Times's correspondents during this period remarked, 'one still searches for a more suitable label'.[21] Only the Daily Telegraph and to a lesser extent the

Daily Express (and their Sunday counterparts) consistently supported the Unionist Party during this time, although their approval was primarily for the leadership rather than the more militant rank and file.

General sympathy for the Catholics was, however, to last only a short while. Within a year, a distinct anti-Irish feeling (first noticeable in right-wing newspapers but soon spreading to most of Fleet Street) became increasingly apparent. The reasons for this reversion to traditional attitudes were occasioned by events - frustration with the lack of Catholic gratitude for the reforms grudgingly conceded by the Northern Irish Government annoyance with Protestant intransigence and a growing lack of comprehension (except only in terms of Irish insanity) as the sectarian violence escalated, particularly following the large-scale riots of August 1969. The introduction of the army confirmed these impressions. The Times, generally renowned for its sober headlines, called one of its editorials on the August 1969 rioting - 'This Madness'.[22] Among the conservative press there was a growing disenchantment with the whole idea of granting reforms to the Catholic community. As early as January 1969, a Daily Express editorial complained: 'Many of these demonstrators could not care less about civil rights. They are either hooligans looking for a punch-up or anarchists with a grudge against society.'[23]

One phenomenon that emerged in the first few months of press reporting, which has continued ever since, was the building up of any British politician connected with Ireland. This contrasted greatly with previous crises, particularly in the nineteenth and early twentieth centuries, when an Irish appointment was considered a political kiss of death and Ireland became a graveyard of reputations. Any British politician is invariably portrayed as moderate, sensible and tolerant - a marked difference to the Irish. Irish politicians, in contrast, have been judged by the yardstick of how much they conform to what are regarded as British standards of behaviour. James Callaghan, Home Secretary from December 1967 to June 1970, was the first British politician to benefit from this process. After a disastrous time as Chancellor of the Exchequer in the period 1964-7 (in which he had often offered his resignation to Harold Wilson), Northern Ireland was substantially to help him in becoming Leader of the Labour Party and Prime Minister (April 1976). His own account of his dealings with Northern Ireland indicates his delight at this new opportunity.[24] Press coverage of Callaghan's term of office was almost ecstatic; no superlative seemed too good to describe his actions. An editorial in The Times, for instance, almost resembled a hymn of praise:

He did indeed descend into the fallen world of Ulster politics like the incarnation of a spirit inhabiting a different plane of political reality. With

a sure political touch he became everybody's confidant, the embodiment of moderation and helpful concern, an object of hope for those who want both peace and justice in the province.[25]
Yet in 1967, when Northern Irish grievances were first presented to him, he, by his own admission, did nothing and, although there is no doubting his subsequent good intentions and political skill, his actions produced no lasting results. Perhaps the best explanation of this change in attitudes towards British politicians involved in Irish affairs lies in the changed position of Britain in the world. The confident Britain of imperial grandeur expected results and acted accordingly when they were not forthcoming. (Only Arthur Balfour, one of the most draconian Irish Chief Secretaries, increased his standing in the nineteenth century as a result of his time in Ireland.) Britain in the last twenty years is much less confident; it now seems enough for British politicians to be able to make ringing speeches about law and order and the need for compromise.

Fleet Street seriously misjudged the principal politicians of this period. Terence O'Neill with his English accent and manner was given more support than his crumbling power base merited. A profile in The Times approvingly described him in the following fashion: 'At 54 he has had a brilliant career of "youngests" and "first"... His background and family history appeal to a large number of Roman Catholics as well as Protestants.'[26] Most newspapers predicted that O'Neill would win the election of February 1969 and beat Ian Paisley who was standing against him in the Bannside constituency; even the left-wing New Statesman, despite reservations, gave the Prime Minister its blessing.[27] In fact, O'Neill's faction of the Unionist Party just scraped home and he beat Paisley by a mere 1,414 votes - only to remain in power a few weeks longer. Ironically, the men who had done most directly to bring down O'Neill's Government - Brian Faulkner and James Chichester-Clark, both of whom had resigned over his reform programme - were then immediately transformed by much of the press into the vacant role of moderate leaders.

Nothing, however, illustrates the British press' basically anti-Irish perceptions so much as their treatment of Bernadette Devlin.[28] She had first come to some degree of prominence in the civil rights and PD movements in 1968 but her election for Mid-Ulster in April 1969 as the youngest ever MP for Westminster made her front page news. Almost the entire press refused to take her seriously, ignoring her views or else presenting them as something of a joke. Fleet Street treated her like some kind of clockwork doll, an amusing diversion from the main stream of Parliamentary life: the general coverage of her early days as an MP combined sexism with trivialisation and a refusal to see her in any other terms than 'swinging youth' and the then fashionable mini skirt. Her arrival at Westminster (April 22, 1969) was greeted by the following headlines: 'Joan from Tyrone' (Daily Mail), 'A Little Miss but a Big Hit' (Daily Mail), 'Miss Protest MP' (Daily Telegraph), 'I believe, that's the story of Bernadette' (News of the World), 'Cassandra in a Mini Skirt' (Observer) and 'A Celtic St. Joan whose soft answer shuts up bigotry' (Sun). Pictures of her on a swing were inevitably captioned 'And She's Certainly Swinging!' (Daily Express) and 'Swinging into Westminster' (Daily Mail). Even when she produced one of the most successful maiden speeches of modern times, it was viewed not so much for its content but for its effect. 'She was a show-biz hit. Nothing like 5 feet tall Bernadette Devlin, 22 today, has been seen in the Commons for years,' gushed Eric Sewell, Parliamentary correspondent for the Daily Mail.[29] It is very difficult to think of any English MP, even if she had been young and female, receiving quite the same trivialising treatment.

If Devlin had been content to play along with the artificial image created by the media, she would probably have enjoyed a few months of publicity and then have been relegated as a news item. It came as an unpleasant shock to Fleet Street to find that she actually meant what she said in relation to Irish nationalism and socialism. Her involvement in the rioting in Londonderry's Bogside in August 1969 completed the newspapers' disenchantment (a widely-publicised photograph showed her breaking a paving stone). Robert Ottway, in the Daily Sketch, when reviewing her autobiography, wrote: 'The trouble with Bernadette Devlin, who must be the daftest lady ever to occupy the weathered green upholstery in the House of Commons, is that she turns her private deprivations into public grievances.'[30] Once the press turned against Devlin, no accusation or innuendo was too nasty to be used against her. Rumours continued to be printed about her private life, particularly concerning an alleged relationship with her agent, Louden Seth. The Evening Standard referred to her almost always in its gossip column, thereby emphasising to its readers that she was not to be taken seriously. This newspaper in particular tried a number of not very subtle ruses in an effort to discredit or embarrass her. It quoted in one snippet of gossip her full address (an attempt to cause her maximum inconvenience from the public) - a practice which is in direct infringement of all British journalists' unions' codes of ethics.[31] The article concerned a trivial story about her using House of Commons notepaper to ask people not to park outside her flat. Her fall from popularity was completed by her subsequent career her fund raising trips to America (August 1969 and February - March 1971), her arrest and imprisonment in June 1970 (the cause of widespread rioting), the birth of an illegitimate daughter (August 1971) and her assault on Reginald Maudling after Bloody Sunday (February 1972). If Devlin did have faults in handling the press, they were faults of inexperience: she was badly organised, unpunctual and often did not answer correspondence. When, however, she refused to conform to the publicity they had created, newspaper reporters angrily questioned her integrity.

Between 1969 and 1973 Northern Ireland was seldom off the front pages of the British press. It now assumed the status of a major story and every newspaper usually had at least one correspondent permanently based in the province. For major crises the number could increase dramatically; the Guardian had eleven journalists covering the Orange Lodge marches of 1970 and both the Observer and Sunday Times had an even larger (but undisclosed) number investigating the circumstances of Bloody Sunday. A number of journalists were to make or improve their reputations reporting Northern Ireland, two (Holland of the Observer and Winchester of the Guardian) were to be given journalist of the year awards. All sides involved in the conflict had something of a love-hate relationship with the press: all were anxious to present their side of the story but suspicious or hostile if those in opposition were contacted. The army, in particular, was anxious to establish good relations with the media from the start. as many British officers believed that American soldiers had been fatally hindered in Vietnam by critical coverage on television and in the press. The army set up a comprehensive information service at their headquarters in Lisburn, staffed by over twenty full-time members,[32] and the press also became accustomed to elaborately staged missions to meet paramilitary spokesmen and even to attend their occasional press conferences. Andrew Stephen, an Observer correspondent in the province at a later date, explained some of the temptations of the journalist's life there:

> Any journalist working in Northern Ireland is practically spoon-fed with news, views and versions of events...
>
> In fact the newspaperman newly arrived in Belfast finds himself courted from every quarter. As likely as not he will soon be whisked off to a genial lunch at the Officers' Mess in Lisburn; a Provisional IRA front man will invite him home where his charming wife will produce hot buttered toast and coffee; and at the Ulster Defence Association headquarters in the Newtownards Road any visiting journalist is assured of ginger cake and a mug of strong tea...
>
> Being an unadventurous journalist in Belfast is very, very easy. The lazy national newspaperman can stay in his hotel room and lift all his material from the comprehensive local radio and television news coverage and the Belfast Telegraph and still appear well informed.[33]

Most journalists succumbed only too easily to these temptations. The Europa Hotel in Belfast, where most journalists were based, became a symbol of the lack of initiative by the press. It was understandable that pressmen should feel justifiable horror at the many bombings perpetrated by the IRA - the carnage made a great impact on the British people. There was sympathy for the unenviable plight of the soldiers in the province. But these circumstances meant that the press too easily allowed itself to report the official view, even when it was at variance with what was taking place. The press generally failed to provide the information and answers to a number of important questions. Why had many Catholics and Protestants turned against the army after initially welcoming it? Why were paramilitaries able to survive and flourish, despite the terrible consequences of many of their actions? Why, despite a massive British presence, which peaked at 21,000 soldiers in August 1972, was the level of violence still rising and a solution to the problems of the province even less likely? By the end of 1973, 928 people had been killed (642 civilians, 242 soldiers and 44 policemen) and in 1972 alone there were 5,171 injuries, while in 1973 the figure was 2,651. Northern Ireland was not the black and white situation that was depicted in most newspapers: to feel revulsion at IRA bombings should not have meant that support was automatically given to British Government policy.

There was very little in British Government policy to justify such support. The Governments first of Harold Wilson and then Edward Heath continued until March 1972 to pin their hopes on introducing sufficient reforms via the Unionist Governments of Chichester-Clark and Faulkner: no Unionist Government could, however, hope to stay in power and command widespread loyalist support, while at the same time introducing sufficient reforms to placate the Catholics. Moreover, the need for reform, although important in itself, was in any case becoming increasingly subordinate to more fundamental problems within the province. The ineffectual, if harmless, Chichester-Clark continued in power from May 1969 to March 1971 with a rapidly deteriorating security situation, yet British politicians and newspapers continued to believe that he could stem the tide.[34] The Spectator, for instance, wrote in an editorial that Chichester-Clark represented: 'The traditional Unionist squirearchy which (pace Miss Devlin) still embodies the best hope for enlightenment in the murky waters of Northern Ireland politics.'[35] Nothing in his record, however, suggested any grounds for such confidence; he had been an ordinary backbencher and, later, Minister for Agriculture and had resigned over O'Neill's reform programme. Chichester-Clark was a weak man, occupying a difficult position at a particularly difficult time: he was not made of the stuff that makes a saviour.

The same illusory hopes were entertained by most of the press and the British Government for Chichester-Clark's successor - Faulkner.[36] Although a much more adept politician, there was little or no chance of his being a success. He also had resigned over the O'Neill reform package (the O'Neill-Faulkner political rivalry was long and bitterly felt) and he had made almost a profession of militant pro-Unionist and anti-Catholic statements. Even if a critic's allegation that Faulkner was once physically sick when talking about Catholics on a public platform is an exaggeration,[37] a list of his statements during his political career on the Orange Order and religion left little chance of reconciling the Catholic community to his Government. For example, in 1960, he told an Orange rally that the slogans 'No Surrender' and 'Not an Inch' '...expressed better than anything the convictions upon which the majority in Ulster speak with one voice'.[38] Fleet Street largely chose to ignore Faulkner's past record and Max Hastings of the Evening Standard summed up the majority's opinion when he wrote: 'Faulkner - the final chance for Northern Ireland.'[39]

British politicians, despite any private reservations, continued to receive little criticism from the press. Nowhere was this more apparent than in the reporting of the Minister mainly responsible for Northern Ireland between June 1970 and March 1972, Reginald Maudling, the Deputy Leader of the Conservative Party and Home Secretary.[40] Maudling showed little interest in the province and his whole attitude was summed up in a remark as he flew back to the mainland after his first official visit (June 1970): 'For God's sake bring me a large Scotch. What a bloody awful place.'[41] It is not surprising that under such leadership Northern Ireland's affairs drifted disastrously. Yet Maudling largely escaped criticism or when the press did attack him, their strictures were of the mildest variety. 'Mr Maudling...,' commented a Financial Times editorial with great understatement, 'has not taken the psychological part of his task seriously enough.'[42] Yet it was not just this part of his task that Maudling had neglected but the whole basic problem and this lack of direction was to have important repercussions.

The British press in the period 1969-73 generally supported a number of policy decisions that had disastrous consequences. There was virtually no condemnation of the Falls Road curfew in Belfast (3rd-5th July 1970), which subsequently led to a number of soldiers being convicted of looting.[43] Yet this was to be the first time the Provisional IRA went on to the offensive and saw the final ending of cordiality between the troops and those living in the Catholic ghetto areas. Far more serious was British newspaper support for internment (August 9, 1971), an almost classic example of how not to conduct anti-guerrilla operations (many soldiers and politicians now, off the record, tacitly admit this).[44] It was implemented on out of date information and was discriminatory as virtually every suspect interned at four o'clock in the morning was Catholic, despite the Protestant contribution to the violence. It was inefficiently carried out as rumours had been circulating for some weeks that the move was coming (the IRA was later to claim that it had been tipped off); most of the main IRA suspects were not at home when the troops arrived and there was a number of innocent people wrongly arrested. Most important of all, any limited military gains were completely outweighed by the furious reaction from the Catholic community: the subsequent riots were the worst to date and the IRA received increased support. On the day after internment all British newspapers, with the exception of the Communist Morning Star, supported the move. Even that traditional champion of civil rights and self-appointed keeper of Britain's conscience, the Guardian, stated in an editorial: 'Internment without trial is hateful, repressive and undemocratic. In the existing Irish situation, most regrettably, it is also inevitable.'[45] (The Observer's editorial next Sunday also did not condemn the move.[46]) The Times's headline to its editorial called it 'A Sad Necessity';[47] while on the right, the press was even more in favour, the Daily Telegraph concluding in an editorial: '...it was overdue to the outraged citizens of Ulster and the hard-pressed troops.'[48] When troops shot thirteen demonstrators on Bloody Sunday (January 1972), Fleet Street almost entirely accepted the army's version of events:[49] if the troops were seen to be in any way at fault, this was excused by the intolerable situation they faced. A Daily Mail editorial asserted: 'British bullets will be found in most of their bodies... but the blood is on the conscience of the irresponsible political leaders and the fanatical IRA.'[50] When direct rule was introduced, the press depicted it as a wise and statesmanlike move, instead of a dilatory action, taken because the Government had run out of alternatives. All of Fleet Street, except the Daily Express and Daily Telegraph, echoed a Daily Mirror editorial which described direct rule as 'right' and 'courageous'.

There were a few exceptions to these general trends in British reporting. The New Statesman in August 1971 became the first major newspaper to call for the withdrawal of British troops after a year's ultimatum.[51] (The Daily Mirror has been, so far, the only major daily newspaper to endorse such a call.[52]) The New Statesman's coverage of events in Northern Ireland improved considerably in July 1972 when Mary Holland began writing nearly all of its articles on the subject. Andrew Boyd in Tribune was one of the few journalists to explain to a British audience the impossibility of Faulkner reconciling Catholics and Protestants in the province.[53] It was the Sunday Times that broke the story of the methods used in the interrogation of people detained during internment, which eventually led to Britain being found guilty of torture in the European Court of Human Rights in 1977.[54] The Morning Star also paid attention to the rise of Protestant paramilitaries in 1971-early 1972 - a subject almost completely ignored by other newspapers at that time. Simon Winchester and Simon Hoggart of the Guardian were, on occasions, prepared to follow up individual allegations against the army, as in the cases of Seamus Cusack and Desmond Beattie. A few journalists, such as Winchester and John Graham of the Financial Times, who were eye-witnesses to Bloody Sunday, were able to demonstrate some of the inconsistencies of the official version, such as the non-existent fusillade of shots from the IRA.[55]

The tendency to see the Irish as 'the enemy', 'aliens' or 'insane' increased throughout the period 1969-73, as British Governments and the army became more embroiled in Northern Ireland. Hostile images of the Irish began to dominate reporting with a growing assumption that they were violent, stupid and non-rational. Although this stereotyping was most pronounced in the conservative press, hardly any newspaper was immune from this development. The Spectator for several years from 1971 was obsessed by the idea of 'the Irish mess'. An editorial explained:

> The Irish mess is the Irish fault and Irishmen will have to clear up the mess. The best and most the English can do is, for a limited time only, to prevent the fault worsening, and prevent the mess spreading.[56]

The Spectator was so taken with the 'mess' image of the Irish that when new developments took place in Northern Ireland, it would often put a headline on its cover 'More Mess'.[57] In this fashion, the Spectator attempted to absolve the British from their responsibility and to depict the Irish as nasty, dirty and inferior. Winchester's book, In Holy Terror, an account of his journalistic experiences in the province, although often informative, has almost an obsession with the smallness of the Irish and the largeness and the commonsense of the English. He described the arrival of William Whitelaw to take over from Stormont after the imposition of direct rule in the following fashion:

> He was, by comparison to those who had gone before, an impressive figure. He seemed very large - Stormont politicians, we suddenly realised then, were all really rather small men, either in physique or in intellect and usually in both. Whitelaw's size, his warmth, his apparent total competence came across hugely well...[58]

In contrast, Desmond Boal is decribed as 'the foxy little barrister' (p.38), Brian MacRoberts - 'the dumpy little gauleiter' (p.44), Joe Burns - 'a small country man of little ability' (p.138), Jack Lynch, who is in fact nearly six foot, 'the diminutive Irish Prime Minister' (p.176) and Billy Hull -

'the slightly ridiculous little fat man' (p.180). It comes as no surprise, therefore, to find the chapter mainly devoted to Brian Faulkner (ch.7) is entitled 'A Cunning Little Man'.

From about 1973 British newspaper interest in Northern Ireland has rapidly diminished. With a few noticeable exceptions, journalists based there are very much 'the second eleven' and some newspapers have no representation at all, relying on the occasional visit for news. The cameraderie of the Europa Hotel has long since passed. Press interest only revives temporarily when something new or spectacular occurs, such as the UWC strike (May 1974), the Queen's visit (August 1977), the La Mon Restaurant bombing (February 1978) and the assassinations of Airey Neave (March 1979) and Lord Mountbatten (August 1979). Three basic reasons appear to exist for this state of affairs. Firstly, repetition tends to blunt most stories, unless the press is prepared to dig a little deeper or look beyond the mechanical reporting of the bare details of a story. Winchester commented about the conditions of reporting as early as 1971: 'the editors tended to want to know how long it would be before the total dead reached a certain, arbitrary figure, rather than the tragic circumstances of each individual death; funerals that rated a page in 1970 rated less than a couple of lines at the base of page three a year later.'[59] Northern Irish stories have increasingly been given smaller amounts of space or have been tagged on at the end of news reports on the television and radio; on a growing number of occasions they have been left out completely. Reading British newspapers today, it is sometimes difficult to realise that there really is a crisis in Northern Ireland at all. Secondly, the press have long since moved on to other stories. It is symptomatic that in 1973 Winchester left Northern Ireland for America to report Watergate. Lastly, the British have lost patience with Northern Ireland, they have become confused and exasperated. John MacKintosh, a former Labour MP, echoed the opinion of many when he stated in 1976: 'the British public are bored to death with Northern Ireland. They want to shut it from their minds ... it is a boring, repetitious series of murders which are going on night after night ...'[60] British public opinion has increasingly oscillated between a 'get tough' policy and a desire to quit Northern Ireland altogether. This growing lack of interest by the British press has not been a uniform process; it was noticeable as early as 1971 that coverage in the 'tabloid' and 'popular' newspapers was declining but the feeling quickly spread even to the 'quality' category as well.

Violence has dominated Fleet Street's reporting of Northern Ireland: the killed, the maimed, the injured and the bereaved make for graphic, sometimes horrifying, detail. But this kind of reporting is inadequate and insufficient; both the responsibility for the violence and its causes are rarely explained to British readers. Newspapers too often tend to blame all the violence in the province on the IRA and reports have seemed increasingly to suggest that the Irish in toto are naturally prone to violence. It is impossible (and possibly always will be) precisely to allocate the responsibility for every act of violence, and the efforts of several well-oiled propaganda machines have not made it any easier. Even the conviction of a person in a law court has not ended speculation over some incidents. However a general pattern can be established, based on careful analytical studies such as those by Michael McKeown and Martin Dillon and Denis Lehane.[61] It is difficult to escape the general conclusion that many journalists are not concerned enough, can not be bothered or do not find the time to investigate independently many of the incidents, even those which involved major loss of life. With a few exceptions, Fleet Street has usually been content to accept official explanations without demur and any critical analysis is quashed by the undoubted horror engendered by many of the actions of the paramilitaries.

A reader relying solely on the British press could be forgiven for forming the impression that the IRA is almost entirely to blame for the violence in Northern Ireland. The IRA has certainly had a major part in the disturbances in the last decade but it is not the only component; yet reporting of the violence used by the Protestant paramilitaries or, on occasions, by the army and the police has largely been ignored or minimised. Successive Governments have been successful in creating an impression that merely to question the official line means the person concerned is automatically an apologist for the IRA. In 1968-9 the IRA made a minimal contribution to the violence; it was weak, divided and had sold most of its arms to the Free Wales Army.[62] It was precisely this lack of action that provoked the split between the Officials and the Provisionals. Yet the press, prompted by officialdom continued to believe that the IRA was a major force in this period. During the August 1969 rioting in Belfast, for instance, The Times commented: 'No doubt they [the IRA] are in the thick of it.'[63] This tendency to blame everything on the IRA increased even further with the formation of the Provisional IRA (December 1969). Many of the subsequent actions of the Provisionals have been horrifying; few would wish to excuse them (certainly not the author of this article) but they were not the only cause of violence in Northern Ireland after 1969. Eamonn McCann, the Irish civil rights and socialist activist, in his study of the British press reporting of Northern Ireland in the years 1968-71 has demonstrated in great detail how Fleet Street was prepared to accept the official version of virtually all incidents.[64] (McCann's pamphlet, on the other hand, dismisses the actions of the IRA in three lines.) McCann's case, however, stands and has not been questioned in detail.

The tendency to blame the Provisional IRA increased even further once it started a major bombing campaign in Northern Ireland and Britain (1971-2). The press, with every reason, condemned these random killings (it has been noticeable that their denunciations increased once the bombings spread to the mainland). Extensive coverage was devoted to major bombing incidents, such as the Officers' Mess at Aldershot (February 1972), Bloody Friday in Belfast (July 1972), two London railway stations (September 1973), the Tower of London (July 1974), and Warrenpoint (August 1979), but these and other incidents too often obscured a more complex picture. When, for instance, a bomb went off at McGurk's Bar, Belfast, killing 15 people, the press largely ascribed it to the IRA, despite a large amount of circumstantial evidence to the contrary. The Times story by John Chartres had its headline 'Blast that killed 15 may have been IRA error',[65] a typical example of the coverage it received. In August 1977, a member of a Protestant paramilitary group was sentenced to 15 life sentences for this killing.

Protestant violence, in contrast, has been minimised by most of the British press. In March 1969 a bombing raid on the Castlereagh Power Station helped to bring down the O'Neill Government; the press too readily accepted that this was the work of the IRA - in fact, it was the responsibility of extreme loyalists. It took Fleet Street a long time to realise that the sectarian assassinations that started in 1972-3 and which have continued on and off to the present day have involved Protestant organisations as well as the IRA. There was a number of reasons for this apparent lack of interest. The IRA, particularly the Provisionals, were by 1972 firmly established in the mind of the British press as the main cause of violence; they were an obvious enemy, working on a familiar pattern. Protestant killings commenced at a time when press interest in the province was diminishing; another death was often perfunctorily reported or not reported at all. The IRA attacked British soldiers and detonated bombs on the mainland, while loyalists usually attacked only the IRA and Catholics in general. The tangled web of IRA (Official and Provisional), IRSP, UDA, UFF, UVF and other similar organisations has sometimes made it difficult to establish responsibility and many newspapers make very little effort to do so. There has been a discernible feeling that if rivalry in the IRA or among Protestant paramilitaries or 'tit for tat' killings between the two communities continues, this simply rids Northern Ireland of a few more militants, even though some of the victims have been picked at random as revenge killings. By far the most informed writer on Protestant paramilitaries was Robert Fisk of The Times, who between 1972 and 1975 gave outstanding coverage of this phenomenon. Occasional articles in similar vein also appeared in the Guardian, Morning Star, New Statesman, Observer, Private

Eye and Sunday Times.

The violence in Northern Ireland is an Irish tragedy within a British framework. For if individual Irishmen deserve condemnation for acts of violence, Britain collectively bears a degree of responsibility for the background against which these deeds take place. Only a few newspapers have been prepared to admit any such possibility of guilt. It has been Britain both in the past and in the present crisis who has determined the very regrettable fact of Irish history concerning violence - it works. Once again in this crisis - as in the past - changes and concessions have been granted after violence or the threat of violence when argument has failed: this lesson has not been lost on either the Catholic or Protestant communities. No connection is seen between British policy (or its lack) and the level of violence in Northern Ireland. British decisions, such as internment, which led to an increase in violence without any long-term benefit. were overwhelmingly supported when they were introduced and conveniently purged from memory when they were seen to fail. The contribution of the soldiers and police towards the level of violence in the province is realised only by a few newspapers. Once again, the British have increasingly come to rely on stock stereotypes of the Irish as naturally being prone to violence. A Daily Mirror 'Assessment' on Ireland asserted that 'the Irish have a deplorable tendency in times of trouble to reach for the gun or petrol bomb rather than the ballot box'.[66] The violence of Northern Ireland is generally presented as the product of 'gunmen', 'thugs', 'psychopaths', 'terrorists' and other such terms of convenience. This view was accurately satirised by Private Eye when it wrote an explanation of the terms used in official hand-outs in the province: 'Gunmen: anybody shot dead by British soldiers.'[67] These impressions are borne out by a detailed survey by Philip Elliot of the reporting of Irish news by British and Irish newspapers in the period September - October 1974 and April - May 1975.[68] He noted that Irish newspapers of whatever background tried to provide more explanation of the violence than did their British counterparts. Another old chestnut, which has also been revived, is the idea of a few subversives being the cause of all the violence. 'The vital point is to deal with the thugs...' insisted Sir Hamar Greenwood to the British Cabinet in 1921,[69] a statement then followed by the traditional plea for a 'get-tough' policy. Yet if this theory is true for the present disturbances, the violence would have ceased long ago as the dead mount and the prisons fill. 'If you could take 300 people out of this country today you would not see another petrol bomber,' wrote Noel Whitcombe in the Sun in 1969.[70] His prediction has not proved correct. The right wing press has also been able to discover large-scale communist subversion, despite the fact that Ireland remains a deeply conservative country. Brendan

Abbott of the Daily Express, for example, believed that Russia was behind both the Official and Provisional IRA:

> Its objects for doing this are devastatingly simple. By backing the more indiscriminately violent Provisionals it hopes to bring the country to its knees as quickly as possible.
>
> By backing the Officials its hope is that the traditional Republican movement and Communist elements in Ulster will eventually take over in the wake of a civil war.[71]

Despite a limited amount of arms being imported from Eastern Europe, these and similar theories rely more on imagination than any factual basis.[72]

Most newspapers contrasted the army with the wild Irish, showing the soldiers as patient, long-suffering and virtuous. Such reporting failed to understand the soldiers' contribution to the violence, the role of the army in the province and the changing conditions it faced. Three periods of reporting the army can be discerned. Firstly, from August 1969, the introduction of the army, to July 1970, the time of the Falls Road Curfew in Belfast, the soldiers won universal backing from every British newspaper. Even those newspapers, such as the New Statesman, which are traditionally suspicious of the army, gave it support.[73] Secondly, the Falls Road Curfew, which provoked numerous allegations of looting (the army later admitted that 60 such incidents did take place), saw the first few qualms being exhibited in certain sections of the press, although the great majority of newspapers still overwhelmingly supported the soldiers. Lastly, the results of internment (August 1971) provoked serious condemnation in a few newspapers and unease in some others, when it became evident that the army had used 'ill-treatment' (to use the terminology suggested by the official Compton Report[74]) in the interrogation of some internees. For the first time, Fleet Street was confronted with hard evidence that the soldiers were not the virtuous peace-keepers of Government hand-outs. The rising level of the violence (the first soldier to die in the province was killed in February 1971 and by August 1980 the total stood at 438 – 104 belonging to the locally recruited Ulster Defence Regiment (UDR)) has meant that the press has increasingly seen the army in terms of war terminology. For most newspapers questioning the troops' basic function in Northern Ireland remains unthinkable; a few newspapers with a liberal stance continue to excuse any particular 'excesses' by the belief that these are the work of a few 'bad apples' or 'black sheep'. Underlying this is the unexamined assumption that if the army was to leave there would be 'a blood-bath'. A very small minority of the press have since 1971 called for the withdrawal of the soldiers.

The British press failed to realise that the circumstances

of the introduction of the troops in August 1969 were only temporary. For Catholics, particularly in the ghetto areas of Belfast and Londonderry, the soldiers represented a guarantee that grievances would speedily be met - when they were not, the soldiers began to be viewed in a very different light. Many Protestants, in their turn, were soon angry that the army was not taking strong enough measures to end what they saw as Catholic 'subversion'. The growing militancy of the IRA, particularly the Provisionals, further aggravated the situation. Fleet Street generally did not understand that nothing in Irish history suggested that British soldiers could act as an impartial force in Ireland: indeed everything suggested the reverse. Nevertheless, there was often a suggestion of World War Two reporting in many newspapers with the British Tommy once again restoring decency against formidable odds. The Daily Sketch caught the initial mood of the press in an editorial:

> British troops, however, have an honourable history of playing Charlie in the middle. They're used to refereeing riots and punch-ups.
>
> The British Army kept Hindu and Moslem apart in India. Malay and Chinese in the Far East. Greek and Turk in Cyprus.[75]

Only a few commentators, such as John Whale of the Sunday Times, predicted that any involvement of troops would be a long term one.[76] The warm welcome the troops received (forever symbolised by cups of tea) did not last for long. The slowness of reforms, the emergence of the Provisional IRA and the spread of violence soon meant that the soldiers were increasingly drawn into conflict with Catholics. Protestants also began to feel disquiet as the army did not appear to crush the IRA. Despite these changes, British newspapers continued to print fulsome tributes and to paint an out-of-date picture. The headline of an article by Rhona Churchill in the Daily Mail was 'When tea and cakes are RC and the bath water's Protestant';[77] this and similar articles provided a false impression of the army's position in the province.

Between August 1969 and July 1970 the British press had to face a situation where the official rationale for keeping the army in Northern Ireland - 'holding the ring' while reforms were introduced - looked less and less realistic. Many newspapers refused to face either the growing unpopularity of the soldiers with both communities or the continuing allegations against some members of the army. The Daily Express commented in an editorial: 'No troops in the world could have done the job better. That should be said again and again.'[78] Starting with Private Eye,[79] a few newspapers, such as the Morning Star, New Statesman and Tribune, began to print allegations against the army. Some of the charges were propaganda - many were not, but most of the press refused to countenance any suggestion against the army. Liberal consciences could be cleared by indicating that any such charges were the exception to the general rule. The Sun in an editorial stated:

> Quite possibly some accusations of looting and destruction may prove justified. Every army has its black sheep.
>
> But we don't doubt either, that most accusations of this kind are exaggerated or even invented. Irishmen tend to have vivid imaginations.[80]

It was the Falls Road Curfew with its widespread and substantiated allegations against the soldiers - many of whom the army later agreed to be in the wrong - that prompted a small minority of the press to be openly critical of the troops. Even some of the journalists who continued to support the army were becoming increasingly uneasy and sceptical in private.

The imposition of internment was a watershed for the army in Northern Ireland. It was not so much the soldiers' part in this inept and bungled operation (many of the army's officers were, in fact, opposed to internment at the time) but the details of the methods used to interrogate the internees that highlighted the problems of the army's presence. The ample evidence of brutality could not be excused by 'the bad apple' strategem: the interrogation techniques had obviously been planned well in advance, permission had been granted by those in authority and the procedures had been duly carried out. Despite these revelations, most newspapers continued to believe that internment and the army's strategy were being successful. Brendan Abbott of the Daily Express, reporting on internment and its interrogation techniques, produced almost a precis of the official hand-out:

> The policy of internment has been a 'roaring success' a senior officer in Belfast told me yesterday.
>
> Enough arms to equip two full battalions of 600 men have been seized as a direct result of the interrogation of suspects by the Royal Ulster Constabulary's Special Branch.[81]

A new argument was, however, beginning to appear in some conservative newspapers. This tacitly agreed that some form of torture had been used but that this was necessary to beat the terrorists. The Daily Telegraph stated in an editorial: 'It is also hard to see how unpleasant measures intended to weaken the morale of those under investigation can be avoided.'[82] Only a small minority of the press openly condemned these methods which provided a heaven-sent opportunity for IRA propaganda. A Sunday Times editorial headlined these interrogation techniques 'A Lowering of Civilised Standards'.[83]

Since 1971 the position of the army in Northern Ireland has essentially remained the same. Instead of being a means to solving the problem it has become part of the problem itself. Actions, such as internment and Bloody Sunday, have done irrevocable harm to political stability and lasting peace. Numerous incidents have harmed the relationship between the soldiers and the man in the street. Of course, the army has been the target of considerable provocation and numerous assaults but this only underlines the point that the soldiers are not seen as a neutral force in the province. The crux of the matter is that the army remains a blunt instrument to perform a very delicate task; soldiers are trained in the use of force - it is not surprising that they have been prepared to retaliate on a massive scale to what they see as terrorism. It may be true that the British army is one of the mildest in the world but this ignores the special circumstances of Irish history. Despite a few reservations, Fleet Street has continued to print the optimistic utterances of the soldiers. Just two weeks before Bloody Sunday and an all time low in Anglo-Irish relations, an army officer told Peter Jenkins of the Guardian:

> We are definitely winning, if we haven't won already. Sporadic violence will continue for a long while probably, but they're reduced to putting their bombs in lemonade carts and empty warehouses. Their recruits are 16-year-old boys. It's turned out an easier job here than it was in Cyprus, and Eoka weren't up to much either.[84]

In October 1977, Roy Mason, the then Secretary of State, announced that the IRA could 'no longer sustain a campaign'. Even army successes, such as Operation Motorman (July 1972), in which the soldiers temporarily occupied Northern Ireland's No Go areas, have had no lasting effect on the province. Serious doubts continue to appear occasionally in some newspapers: John Graham, for example, of the Financial Times commented in 1971:

> The British forces, if given the chance, will win the present campaign; but they will at the same time create the IRA of the 1980s, if indeed they have not already done so...
>
> And for every IRA man lost - either shot by the British or captured and interned - there are two or three recruits...[85]

Nevertheless, only the Daily Mirror (despite it being a jingoistic supporter of the soldiers), the Morning Star and the New Statesman have called for the withdrawal of the troops. Subsequent events have only underlined the futility of the army's presence. In May 1974, the army watched as militant Protestants virtually took over the running of the province during the UWC Strike, backed by wide-scale intimidation, and overthrew the legally elected power-sharing

Executive. Although the army's presence is now nearly half of what it was in 1972, it is still a considerable force. Moreover, the policy of 'Ulsterisation' the handing back of responsibility for security to the Police - is only a tacit way of giving back the control of the province to the Protestants. But the press has long since given up the debate of such issues, even the death of another British soldier often getting little or no coverage, to say nothing of the policy that put him there in the first place.

Nearly as important as what has been included by the press is what has been left out or only given scant coverage. There has been hardly any mention of religion or religious issues, such as censorship, contraception, church-state relations, divorce, education, mixed marriages, papal infallibility and the Orange Order. Yet this is a major omission in looking at a problem where the two sides have religious labels and religion plays such an important part in everyday life. Too often when the British press has discussed religion in Ireland, it has been simply to dismiss Irish belief as 'bigotry', 'sectarianism' and 'prejudice'. (The only noticeable exception to this generalisation has been the Catholic weekly, The Tablet.) There is a contradiction in this approach, for though the press appears to believe the problem to be non-religious, there have been repeated calls by Fleet Street for the various denominations to use their influence to end the violence. The News of the World, for instance, is just one newspaper that has urged the clergy 'to speak out from the pulpit'.[86] It is interesting to note the degree of latent anti-Catholicism that still exists in Britain. Some of the prejudice has been unheeding, as in the almost universal use of the form 'Roman Catholic', a source of offence to many Catholics. A letter writer to the Guardian expressed the opinion: 'The Roman Catholic Church has many good points but the urge to give a fairly accurate account of a physical fact is not one of them.'[87] On the few occasions that Catholicism in Ireland has been discussed, it has been simply to dismiss it as 'illiberal' in the centre and left-wing press and as 'subversive' on the right.

A clearer understanding of religious issues might have helped a British readership understand the career of Ian Paisley.[88] Before 1968 he was usually presented, even in the quality press, as an aberration, a throw-back to some dimly remembered age, a freak. From 1968 Paisley was denounced by all sections of Fleet Street as a 'bigot', 'zealot', 'fanatic' and 'rabble-rouser'. The Daily Sketch, for example, denounced him as 'the snarling zealot of Ulster',[89] while to the News of the World he was a 'Merchant of Hate'.[90] Whatever Paisley is, he is certainly not a thick-skinned buffoon but an efficient and intelligent politician, however inflammatory his message. He is, therefore, a far more complex and dangerous individual than the narrow-minded bigot depicted in most British newspapers. Paisley may appear outlandish in Britain but he does not appear so in Northern Ireland where he is but one in a long line of Protestant fundamentalist preachers, such as Hugh 'Roaring' Hanna and Henry Cooke. From 1972 the press even began on occasions to portray Paisley as something of a moderate - a man tamed by the British system; this was to be a serious misjudgement. Walter Terry of the Daily Mail heralded in the headline to a profile: 'This astonishing transformation in the life of Rev. Ian Paisley... Exit the Bully Boy Enter a Man of Stature.' It continued:

> We underestimated his shrewdness as did many fellow politicians. And somewhere among the tortured politics of his province, Ian Paisley changed - enough to see the obvious; that reason makes more sense in a mad situation than blind denunciation from a pulpit.
>
> Subtlety became his weapon; skill and patience took charge of the demagogue.[91]

Apart from Paisley's own assurances, it is difficult to discover on what evidence this and similar statements have been made, but they are difficult to reconcile with the man who in January 1974 would help wreck debate in Northern Ireland's elected Assembly and would take an active part in the UWC strike and the attempted Protestant strike of May 1977. By not trying to understand the role of religion in Ireland, except in the most simplistic terms, the British press has failed to understand a fundamental dimension to the problem.

Other stories that have received little or no coverage are paramilitary links with suppliers of arms (particularly in America, Europe and the Middle East), paramilitary protection rackets, illegal drinking dens in the province, Protestant paramilitary links with the UDR and RUC and the funding of the IRA by large-scale bank robberies. There has been scant attention paid to 'black' propaganda and illegal intelligence activities by the army, as in articles by David Blundy of the Sunday Times in 1977[92] and Howard Monks, Stephen Scott and Duncan Campbell in the New Statesman in 1979.[93] Blundy, for example, gave evidence of how the army had attempted to sabotage the Northern Ireland Office (NIO) dialogue with the Provisional IRA by leaking a fake intelligence summary which gave ammunition to Paisley to attack the NIO as 'soft' and how Merlyn Rees had been led to believe that four guard dogs had been burned to death by internees after the burning of Long Kesh - prompting him into making a powerful speech condemning this 'sadistic' - and fictional - atrocity. He also revealed official efforts to blacken loyalist politicians, such as William Craig and Ian Paisley, the detonation of explosions in order to blame the IRA, the planting of ammunition and the use of non-standard weaponry to shoot at civilians. The Sunday Times also showed in 1977 that the army had been using faked National Union of Journalists (NUJ) cards for soldiers posing as photographers.[94] Another issue that has not been investigated in sufficient depth is the conditions in H Block, Long Kesh, where prisoners have been conducting a campaign for political status by total non-cooperation with the authorities. When in August 1978, for example, Dr Tomas O'Fiaich, the Catholic Primate of All Ireland, made an attack on the H Block system, it received little coverage in the press. Those newspapers that did report the Primate's words dismissed them in a few paragraphs; two of them (the Daily Express and Daily Telegraph[95]) used the Anglicised version of his name as a deliberate insult. In general, it has been the 'fringe' press, such as the Leveller and Time Out, which has been prepared to tackle this kind of issue.[96]

Journalists in Northern Ireland have also been subject to editorial and official pressure. In 1978, the Observer, for example, pulped an entire edition of its colour supplement because the Editor-in-Chief, Conor Cruise O'Brien, disapproved of an article by Mary Holland about a Londonderry woman, Mary Nelis. Some journalists who have bucked the system, even in a minor fashion, have been refused any form of co-operation from the authorities and other forms of pressures have also been placed on them. When Andrew Stephen, an experienced reporter on Northern Ireland, joined the Sunday Telegraph from the Observer, the NIO telephoned one of his editors and suggested that he be switched to another story. Officialdom, the editor was told, considered Stephen 'irresponsible', 'not helpful' and 'misguided'.[97] Robert Fisk, Simon Winchester and Simon Hoggart have all on different occasions been refused access to army briefings. The then Head of the Army PR unit, Peter Broderick, even wrote to The Times's office, describing Fisk as 'a hostile reporter'.[98] By leaking information in advance to sympathetic newspapers, the Government of the day was able to defuse press criticism concerning the Widgery Report on Bloody Sunday and the European Court of Human Rights's verdict on the interrogation of suspects during internment. The Daily Mail's front page headline, for instance, on the day of the Widgery Report's publication was 'Widgery Clears The Army' and it was not until pages fourteen and fifteen that the reader discovered, in much smaller print, that it had also criticised the soldiers.[99]

The British press has generally failed to provide its readership with the information and the analysis needed to make up its mind on Northern Ireland. Alternatives to the present bi-partisan policy, such as troop withdrawal, a United Nations or neutral peacekeeping force and redrawing the province's boundaries, have received little or no consideration. For over ten years, Labour and Conservative Governments have striven for the well-intentioned but

194

unachievable goal of power-sharing within the present structure of Northern Ireland: yet nothing has indicated that this goal is achievable, everything suggests the reverse. Green and White Papers, voting reforms, referenda, the Assembly, the Convention and other constitutional proposals have all failed to alter the basic electoral arithmetic of the province. Over a decade of community strife has hardened centuries-old divisions, not brought the two communities together as the British fondly hope. Fleet Street has alternated between periods of unreasonable optimism and dark despair. 'The middle opinion,' wrote the Economist in January 1969, 'is still the majority in Ulster.'[100] There is little or no middle ground in Northern Ireland and a solution based on such hopes, however worthy, has virtually no hope of success. Irish politics are not based on the British virtues of compromise and moderation. When each attempt to produce such a solution has failed, Fleet Street has reacted with anger and contempt. After the success of the loyalist strike in 1974, the Daily Mail wrote: 'Hope, like the lights, seems to have been finally snuffed out.'[101] 'What do we want for Northern Ireland, this wretched God-stricken back alley of Europe where they shoot peoples' kneecaps?' rhetorically asked the Daily Express on Christmas Eve 1977, but could provide no answer.[102] Hopes for compromise policies are grasped at like straws. Each constitutional proposal or reform has been billed as 'the last chance' - the Guardian even managed in 1972 to give Northern Ireland two last chances in the space of six months.[103] The reporting of the Peace Movement in 1976-7 is a classic example of a sincere and well-intentioned movement, built up by the British media out of all proportions to its actual strength in the province. Andrew Stephen of the Observer correctly noted in January 1977: 'It is a telling paradox that both the movement and its leaders receive more recognition the further they are away from the Northern Ireland ghettos, where they are viewed with increasing cynicism if not downright detestation.'[104] This is not to argue that the Peace People did not desire worthwhile goals but there was little chance of these objectives being achieved. Yet the politicians and the press continue to feel that British policy is working. Richard Crossman, a member of the Labour Cabinet, was to write in his diary in November 1969: '...I couldn't help reflecting on what an amazingly good job the Labour Government has done in Northern Ireland.'[105] William Whitelaw, the Northern Irish Chief Secretary in 1972-3, received paeans of praise from nearly every newspaper. The Daily Mail wrote in 1973: 'Mr Whitelaw has brought off the impossible... It took the Northern Irish 350 years. It took Willie Whitelaw 20 months.'[106] (When Whitelaw ran for the office of Leader of the Conservative Party in February 1975, his 'success' in Northern Ireland was greatly used by his supporters to argue his claim. Yet his power sharing arrangements lasted only five months and collapsed in failure.) The Daily Express, never a newspaper generally to enthuse over Labour politicians, wrote in 1977 that Roy Mason is 'easily the best, toughest, least tractable and most effective Secretary of State ever'.[107] Despite growing cynicism in private, most journalists continue to report the official line. 'Tension has gone from most parts of Ulster,' reported the headline to an article by Christopher Thomas in The Times in August 1980.[108] A few days later the same journalist's article from Northern Ireland had the headline 'Four killed, 22 hurt in Ulster'.[109] Above all else, British newspapers have generally failed to explain that a solution to Northern Ireland must start in Britain, not in Northern Ireland.

Notes

1   This study of British newspapers is based on all London-based national daily newspapers, the two London evening newspapers (these were reduced to one in 1980). seven weeklies (Economist, Listener, New Statesman, Punch, Spectator, Tablet and Tribune), all London-based national Sunday newspapers and one fortnightly (Private Eye).
2   Useful analysis is provided in Campaign for Free Speech in Ireland, The British Media and Ireland (London, 1979) and E. McCann, The British Press in Northern Ireland (London, Northern Ireland Socialist Research Centre, 1972).
3   The Sunday Times Insight Team, Ulster (Harmondsworth, Penguin Books, 1972).
4   R. Fisk, The Point of No Return: The Strike which Broke the British in Ulster (London, Times Books and Andre Deutsch, 1975).
5   For Winchester's experiences of reporting in Northern Ireland, see S. Winchester, In Holy Terror (London, Faber and Faber, 1974).
6   P. Knightly, The First Casualty (London, Andre Deutsch, 1975), p.383. For an 'American' view of Northern Ireland, see A. Bailey, Acts of Union: reports on Ireland 1973-79 (London, Faber and Faber, 1980). (Bailey is, in fact, English but is based mostly in America and his book comprises reports for the New Yorker.)
7   Time Out, 29 September 1978.
8   For British newspaper coverage of the last Anglo-Irish crisis, see D. Boyce, Englishmen and Irish Troubles (London, Jonathan Cape, 1972).
9   C. Seymour-Ure, The Political Impact of Mass Media (London, Constable, 1974), p.209. Seymour-Ure points out, however, that four out of five adults in Britain read some form of newspaper on a regular basis.
10   B. Inglis, West Briton (London, Faber and Faber, 1962), p.177.

11   Observer, 26 May 1968.
12   R. Harris, Prejudice and Toleration in Ulster
(Manchester, Manchester University Press, 1972) and R.
Rose, Governing Without Consensus (London, Faber and
Faber, 1971).
13   The Cameron Report, HMSO Belfast. Command 532. 1969.
14   The name of Northern Ireland's second city has remained
disputed over several centuries - 'Londonderry' is used by
Unionists and 'Derry' by Nationalists. I use 'Londonderry' as
that is its official title; no political connotation is intended.
15   M. Davies, 'The Role of the Press in the Recent
Northern Irish Crisis', unpublished dissertation for
B.Sc.(Soc.), London School of Economics, 1970.
16   M. Hastings, Ulster 1969 (London, Victor Gollancz,
1970), p.197. For another journalistic account of events in
Northern Ireland during 1968-69, see M. Wallace, Drums and
Guns - Revolution in Ulster (London, Geoffrey Chapman,
1970).
17   Danny Cohn Bendit was one of the main student leaders
prominent in European demonstrations in 1968.
18   Daily Mail, 22 February 1969.
19   Hastings, Ulster 1969, p.197.
20   Daily Mail, 24 April 1969.
21   The Times, 15 August 1969.
22   The Times, 14 August 1969.
23   Daily Express, 7 January 1969.
24   J. Callaghan, A House Divided, The Dilemma of Northern
Ireland (London, Collins, 1973).
25   The Times, 30 August 1969.
26   The Times, 1 February 1969.
27   New Statesman, 21 February 1969.
28   For Devlin's own account of this period, see B. Devlin,
The Price of my Soul (London, Andre Deutsch, 1969). Some
useful information is also contained in G. Target, Bernadette
(London, Hodder and Stoughton, 1975).
29   Daily Mail, 23 April 1969.
30   Daily Sketch, 21 November 1969.
31   Target. Bernadette, p.305.
32   For a critical assessment of the army's PR operations,
see S. Hoggart, New Society, 11 October 1973.
33   Observer, 29 February 1976.
34   For Chichester-Clark's views of this period, see the
interview with him in W. van Voris, Violence in Ulster
(Amherst, University of Massachusetts, 1975).
35   Spectator, 2 May 1969.
36   For two accounts of Faulkner's life, see D. Bleakley,
Faulkner: Conflict and Consent in Irish Politics (London,
Mowbrays, 1974) and A. Boyd, Brian Faulkner (Tralee, Anvil
Books, 1972). For Faulkner's own account of his career, see
his posthumously published autobiography (he died as a
result of a hunting accident in 1977), B. Faulkner, Memoirs

of a Statesman (London, Weidenfeld and Nicolson, 1978).
37   O. Dudley Edwards, The Sins of Our Fathers (Dublin,
Gill and Macmillan, 1970), p.40.
38   Boyd, Brian Faulkner, p.24.
39   Evening Standard, 23 March 1971.
40   For Maudling's own account of his dealings with Northern
Ireland, see R. Maudling, Memoirs (London, Sidgwick and
Jackson, 1978), ch.2.
41   Sunday Times Insight Team, Ulster, p.213.
42   Financial Times, 24 March 1971.
43   For a critical account of these days, see S. O'Fearghail,
Law (?) and Orders: The Belfast Curfew of 3-5 July 1970
(Dundalk, Dundalgan Press, 1970). See also Sunday Times
Insight Team, Ulster, pp.215-21.
44   For two critical accounts of internment, see D. Kennally
and E. Preston, Belfast, August 1971: a case to be answered
(London, Independent Labour Party, 1971) and J. McGuffin,
Internment (Tralee, Anvil Books, 1973) (McGuffin was one of
those detained on 9th August.)
45   Guardian, 10 August 1971.
46   Observer, 15 August 1971.
47   The Times, 10 August 1971.
48   Daily Telegraph, 10 August 1971.
49   For two largely conflicting accounts of Bloody Sunday,
see the Widgery Report, HMSO, London, House of Lords 101
and House of Commons 220, 1972, on the one hand, and on
the other, S. Dash, Justice Denied - A Challenge to Lord
Widgery's Report on Bloody Sunday (New York, The Defence
and Education Fund of the International League for the Rights
of Man, 1972); E. McCann, What happened in Derry?
(London, Socialist Worker Pamphlet 1972); and NICRA,
Massacre at Derry (Belfast, NICRA, 1972).
50   Daily Mail, 31 January 1972.
51   New Statesman, 13 August 1971.
52   Daily Mirror, 14 August 1978. As early as 1972, the
Daily Mirror had suggested the substitution of a United
Nations force in Northern Ireland; see Daily Mirror, 3
February 1972.
53   See, for example, Tribune, 26 March 1971.
54   Sunday Times, 17 October 1971.
55   Winchester, In Holy Terror, pp.191-211.
56   Spectator, 29 May 1971.
57   See, for example, its cover after Bloody Sunday,
Spectator, 5 February 1972.
58   Winchester, In Holy Terror, p.234.
59   Winchester, In Holy Terror, p.94.
60   The Campaign for Free Speech in Ireland, The British
Media and Ireland, p.7.
61   M. Dillon and D. Lehane, Political Murder in Northern
Ireland (Harmondsworth, Penguin Books, 1973) and M.
McKeown, The First Five Hundred (Belfast, Michael McKeown

(own publisher), 1972).

62   For a history of the IRA, see J. Bowyer Bell, The Secret Army. History of the IRA. 1916-1974 (Cambridge, Mass., MIT Press, 1974) and T. Coogan, The IRA (London, Fontana, 1971).

63   The Times, 18 August 1969.

64   McCann, The British Press and Northern Ireland.

65   The Times, 16 December 1971.

66   Daily Mirror, 27 August 1969.

67   Private Eye, 27 August 1971.

68   P. Elliot, Reporting Northern Ireland, Ethnicity and the Media (Paris, UNESCO, 1978).

69   Quotes in P. O'Farrell, England and Ireland since 1800 (London, Oxford University Press, 1976), p.157.

70   Sun, 15 August 1969.

71   Daily Express, 20 November 1971.

72   The United States and to a lesser extent Australia and New Zealand, remain the most important overseas sources of arms and money for the IRA. Most of its money for arms does, however, come from Ireland itself (often through robbery). There has been very little examination by newspapers of funding for paramilitary activity. For some exceptions to this generalisation, see Daily Express 3 September 1971, and The Times, 9 January 1973.

73   New Statesman, 12 September 1969.

74   The Compton Report, HMSO, London, Command 4823.

75   Daily Sketch, 14 August 1969.

76   Sunday Times, 24 August 1969.

77   Daily Mail, 24 June 1970.

78   Daily Express, 30 September 1969.

79   Private Eye, 10 October 1969.

80   Sun, 7 July 1970.

81   Daily Express, 20 October 1971.

82   Daily Telegraph, 17 November 1971.

83   Sunday Times, 21 November 1971.

84   Guardian, 17 January 1972.

85   Financial Times, 30 November 1971.

86   News of the World, 14 November 1971.

87   Guardian, 25 August 1971.

88   For details of Paisley's life, see P. Marrinan, Paisley: Man of Wrath (Tralee, Anvil Books, 1973).

89   Daily Sketch, 24 January 1969.

90   News of the World, 31 August 1969.

91   Daily Mail, 7 June 1972.

92   Sunday Times, 13 March 1977.

93   New Statesman, 13 July 1979.

94   Sunday Times, 31 July 1977.

95   See Daily Express, 3 August 1978, and Daily Telegraph, 2 August 1978.

96   See, for example, Time Out, 29 September 1978 and 10 August 1979, and Leveller, June 1978.

97   The Campaign for Free Speech in Ireland, The British Media and Ireland, p.27.

98   Hoggart, The Army PR Men of Northern Ireland.

99   Daily Mail, 19 April 1972.

100   Economist, 18 January 1969.

101   Daily Mail, 28 May 1974.

102   Daily Express, 24 December 1977.

103   Guardian, 28 March 1972 and 12 June 1972.

104   Observer, 2 January 1977.

105   R. Crossman, Diaries of a Cabinet Minister, vol.3 (London, Hamish Hamilton and Jonathan Cape, 1977).

106   Daily Mail, 23 November 1973.

107   Daily Express, 24 December 1977.

108   The Times, 8 August 1980.

109   The Times, 11 August 1980.

Essay ten

ULSTER TERRORISM:
THE US NETWORK NEWS COVERAGE
OF NORTHERN IRELAND 1968-1979[1]

Ken Ward

On August 12 1979 NBC Nightly News carried a story from its
reporter in Northern Ireland, Steve Mallory, commenting on
the tenth anniversary of the introduction of British troops
into the province as a peace-keeping force. It encapsulated
the history of the previous decade in ninety seconds: the
police had been unable to cope with sectarian violence and the
introduction of the troops was welcomed by the Catholics who
'turned on the British troops shortly after their arrival. They
were viewed as oppressors. The Provisional IRA went to war
against the British and Protestants.' He concluded

> Catholics generally want the British out. They want
> to be reunited with the Republic of Ireland; the
> Protestants don't, they want to remain a part of
> Great Britain. These differences have sparked a
> decade of violence, and there are few indications
> that the situation is going to change in the next
> ten years.[2]

Here were reiterated the two main themes around which
reporting of Northern Ireland had been structured in the
previous decade on the three national network evening news
in the United States. Firstly, the incipient civil war between
two religious group; secondly, the armed struggle of an
insurgent force against a colonial power which was backing
one of those groups. They had not developed simultaneously
but had become the interwoven framework in which events in
Northern Ireland could be conveniently situated.

It has been argued by Galtung and Ruge that foreign
events must meet a number of criteria in order to be seen as
newsworthy in a communications medium. Frequency,
intensity, lack of ambiguity and relevance are of importance
and inter-related. To these must be added both a predictive
and 'unexpected' element which must still be 'meaningful'.[3]

Gans reinforces these aspects in suggesting that foreign
news stories are of importance in the United States only if
they are 'thought relevant to Americans or American
interests; with the same themes and topics as domestic news,

201

or when the topics are distinctive, with interpretations that apply American values'.[4]

Events in Northern Ireland, having been seen to have relevance to an American audience in October 1968, became more frequently reported, grew in intensity of action and violence, and appeared unambiguous in interpretation. If their relevance was related to U.S. domestic concerns the perceptions of that relevance was created by reporters and news presenters. It is the argument of this paper that the developing interpretation of Northern Ireland appears to have been founded on perceptions of American involvement in Vietnam.

This study is concerned only with stories on Northern Ireland presented on CBS Evening News, NBC Nightly News and ABC Nightly News between 1968 and 1980. Each of these broadcast for thirty minutes in the early evening of each weekday, at a fixed time, through more than 550 local affiliated stations to an estimated audience, in 1969, of 57.5 million viewers.[5] Such a global figure takes no account of interest or undivided attention and there is very little information about the nature of the news audience. The result is the development of an audience-image among television journalists; essentially that of a disinterested group spanning all ages and educational levels, a group using the news for reassurance that the world is safe.[6] In the 23 minutes devoted to news, in the half-hour, the information provided would fit easily on the front page of a newspaper.[7] The constraints of time must be considered in relation to the audience and the financial structure of American television. The role of the news programmes is not merely to inform, but to entertain; to keep or capture an audience which would move on to 'prime-time' programming on the same network.

Thus the national audience is given a news package with, according to Reuven Frank, every news story requiring 'the attributes of fiction, of drama. It should have structure and conflict, problem and denouement, rising action and falling action, a beginning, a middle and an end.'[8] Frank had initiated a half-hour national news programme on CBS in 1963 against much opposition from affiliate stations who counted lost revenue from local sponsors in thousands of dollars. NBC and ABC quickly followed suit and by the end of the decade the nightly news were prestige programmes, often bringing fame and fortune to their news presenters, the anchormen. That each network should follow the same format is one further example how competition encouraged conformity; against Walter Cronkite on CBS could be placed David Brinkley and Chet Huntley on NBC or Howard K. Smith on ABC. News presenters were an essential element in the news package since it was widely believed, and often substantiated from surveys, that the audience identified with, and related to, the personalities of the anchormen.[9] They invariably wrote their own introductory remarks, setting the 'tone' of film stories, and keeping the topic in the public view through 'tell' stories of ten to twenty seconds duration, straight to camera, with a caption, but without film. The apparent power of the anchormen in U.S. politics is suggested by the story that Lyndon Johnson considered he had lost the country over Vietnam once he had lost Walter Cronkite.[10] Yet Cronkite had to go to Vietnam to be convinced in his own mind of the futility of American policy; for foreign news the presenters are normally dependent upon correspondents in the field. Northern Ireland was, in general, covered by the London-based network correspondents who would either comment on immediate events by satellite (an expensive business in the early seventies), or prepare film reports which would be available and used on a suitable peg if time was available in the news broadcast. In either case, Reuven Frank's admonition was of paramount importance; they were to underline the drama and present the conflict within the wider framework understandable to the unknown audience who would have no first-hand knowledge of the background to the events. Large minorities of interested viewers, for instance, the Irish-Americans, would have a very different framework in which to place events in Ulster and television news was more likely to confirm their own prejudices. We are concerned in this paper with the images of Northern Ireland presented to the wider, disinterested audiences with no particular view of Ulster but a desire to place it within their own domestic experience.

It is no surprise, therefore, to see Northern Ireland being treated as part of two running stories in October 1968. The trouble in Londonderry, reported by Cronkite in a 'tell' story, on 7 October had arisen out of a civil rights march, and followed the wider European disturbances of the spring and summer. NBC sent a film crew to Londonderry specifically to film a 'civil-rights' story to include 'boarded-up windows, riot damage and a protest march'.[11] The report by George Montgomery was shown on 7 November with the presenter's lead:

> Last month there was violence in Londonderry in Northern Ireland when Catholics demonstrated for a greater voice in the local government. They clashed repeatedly with riot police.

Emphasis in Montgomery's report was laid on the intransigence of the Protestant population and government, and the legitimacy of the Catholic demands for civil rights. Yet the tone was sardonic and presages a future element in the coverage:

> Paisley's followers went through their patriotic antics around the City Hall. They waved their Union Jacks in loyalty to a Britain which usually does not like to interfere in the quaint goings on

here.

There was not merely the civil rights element in the story, but an allusion to British colonial power linked to the Protestant extremists which would have struck a chord in a country which had continually seen Britain as an imperial aggressor, if not an imperial rival. It was however the '400 years of bigotry and bitterness' in Northern Ireland with which Bill Beutel concluded his report for ABC on 22 January 1969 which again underlined the Catholic-Protestant antagonism. The presenter had emphasised the same point in his introduction:

> Fires fed by religious hatred ended in attacks on police and have caused a national crisis. Some observers have compared the plight of ghetto residents in Northern Ireland to ghetto residents in this country.

With Beutel talking over the singing of 'We will overcome', and the main demand of Catholics expressed as 'One man, one vote' the relationship to the U.S. domestic environment is obvious. However there was one further element in this report which provided a key to future newsworthiness, the prediction of further disorder. It was, in his view,

> the extremists of both sides, especially the Protestant extremists, who are being allowed to push Northern Ireland, if not into civil war, at least into a breakdown of law and order.[12]

Morley Safer explained the position of the police in a satellite report to CBS viewers on 21 April 1969. They

> represent to most Catholics in Northern Ireland the armed weapon of Protestantism.

His report contained film of youths fighting police in Londonderry - 'By mid-afternoon it had turned into civil war, holy war, hundreds of police versus young Catholics armed with crowbars and firebombs.' Over film of youths marching past the camera with sticks he concluded 'the people of Londonderry prepare to do battle'.[13]

Safer was a very experienced television journalist, who had become famous for his reporting from Vietnam, particularly the burning of Cam Ne by U.S. Marines in August 1965.[14] Working now from London he immediately identified a civil war situation in which the forces of the state were ranged with the Protestant majority. It was a view reiterated on other networks - 'one step nearer to civil war' on ABC on 23 April, and on the 24th Lou Cioffi presented a film, by satellite, on the situation in Londonderry, using the gable-end wall paintings of Protestant victories to signify more graphically the divisions in the community. Londonderry offered other images of division and subservience which were quickly used by directors and reports. In the same film Cioffi's comment that 'today the Catholics are outside the Protestant walls' was backed by pictures taken from above the

Catholic Bogside area 'which had become their fortress'.15

It was clear to Cioffi in a report on ABC on 14 July that the divisions could only lead to further violence. There had been constant predictions of continuing conflict in news reports during April and the events of August although violently explosive, were not unexpected to the news programme audience. The inherent antagonism of one group for another was apparently the major factor in Northern Ireland affairs.

The prophecy was fulfilled between 12 and 15 August 1969, and the disturbances were to mark a turning point in the development of the political situation, and its coverage by the networks. On 5 August Bill Beutel had commented on the role of the British Army in a background report.

Fifty years ago the British Army fought the Catholics to keep Northern Ireland Protestant and part of the British Empire. The Catholics have never forgotten that.16

Within ten days the Army had arrived as a peace-keeping force - and Bill Beutel's follow-up 'background to the fighting' reiterated his points of the 5th. The British and Protestants were seen by Catholics as a 'foreign army of occupation' and the only solution to Catholics lay in one Ireland 'free of Britain and Catholic'.17 This was a view shared by the Irish Republican Army, 'the underground organisation which has long used terror in its bid to force the unification of Ireland'.18

The news reports from Northern Ireland between 12 and 15 August on all three networks brought graphic pictures of urban unrest: burning buildings, petrol bombing, police activity. Again, the vantage point of roofs of flats in Londonderry provided the networks with the image of a community under siege - even flying the American flag.19 The arrival of British troops brought relief to Belfast and Londonderry, and the images were of the aftermath of war. NBC News on the evening of the 15th concentrated on the destruction in the Bogside and the indomitable spirit of the inhabitants, allowing a young woman, sweeping up debris, to speak direct to camera for a full minute. This was Bernadette Devlin, recently elected a Member of Parliament, and personified in the report as the down to earth spokeswoman of the Bogsiders. The police were castigated as a

bunch of armed, uniformed hooligans, defenders of the Unionist party; and they are supposed to be the civil forces acting between civilian and civilian: they are the armed wing of the Unionist party. Until we have established justice in this community we want the constitution suspended forthwith - I want to get on with my cleaning.20

Here was the perfect example of the personification of foreign news - the representative individual responding to events and articulating the thoughts of the community.

Yet if the crisis was becoming assessed in nationalist/ imperialist terms Chet Huntley took the opportunity to reiterate the older context in a commentary on 15 August. In many ways unusual to U.S. television such personal views were a feature of news programmes, invariably placed as the last item and drawing conclusions for the audience. He stated categorically:

> The white Catholics in Ulster are the same as the blacks in the United States; they've been deprived of their rights, hurried into slums, and denied jobs, hurt and slashed, ever since the Battle of the Boyne. And like the blacks they've revolted... and like the blacks they're burning down the very ghettos that were built to contain them, and like the blacks they're being shot down. So the lesson is attention must be paid.., And those in power, once more, will profess either to see a conspiracy, or simply be surprised that it all happened. Good night from NBC News.[21]

The domestic inference was clear: Northern Ireland was the peg for a wider discussion of inequalities in society and the simplistic editorial took no account of the factors which were being identified in the news reports. The incipient identification of the ultimate aspirations of the Catholic population with the IRA and the defensive character of the violence of the Bogside would legitimise the future presentation of terrorism from the Republican side. The social issues identified by Huntley were to be submerged in a wider colonial conflict.

In fact, it is difficult to follow the development of such a framework through news reports from August 1969 to February 1971. During 1970 there were no more than a dozen references to Northern Ireland on all three networks, most of the reports being 'tell stories' with no background information. There was political activity but as the NBC correspondent pointed out to Edward Jay Epstein, in 1969,

> We cover Northern Ireland, but the stuff that gets on the air is the rough stuff. If there's something fairly peaceful, or something that involves their parliament, it's hard to get it on.[22]

'Direct attacks by Irish citizens upon British troops'[23] in February 1971 heralded a new direction and required some explanation. It was provided by IRA personnel on NBC:

> The British Army are the terrorists. They introduced the terror situation, not us, and if they terrorize the population we will terrorize them.[24]

The situation was now described as 'urban guerrilla warfare'.[25] The objective of the IRA was clearly 'to wrest Northern Ireland from British rule',[26] and John Laurence in a background report for CBS underlined the depth of resistance in the Catholic population. Following film of the preparations of the Belfast Brigade of the Irish Republican Army for 'full scale guerrilla warfare' he reported on the scene in a Belfast bar 'where poor Catholics meet at night', singing songs, carrying on 'the spirit of the Republican movement to unite Ireland... while out in the streets at night the secret army they support is fighting'.[27]

Laurence had been a compatriot of Safer in Vietnam and recognised as another outstanding television journalist - yet the view became current by the mid-1970s that, like Bob Dylan, Laurence continued to sing his songs of the 1960s, but the words and music had changed.[28] Laurence was not alone in setting the Northern Ireland problem in the context of an armed struggle against an occupation army, as well as that of a civil war. George Montgomery for NBC on 11 March emphasised the split in the IRA between the 'tough minded Provisionals' and the 'milder Official' wing.[29]

While urban terrorism was a world-wide phenomenon by the 1970s and would be the obvious frame of reference for the IRA the presence of civil war and armed struggle was redolent of the Vietnam conflict, particularly to reporters who had worked in that theatre, and who could present a clear image of such a conflict for the domestic population.

With the introduction of internment by the Northern Ireland government in August 1971 the imagery was compounded further. George Watson, for ABC, stood in front of the camp which housed 'dozens of suspected terrorists' and resembled 'nothing more than a concentration camp complete with barbed wire, watch towers and snarling guard dogs'.[30]

In September and October Watson reported on the attempts by British soldiers to seal the border with the Republic, 'a futile, almost farcical situation' needing 20,000 men for an effective blockade.[31] George Montgomery, for NBC, was covering the same ground, by helicopter, in November, assessing the capabilities of both sides, the IRA and British Army.[32] It was not until 1974 that Watson articulated this frame of reference for American viewers with the direct statement:

> Just as Americans grew weary of war in Vietnam
> the British today are getting tired of their costly
> commitment to Northern Ireland.[33]

Yet the symbolism of Vietnam was in virtually every film story from 1971. The actions by British paratroopers in Londonderry on 30 January 1972 was one further element - predictive within the context of an occupation army, unexpected by the scale of death in one incident. Bernadette Devlin, once more, spoke straight to camera on 31 January:

> The British government ordered the British Army to
> shoot down Irish civilians.[34]

and irrespective of the accuracy of the statement, she suggested two days later that the facts were not important

because
> Bloody Sunday enters into Irish mythology and will
> be a rallying cry for Irish nationalists for many
> years to come.[35]

Once again the tragic news from Londonderry was personalised through Bernadette Devlin, outspoken, committed, and
arguing that the only way forward was by force.[36] As Walter
Cronkite told it in the lead story on 1 February, the dead
from Bloody Sunday had hardly been counted 'when the
outlawed Irish Republican Army vowed revenge',[37] the
aspirations of the nationalist, Catholic population were now
apparently synonymous with the aims and actions of the IRA
in the future generation of Northern Ireland.

From February 1972 the chronicle of violence, sporadic
at times, alleviated by attempts at political compromise,
displayed a sense of hopelessness in a situation where
innocent people, the silent majority, were portrayed as the
victims. Anniversaries became occasions for progress reports:
on 30 January 1973 Garrick Uttley, news presenter on NBC,
commented

> In Northern Ireland the bombing, the killing
> continues. In the past 24 hours three men have
> been murdered in the Irish vendetta between
> Catholics and Protestants. Everything you can say
> about Northern Ireland has been said – the
> violence, the killings, the hate · it all defies
> rational thinking and it mocks human compassion
> but it goes on.

and as Robert Hager concluded his film report in the same
story, the suffering seemed no closer to an end 'than last
year, or the year before, or the year before that'.[38]

The reasons were still presented as emanating from the
position of the British government and British Army: and the
unwillingness of the former to stand against the tactics of the
Protestant population in the North; particularly in the general
strikes of February 1973 and May 1974. The comparison with
the treatment of Catholics was highlighted by Bob Simon of
CBS in a profile of Maire Drumm, a militant Republican from
Andersonstown, but 'known to be warm, understanding,
compassionate... the kind of woman people instinctively bring
their problems to'. Yet, she was harrassed by the Army, and
spent time in prison. As Simon commented:

> Maire Drumm doesn't pretend to know or care about
> Vietnam, about the Middle East, about anything or
> anywhere, but Ireland. Her politics are provincial,
> uncompromising and incredibly simple – Ireland's
> problem to Maire Drumm is the border, the border
> is maintained by the British; the British have to
> go.

and then the clinching argument, 'To Maire Drumm the only
meaning of the IRA bombing campaign which has killed dozens

of innocent people is that it hastened the downfall of Ulster's Protestant-dominated government and brought a united Ireland one step closer.'[39]

As Bernadette Devlin had personalised one aspect of Catholic defiance, so Maire Drumm signified the depth of resistance, and the simplicity of the causes of, and solutions to, the violence.

The end of the Stormont government in March 1972, the imposition of direct rule, and the creation of a power-sharing executive through 1973 and 1974 were covered by reports and film stories, but the overwhelming impression created by 'tell' stories was of continuous violence - summed up by a typical lead to a filmed report on NBC:

> The news from Northern Ireland is the usual, more violence and death. What is unusual is the number. Nine people killed, shot, and about twenty more wounded last night in Belfast.[40]

Newsworthiness lay in the scale of death; tit-for-tat killings of fifteen Catholics and Protestants in Co. Armagh, in January 1976, provided all three networks with opportunities for further analysis of the problem. The spiral of violence was now identified with the country areas and 'Britain's crack anti-terrorist force' was being sent 'into the lawless district for the first time'.[41] John Laurence made a more direct comparison on CBS - 'the British Army's most elite counter-insurgency unit the Special Air Service - similar to the US Special Forces...'.[42]

Five days later visual images backed descriptive commentary in placing the conflict squarely within the American experience. Walter Cronkite introduced a film report from John Laurence with the comment

> The escalating violence in Northern Ireland has revived demands in Britain that British rule of the troubled territory be ended...

Laurence himself was out on patrol, by helicopter, in South Armagh. There was a 'search and destroy' operation, aware of potential ambushes, and

> Again, it looks a little like the Vietnam War... Militarily the British Army has been forced to adopt some of the same tactics as the American Army, but not by choice... the British Army may find itself bogged down, not only in South Armagh, but all of Northern Ireland; much like the U.S. Army in South East Asia.[43]

Four years earlier Garrick Uttley, on NBC, had commented, in the aftermath of Bloody Sunday that 'two and a half years of British pacification have neither defeated the Catholics nor won them over' and Northern Ireland could become Great Britain's Vietnam.[44] Here was a consistency of perceptions across networks and over years.

The willingness of Great Britain to hold on was asserted

in the response to the Queen's Jubilee of August 1977.

> Elizabeth the Second. Queen of Great Britain and Northern Ireland, is determined to go to Northern Ireland tomorrow, even though there are warnings that it is too dangerous.[45]

remarked David Brinkley on the 9th, and Richard Threlkell for CBS on the 10th suggested that 'the British Government dare not admit there's an inch of British soil which the Queen cannot safely set foot'. Garrick Uttley on NBC was even more categorical about the importance of the visit.

> Her Majesty's Government, though, is determined to rule Northern Ireland, the army provides its muscle, the Queen provides the symbol. That is the importance of her visit here...[46]

However, if there was one major element missing in reports from Northern Ireland in the decade it was an examination of the position of the British government. Its presence was signified by the Army, but the general aims and viewpoints of the politicians were never explored. The arguments for the British presence had been summed up in 1969 and were never subsequently contradicted or examined in depth. The continuing violence was the element which dominated the reports, and the complexities of politics had no attraction for a medium which could best illustrate conflict than explore the dilemmas of a democratic state.

There was one major exception to the general tenor of reports. In 1976 all three network news ran stories, carefully prepared, on the possible gun-running link between Irish-American charity organisations in the United States, and the IRA. ABC produced their story on 2 and 3 February, NBC on 9 April, and CBS, most appropriately, on 17 March, St Patrick's Day. A clear connection was suggested in all the reports between the military effectiveness of the IRA and financial support from the United States. The message to Irish-Americans was clear; do not give money to pseudo-charities. Such reports stand out by their infrequency: in the majority of cases the relevance of Northern Ireland to the United States was oblique and distant.

However one international stance of President Carter after 1977 might be seen to have direct relevance to Americans as a challenge to British superiority. With human rights a major constituent of the U.S. foreign policy perspective the question of prison conditions, and political status in Northern Ireland could be seen as of direct interest to Americans. The movement from a dirty-protest to hunger strikes again personalised the issue, but the framework was still that of the early seventies.

Britain was still recognisable as a power trying unsuccessfully to preserve a status quo within a disintegrating society. The terrorism of the IRA was justified by the cause for which it was fighting - unification of a partitioned country: Protestant activists were the privileged minority supported by the imperial power. By 1972 the consequences of the Vietnam War were clear to Americans commentators could legitimately draw conclusions about that experience and apply them to Northern Ireland.

It would be simplistic to accuse the network news organisations of bias towards the IRA: selection of news from abroad will always favour social disorder and distant conflict: the IRA could capture interest in a way that democratic politicians could not. It has also been noted that foreign news is generally treated with less detachment than domestic news, explicit value judgements being offered which overtly comment on a domestic parallel.[47] It might be argued that the experience of Vietnam made Northern Ireland provide a framework of understanding for U.S. news reporters and the American public, and provided a platform for views which had not been expressed during the war itself.

Notes

1   Research for this chapter was conducted in the TV Archive of Vanderbilt University, Nashville, Tennessee with funds from the International Communication Agency and the Research Committee, N.U.U. I would like to thank James A. Pilkington, Director of the TV Archive, and his staff, for their outstanding assistance, and my colleague John Short for timely advice.
2   NBC Nightly News, 12 August 1979.
3   Johan Galtung and Mari Holmboe Ruge, 'The Structure of Foreign News', in Jeremy Tunstall, ed., Media Sociology (London, 1970), pp.259-98.
4   Herbert J. Gans, Deciding What's News (London 1980), p.37.
5   Edward Jay Epstein, News from Nowhere (New York, 1974), p.4.
6   Gans, p.226.
7   Erik Barnouw, The Sponsor (Oxford, 1979), p.126.
8   Epstein, pp.4-5.
9   Jeffrey Feinman The Newscasters (New York 1977).
10   Gary Paul Gates, Air Time (New York, 1979), p.222.
11   Epstein, p.110.
12   ABC Nightly News, 22 January 1969.
13   CBS Evening News, 21 April 1969.
14   David Halberstam, The Powers That Be (New York, 1980), pp.678-85.
15   ABC Nightly News, 24 April 1969.
16   ABC Nightly News, 5 August 1969.
17   ABC Nightly News, 14 August 1969.
18   ABC Nightly News, 15 August 1969.
19   NBC Nightly News, 14 August 1969.
20   NBC Nightly News, 15 August 1969.

21   Ibid.
22   Epstein, p.247.
23   CBS Evening News, 6 February 1971.
24   NBC Nightly News, 9 February 1971.
25   ABC Nightly News, 16 February 1971.
26   NBC Nightly News, 11 March 1971.
27   CBS Evening News, 20 February 1971.
28   Gates, p.173.
29   NBC Nightly News, 11 March 1971.
30   ABC Nightly News, 12 August 1971.
31   ABC Nightly News, 20 September 1971.
32   NBC Nightly News, 26 November 1971.
33   ABC Nightly News, 5 June 1974.
34   CBS Evening News, 31 January 1972.
35   ABC Nightly News, 2 February 1972.
36   CBS Evening News, 31 January 1972.
37   CBS Evening News, 1 February 1972.
38   NBC Nightly News, 30 January 1973.
39   CBS Evening News, 8 February 1973.
40   NBC Nightly News, 4 February 1973.
41   ABC Nightly News, 7 January 1976.
42   CBS Evening News, 7 January 1976.
43   CBS Evening News, 12 January 1976.
44   NBC Nightly News, 6 February 1972.
45   NBC Nightly News, 9 August 1977.
46   NBC Nightly News, 10 August 1977.
47   Gans, p.31.

Essay eleven

'TERRORISM', THE MEDIA,
AND THE LIBERAL-DEMOCRATIC STATE:
A CRITIQUE OF THE ORTHODOXY

Philip Schlesinger

The government must promote its own cause and
undermine that of the enemy by disseminating its
view of the situation, and this involves a carefully
planned and co-ordinated campaign of what for want
of a better word must regrettably be called
psychological operations.

Major-General Frank Kitson[1]

The Conference succeeded in bringing about a
better understanding of the respective problems
faced by newsmen and government officials in
dealing with terrorism. Most participants agreed
that a postponement of information for a few days
was acceptable if either human life or national
security were at stake. While there will always be
some degree of mutual suspicion between press and
government in a democratic system, mutual
cooperation and proper working procedures in times
of crisis can produce an acceptable balance between
the interests of the state and the press.

Mr Peter Galliner,
Director, International Press Institute[2]

This essay explores an issue which has received little
systematic attention within the sociological literature: the
media reporting of terrorism in Western democracies. In what
follows I shall pursue three themes. First, I will indicate how
the term "terrorism" is conventionally related to the question
of legitimate political activity and to the concept of practical
rationality. Such a semantic dimension is relevant for
understanding how media discourse may routinely reproduce
dominant meanings. Next, the essay turns to an examination
of official and semiofficial orthodox views on the role of the
media in reporting terrorism. And finally, to reinforce the
arguments of the second section I shall make some points
about the control of the media reporting of terrorism in the
United Kingdom as this is a particularly good test case which

213

confutes the easy generalizations of the antiterrorism experts. I shall conclude by stressing the need for careful further investigation of the issue, particularly through a comparative analysis of state systems in articulation with their national media and through an analysis of the specific causes of political violence.

TERRORISM: OFFICIAL AND UNOFFICIAL

The language used by the media in describing acts of political violence is of crucial importance in the eyes of state agencies. The standard official view was clearly stated at the International Press Institute's 1978 conference on "Terrorism and the Media" by Lord Harris, then Minister of State in the British Home Office. In an "off the record" contribution he is reported to have said that "the Italian media allowed themselves to be caught up in the language of the Red Brigades which had kidnapped and murdered Aldo Moro. The so-called communiques of the Red Brigades were just an example of play-acting staged for the benefit of the media, which accepted them with too little caution. 'Terrorists... are common criminals: they do not have courts, they do not issue communiques, and they do not have the status of public servants.'"[3]

The rest of Lord Harris's views are, unfortunately, not publicly available. However, Dr Conor Cruise O'Brien provides a reasoned elaboration of this position, one which is not without interest given his former post as Minister for Posts and Telegraphs in the Irish government and his advocacy of censoring broadcast interviews with IRA spokesmen. Dr O'Brien states a central axiom which stands neatly for virtually all the thinking done on this subject: "The force used by a democratic state is legitimate while the violence of the terrorist is not legitimate."[4] Thus a controlled political discourse is an essential part of the liberal-democratic state's fight against its enemies:

> The terms "force" and "violence" are... like "terrorist" and "freedom-fighter" largely emotive propaganda terms; which we use about a given act depends, not on the degree of force or violence, but on a view of its justification.[5]

Talking principally about the IRA, Dr O'Brien argues that as both the British and Irish states pursue rational procedures for solving political problems they are legitimate, and the IRA's campaign of violence is not justified. In this view, liberal democracies are embodiments of rationality while terrorists, being violent, are quintessentially irrational. Their notions of liberation, whether universal or nationalistic, are but quasi-millenerian; they concern articles of faith, not practical reason. Hence, political debate with a terrorist should be refused, for "though he can argue fluently from his own peculiar premises, he is not accessible to rational argument on premises other than his own".[6] Terrorists should receive no publicity and should be dealt with by military rather than political means.

Whatever their undoubted advantages, liberal democracies are not embodiments of rationality. For one, proper adherence to democratic practices coupled with widespread inequality, suffering, and the anarchy of production might, on other criteria, be thought less than fully rational, if not positively irrational. Moreover, Dr O'Brien fails to question the use of force in the pursuit of national security. Must it invariably be above suspicion? On his view, yes, for he engages in a definitional sleight of hand in which rationality and democratic institutions mutually imply one another. It is, furthermore, important to recognize that political violence employed against the liberal-democratic state is not <u>inherently</u> irrational. It depends upon the likelihood of a successful outcome, which may be a morally unappealing view but is nonetheless attuned to current political realities. In short, the use of political violence by those opposed to the state is <u>prima facie</u> evidence neither of rationality nor of irrationality.[7]

Lord Harris and Dr O'Brien propose a form of linguistic surgery in order to effect an ideological closure in which the good elements within the polity are radically distinguished from the bad, the orderly from the chaotic. This rigorous drawing of the conceptual lines has attendant dangers. By being overwhelmed by moral repulsion and by criminalizing politics, one is apt to overlook the possible political rationale of those acts which one rejects. A general presumption of political rationality would seem to be an important precondition for analyzing a "terrorist problem". Moreover, the dehumanization of the state's enemies endangers civil liberties. These positions have been eloquently argued by Professors Edmund Leach and Franco Ferrarotti.

Leach observes that there are problems when divergent concepts of rationality, order, and criminality coexist "within the matrix of a single political domain". Although real consensus may be absent, the legal apparatus is obliged to produce a consensual view which identifies and treats criminals not merely as unheroic but also as inhuman. Thus,

according to the value system which is taken for granted by the press and radio, anyone who refuses to accept the prevailing conventions of how hostilities should be conducted should automatically be categorised as a criminal, lawless, barbarian, terrorist, a savage who can properly be likened to a reptile or a wild beast.[8]

In the cast of mind of those who engage in indiscriminate terrorism, thinks Leach, potential victims are thought of as "'people quite unlike us', sub-human others, people to whom

<u>my</u> rules of morality do not apply".[9] This refers both to agents of the state and to its opponents. For states engaged in counterterror there is the peril of mounting "crusades of reprisal" and of obscuring the sources of political violence:

> However incomprehensible the acts of the terrorists seem to be, our judges, our policemen, and our politicians must never be allowed to forget that terrorism is an activity of our fellow human beings and <u>not</u> of dog-headed cannibals.[10]

This humanistic caution would seem to be well made at a time when liberal-democratic states such as Britain, Italy, and West Germany have acquired "exceptional" legal powers such as the Prevention of Terrorism Act, the <u>Berufsverbote</u>, and the <u>Legge Reale</u>.[11]

Franco Ferrarotti has gone further than Leach in trying to outline a set of humanistic assumptions within which violence, including political terrorism, should be evaluated. First, in terms redolent of Leach, he argues that "the violent are not 'mad wolves' but fully human beings". Second, he suggests that violence has a "specific historical determination" and that its causes require empirical exploration. Last, he proposes that violence is the "perversion of a virtue" and a search for meaning in order to escape the straitjacket imposed by a rational, bureaucratic society. It is this deeper metaphysic which leads him to be sceptical of those who would treat violence as the symptom of a "sickness". Mere repression, he suggests, is a theoretical error with the likely consequence of eventually increasing violence rather than abating it.[12] One might add that the manipulation of the media by states pursuing short-term "psywar" goals will also come home to roost.

As Professors Noam Chomsky and Edward Herman have pointed out, the dominant assumptions about order, legitimacy, and rationality embed themselves in a "semantics of 'terror'".[13] Like Dr O'Brien they recognize the importance of language in propaganda battles. But rather than endorse the liberal-democratic state as perfectly rational, they are concerned to point to U.S. support for repression in the Third World and the ideological function of "human rights" rhetoric. While the substance of their study extends well beyond the performance of Western media reporting of violence, it is their focus upon this theme which makes it relevant here.

Chomsky and Herman argue that U.S. policy toward Third World states provides, at any given time, an ideological framework within which "the spectrum of acceptable and unacceptable bloodshed" may be defined. Central to this framework are "the words 'terror' and 'terrorism'" which "have become semantic tools of the powerful in the Western world".[14] These terms, they rightly contend, "have generally been confined to the use of violence by individuals and marginal groups. Official violence which is far more extensive in both scale and destructiveness is placed in a different category altogether."[15] In the public discourse of the West, those who oppose established orders are the terrorists, while state terrorism is a category virtually never employed, unless it refers to the Communist bloc. In the course of their analysis Chomsky and Herman develop a provocative distinction. They talk, on the one hand, of "official violence" as resulting in "wholesale terror", and on the other of "unofficial violence" as producing "retail terror". If adopted, this quantitative criterion would doubtless lead to a transvaluation of present values about terrorism in Western democracies. But it is unlikely to be persuasive either to the Western media or to the "accredited spokesmen" in Stuart Hall's apt phrase, who provide the primary definitions of social reality which the media largely reproduce. Instead, as Chomsky and Herman argue, the Western media have for the most part fallen in with the officially endorsed usage, which, in "the 1970s has been institutionalised as a device to facilitate the exclusive preoccupation with the lesser terror of the alienated and the dispossessed, serving virtually as a disguised form of apologetics for state terror and client fascism".[16]

A caveat is in order, lest in acknowledging the justice of Chomsky's and Herman's critique we uncritically go overboard for the "alienated and dispossessed". An acceptance of the quantitative critique and its implications for linguistic reform does not mean abandoning the need for moral and political opposition to indiscriminate political violence by the repressed. E.P. Thompson puts it well when he observes that

in conditions of extreme repression, democrats and socialists may be forced to take arms in self-defence or in a strategy of insurrection. And in such conditions they merit our solidarity. But where other measures of organization and agitation remain open, the recourse to terrorism is at best romantic, self-defeating and profoundly elitist (people who cannot be moved by arguments must be terrorized by guns), and at worst merely sick and villainous.[17]

Although this essay is concerned with, in Chomsky's and Herman's terms, "retail terrorism", one should bear in mind the integral links between the internal policing of dissent through mechanisms of control such as the media and the international dimension. Chomsky and Herman make some relevant points here. First, and most Northern Ireland coverage in the British media has taken this form, by commonly representing revolutionary terrorism as the initiating force, state violence may be seen as purely "responsive" and states therefore as justified in riding roughshod over civil liberties. Second official violence in, for instance, Latin American states such as Brazil and Uruguay is redefined in the Western media and thus implicitly endorsed. Again, to take an "internal" example, in Northern Ireland state-sanctioned torture of prisoners was redefined first by a judicial inquiry, and then by the media, as "inhuman and degrading treatment". Third, retail terrorism is presented as an irrational activity, and its seeming irrationality the more persuasively presented in virtue of inadequate contextualization. Finally, they note, in the United States supporters of the anti-Vietnam War movement were effectively discredited by being labelled as "terrorists". Again, in Britain and elsewhere, the expanded category of "subversion" elides the distinction between legitimate and illegitimate dissent in much the same way.

THE ORTHODOX CONSENSUS AND ITS LIMITATIONS

The debate about the media reporting of unofficial terrorism in Western capitalist democracies has primarily developed within the compass of the psychological warfare aims of the state.[18] In this respect there are significant parallels with the way in which information policy is located in Latin American states governed according to an ideology of "national security" which is fixated upon the "enemy within".[19] During the past decade, and especially since the mid-1970s, an international conventional wisdom has been elaborated within official and semiofficial circles in which the media are conceived of pragmatically, as instruments which can contribute to, or impede, final victory. Although mere expediency might seem to dictate outright censorship in order to deny violent opponents of the state the supposedly clear-cut advantages of publicity, matters are not so simple. Overt censorship threatens the legitimacy of the liberal-democratic order, one in which the received conception of press freedom is that the media are completely separate from the state. Hence, it is advantageous for the state to set in train an information policy which integrates the media into a national-security design while, at the same time, preserving the necessary appearance of separation. The dominant view in the current orthodoxy has been succinctly expressed by Major-General Richard Clutterbuck, the British counterinsurgency expert:

> The television camera is like a weapon lying in the street. Either side can pick it up and use it. If governments use it in this way   encouraging their officials, policemen and soldiers to help the media-men, and to answer their questions - it is far more effective than any kind of censorship or government control.[20]

Aside from seeking media cooperation there would seem

to be two possible options. First, there is overt censorship. But this is rarely argued for in an across-the-board manner - except where "news freezes" are sought, and even then media compliance is usually forthcoming. In general, open censorship is advocated for broadcasting rather than the press, and in such limited contexts as refusing to allow interviews with spokesmen of illegal organizations engaged in political violence. Dr O'Brien has persistently pursued this line in Britain and the Irish Republic as part of his wider argument that "a liberalism, relevant to the dangers of the day should be concerned to support and strengthen the principle of authority under the law."[21] It has also been advocated by some counterinsurgency theorists and the London-based right-wing Institute for the Study of Conflict.[22]

Falling outside the orthodoxy is the much less frequently stated libertarian case as proposed, for instance, by the U.S. political scientist Bernard Johnpoll: "It is useless to discuss what the media can do about terror. The media are not judicial institutions; their sole role in modern society is to transmit information. How to erase terror is a judicial and ethical question; not a question of the media."[23] Perhaps this could be seriously argued only in the United States, and, moreover, by a confirmed believer in the separation-of-powers doctrine both as reality and as ideal.

In U.S. law-enforcement circles different grounds are advanced for noninterference. Patrick Murphy, a New York police chief, offers three reasons: censorship "concedes a victory to terrorists" by suppressing freedoms; the media "can and do play an important and positive role" by stilling rumours and speculation; and the government does not have the expertise to "fine tune" the media.[24] The last point is particularly disingenuous, and the other two are plainly informed by a long-term psywar outlook. H.H.A. Cooper of the Task Force on Disorders and Terrorism also argues for noncensorship in news reporting, but advocates "care" in commentaries and investigations, suggesting that the media should recognize the possibility of their being abused and therefore be "responsible".[25]

This argument for "socially responsible" media is developed against the background of some highly questionable assumptions about the nature of the contemporary liberal-democratic state and the operations of the media within it. These are: that liberal democracies are very vulnerable and they do not censor news; that the media are willing victims of terrorist propaganda and function as open conduits for such views; that media coverage has a "contagion effect". As noted, Conor Cruise O'Brien has argued, in effect, that liberal democracies need to take on an "exceptional" character, "relevant to the dangers of the day". This is but an extension of the view that such states are presently highly vulnerable, especially when confronted by publicity-seeking terrorists. They are presumed to lack an effective repressive apparatus and to be perfectly open. This line has been canvassed by Professor Walter Laqueur of the Center for Strategic and International Studies, Washington, D.C., and Dr J. Bowyer Bell of the Institute for War and Peace Studies, Columbia University, both of whom are prominent writers on political violence.[26]

However, this assumption needs to be critically evaluated by reference to the recent growth of research suggesting that there have been significant alterations within the liberal democracies in the direction of what is variously termed a "strong state", "authoritarian statism", or the "national security state". The development of European antiterrorism legislation and police and military cooperation for "internal defence", the weakening of the rights of defendants in both criminal and political trials, the growth of high-technology police surveillance of whole populations, the expanded category of "subversion", restrictions upon the rights of trade unions and of political demonstrations, the use of repressive technology in civil policing are all manifestations of this shift.[27] Against such a background, which, to be sure, in part represents a response to unofficial political violence, it is difficult to concur with the picture of present vulnerability which is drawn in the writings of the "terrorism studies" experts – where, indeed, one rarely finds any analysis at all of the operations of the present advanced capitalist state.[28]

But where the vulnerability-of-liberal-democracy thesis is retained it is but a small step to promote the role of the media of communication in exacerbating that weakness to one of crucial significance. Thus Professor Laqueur remarks:

> Terrorists have learned that the media are of paramount importance in their campaigns, that the terrorist act by itself is next to nothing, whereas publicity is all. But the media, constantly in need of diversity and new angles, make fickle friends. Terrorists will always have to be innovative. They are, in some respects, the superentertainers of our time.[29]

These few remarks command widespread assent. Bowyer Bell links the centrality of the media to subversive strategies for publicity: hence "it matters a great deal not only why and how a rebel kills, but also where and when. The television terrorist understands prime time, the need to escalate his deed, to manipulate the media, to reach the masses."[30] He goes on to argue that manipulation of the media by terrorists requires that several conditions be satisfied. First, there should be a good locale with communications facilities, such as the Munich Olympics in 1972. Second, the media need to be enticed by the prospect or actuality of violence. And finally, in order to hold the media's attention a terrorist "spectacular" should contain frequent shifts of scene, as in, say, an aircraft hijack.[31]

For Bowyer Bell the terrorist is a publicist or showman. This dramaturgical perspective is present throughout similar writings. So Laqueur talks of "superentertainers", while Brian Jenkins, the Rand Corporation's expert on international terrorism, likewise observes: "Terrorists choreograph their violence. Terrorism is theatre."[32] In a perspective which sees political violence as unambiguously effective drama it is not surprising that media coverage is accorded such importance. Assuming the simple convergence of terrorist actions and the values and needs of capitalist media, it is no great step to the view that the media are the willing victims of the superstars of violence. However, Laqueur does qualify this by noting that they are "fickle".

In the orthodox view, then, liberal democracies are seen as uncensored with media engaging in the untrammelled pursuit of news values stressing violence and drama, the result being disproportionately great publicity. But this argument runs against actual developments where some liberal-democratic regimes, in strengthening their repressive apparatuses, have also developed sophisticated policies for the management of publicity. State strategies toward the media in West Germany are a case in point.

Mr Armin Grünewald, the West German government's official spokesman, has observed that the media "play a substantial part in the terrorists' logistic organization" and that the state therefore has a right to insist on collaboration from the press and broadcasting. In the 1970s "information policy has become a stable component of every consultative moment of the situation", and principles of collaboration between the media and state have been developed involving centralized channelling of information. He has illustrated this process control revealingly. During the month-long "news freeze" during the kidnapping of Hanns Martin Schleyer, head of the West German industrialists' organization,

> the Secretary of State, Herr Bölling, granted dozens of interviews, made statements and took part in a series of debates almost entirely centering round the meaning and legitimacy of these restraints. This was not only a quest for understanding but a conscious calculation. Self-restraint by the media, the most important element of the news operation, is feasible only if they are urged to deal with questions that are not dangerous for police tactics.[33]

Successful control of media coverage was achieved without legal compulsion, for such powers did not exist.

The Vice-Chairman of the Bonn Criminal Police, Mr Reinhard Rupprecht, has given a similarly frank account of the control of news during the Schleyer kidnapping. Preferring the more euphemistic "deferment of news" to "news freeze", Mr Rupprecht argues that the media were of crucial importance in achieving public cooperation in the hunt for those suspected of the kidnapping. A few minutes after Schleyer's body had been found a police information film was broadcast and the entire press carried a

> whole-page insert with photos and distinctive characteristics of the 16 wanted terrorists, together with summaries of certain pieces of evidence and details which would on the one hand arouse suspicion should the terrorists rent flats that could be used as meeting or hiding places or purchase used cars, and on the other be useful in recognising any forgery of passports, identity cards and driving licences.

Other aspects of this public mobilization for "national security" included a further nine police films broadcast on television at prime time on nine consecutive days "with no need to have recourse to the right of divulgation on radio and television which was reserved to the Federal government".[34] Special research on the use of pictures and graphics was commissioned in order to make this "search operation" more effective. When one considers evidence such as this of the effectiveness with which the media may be subject to state direction at times, it is hard to accept the general picture of limp-wristed liberal democracy current in the orthodox view.[35]

Let us now turn to the last standard assumption - that the media, by reporting terrorist acts, have "contagious effects". This has been advanced, for one, by Professor Yonah Alexander of the State University of New York. But while he says that publicity legitimizes terrorism, he provides no sound evidence to support this contention. For instance, he cites the results of two U.S. public-opinion polls which indicated "greater awareness" of the PLO during 1974-75, years when that organization was attracting lots of media attention. However, he seems not to realize that public recognition of a group's existence does not indicate that its goals are now publicly favoured. Nor, indeed, does recognition mean that the public necessarily understands the political aims of the group in question in terms that it itself would wish. For the media treatment of sieges, bombings, and hijackings may well result in their ostensible rationale being either excluded entirely, ridiculed, challenged, distorted, or played down.[36]

A further variant of this naive "effects" argument is Alexander's suggestion that publicity for terrorism leads to the exportation of violent techniques which are taken up elsewhere. Yet the evidence cited is exiguous indeed: we are merely told that Nelson Rockerfeller, Andrew Young and

Major-General Clutterbuck believe this to be so. The following illustration is offered:

> Several weeks after Argentina's Montoneros removed the body of ex-President Pedro Aramburu to secure the return of Eva Peron's body from Spain, Burmese terrorists stole the body of U Thant for the purpose of using it in negotiations with the Burmese government.[37]

But surely a particular technique, body-snatching, cannot be considered in total isolation from the social relations in which it occurs. One must specify the mediating conditions which explain why such acts occur. It is not enough to assert loose correspondences between actions in Latin America and in Asia with the supposed explanation that terrorism is a "world-wide theatrical attraction [which] tends to encourage angry and frustrated groups beyond a particular country to undertake similar acts out of their helplessness and frustration".[38] Which angry groups? Why them especially? In which societies and in which circumstances do they use such techniques? Do they have alternatives? Such basic questions for research cannot be made to vanish by the magical invocation of media effects.

In fact, Professor Alexander's argument is yet another variant of the venerable and quite unproven contention that the portrayal of violence on television, or in the cinema, or before that in the nineteenth-century theatre, has had deleterious effects, especially upon impressionable children. There has been a long-standing debate on this question in cultural criticism and mass-communication research which makes it plain that no simple cause-effect relationship between the portrayal of violence in the media and a given social response has so far been established. Indeed, to conceptualize the problem in those terms at all is to leave out any study of popular attitudes, their production by given social relations, and the highly complex process of the mediation of meaning which communicative activities entail.[39] When Alexander asserts that "by providing extensive coverage of incidents the media give the impression that they sympathize with the terrorist cause thereby creating a climate congenial to further violence",[40] he is actually posing a problem for future research into the reporting of political violence and its public interpretations, not stating an established proposition.

SOME ASPECTS OF THE BRITISH MODEL

The "terrorism studies" experts' views on the media reporting of political violence are entirely innocent of any serious analysis of the process of news production and the constraints it faces in a liberal democracy shifting to an "exceptional" modality of rule armed for psychological warfare. The British model of media control during the past decade provides a particularly good illustration of how crass overt censorship by the state may be avoided and instead be substituted by indirect control coupled with media self-censorship. The appeals of this solution are international. At the 1978 IPI conference on "Terrorism and the Media" it was widely hailed as an example worth following. One can readily see why. For by avoiding evident censorship the state's ideological capital remains intact, and the media, by being socially responsible and by pursuing voluntary self-restraint, also retain their public credibility. And yet the solution does have its costs for the state, for, at given moments, the institutional imperatives of the media supervene over the doctrine of national security, and so they rock the boat. This contradictory situation may be illustrated with reference to the coverage of the continuing crisis in Northern Ireland, one which has involved British troops in fighting an undeclared "small war" for the past decade.

The sociological impasse in Northern Ireland has contributed to a wider "crisis of legitimacy" within the British state at the root of which lies the continuing inability of successive governments to discipline labour and to restore adequate profitability to capital. The drift toward more authoritarian forms of rule has made much more crucial the role of the media in winning consent for increasingly coercive policies. Since the late 1960s, a framework of interpretation for quite separate forms of dissent has been elaborated, based upon the notion of a society suffering from the malaise of violence. Industrial-relations conflicts (notably picketing), street crime, juvenile hooliganism, political demonstrations, and antistate violence (such as the continuing IRA campaign) have all been assimilated to the "violent society" framework.[41] It is in such a context that state strategies toward the media should be seen. I shall touch only very selectively upon several instances which cast further doubt upon the standard assumptions of the experts.

The coverage of Northern Irish affairs in the British media, as Philip Elliott has pointed out, has tended to simplify violent incidents, to avoid historical background, to concentrate upon human-interest stories, and to rely heavily upon official sources. Even during the periods of the most intense constitutional political activity, the story has been preeminently one of violence, and of irrational, inexplicable violence at that.[42] Aside from weakness in the journalistic practice of the British media, there can be little doubt that the one-dimensional coverage reflects, at least in part, the effective long-term strategy of attrition waged by the British state in its psychological-warfare campaign, one which has involved increasingly sophisticated public-relations techniques.

Most public attention in Britain has focused upon the British state's repeated efforts to control broadcast news and current-affairs coverage without stepping over that fatefully delegitimizing line into overt censorship. It is a struggle which has been waged patiently and with skill, and, moreover, one which has aroused little public disquiet. As both main political parties have been involved in prosecuting the war effort, opposition has come from within the media themselves and from civil libertarians. Aside from those trade unionists directly involved in media production, however, it has no mass character at all.

It is impossible to do justice to this complex history here, but at the risk of oversimplification some general indications of its course may be given.[43] In general the British state has been largely successful in inducing the broadcasting organizations to censor themselves under the guise of "responsibility". Television, as the medium with the largest news audiences and the highest credibility, is seen as especially important in the psychological-warfare campaign. The public service British Broadcasting Corporation (BBC) and the commercial Independent Broadcasting Authority (IBA) are responsible for all radio and television programming in the United Kingdom. The BBC is financed by a license fee levied by the state, but has a charter of independence from government. The IBA's finances are regulated by the government, which takes a levy from its advertising revenue, and it is subject to a Broadcasting Act. The public legitimacy of these central cultural institutions (which is great) derives from their formal independence from the state and from their obligation to provide "impartial" and "balanced" news and current-affairs coverage.

At the beginning of the 1970s the formal adherence to impartiality, which had only formerly been waived over race-relations issues, was abandoned over Northern Ireland. This shift came at a time when the British Army became increasingly involved in direct conflict with the IRA. As state pressure for "responsible" broadcasting mounted, the broadcasting authorities began to develop detailed internal guidelines for reporting the conflict. These included a virtual ban upon interviews with members of illegal organizations, one which has been so effective that only four such interviews have taken place on the BBC to date. More importantly, Irish Republican views, without knowing which the conflict cannot be understood, have received little serious analysis. Both the BBC and the IBA tightened controls on programmes about Northern Ireland. The BBC, for instance, developed a system of "reference upwards" under which editors and reporters wishing to produce stories about Northern Ireland had to take their requests to the highest editorial levels of the organization. This had the undoubted effect of deterring investigative reporting of abuses by the state, such as the

employment of torture or "dirty tricks" by the security
forces. Moreover, it has inhibited an examination of the
essentially political character of the crisis, resulting in an
overemphasis upon manifestations of violence. The IBA, too,
insisted upon viewing potentially controversial stories made by
the companies it regulates and, like the BBC, has banned,
censored, and delayed several programmes. It is important to
note that not only have news and current-affairs reporting
been inhibited but also dramatic works and major historical
documentaries dealing with the roots of the Irish crisis have
been censored or banned. Thus the effective restriction of
public enlightenment has operated across the spectrum of
programming, reinforcing the deficiencies of the educational
system and of the wider culture, which provide no basis for
an understanding of Britain's imperial role vis-a-vis Ireland.

Over the years, the broadcasting authorities have
developed a "public order" policy on Northern Ireland which
contains three elements. First, they generally support the
efforts of the security forces in law enforcement. Second,
they delegitimize "extremism" and "terrorism", especially that
of the IRA, which is presented as the principal enemy and as
the initiating cause of violence. Finally, there is a stress
upon the avoidance of "inflammatory" coverage. The first two
characteristics are shared by much of the press.

Nevertheless, there are real tensions in the relationship
between broadcasters and the state, and the past decade has
been spotted with a number of quite dramatic rows. One
typical instance occurred in July 1979. A BBC television
programme interviewed a member of the group which claimed
to have assassinated the Northern Ireland spokesman of the
Conservative Party a few months earlier. The interview,
given the virtual ban in force, was really quite exceptional.
Its transmission produced an outburst of rage in Parliament,
with the Conservative Prime Minister, Mrs Thatcher, saying:
"I am quite appalled it was ever transmitted." The opposition
Labour Party home-affairs spokesman joined in the chorus of
condemnation, calling the decision a "grave error".

In its defence the BBC pointed out that it had
considered the matter carefully and that the last such
interview had taken place five years earlier. The BBC's
Director of News and Current Affairs argued that from time
to time it was right "to show the public by way of reminder
who and what the extremists are" and that

> the media have a very real contribution to make, in
> particular, a contribution to the maintenance of the
> democracy which is under threat, both by providing
> a forum where the harshest differences of opinion
> can be aired, and by reporting and courageously
> investigating the unpalatable truths which underly
> the problems of the province.[44]

This typical liberal defence did not impress the government

which instructed the Attorney-General to investigate whether the BBC could be prosecuted under the Prevention of Terrorism Act for withholding information likely to lead to the apprehension of a terrorist. No prosecution was to eventuate. However, a further twist was given to the existing techniques for the intimidation of broadcasters.

The highly "responsible" way in which the British media have reported political violence in Northern Ireland hardly gives credence to that favourite argument of the counterinsurgency experts and the politicians that the media (somehow) produce violence on the streets. The political causes of such disaffection lie elsewhere in fact, and far from producing deleterious "contagious effects" one might instead argue that the media frequently rally behind the state. Such a process occurred when, for instance, Lord Mountbatten was assassinated. Philip Elliott has labelled this an "affirmatory ritual", one in which press and broadcasting have emphasized the integrity of the social order. Terrorism is represented as inhuman and irrational and as the very embodiment of encroaching chaos.[45]

A few illustrations from the press coverage of Lord Mountbatten's assassination in August 1979 will make this point more correctly. The tone of the coverage was highly reverential, almost sacral, given his kinship to the Queen. Mountbatten was presented as the epitome of the finest British qualities: soldier, hero, noble, statesman, family man par excellence. His passing was widely referred to as the "end of a legend". The newspaper and television programmes ran stockpiled obituaries, interviews with acquaintances and friends, and tributes from across the globe. The act of killing was widely interpreted as irrational. as that of "evil men" (Daily Mail), "wicked assassins" (The Sun), "psychopathic thugs" (Daily Express), "murdering bastards" (Daily Star), as "cowardly and senseless" (Financial Times) and as the product of "diseased minds rather than political calculation" (Daily Telegraph). There was, therefore, a counterpoint between, on the one hand, the irrational and evil forces threatening the state and, on the other, the virtues of an exemplary citizen whose death is inexplicable.

Much less prominence was given to the simultaneous disaster which befell the British Army. namely, the killing of some 15 crack troops in an IRA ambush. A close reading of some papers disclosed that sources in the security forces, far from seeing the two linked incidents as an irrational exercise, saw them rather as indicative of a more sophisticated strategy of armed struggle. Only one newsparer printed in full the IRA communique which specified the reasons for Mountbatten's killing. This talked of his assassination as "one of the discriminating ways we can bring to the attention of the British people the continuing occupation of our country".[46]

This brief sketch suffices to make the point that the

orthodox view of the media as "willing victims" of the terrorists is without foundation. It fails to attend to how the media routinely deny the rationality of antistate political violence and how in some circumstances they invoke the sacred dimension of nationhood to ward off subversive evil. The question of the extent to which the public accepts the invitation to participate in such rites remains open to investigation. The points made here are by no means peculiar to Britain; Lavoinne, for instance, has argued much the same for France.[47]

The process of ritual affirmation is quite spontaneous and located within the hegemonic ideology. To indicate further how conscious strategic calculation is at work in the British model too, let us consider a last example. A good instance is that of the development of "voluntary self-restraint" by the press in the reporting of sieges, kidnappings, and hostage-takings. An agreement between the national media and the police in 1975 was initiated by the then Commissioner of the Metropolitan Police, Sir Robert Mark. The media were asked to be "responsible" in their reporting in the interests of saving human life. In practice, what was required was for them to withhold, at the police's request, information deemed to be of use to kidnappers or hijackers.

The policy was rapidly tested at the Spaghetti House and Balcombe Street sieges and in the case of a girl kidnapped for ransom, incidents all of which occurred in 1975. During the first siege, the media agreed to suppress news of the capture of one of the gunmen's accomplices. In the second, the BBC, at the request of the police, broadcast the news that a crack Special Air Service squad was present at the scene. The IRA gunmen who were tuned in to radio broadcasts surrendered rapidly. In the kidnapping case, the police succeeded in achieving a total news freeze for nine days in return for daily press briefings, and the story was published only when the girl was finally released unharmed. Such extensive cooperation was unprecedented, and its success led to the London model being extended to the provincial media.

Even greater cooperation was achieved during the siege of the Iranian embassy in 1980.[48] In this case, radio, especially the BBC's news service, was of crucial importance. This was because one of the express objectives of the gunmen was to achieve some publicity for their views. The authorities had an equally express strategy of preventing them from communicating their demands. One way in which this was achieved was by cutting off all telex and telephone links between the embasssy and the outside world: these had been used at first by the media to make contact with the gunmen. The gunmen had radio receivers and constantly monitored them to listen for news of their demands being met, so the process of attrition could be aided by delaying the achievement of publicity objectives. The security forces knew what these were because they had the embassy bugged. One of the extraordinary twists in the tale lay in the fact that two BBC television newsmen were among the captured hostages. It was they who transmitted the gunmen's initial demands to their newsroom. One of these demands - a request for mediation by the ambassadors of several Arab countries - was suppressed by the BBC at the request of the British government, which was unwilling to yield its control over the bargaining process. In return, the BBC was taken into the confidence of the authorities, it would appear, and its top officials were privy to special security briefings. The BBC became more deeply involved when one of its senior news executives was brought into the bargaining process and was instrumental in ensuring that publicity was traded for the release of some hostages. The close cooperation of the BBC and the Independent Television News Service with the security forces seemed to mark a further step forward in the absorption of the broadcast media into the crisis-management apparatus of the state. But such a development could occur only because of the longer-term strategy of seeking cooperation which had been pursued throughout the decade. The control of publicity at the Iranian embassy was an integral element in a siege-management approach which eventually led to a shoot-out using the Special Air Service.

FUTURE DIRECTIONS

This essay has presented a critique of the orthodox assumptions concerning the media reporting of what Chomsky and Herman call "retail terrorism". Given the evident importance of this topic, there is surprisingly little writing on it which has been informed by any focused research. There would seem to be an urgent need for an investigation into existing policies and national debates on "terrorism and the media" in Western capitalist democracies. The orthodox arguments, which derive from the instrumental preoccupations of a national-security-minded officialdom point in the perilous direction of increased censorship and enhanced secrecy. Before further progress is made down that restrictive road, some dispassionate analysis, addressed to the widest possible public, of the real significance of publicity in present struggles to "suppress terrorisim" would seem to be called for.
    Some of the lineaments of an approach to the problem have been set out here. Unquestionably, we need to pay careful attention to the specific forms of political violence within a given state and to their causation. Detailed attention needs to be given to the organization of national media systems and the ways in which they articulate with the state.

A comparative approach would have the merit of highlighting how national peculiarities have affected the evolution of psychological-warfare strategies. Such a systematic study of the dialectical interplay between media, political violence, and the state has hardly begun.[49]

Notes

1   Maj.-Gen. Frank Kitson, Low-Intensity Operations (London: Faber, 1971). General Kitson is Britain's most celebrated "counterinsurgency: theorist and practitioner of "psyops".
2   Terrorism and the Media (London: International Press Institute, 1980). This contains the proceedings of an international seminar held in Florence in 1978 under the auspices of the International Press Institute and Affari Esteri (Rome). As the book is unpaged, all references will be to particular articles.
3   Claudio Pontello, "Terrorism and the Media", in Terrorism and the Media.
4   Conor Cruise O'Brien, "Liberty and Terror: Illusions of Violence, Delusions of Liberation", Encounter 49 (October 1977), p.38.
5   Ibid., p.35.
6   Ibid., p.38.
7   Cf. Ted Honderich, Violence for Equality: Inquiries in Political Philosophy (Harmondsworth: Penguin, 1980).
8   Edmund Leach, Custom, Law, and Terrorist Violence (Edinburgh: Edinburgh University Press, 1977), p.26.
9   Ibid., p.30.
10 Ibid., p.36.
11 Cf. S. Cobler, Law, Order, and Politics in West Germany (Harmondsworth: Penguin, 1978); Suzanne Cowan, "Terrorism and the Italian Left", in Carl Boggs and David Plotke, eds., The Politics of Eurocommunism: Socialism in Transition (London: Macmillan, 1980); Brian Rose-Smith, "Police Powers and Terrorism Legislation", in Peter Hain, ed., Policing the Police (London: John Calder, 1979), vol.I.
12 Franco Ferrarotti, "On Violence: Paradoxes and Antinomies", typescript translation of ch.7 of his L'ipnosi della violenza (Milan, 1980). Also cf. "Anche i terroristi sono esseri umani", La critica sociologa 43 (Autumn 1977).
13 Noam Chomsky and Edward Herman, The Washington Connection and Third World Fascism and After the Cataclysm, vols.1 and 2 of "The Political Economy of Human Rights" (Nottingham: Spokesman Books, 1979).
14 Ibid., I, p.85.
15 Ibid., I, p.6.
16 Ibid., I, p.87.
17 E.P. Thompson, Writing by Candlelight (London: Merlin, 1980), p.171.

18 I have so located it in my essay "On the Shape and Scope of Counterinsurgency Thought", in G. Littlejohn et al., eds., Power and the State (London: Croom Helm, 1978) esp. pp.112-14.

19 Armand and Michele Mattelart, "Information et etat d'exception", in De l'usgae des medias en temps de crise (Paris: Alain Moreau, 1979).

20 Maj.-Gen. Richard Clutterbuck, Living with Terrorism (London: Faber, 1975), p.147. Cf. his Guerrillas and Terrorists (London: Faber, 1977), where he advocates treating the media as "allies and friends".

21 Conor Cruise O'Brien, "Freedom and Censorship", a lecture at the Independent Broadcasting Authority, London, March 28 1979, p.9.

22 E.g. Paul Wilkinson, Terrorism and the Liberal State (London: Macmillan, 1977), p.169, and Television and Conflict (London: Institute for the Study of Conflict, 1978).

23 Bernard Johnpoll, "Terrorism and the Mass Media in the United States", in Yonah Alexander and Seymour Maxwell Finger, eds., Terrorism: Interdisciplinary Perspectives (New York: John Jay Press, 1977), p.160.

24 Patrick Murphy, "The Case of the United States", in Terrorism and the Media.

25 H.H.A. Cooper, "Terrorism and the Media", in Alexander and Finger, Terrorism. He uses typical psywar language: "he who controls the media is most powerfully equipped to win the hearts and minds of the people" (p.145); "The terrorist needs the media as a fish needs water" (p.150).

26 Walter Laqueur, Terrorism (London: Weidenfeld & Nicolson, 1977), pp.109-10; J. Bowyer Bell, A Time of Terror: How Democratic Societies Respond to Revolutionary Violence (New York: Basic Books, 1978), p.78.

27 In Britain there has been a spate of concerned literature, including C. Ackroyd et al., The Technology of Political Control, 2nd edn. (London: Pluto Press, 1980); T. Bunyan, The History and Practice of the Political Police in Britain (London: J. Friedmann, 1976); Thompson, Writing by Candlelight. Cf. also Nicos Poulantzas, State, Power, Socialism (London: New Left Books, 1978) and Hans-Magnus Enzensberger, "An Address on German Democracy to the Citizens of New York", New Left Review 118 (November-December 1979).

28 A notable exception in Bowyer Bell's still rather cursory analysis of the Italian and Iris states in A Time of Terror.

29 Laqueur, Terrorism, p.223.

30 Bowyer Bell, A Time of Terror, p.54.

31 Ibid.. pp.110-16.

32 Brian Jenkins, "Responsibilities of the News Media - I", in Terrorism and the Media.

33 Armin Grünewald, "Government and the Press: National

Security and the Public's Right to Know", in <u>Terrorism and the Media</u>; emphasis added.

34   Reinhard Rupprecht, "The Case of Federal Germany I", in <u>Terrorism and the Media</u>.

35   Not all states have such effective systems of control, it is true. The continual leaking of information during the Aldo Moro kidnapping to the Italian press has led to calls for news freezes and for a code of practice. Cf. Robert Sole, <u>Le defi terroriste: lecons italiennes a l'usage de l'Europe</u> (Paris: Seuil, 1979), esp. pp.221-30.

36   As occurred for instance with the "Angry Brigade" in Britain. Cf. S. Chibnall, <u>Law-and-Order News</u> (London: Tavistock, 1977), pp.95ff.

37   Yonah Alexander, "Terrorism, the Media, and the Police", <u>Police Studies</u> 47 (June 1978). Given his energetic promotion of "terrorism studies" and his editorship of the journal <u>Terrorism</u>, Alexander's views are probably quite influential.

38   Ibid., p.47.

39   Cf. James D. Halloran, "Mass Communication: Symptom or Cause of Violence?", <u>International Social Science Journal</u> 30 (1978); Stuart Hall, "Culture, the Media, and the 'Ideological Effect'", in James Curran et al., eds., <u>Mass Communication and Society</u> (London: Edward Arnold, 1977).

40   Alexander, "Terrorism, the Media, and the Police", p.51.

41   For elaboration of this argument, cf. Stuart Hall <u>et al.</u>, <u>Policing the Crisis</u> (London: Macmillan, 1978) and Chibnall, <u>Law-and-Order News</u>.

42   Philip Elliott, "Reporting Northern Ireland", in <u>Ethnicity and the Media</u> (Paris: UNESCO, 1977).

43   For a detailed account cf. Philp Schlesinger, <u>Putting "Reality" Together: BBC News</u> (London: Constable, 1978), esp. ch.8. Cf. also Anthony Smith. "Television Coverage of Northern Ireland", <u>Index on Censorship</u> 2 (1972). Informative articles are contained in <u>The British Media and Ireland</u> (London: Campaign for Free Speech on Ireland. 1979).

44   <u>The Listener</u>, July 17 1979, p.74.

45   "Press Performance as Political Ritual", <u>The Sociological Review Monograph on the Press and Journalism</u>, Keele University, forthcoming.

46   <u>The Daily Mirror</u>, August 28 1979.

47   Yves Lavoinne, "Presse et cohesion sociale: le cas des prises d'otages", <u>Revue francaise de communication</u> (Winter 1979), pp.35-41.

48   This account draws upon my analysis of this siege, its implications, and the wider background to it. Cf. my paper "The Media Politics of Siege-Management: Princes Gate, 1980", in <u>Screen Education</u> (Winter 1981).

49   A research project along the lines indicated, which I am codirecting, is in its initial stages at Thames Polytechic.

PART FOUR

THE FUTURE OF TERRORISM

Essay twelve

THE PROBLEM OF ULSTER TERRORISM:
THE HISTORICAL ROOTS

Paul Bew

This paper is based on the conviction that Ulster terrorism must be analysed primarily in the context of the particular local political history in which it has evolved. It is highly sceptical of explanations which place much stress on either psychological or international considerations.[1] This is not to deny that these factors have had some effect in the development of the Ulster crisis. Nevertheless, they have been secondary to say the least. The fundamental basis of the current conflict in Ulster is a history of tension between the forces of Irish nationalism/catholicism and Irish unionism/protestantism.

What is the historical origin of the modern Ulster question? At what point did the partition of Ireland become inevitable? It makes no sense to put this any earlier than 1886 when Gladstone's first home rule bill opened up for the first time the serious possibility that self-government might be granted to a parliament in Dublin. Irish protestant and unionist opinion mainly concentrated in the north-east strongly resisted Gladstone's concession to predominantly catholic Irish nationalism. Partition, always a strong possibility after 1886, became a political fact in 1921, when two new states were established in Dublin and Belfast.

How are we to explain Unionist opposition to home rule? This problem gives the historiography of the period a unique interest. Professor Joseph Lee, in his recent highly influential 'The Modernisation of Irish Society 1848-1918' (1973) - a work which in its modernising zeal is by no means a textbook of Irish nationalist piety - has offered an explanation. Discussing the dilemma of John Redmond, the leader of the constitutional nationalists for most of this period, Professor Lee writes

> It is true that Redmond was prepared to make what he considered generous concessions towards Scotch-Irish susceptibilities virtually amounting to "home rule within home rule" as long as the Unionists acknowledged ultimate allegiance to the sovereignty

of a Dublin parliament. But Redmond forgot that it was not equality, but superiority, the Orangeman claimed as his birthright - and home rule, however generous the "special considerations for Unionists" certainly threatened a blow at the master-race syndrome.[2]

This is a concise enough definition of the Ulster problem. There are many who would insist that it is an accurate description of the Ulster protestant mentality today. Indeed, given the clear existence of protestant suprematist traditions in north-east Ulster - today exemplified by the Rev Ian Paisley - there is clearly an element of truth in these observations. But is it the whole truth and can we be satisfied with Lee's analysis as a definitive statement?

A few pages later Professor Lee declares equally uncompromisingly that "Orangeism was racism". He writes of Sinn Fein who replaced the Irish parliamentary party as the dominant force within nationalism in 1917:

It remained to be seen in 1918 what policy Sinn Fein would adopt towards the Scotch-Irish in Ulster. The nationalist attitude, republican and home rule alike, was a remarkable one. Almost alone among the peoples of Europe Irish nationalists aspired to integrate, rather than expel the settler race.[3]

We may perhaps begin our attempt to shed some light on this problem by pointing out that this account is misleading. In the first place, by 1918 Sinn Fein policy towards the Ulster Unionist was absolutely clear cut and was in no way shrouded in secrecy. In the second place, these policies were by no means so generous in tone as Professor Lee's passage implies.

Eamon de Valera, Sinn Fein's leader, had declared in Dublin in the middle of July 1917:

The newspapers stated that the Sinn Fein party wanted to coerce Ulster. Now, he did not want to mince matters, and if Ulster stands in the way of Irish freedom, Ulster should be coerced. Why should she not be?[4]

The same speaker topped this a few days later when he said:

If the minority stood in their way to freedom they would clear them out of it. They did not want to be forced to do so, but if it came to that they would not hesitate.[5]

Then in the early autumn, speaking at Cootehill, Co Cavan, Eamon de Valera became if possible even more frank:

We say to these planters... if you continue to be a garrison for the enemy... we will have to kick you out. I am not out to raise differences between the Irish people.[6]

These enthusiastic declarations were not confined to de Valera. They were to be found on the lips of many of the leading Sinn Feiners. They counterposed to the old and fading parliamentary party's queasy and embarrassed acquiescence in partition their own militant but entirely unrealistic intentions of 'dealing' with the large protestant minority by force. Arthur Griffith, for example, joined in the chorus in a Belfast speech in September 1917:

> The Unionists of Ulster had to take one of two courses... to accept the fact that they were part of the Irish nation, and must throw in their lot with that nation, or else stand deliberately out as an English garrison. If they did the latter they stood out as enemies of the Irish nation and the Irish nation must deal with them.[7]

It is difficult to assess the precise political role of such statements. They were after all made at a time when the Sinn Fein's leadership's attitude towards the future role of armed struggle anywhere in Ireland was ambiguous. (Even as late as the general election of December 1918 Sinn Fein limited itself to promising abstention from Westminster and attendance at the Versailles peace conference.) Threats to use force in the north therefore rang more than a little hollow. Perhaps it was felt to be enough to put the Irish parliamentary party on the defensive by suggesting that partition was yet another one of its shabby and corrupt compromises with the British state. In this it was probably successful as the party leadership's apparent backtracking on the issue would appear to indicate.

Within a few years, however, when the parliamentary party was safely removed from the scene both de Valera and Griffith in their different ways felt free to associate themselves with a much softer line towards Ulster.[8] Even in 1917/18 there was however an interesting more heterodox strain in Sinn Fein thinking in Ulster. This was to be found at the level of the second rank cadre. One prominent metropolitan intellectual, Arthur Clery, in his Dublin Essays (1917) revealed himself as an explicit partitionist who honestly acknowledged the sectarian elements within both Irish communities.[9]

Even more interestingly, there is the case of Father Michael O'Flanagan. Father O'Flanagan emerged in early 1917 as the most important pro-Sinn Fein priest in Ireland. In February 1917 the Sinn Fein candidate Count Plunkett won the North Roscommon by-election comfortably against the Irish party. This was Sinn Fein's first, and therefore politically vital, demonstration of its electoral popularity. Plunkett, in his victory speech, went out of his way to thank Father O'Flanagan who was declared to be 'the best priest in Ireland'.[10]

Yet Father O'Flanagan's views on the Ulster question were not those of the Sinn Fein leadership. In 1916 he had made it clear that he looked on partition as obvious and rather inevitable. Father O'Flanagan had pointed out that a geographical entity is not necessarily a political entity. He had written:

> If we reject Home Rule rather than agree to the exclusion of the Unionist parts of Ulster what case have we to put before the world? We can point out that Ireland is an island with a definite geographical boundary.... Appealing as we are to continental nations that argument will have no force whatever. National and geographical boundaries scarcely ever coincide. Geography would make one nation of Spain and Portugal; history has made two of them... Geography has worked hard to make one nation of Ireland, history has worked against it. The island of Ireland and the national unit of Ireland simply do not coincide.[11]

Later in the year Father O'Flanagan expressed the same idea:

> I agree that the 'homogeneous Ulster' of the Unionist publicists is a sham and a delusion. But if there be no homgeneous Ulster, how can there be a homogeneous Ireland? ...A more accurate description of Ireland for the past two hundred years would be an economic and social duality.[12]

The fact that Sinn Fein was prepared to clutch such an obvious 'two nations' heretic to its breast in order to win in North Roscommon is a revealing index of its priorities. It wanted above all things, including the unity of Ireland, to establish its dominance in the Southern Irish body politic. After all, did not Eamon de Valera declare publicly in the same county a year later at Elphin that the northern catholics had been 'contaminated' by the Orangemen and the 'melt had been broken' in these people?[13]

There is in other words implicit in the thinking of those men who were to found the new Irish state – and dominate its life until at least the nineteen fifties in the case of Eamon de Valera – an implicit 'two nations' logic. Professor Lee grasps this in what is by far his most subtle and insightful comment on the Ulster question:

> While claiming the Scotch-Irish as Irish, they behaved as if all their traditions and not merely Orangeism, was irreconcilably alien to everything Irish. The nationalist reluctance to salute the Shankill's sacrifice on the Somme in July 1916 reflected Southern Ireland's implicit belief, despite its denials, in one 'two nations' theory. The slaughter of the Somme, where the stupidity of the generals was surpassed only by the indomitable bravery of the officers and men of the 36th (Ulster) Division, bereaved thousands of Ulster

homes. Nationalists frigidly ignored the tragedy.[14]

In this passage Professor Lee acknowledges not only the existence of an implicit 'two nations' logic on the part of the southern Irish but also notes the importance of non-Orange traditions among the Unionist population in the north of Ireland. These two points are of vital importance. In the first place, the attitude of some thousands of Irish protestants towards Irish nationalism was not so much passionate hostility as passionate incomprehension: an exquisite sense of not belonging. When Eamon de Valera had spoken of coercing Ulster in mid July 1917 he had gone on to make it clear that all this strife was necessitated by the need to save the Irish language. He thus quite successfully conjured up an image of a Gaelic society - an enclosed world with its own interesting but - to the northerner - irrelevant concerns. This leads us on to our second point. Even the most passing scrutiny of Ulster election results through from the 1880s points to the existence of important non-Orange electoral forces of a Liberal, later Liberal Unionist and Labour kind.

It is a fundamental error if one equates Unionism with Orangeism conceived as religious bigotry. In fact - to succeed in the face of such a strong nationalistic threat - Unionism had to embrace many thousands of Protestants with non-Orange, Liberal or Labour electoral traditions.[15] In consequence, the leadership - as the intelligent nationalist William O'Brien pointed out - was by no means exclusively Orange.[16] Unionism did make an appeal to religious or sectarian feeling. But its success as a truly broad mass movement lay in its ability to articulate the uneven development of Irish capitalism in a particular way. The hegemony of Unionist ideology lay in the contrast it was able to make between Ulster's expansionary regional capitalism and Southern underdevelopment.[17]

There is now a substantial historiography which draws attention to the pertinence of political and social divisions within the Ulster protestant community and demonstrates their real effects on the overall development of relationships between Irish catholics and protestants.[18] It will be said that the 'anti Orange' tendency in its various forms has never been able to establish its dominance. This is perfectly true as far as it goes. But it is also true that the peculiar ambiguities of Irish nationalist strategy - that strange mixture of violence, friendship and indifference - have been almost perfectly designed to strengthen the forces of reaction within the protestant community. We have presented here the case of Sinn Fein in 1917/18 and it is by no means the only example.

The dominant position within nationalism has consistently rejected opportunities to follow a policy of conciliation of the Unionist minority. Most strikingly the opportunity created by the Conservative government's serious attempt in 1903 - with the support of a section of the Irish landlord class - to end the bitterness generated by the land question was deliberately spurned. The party instead took a turning towards a doctrine of agrarian class conflict with which it was never really comfortable - with serious consequences for its long term credibility. This allowed the Unionist right in the north to recoup its political losses by 1910. The policy of building tactical alliances with moderate Unionists had only one major supporter - William O'Brien - who in November 1904 threw open his paper, the Irish People, to these and other shades of political opinion. For the first time serious attempts were made to explain to a nationalist audience the basis of popular Unionism - 'the northern working man is not a conservative, he is a radical with a monomania about the Pope',[19] T W Russell, the Liberal Unionist, explained helpfully - but it was to be a short lived experiment. The strategy of conciliation while inevitably long term and fraught with massive difficulties was never really tried.

Professor Lee, in common with many other writers, observes that nationalist resort to political violence in 1916 had been preceded by the earlier unionist gun running. This is a perfectly fair point. However, as Dr P J Bull has pointed out, it is at least as legitimate to say that the nationalist rejection of conciliation of 1903/4 paved the way for the unionist rejection of conciliation in 1912.[20] Many prominent parliamentary nationalist leaders enjoyed their finest hour in 1917 and 1918 when they fought Sinn Fein's belligerent attitude towards the Unionist minority. John Dillon commented on de Valera's position: "Well, I have been all my life fighting the Unionists of Ulster and I know something about them. I tell him that they will have a very stiff job with the Unionists of Ulster and if that be their idea of uniting Ireland, they are very young and very foolish."[21] John Fitzgibbon equally assured his Sinn Fein critics it was impossible to 'overestimate' the value of a policy of conciliation of Unionist opinion.[22] Yet both men had played a major role in sabotaging earlier attempts at compromise. Their defence was to say that earlier occasions had not been sufficiently auspicious but it is hard to conceive of any less auspicious occasion than the fraught years of 1917/18 bedevilled as they were by repression, hunger strikes and fear of conscription. If conciliation was the only sure policy in 1918 it is difficult to believe it was not the only sure policy in, say, 1903/4 when both Dillon and Fitzgibbon played leading roles in fighting it.

There is no doubt that the establishment of the Northern Irish state had unhappy consequences for the northern Irish catholic minority.[23] The present writer in collaboration with others has stressed the effects of discrimination. It is especially important to note the economic context in explaining the current violence.

Starting from a position in 1911 in which they were disproportionately over-represented as semi-skilled manual and non-manual occupations, and under-represented in skilled manual and non-manual ones, Catholics have moved towards a position today where they are over-represented in unskilled manual occupations and under-represented in semi-skilled non-manual ones. In other words, Catholic 'wastage' from semi-skilled non-manual and skilled manual occupations has been polarised into skilled non-manual and unskilled manual ones. This trend is in marked contrast to changes in the Protestant social structure, where skilled manual labour has been displaced fairly evenly with all the other strata except the unskilled. The proportion of unskilled Protestant workers has indeed actually fallen.[24]

To put it more explicitly, while in the Protestant community the unskilled section of the working class was diminishing as a proportion of the work force during the life of the northern Irish state, in the catholic community it was actually increasing. By the 1970s no less than a quarter of the non-agricultural work force was consigned to the residuum of unskilled labour, excluded not only from political life but from social rewards. This sector constituted an immense reservoir of opposition to Unionism and indifference to moderation.

This is why the Provisional IRA have a seemingly inexhaustible supply of recruits. The dominance of catholic political culture by a simplistic nationalist rhetoric - which we have attempted to analyse in this paper - provided one other necessary cause of the campaign. Neither factor - economic disadvantage or simplistic nationalism - on its own would have been sufficient. Finally, the obvious ambivalence of the British state towards Ulster Unionism gave a further impetus.

This paper has laid much stress on the effects of nationalist strategy on the unionist bloc, and of unionist strategy on the nationalist bloc. This might seem to be a relatively obvious way of approaching the problem. But in fact so much of the discussion of terrorism in Ulster lacks historical specificity. Most writers - particularly leader writers and politicians - prefer to talk in general theories or analogies. There are general theories of British withdrawal as if this were simply another example of 'decolonisation'. Again there are more subtle analogies - which in some way acknowledge mass protestant opposition before dismissing it - the most popular being the case of Algeria.[25] This particular analogy is often intended to appeal to the generous impulses of a radical audience. Less often heard these days is the nationalist analogy of the late thirties - that of support for Hitler and his case over the Sudeten Germans as being analogous to Dublin's over the northern catholics.[26]

All these analogies are deeply misleading. These exotic examples serve only to distract from the prosaic realities. They fail to respect the facts of the case. Would the expulsion of the large Irish protestant minority from the UK reduce the current level of violence in Ulster? It seems on the face of it a most unlikely development.

Yet - whatever course is taken - the outlook remains bleak. The period from 1973 to the end of 1980 saw very broadly a slow decline in the capacity of the Provisional IRA to make major military or political gains. The leadership had declared 1974 to be the 'year of victory' but no such victory had ensued. To be sure they retained a certain military capacity but the long term political rationale of the campaign was in doubt. The hunger strike, despite a relatively apathetic initial response from the catholic masses, and despite the British government's 'victory' over the first batch of strikers just before Christmas 1980 has changed all that. The death of Sands and his fellows, the election of Sands as an MP and the election successes of many Provisional fellow travellers has transformed the situation. Moderate catholic opinion finds itself in a similar electorally vulnerable position to that of the Irish parliamentary party in 1916 or 1917 - though it is not quite summer 1918 yet. There is little likelihood of any stability, let alone seriousness, in British policy.

The Provisionals themselves have been some time in a triumphalist mood. After the murder of Lord Mountbatten, a "spokesman" in a special Irish Times interview openly boasted that protestant resistance was dependent on British support.[27] A few months later another "spokesman" told Magill magazine that not only was the Northern Irish state irreformable but so also were northern protestants![28] The feeling on the other side of the divide is, of course, equally bitter.

Such a deepening of sectarian polarisation has the most serious implications for democracy in Ireland. Democratic liberties have been seriously infringed in Ulster in the seventies. Unfortunately these liberties are likely to be even more under threat in the eighties. That is, unless the triumphalist element in both the main political blocs can be substantially weakened.

Notes

1   See Claire Sterling, The Terror Network: The Secret War of International Terrorism (London, 1981). See also Maurice Tugwell, "Politics and Propaganda of the Provisional IRA', in Paul Wilkinson, ed., British Perspectives on Terrorism (London, 1981). As for the international aspects of the Ulster question, it is painfully obvious that the interests of the Soviet Union are mainly ideological: to extract the maximum propaganda benefits from the embarrassments of the British over questions such as internment and the hunger strike. The Provisional IRA is after all the only 'marxist influenced' terrorist organisation in the world whose main

objective at least is supported by the Reagan government. For a level-headed rebuttal of psychological explanations, see Ken Heskin, Northern Ireland: A Psychological Analysis (Dublin and Columbia, 1980).

2 Lee, op.cit., p.134.

3 It may be necessary to say a word about Paisleyism itself. As Henry Patterson has cogently argued: 'The continuation of Provisional IRA violence would not, in itself, have guaranteed Paisley his success. This came as a result of the effects of the abolition of Stormont on the Official Unionists. As possession of the state apparatuses had served the function for traditional Unionism in producing Protestant unity, its loss of control of the state was to produce a profound disorientation.' The Official Unionists have been seriously divided between 'integrationists' and 'devolutionists', and as Patterson concludes: 'DUP strength is therefore the product of its apparent strategy in comparison to the fumbling of the Official Unionists.' The DUP also, it should be noted, tends to take a firmer line in opposition to the monetarist policies of the Thatcher government. The real problem for Paisleyism is a long term one: none of its objectives such as a return to the old Stormont system are even remotely likely to be achieved. Patterson's remarks are taken from his "Paisley and Protestant Politics", Marxism Today, January 1982, pp.26-31.

4 Weekly Freeman, 21 July 1917.

5 Ibid., 28 July 1917.

6 Ibid., 29 September 1917.

7 PRO CO 904-1-6, 13 September 1917.

8 For the Ulster policies of the Dublin government of which Griffith was a member, see Paul Bew, Peter Gibbon and Henry Patterson, The State in Northern Ireland 1921-72 (Manchester, 1979), pp.63-70. For de Valera, see John Bowman's valuable "De Valera and the Ulster Question: 1917-73", Unpublished PhD thesis, University of Dublin, 1980.

9 On this point see Brian Girvin, "Irish Nationalism, Partition and the Demise of the Home Rule Party 1910-18", Retrospect (Dublin), N.S. 1, p.31.

10 Weekly Freeman's Journal, 10 February 1917. O'Flanagan was later to assume for himself the role of the conscience of Sinn Fein. See Tom Garvin, The Evolution of Irish Nationalist Politics (Dublin, 1981), p.153.

11 Freeman's Journal, 19 June 1916.

12 The Leader, 2 September 1916.

13 Roscommon Herald, 9 February 1918.

14 Lee, op.cit.

15 See on this point Paul Bew, "Britain's modern Irish question", Economy and Society 10/4, pp.481-87. See also Paul Bew and Frank Wright, "The Agrarian Opposition in Ulster 1846-1887", in S. Clark and J.S. Donnelly, eds., Irish Peasants, forthcoming.

16   William O'Brien, The Responsibility for Partition (Dublin, 1921), p.21.
17   For an attempt to argue this, see Paul Bew, C S Parnell (Dublin, 1980), pp.131-32.
18   Note in particular the works of Peter Gibbon, The Origins of Ulster Unionism (Manchester, 1975), and Henry Patterson, Class Conflict and Sectarianism. The Protestant Working Class and the Belfast Labour Movement (Belfast, 1980). See also the present author's "A protestant parliament for a protestant people: some reflections on government and minority in Northern Ireland 1921-43", in A. Cosgrove and R. Fanning, eds., Parliament and Community, forthcoming.
19   J.V. O'Brien's William O'Brien and the Course of Irish Politics (California, 1975) is a most valuable work. It does however give O'Brien's conciliation policy a somewhat harsh treatment.
20   P.J. Bull, "The Reconstruction of the Irish Parliamentary Party 1895-1905: An analysis with special reference to William O'Brien", unpublished PhD thesis, Cambridge, 1972, pp.384-94.
21   Weekly Freeman, 29 September 1917.
22   Mayo News, 29 June 1918.
23   There is now a substantial literature, see Bew, Gibbon and Patterson, op.cit., and Patrick Buckland, A History of Northern Ireland (Dublin, 1981). Useful review essays: H. Cox, "Stormont Revisited", Parliamentary Affairs XXXIV (Winter 1981); P. Hillyard, "The State in Northern Ireland", Marxism Today, January 1980, Richard Chessum, "Marxism, the State and Northern Ireland", Ireland Socialist Review 7 (Spring 1980); G. Eley, 'The Left, the Nationalists and the Protestants', Michigan Quarterly Review 22, no.1 (winter 1983). See also the comments by Gearoid O Tuathaigh in his contribution to J.J. Lee, ed., Irish Historiography 1970-79 (Cork, 1981).
24   British Journal of Sociology 32/3 (September 1981), pp.362-80. For a more measured account, see John Whyte, "How much discrimination was there under the Unionist regime?", in The Journal of Contemporary Irish Studies, forthcoming.
25   Irish Nationalism (Dublin, 1981).
26   This point is borne out by the matter concerning civil rights leaders' attitudes discussed in Paul Bew, Peter Gibbon and Henry Patterson, "Some Aspects of Nationalism and Socialism in Ireland 1968-78", in A. Morgan and R. Purdie, eds., Ireland: Divided Nation, Divided Class.
27   Bew, Gibbon and Patterson, The State, op.cit., pp.166-67.
28   For example, see R.W. Johnson, "Ireland and the runcible man" for a remarkably benign 'Algerian' unscenario: "It is possible that Ian Paisley and the UDF [sic] will behave like the OAS and many innocent people will die. But once it

is clear that they face a catholic majority and the british army, they'll give up surprisingly soon". New Society, 25 June 1981. This writer seems to be unburdened by any knowledge (UDF indeed!) as are many of the commentators in the weeklies. Ireland still remains the subject on which it is positively de rigeur to talk fanciful nonsense.

Essay thirteen

THE PERSISTENCE OF IRA TERRORISM[1]

Martha Crenshaw

> A physical force movement in Ireland which ends
> without a fight has a more demoralizing influence on
> the people than a fight that fails.[2]

The Irish Republican Army has the distinction of being the
longest-lived organization in history, exhibiting a remarkable
continuity in both goal and method. The roots of violence in
Ireland are tangled and deep; understanding their growth is
essential to explaining the extraordinary tenacity of the IRA.
The Provisional IRA's persistence since its inception in 1970
lies in the historical development of Irish Republicanism.
Terrorism in the formative period of the Provisional IRA
(1970-1972) stemmed not only from the events which
immediately precipitated violence but also from a set of
preconditions that both made terrorism possible and provided
motivations for its practitioners and supporters. The IRA's
collective perception, definition, and interpretation of events
and background conditions were also critical, as was the
character of the organization and the relationships among its
members. How and why IRA terrorism has continued into the
1980s, despite its obvious lack of success in achieving the
goal of a united Ireland, forever free of the British presence,
requires another explanation. The consequences of IRA
terrorism, which are one reason the IRA persists, also
deserve close scrutiny if we are to discover the limits to the
effectiveness of terrorism.

THE PRECIPITANTS OF TERRORISM

The events that led to the creation of the Provisional IRA,
with its determined dedication to the use of terrorism to expel
the British from Northern Ireland and unite the island,
include a sequence of steps, beginning with the formation of
the Northern Ireland civil rights movement and culminating in

246

British violence against civil rights demonstrators. The violent Protestant response to Catholic assertiveness, the subsequent introduction of British soldiers into the province, and the policy of internment were intermediary steps.

The civil rights movement in Northern Ireland, which came into the headlines in 1968, sought to remedy a situation of institutionalized social, political and economic inequality for the Catholic minority. Under the Stormont regime, the semi-autonomous government of the North dominated by the Protestant Unionist party since the partition of Ireland in 1920, local and regional government was an exclusively Protestant domain. An elaborate system of gerrymandering and property qualifications for voting ensured that Catholics, even in areas such as Derry where they constituted a majority, were under Protestant control. Decisions on matters such as housing - the immediate issue that provoked Catholic resentment - were in Protestant hands. Protestant employers also discriminated against Catholics in their hiring practices.

Catholic frustration was heightened in the late 1960s. Expectations of change had risen in response to liberal overtures made by the O'Neill government (1963-1969), which, in a move to bring economic prosperity to Ulster, attempted to incorporate Catholics in the formation of a modern industrial economy. At the same time the civil rights movement in the United States provided a model of apparent success, while student radicalism sharpened the mood of political activism. Many members of the Northern Ireland Civil Rights Association, like Bernadette Devlin, were students, others were middle-class Catholics. The IRA had no conection with the organization, which adopted the American tactics of non-violent civil disobedience, mass demonstrations and protest marches.

The assertion of Catholic rights was met with violence from Protestant extremists. Assaults on marchers and demonstrators, mob attacks on Catholic neighbourhoods, burning houses and other damage and harm went largely unchecked and sometimes aided by the Protestant security forces, the Royal Ulster Constabulary and its citizen auxiliaries, the "B-Specials". Catholic provocations and riots followed Protestant demonstrations, Protestants then retaliated in kind. Besieged Catholic areas of Belfast and Derry threw up barricades and defended themselves with petrol bombs and paving stones.

Confronted with a situation where the RUC was unable or unwilling to maintain law and order, Britain was compelled by August 1969 to commit troops to keep the peace, primarily by protecting the Catholic population. The Stormont regime was induced to replace the hated B-Specials with a new Ulster Defence Regiment and to implement local reforms.

For a combination of reasons, including the appearance of the revitalized Provisional IRA on the scene, the British were unable to restore order. Frustrated at involvement in what became more and more of a civil war, the British government in 1971 introduced the policy of internment without trial for those suspected of involvement in illegal violence. This policy and its clumsy implementation appeared prejudiced to Catholics, although the policy nominally applied to Protestants as well. Internment symbolized the final split between Catholics and the British government.

A last catalyst came in early 1972, on January 30, "Bloody Sunday", when British troops fired on Catholic demonstrators in Derry. The unexpected violence of the British retaliation against a demonstration no different from countless predecessors over a two-year period left the Catholic population stunned at the thirteen civilian deaths that resulted. This unfortunate incident, the reasons for which remain obscure despite an official British investigation, produced such a degeneration in security that Westminster instituted direct rule of Northern Ireland in March.

The IRA gained a hold for its present terrorist campaign on the coat-tails of the civil rights movement. The IRA initially posed as the defender of Catholics, first against the Protestants, then against the British. Yet why an organization like the IRA existed, waiting in the wings, and why it could step so naturally into the role of protector, can only be explained by deeper background factors. The support of the Catholic community has been particularly critical to the IRA's activity. Situational factors also made terrorism physically possible for the IRA and crippled the British response. Though the events outlined above could have happened differently, the long-range conditions to be discussed now were not matters of choice by the 1969-1972 period. Over time some of them could be changed by human manipulation; others appear eternal. However, they did not determine terrorism; they existed before terrorism began. Much of the importance derives from their relationship to the specific events of 1969-1972.

THE PRECONDITIONS OF TERRORISM

A condition that both inspired IRA terrorism after 1920 and enabled the IRA to retain a minimal level of popular support was the objective fact of genuine Catholic grievances in Northern Ireland. Discrimination by the Protestant majority against the Catholic minority stemmed from the nature of the partition arrangements, which allowed the Stormont regime almost complete authority in matters of domestic governance. Autonomy for Ulster inevitably meant the denial of Catholic participation in political decision-making and the perpetuation of social injustice. Clearly, Northern Ireland was a case of "relative deprivation", made more acute by the civil rights movement and undoubtedly by comparison with the political freedom, if not the economic benefits, of fellow-Catholics across the border in the Republic.[3] Inequality and injustice resulted in Catholic alienation from the regime. Their lack of loyalty to Stormont and their voluntary adherence to patterns of segregation along religious lines were deeply ingrained. That Irish nationalism and Catholicism should be equated and that there could be no common political identity in Northern Ireland were results of the extreme lack of consensus in the political system.[4] The communities remained divided, at best uneasily co-existing.

The role of myth as an inspiration for terrorism is as important as the minority status of Catholics in the North.[5] IRA terrorism is firmly anchored in the physical force tradition of Irish Republican nationalism with a continuous history that goes back to the French Revolution. The heritage of belief on which the IRA relies prescribed the desired end, explains how to attain it, and identifies the enemy to blame for the present state of injustice and thwarted aspirations. These elements of the myth are confirmed by the lessons of history and sanctified by the blood of martyrs. Irish mythology directly motivates the IRA and makes its terrorism possible by insuring that many Irish Catholics, North or South, and Irish-Americans will either support or not oppose the IRA. Myth and history confer legitimacy on what otherwise might be a highly dubious adventure.

The Provisional IRA traces its ancestry directly back for at least a century, to the formation of the secret Irish Republican Brotherhood (IRB) in 1858. The IRB, also known as the Fenians, was an oath-bound secret society dedicated to the achievement of Irish independence from Britain through military means. The following description of it fits the contemporary IRA with remarkable exactness:

> The essential principles of Fenianism were that nothing could be achieved for Ireland by constitutional means, that British power must be overthrown by force, and that any delay in action would be dangerous.... Though it throve on social discontent, Fenianism had no programme of reform – it would be time enough to think of that when national independence had been won; and though its leaders often claimed to be acting on behalf of "the Irish people", it was in no sense democratic.[6]

The Fenians relied strongly on terrorism, including attacks in England as well as Ireland.[7] The organization benefited, as does the contemporary IRA from the existence of an American Irish community that provided refuge and financial support.

The physical force tradition in Irish politics dates back even further than the Fenians to Wolfe Tone and the abortive revolution of 1798, inspired by events of 1789. Whereas the early rebels emphasized the development of popular support and mass uprisings, the IRB along with other nineteenth century Republican undergrounds in Europe, recognized that attempts at mass insurrection had consistently and dismally failed and turned to the idea of conspiracy. The IRB and their IRA heirs were convinced that they knew the right for Ireland, regardless of what the majority of its people might think. Revolutionary action could not wait for mass mobilization.

The modern IRA was formed during the events which led to the creation of the Irish Free State in 1922. It combined the IRB and an above-ground paramilitary organization, the Irish Volunteers, formed in 1913 in response to the creation of an Ulster Volunteer Force as a Protestant means of combatting the prospect of home rule for Ireland. In 1914, Britain shelved plans for limited Irish autonomy until the end of the war. IRB leaders, however, saw the hostilities as an ideal opportunity. Having gained some control over the Volunteer movement, they laid plans for insurrection. Consequently on Easter Monday 1916, a group of Volunteers, led by the IRB, seized the Dublin Post Office and other central buildings. The rebels held out against government troops until Saturday, then surrendered without having made any significant impact on public opinion It was the British government's response, the execution of fifteen captured leaders, that gave nationalism its force by creating martyrs to the cause. Patrick Pearse, one of the executed leaders, had predicted that only a blood-sacrifice could save the Irish nation, and by providing it Britain forever imbued Irish Republican nationalism with the aura of self-sacrifice and martyrdom. As historian J.C. Beckett has described it Ireland now passed under the most dangerous of all tyrannies, the tyranny of the dead.[8]

In early 1919, the reconstituted Volunteers became the IRA under the leadership of Michael Collins, also head of the IRB. The IRA conducted a well-orchestrated guerrilla and terrorist campaign against the police, army and English landowners.[9] Collins was particularly adept at undermining British intelligence through the selective assassination of agents. Ambushes and other hit-and-run guerrilla tactics proved successful in rural areas. The IRA enjoyed a high level of popular support, due to its efficiency and discipline, popular anger at Britain for trying to introduce conscription to Ireland in 1918, its association with the secessionist Irish Parliament or Dail, representing the constitutionalist side of Irish nationalism, and the brutality of the British military response. British forces, the ignominious "Black and Tans" and an Auxiliary division, were sent to aid the Royal Irish Constabulary; hastily recruited, unruly and hated by the population, their principal response to the rebellion consisted of reprisals against civilians.[10]

The result of the war of attrition was partial victory for the IRA. The British opened negotiations which ended in the constitution of the Irish Free State in 1922. It was, however, a truncated state, as the Six counties of Ulster, where Protestant loyalist settlers were concentrated, were split off by the terms of the Government of Ireland Act of 1920 as a separate province to remain part of the United Kingdom.

It was predictable that a faction of the IRA should reject the settlement and that the civil war of 1922-1923 should result in the defeat of the rebel IRA by Free State forces. The majority of the recalcitrants eventually became reconciled to the state; when their leader, Eamon de Valera, became Prime Minister, he led the drafting of a new constitution, and the government outlawed the IRA. The IRA is thus characterized by consistent opposition to government authority, whether British or Irish, and a stubborn refusal to die out. There was a brief flurry of terrorism in England in 1939, and in 1956-1962 a campaign of terrorism along the border with the North. The IRA holds that the revolution is incomplete. Republican faith in a future united Ireland and the certainty of the Provisionals that the principal requirement is driving the British out by the war of attrition that worked in 1921 are based on years of tradition, myth and symbolism. IRA beliefs combine political naivete, unyielding conviction and mystical faith in Irish unity. There is little practical consideration of the intervening steps between throwing the British out and bringing a million Protestants, not to speak of the very disparate Catholic populations of North and South, into a united Ireland.

The genealogy of the IRA must be seen in the light of historical Irish antipathy toward British authority and toward the Protestant settler "ascendancy", dating principally from the time of Cromwell's conquest. In 1652, the Act of Settlement expropriated Irish landowners who had participated in the rebellion and awarded their estates to Protestant settlers. The victory of William of Orange over James II is still heralded by the Protestants of Ulster. A series of penal laws in the early eighteenth century effectively prevented Catholics from acquiring land, holding public office, or educating their children. The Great Famine of 1845-1848 also embittered relations between the Irish people and the British government, as many felt that the British showed a callous disregard for Irish misery. Furthermore, the great distress led to mass emigration to the United States, where the new Irish Americans tended toward an extreme nationalism that funded many ill-fated Fenian plots of the nineteenth century.

The appeal of the physical force tradition, hatred for the British overlord, suspicion and mistrust between Protestants and Catholics and demonstrable Catholic grievances combined to ensure not only a small number of militants willing to use force to achieve the goal handed down to them by their ancestors, but also three different populations willing and able to provide at least passive support for a violent movement. Many inhabitants of the Republic, Catholics of the North and Irish-Americans were and are sympathetic to the cause. Their sympathy may not extend to approval for acts of terrorism, but it does extend to occasional moral and financial, and sometimes active, support.

Thus, among the given factors that permit if they do not encourage terrorism is geography. the contiguous border between Northern and Southern Ireland. That British or Ulster security forces do not have the right of pursuit into the Republic, that IRA members, money and weapons may move freely back and forth, that robberies in the Republic fund the IRA's Northern operations – these are conditions largely independent of the Republic's official policies but which aid the IRA. The government of the Republic, in which the IRA has been outlawed much longer than it has in Great Britain, unwillingly provides sanctuary, a conduit for arms and funds, and staging bases – functions highly important to the operations of the IRA – but dares not move more strongly because public opinion does not consistently favour the repression of Republicanism.

The general availability of weapons and explosives is also a significant factor in enabling the IRA to act. IRA sympathizers in the United States are instrumental in this regard; the Armalite rifle, a favourite of the IRA, is commercially produced in the United States and most IRA purchases come from New York.[11] Small conventional arms – machine and submachine guns, light rifles and revolvers are easily obtainable for the IRA as for most modern terrorist organizations. Explosives are even more easily acquired: thefts from military and especially commercial sources are relatively common, and explosives can be constructed by using gardening chemicals. Radio fuses and electronic timers can also be adapted to bombs. Gelignite and dynamite are quite effective without sophisticated manipulations. The IRA has proved extraordinarily adept at incendiary bombs, car bombs, mines and booby traps. The supply of weapons and explosives is extremely difficult for governments to control. The prohibition of small, silent, high-powered rifles and of remote-control, timed explosives is impossible; this factor of technological modernity in the means of destruction favours terrorists everywhere.

The urbanization of Northern Ireland has also made terrorism easier for the IRA, while rural terrorism occurs most seriously in border areas such as Armagh.[12] Over half of the population of Northern Ireland; over 500,000 people live in greater Belfast. Catholics are also concentrated in Derry.

A last factor which facilitates IRA terrorism is political:

the democratic restraints on the British response. Although complaints have been lodged against specific British practices, British policies remain those of a democractic liberal state, concerned with protecting the rights of the individual. The IRA profits by the limits democracy imposes; all liberal states combatting terrorism, including most prominently West Germany, Italy and Spain, face similar problems. Governments confront a difficult choice between tolerating a certain level of terrorism or instituting rules and security procedures that jeopardize the political order that is being defended against terrorism.

TERRORIST ORGANIZATION, AIMS AND METHODS

The people who become terrorists or assist terrorists are a very small number of those who collectively experience the events and conditions outlined above. At its highpoint in 1972, the IRA numbered about a thousand activists, it is currently thought to be in the range of three to four hundred, apparently showing some diminution since a 1979 figure of five hundred.[13] The Irish National Liberation Army, a recent manifestation of Irish nationalism that evolved from the Official wing of the IRA, has only a hundred members.[14] To understand the resort to terrorism, we must look at the terrorists' perceptions of the environment, their reasons for terrorism, their interpretations of the situation, their goals, their strategies and their organization.

Terrorism is a rational choice, deliberately made for reasons that are comprehensible if not justifiable to the outside observer. Furthermore, terrorism is best understood as the collective choice of an organization than as the decision of a single individual. Terrorism is not a form of deviant psychology; examination of personality types is unlikely to provide a satisfactory explanation. In the words of a British military intelligence report, the IRA consists of well trained, skilled militants led by "a strata of intelligent, astute, and experienced terrorists".[15] Most observers agree that there is no unifying personality characteristic among terrorists, much less some pathological drive that would make terrorism a form of expressive rather than instrumental violence.[16] IRA leaders impress observers as being genuinely dedicated to the cause, not as individuals attracted to violence for its own sake.

Psychological motives for terrorism and social and psychological rewards for participation in terrorist activities play some role, although they are not dominant factors. Vengeance against the enemy is a strong emotional motive, one which many terrorist groups share.[17] Also, in the Irish context, the role of an IRA member is one that earns a definite reinforcement. The solidarity and comradeship of belonging to a paramilitary organization, an in-group blessed by history and myth, as well as the wider social respect that the IRA receives (a form of approval and awe that most other terrorist groups operating in democracies do not elicit), are important rewards. The IRA gunman can become a legend in his own time.

Such factors partially explain why individuals are attracted to terrorism. They do not explain why the terrorist organization decides and acts as it does. The role of the leadership is extremely important in determining goals and strategies, although leaders are pressured by followers and by public opinion.

The Provisionals, as we have argued, inherited the goal of a United Ireland and the strategy of physical force. However, the Provisional IRA deliberately chose the time and the form of violence. When the civil rights movement broke out in 1969, the IRA formally adhered to a programme emphasizing social revolution and Marxist doctrine rather than violence. The organization was centred in the Republic of Ireland, and its leaders had apparently concluded from the failure of the 1956-1962 border campaign that the conditions were not ripe for revolution. The IRA of the time favoured tolerating the Stormont regime (presumably on the grounds that the greater the oppression, the quicker the arousal of a revolutionary consciousness among the masses), collaboration with other leftist parties, and the mobilization of working class support.

The Catholic-Protestant clashes which grew out of civil rights activism split the IRA into two factions, the "Officials", who clung to their strategy of waiting for appropriate conditions, and a new Provisional wing determined to take advantage of what was perceived as a unique opportunity. Sean MacStiofain, leader of the Provisionals, argued that immediate action was imperative. Protecting the Catholic population against Protestant attacks would enhance IRA prestige and support; passivity would be disaster. Defending the Catholic minority was an intermediate goal, justified in the short run by the necessity of maintaining the IRA's credibility, and in the long run as a step toward abolition of the Stormont regime, expelling the British, and unifying Ireland.

The Provisional faction also rejected the increasingly Marxist orientation the old IRA had taken. To the orthodox Marxist, revolution can occur only when the situation brings about a mass uprising with only limited assistance from a vanguard party. Historical forces, not individual actions, create revolutionary conditions. Terrorism can play little part in this scenario, and it has historically been at this juncture in decision-making that terrorist groups have split from larger revolutionary movements.[18] Most terrorist organizations believe that the violence of an underground organization can bring about revolutionary conditions. MacStiofain impatiently expresses this doctrine when he states:

> Thinking back over the history of the movement I realised that although the revolutionary chain had remained unbroken ever since Wolfe Tone had defined the Republican objective of independence from England in 1798, the strength of popular support for it had varied from time to time. It seemed to bear out a focal theory of revolution long before it was spelled out by Che Guevara and others. Guerrillas who want to bring social and political change do not wait for conditions to become "ripe" for revolutionary action, because they could be waiting forever. Instead, they take the field and gradually build up popular support through their successes.[19]

Thus, the differences between the Provisionals and the Officials were both ideological, the Provisionals being more simply nationalistic and definitely anti-Marxist though vaguely socialist, and they differed on the interpretation of events and on how the IRA ought to react. Given the small size of the IRA and its commitment to immediate action, terrorism was a logical and time-honoured choice.

The IRA's strategy centres on two related goals, which are thought to pave the way to an independent, united Ireland. The first is to obtain the allegiance of the Catholic population, principally in the North and secondarily in the South. Their second aim is to mount a successful war of attrition against the British, following the precedent of Michael Collins. Thus the IRA intends to undermine British rule, by demoralizing military forces in Northern Ireland, by "bringing the war back home" to England as painfully as possible, and by making the war effort costly financially as well as politically. Ironically, the IRA wishes to keep British forces in Northern Ireland until the nation sickens of the task of keeping order. In most ways, the IRA sees the Protestants of Northern Ireland as minions of the British, not as an autonomous force. Thus IRA leaders conclude that were the British to pull out entirely, unification would result regardless of Protestant wishes. The power of Protestant paramilitary forces is disregarded.

In this strategic context, the IRA seems also to be preoccupied with demonstrating a "position of strength" and, as a corollary, never appearing weak. Maria McGuire explains, for example, that while negotiations and truces were often desired or even anticipated, the aim of negotiating from strength, of never letting it be thought that the IRA was in a position of weakness, dominated IRA decision-making. The fear of appearing weak sometimes counteracted fears of alienating Catholic opinion, as it did when MacStiofain refused to call off the IRA's "military campaign" after the British suspended Stormont.[20]

The form of terrorism the IRA has chosen has not been particularly inventive; it rarely deviates from the assassinations and bombings employed by Fenians, IRB and original IRA. The changes are more in the exploitation of technical means than in targeting or aims. The IRA's traditionalism in these matters and their lack of interest in the international situation have meant that modern forms of terrorism - such as kidnappings and hijackings that gain world attention - are not practiced.

IRA activity since 1970 has consistently focussed on the security forces: the British army, the Royal Ulster Constabulary, the Ulster Defence Regiment, and its predecessor, the B-specials. These attacks accord with the IRA's goal of demoralization and diversion, are consistent with the historical image of the IRA as an army, and are justifiable to the IRA's constituency. Initially the IRA restricted its attacks to armed, uniformed security personnel, but in late 1971, off-duty military and police were also subject to attack. Sean MacStiofain argued that treating unarmed RUC, UDR and British forces as "legitimate combatant targets" was a result of the government's policy of internment, introduced in August.[21] The "combatant" category of victim proved quite elastic and was expanded further to include civilians who directly support the military effort: prison guards, canteen workers, former RUC reservists, civilian employees of the military, and their dependents. Opposition politicians are also considered "legitimate" victims.

The modus operandi has become standardized: mining roads British patrols must travel on, snipers firing single shots at the military on patrol in urban neighbourhoods, and masked men shooting UDR members as they plough their fields or sit with their families. Occasional attacks on security forces have also taken place outside Northern Ireland. The bombing of the Aldershot military base in February 1972 was, however, the work of the official IRA, who engaged in the brief campaign of terrorism probably in an attempt to wrest leadership of the militant nationalist movement from the Provisionals.

The IRA has also engaged in extensive property destruction. Bombings of material targets, either of economic value such as shops or of military importance such as roads and bridges, are as standard and as appropriate to the IRA's goals as attacking security forces. Incendiary bombs have proved particularly versatile.

Indiscriminate assaults in clearly civilian targets, however, have been more problematic for the IRA. Bombings have affected two groups: Protestants in Northern Ireland and the English population.

Sean MacStiofain gave two reasons for introducing the car bomb to Belfast in 1972. First, he said that the IRA had acquired the ability to manufacture its own explosives, which made massive explosions possible. Second, he cited the war of attrition against the British: the bombs were intended to complicate the government and administration of Northern Ireland, to strike at the "colonial" economy, since the British government was responsible for compensation for bomb damage to commercial and industrial targets, and to tie British troops to guarding the centre of Belfast, not pursuing the IRA.[22]

Maria McGuire provides more political reasons for urban bombings. She cites the IRA's aim of causing "confusion and terror": "Half a million people in Belfast would be kept wondering where the Provisionals would strike next and would be forced to tell the British to make peace with us."[23] She also mentions the temptation of "so many targets" in Belfast and the desire to divert British troops from Catholic neighbourhoods, to demonstrate that the British could no longer govern and that the Provisionals would continue despite military efforts, to disrupt the life of the city (especially by mixing false alarms with real bombs), to drive out foreign investors, and to make the conflict costly for Britain.[24]

In its civilian bombings, the IRA was also acting in terms of its role as defender of the Catholic population and in the context of the sectarian struggle that the war had become by 1972. There were 115 civilian deaths in 1971; 322 in 1972. The communal nature of the conflict grew out of Protestant retaliations against the IRA, acts of revenge or aggression that as often as not struck anonymous Catholics indiscriminately. The Ulster Defence Association, founded in 1971 and the only legal Protestant paramilitary organization, admitted in 1975 that in the "tit-for-tat" period of 1971-1973, only two in ten of the Catholics killed by the UDA had anything to do with the IRA.[25] Under such circumstances, the IRA undoubtedly felt compelled to act dramatically in order to maintain its position as a Catholic opinion leader. Rather than being part of a coordinated strategic plan, the 1972 bombings may have been a response to increased capability and Protestant provocation.

The ambivalence the IRA leadership seemed to feel about this tactic reflected a sensitivity to the image of the organization and to the possibility of a backlash effect among supporters. The IRA, which never neglected propaganda, always insisted that adequate warning was given and that the responsibility for casualties lay with the British who failed deliberately to evacuate buildings.[26] MacStiofain claimed that in late 1972, the IRA cut back on the use of bombs because "there were too many unexplained bombings and provocations going on" and the IRA did not wish to be confused with Protestant extremists.[27] In March 1972 the IRA had denied a role in the bombing of the Abercorn Restaurant in central Belfast, when two people were killed and a hundred and fifty injured. In early 1978, the IRA even apologized for the bombing of the La Mon House Restaurant, and since then there have been no equivalent numbers of civilian casualties.

"Bringing the war home" to England has included bombings in urban centres such as London and Birmingham, involving car-bombs, bombings of pubs and underground stations, and even the Tower of London and the House of Commons. Such campaigns have been short-lived, but it is difficult to know whether their brevity and infrequency is due to logistical problems for the IRA, the efficiency of the English police and intelligence services, or the negative reaction such indiscriminacy engenders.

The IRA has also, but rarely, resorted to selective attacks on prominent civilian victims. For example, in 1973, a letter-bomb was sent to the British Embassy in Washington – an act that was not repeated, due surely to the danger of alienating American opinion, shocked at the injury done to the secretary who opened the letter intended for the Ambassador. In 1976, the IRA assassinated the British Ambassador to Ireland in Dublin, and in 1979, Earl Mountbatten at his Irish home.

A partial explanation for the untypical assassination of a popular figure such as Mountbatten, an act that also killed members of his family and which was by no means as publicly justifiable for the IRA as attacks on official representatives of British policy, lies in the existence of parallel Republican terrorist groups. Just as Provisional attacks on military targets in England may have been inspired by the Officials' actions, the Irish National Liberation Army, created in 1975, may have provoked the IRA to a violent rivalry.[28] The INLA cooperates with the IRA in Northern Ireland; it is, however, more internationally-oriented. In 1979 it was responsible for the assassination in London of Airey Neave, the Conservative Party spokesman on Northern Ireland, and also of the British Ambassador in the Hague. Here again, self-maintenance may be a motive for IRA terrorism.

The IRA has also tried consistently to establish itself as a counter-government in Catholic areas of Northern Ireland, enforcing obedience as well as demanding loyalty. It controls certain rackets, operates some honest businesses, and collects protection money. Petty crime and treachery are dealt with by knee-capping offenders or dropping concrete blocks on their limbs.

Although the IRA relies heavily on terrorism, violence is not its sole recourse. Great emphasis is placed on propaganda and fund-raising. The "blanket" strike of IRA prisoners and most significantly the 1981 hunger strike were non-violent attempts to achieve IRA goals. The IRA has also on occasion, notably in 1972, engaged in what might be termed diplomatic negotiations with the British. There has, however, been no close alliance between the IRA and other movements representing Catholic opinion; the SDLP has been perceived as a rival rather than a collaborator. The Irish government remains an enemy. The IRA is not part of a broadly based social movement.

THE POLITICAL EFFECTS OF IRA TERRORISM

It is difficult to evaluate the consequences of IRA terrorism, mingled as they are with the effects of other actions and events in a dynamic process of political change. Such limitations, however, should not preclude analysis of the outcomes of terrorism, especially its impact on stability and democracy in Northern Ireland and in Great Britain.[29] The IRA constitutes an important example of indigenous terrorism at its most intense in a developed, industrial Western democracy: what difference has it made to the governance of the state?

The case of the IRA represents an unusual situation. Despite Northern Ireland's operational autonomy in the period before 1972, it remained a part of a larger whole which could reinstitute the prerogatives of sovereignty when it chose. Furthermore, while the province of Ulster was itself not democratic, the larger entity of which it formed a part was. The combination of these two circumstances means that terrorism was not in this case a direct threat to a homogeneous political entity, as it has been in West Germany, Italy and Spain.[30]

If we look narrowly at the effect of terrorism on the structure of power in Ulster, then the British imposition of direct rule marks a radical change. The rules by which Ulster was governed and the elites who had constituted regimes were, in essence, peacefully overthrown from above.

Direct rule was meant not only to restore order in the strict sense by making the British government responsible for security - this could be done without suspending Stormont - but to implement political reforms which would extend democracy to the province by guaranteeing equal rights and opportunities to Catholics. The early civil rights agitation had caused Britain to pressure the Stormont government to hasten reforms that had started under O'Neil. Moderate Unionists, however, found themselves constantly outflanked on the right, notably by Ian Paisley, head of the Free Presbyterian Church of Northern Ireland. In 1969, O'Neil was replaced by James Chichester-Clark, who in turn was replaced by Brian Faulkner. Faulkner's brief tenure was undermined by the introduction of internment, which provoked IRA violence, an SDLP boycott of Parliament, and SDLP sponsorship of a civil disobedience campaign. Both political stalemate and the breakdown of law and order brought about direct rule in March 1972.

The British government then took on the role of conflict

mediator, trying to reconcile the antagonists and to establish a democratic structure in Northern Ireland. Efforts to bring about "power-sharing" in 1973, 1975-76 and in 1982 have so far resulted only in disappointment and frustration. The principal obstacle to compromise remains the lack of consensus that Richard Rose cited in the 1960s.[31] The British government has found that it cannot bring about consensus and that in its absence, democracy implies irreconcilable political demands for Protestant and Catholics. Local government reforms, however, have been implemented from the top, and there is no question that Catholics possess more rights and opportunities for participation under British than under Protestant rule.

The Protestant reaction both to Catholic assertiveness and to IRA terrorism lies at the heart of the failure of power sharing. There is no doubt that terrorism has played a major role in thwarting British attempts to replace direct rule, although it would be reckless to argue that without the IRA, Protestants would meekly agree to compromise. The Protestant majority of Ulster rejects power-sharing as a thinly veiled step toward Irish unity; this rejection is expressed in collective strikes and demonstrations as well as the violence of such extremist groups as the UDA. For example, the final blow to the executive in which the Unionist and SDLP parties shared power was a general strike by Protestant workers' associations in May 1974 that paralyzed the province. Nevertheless, terrorism seems to have heightened the dilemma of loyalty; Protestants equate disloyalty, Catholicism, nationalism and Republicanism. The differences between those who espouse peaceful means to unity and those who choose violence are blurred as polarization of opinion intensifies. Protestants react as a besieged minority; they dread integration with a Catholic state and the submersion of their identity with an alien political and religious community. Terrorism only increases Protestant intransigence and suspicion; they prefer insecurity in a system under British or home rule to peace in a context of Irish unity.

Furthermore, Protestant extremists have learned the lesson that violence pays. Part of this lesson derives from the early political experience of the Ulster Volunteer Force that successfully protested against the early Irish home rule proposals. In the contemporary era, Brian Faulkner, a moderate voice, observed that the activities of the UDA were predicated on the assumption that violence pays: "The objective of the Protestants involved was clear; they were telling the Government that if it was thought peace could be bought cheaply by a deal with the IRA, they would be buying more trouble from another source."[32] Even he concluded that "It is sad, but true, that the real determination of Unionists not to join a united Ireland seems only to have been fully believed when Protestant assassins started killing

Catholics."[33] When, in 1979, the UDA announced a return to paramilitary action, blaming the failure of the security forces to check the IRA, their leaders asserted that "the only thing that pays in this country is violence".[34]

There is another side to the British policy response to terrorism: the use of military forces to restore order and quell terrorism. Democracies only infrequently and reluctantly intervene in domestic politics by sending in the army to perform police functions. The British have been in Ulster for so long that many tend to view their involvement as commonplace. Yet continued military intervention is a significant result of a prolonged terrorist campaign.

British security measures against the IRA have involved a mixture of confrontation and, if not always cooperation, tolerance. The first bargain the British struck was in allowing the IRA to establish "no-go" areas in Belfast and Derry, which enabled the IRA to implant itself among Catholics. This permission was eventually lifted in response to Protestant pressure, and in July 1972 21,000 troops, participating in "Operation Motorman", destroyed the barricades without incident. The IRA put up no resistance, since their points, gaining authority over Catholic areas and general prestige, had already been won. Other examples of tacit cooperation include observing IRA truces and ignoring the publicized appearances of IRA leaders in the North. Formal cooperation with the IRA has also occurred. Negotiations between IRA leaders and British officials have occurred on and off and sometimes resulted in temporary cease-fires. From 1972 to 1976, IRA prisoners were accorded special status. The Provisional Sinn Fein, the IRA's political wing, is a legal organization (as is the UDA, for that matter).

It is difficult to assess the effectiveness of conciliation in controlling the IRA. Most damage was done by the laissez-faire attitude that allowed no-go areas. Dealing with the IRA has the historical precedent of 1920-1921, and the directness of the idea is appealing, yet it seriously compromised the British with Protestant opinion. Nor was the IRA ever persuaded to relent on its insistence that the British get out, and so by enhancing the IRA's reputation and self-regard, bargains strengthened the IRA. Furthermore, it is politically difficult to renege on concessions once granted. IRA protests against the denial of special status to prisoners culminated in the 1981 hunger strike, after which the British government granted several IRA demands.

Internment without trial, which lasted from August 1971 to December 1975, was the chief British security measure aimed at destroying the IRA. Although the policy was supposed to affect Protestants as well as Catholics, of the total of 1981 people held, only 107 were Protestants.[35] Internment had the worst possible combination of effects. Its unfair administration alienated the Catholic population and pushed them into the arms of the IRA; imprisonment created martyrs to the cause and provided indoctrination for future IRA militants thrown together in prison; arrests failed to decapitate the IRA, since they were fairly random and missed the top leaders; and the policy did not even pay off by appeasing Protestants. In general, internment strengthened the IRA and exacerbated the conflict between Protestant and Catholic communities. Although judicial prosecution of terrorists is often hampered by terrorist intimidation of witnessess, jurors and judges, internment cannot be an effective answer without excellent intelligence which enables the government to pinpoint the responsible terrorist leaders. Otherwise it aids terrorist recruitment and the acquisition of popular support.

Another problem the British and Ulster security forces have faced also relates intelligence failures to the task of obtaining convictions. If witnesses are unavailable, then a suspect's confession is the best evidence. Accusations of torture and brutality during the interrogation of arrested persons have embarrassed Britain internationally, won sympathy for the IRA, and made military and police personnel defensive. Specific objectionable practices such as sensory deprivation techniques were consequently abandoned and reforms of the RUC's interrogation procedures were instituted. The critical publicity that any transgression receives is an inevitable consequence of combatting terrorism in a democracy.

Another set of problems stems from army and police efforts to protect the population and themselves from terrorist attacks; routine security measures such as searches, identity checks, roadblocks, and patrols upset civilians. Catholics in Northern Ireland never expected fair treatment from the Protestant Ulster police auxiliary forces, who were reputed to treat Catholics harshly, ignore the violence of their co-religionists, and even on occasion join in mob attacks on Catholics. Catholic attitudes toward British troops shifted from benevolence to hostility for a combination of reasons including historical tradition, experience with military roughness, and the perception that the British were biased toward Protestants. It proved difficult for the army to remain impartial and open-minded when a third of the population hated them and the other two-thirds welcomed them. In combatting terrorism, security forces inevitably come to feel that the people from whose midst the terrorists come and who fail to inform on them are also the enemy.

In an effort to reduce the army profile, Britain adopted a policy of "Ulsterization", turning more security duties over to an upgraded RUC, but Britain maintains troops in West Belfast, Derry and south Armagh, where the RUC is still unacceptable and the IRA active. Attempts to recruit more

Catholics into the RUC have not been outstandingly successful. Despite emphasis on intelligence-gathering and analysis and the establishment of a special telephone number for callers who wish to give information anonymously, acquiring accurate information on the IRA remains a key problem. The British government is apparently reconciled to a policy of containment and the tolerance of a low level of violence for an indefinite future.

The British policy response has also involved greater cooperation with the Republic of Ireland than existed before the Troubles. Politically the British government has shown an enthusiastic willingness to associate the Republic in finding a solution, and the Republic has expressed eagerness to be included. The relationship is a delicate one, but both countries share the view that the IRA must be repressed, that unity can come about only through consent, and that for the present direct rule is the only feasible policy. In the area of security, cooperation between police forces on either side of the border has improved. However, the Republic does not extradite terrorist suspects or allow Northern Ireland forces the right of pursuit across the border. The South still provides a convenient sanctuary and base for both IRA and INLA, a source of funds, and a channel for arms. Irish popular enthusiasm for the cause of Catholics of the North died down as internment and official discrimination ended, as IRA bombings and assassinations outraged public opinion, and as the hunger strike ended with little credit for the Republican movement. Nevertheless, the idea of Irish unity remains powerful. The failure of the British and Irish Prime Ministers to agree on common security measures even when confronted with the crisis of finding a response to the assassination of Mountbatten demonstrates the limits of cooperation. The policy of the Irish government is that political resolution of the conflict is an essential precondition for the eradication of terrorism.

Terrorism has little effect on the domestic political structure of Great Britain or Ireland; for example it is not an election issue in either country. However, it has resulted in policy changes oriented toward suppressing the IRA. The IRA only became an outlawed organization in Great Britain in 1974 as a result of bombings in Birmingham. The Prevention of Terrorism Act (which also applies to Northern Ireland) involves restrictions on civil liberties such as government exclusion powers by which suspected terrorists can be expelled from Britain. Persons may also be detained for questioning for up to a week. More stringent measures were taken in the Republic, where a Special Criminal Court was established, the defendant's presumption of innocence abolished in the case of IRA membership, and spokesmen for the IRA prohibited from appearing on radio or television or being quoted in the press.[36]

Equally as important as the effects of terrorism on formal power structures and government policies is its impact on popular attitudes and on participation. Among the Protestants of the North, terrorism has only stiffened preexisting attitudes of resistance to any compromise that hints of a drift toward Irish unity. Among the IRA's potential Catholic constituency, there seems to be every indication that although terrorism did spark a brief Peace Movement, which expressed a strong revulsion for violence, over the past decade a residual amount of support for the IRA remains constant. This apparent anomaly, which exists in the Republic, Northern Ireland, and among Irish-Americans, can be explained by the fact that many Catholics preserve a strong feeling of support for the IRA's goals while repudiating their means.[37] Thus, the disapproval the IRA may be subjected to in the immediate aftermath of an atrocity is ephemeral. The predominant feeling seems to be that the struggle is just, and that therefore the means must at least be tolerated. Paradoxically, by keeping the struggle alive, terrorism reminds the populations of the salience and the justice of the IRA's ends, thus invoking deep emotional sympathy while perhaps provoking short-term condemnation. Terrorism helps keep the Fenian flame burning.

Terrorism also has general and diffuse consequences for the long-term prospects for democracy and stability; in particular, it affects the quality of life, patterns of political socialization, and political culture. Such subtle effects are extremely difficult to gauge. Most observers first notice the extraordinary resilience of the social order in Northern Ireland: life goes on despite high levels of violence. Dervla Murphy, for example, while characterizing the atmosphere as "posionous" and "spiritually destructive", seems to feel that the appearance of normality is superficial:

> Everybody seems unselfconsciously matter-of-fact about the extraordinary way they live now. Yet the process of adapting to this sort of permanently watchful existence must be damaging. The annual statistics say that Northern Ireland's citizens are not more at risk from bombs and bullets than from road accidents. But it's the nature of the threat that creates tension, not the numbers of victims.[38]

Yet there is little concrete evidence of distress. Many researchers fear that violence has reinforced anti-social behaviour, but such reinforcement occurs as much from watching violence on television as from experiencing it, and furthermore there is little crime or delinquency in Northern Ireland. Data on the incidence of mental illness in Belfast are mixed. Certainly the actual victims of explosions suffer more acute disturbances, but their recovery rate is remarkably rapid. In general, the evidence supports a theory of adaptation rather than social upset. The problems may lie in the strain of coping and adapting and in the consequences of growing to tolerate violence.[39] Such effects have been little studied, and it is impossible to say how they will influence the future politics of Northern Ireland.

EFFECTIVENESS AND LEGITIMACY

The IRA is further than ever from its goal of a united Ireland, although it achieved its instrumental objective of ending Protestant rule in Northern Ireland. It has been unable to move beyond this point, no more than the British have been able to institute a power-sharing system. How does one explain the fact that although the "war of attrition" has failed, violating precedents in Ireland, in Palestine, in Aden, and in other colonies,[40] the IRA endures and retains an unexpected and unprecedented strength and negative capacity for affecting events?

Organizations like the IRA that seek political power cannot attain it through force of arms. The IRA cannot and never could challenge the British army and the Ulster security forces on a military level, despite the IRA's perception of itself as an "army". The hope of the weak in such circumstances is to erode the legitimacy of the government and simultaneously to establish their own legitimacy. Terrorism can be considered effective in so far as it accomplishes this aim.

First, the IRA's efficiency as an organization – its discipline, training and expertise – is a prerequisite for success. The goals of the IRA are also conducive to effectiveness. As Conor Cruise O'Brien aptly noted: "The formidable thing about the new I.R.A. – the Provisionals – was its simple relevance to the situation." Their straightforward policy of throwing the British out was not tainted with the "Communism" of the Officials or the anti-sectarian pacifism of the civil rights leaders. "The Provisionals weren't telling people to turn the other cheek if a misguided Protestant brother had a bash at them."[41] Although the fall of Stormont diminished the IRA's relevance, as long as British troops are present in Ulster, and as long as there are Protestant extremists to occasionally take bashes at Catholics, the IRA will maintain some appeal. There is evidence that the IRA is sensitive to this predicament and has attempted to reinforce its message. IRA leaders may perceive that over time the British presence has come to seem more tolerable, or at least acceptable, that Catholic grievances have diminished under direct rule, and that Protestants seem less threatening. The prison protests and hunger strikes were an attempt to restore or enhance the IRA's legitimacy. There is some indication that they failed, as the ending of the hunger strikes marked a division between the Catholic church and the IRA that may drive Catholic public opinion away from the Republicans.[42]

Another limit on the IRA's potential legitimacy is its failure, despite the attractiveness of its ambitions to Catholic Irish, to form an alliance with peaceful or constitutional nationalists. Were the IRA allied with nationalist political parties or the government of the Republic of Ireland, its chances of attaining its goals would be much greater.

The hunger strikes raised an issue that is also important with regard to terrorism. The means of the IRA must seem congruent with the ends if terrorism is to be effective. Terrorist attacks on the British military and on the largely Protestant police forces of Ulster can be justified as striking at the enemy and also as having military significance. But, just as the deaths of more than ten IRA or INLA prisoners seemed increasingly inappropriate to the aim of changing British policy, so does terrorism against anonymous civilians seem only vaguely connected to the IRA's goals. Acts such as the assassination of Earl Mountbatten or bombings of pubs or restaurants have consistently proved counterproductive and have provoked dissention among IRA leaders. Targeting security personnel remains a fallback position; sporadic forays into killing civilians are apparently motivated by considerations such as British pressures (as, for example, announcing that the IRA is on the run) or rivalry with the INLA.

The political situation of the North is of course what gives the IRA its relevance. The IRA embodies a myth. Audiences with sympathetic predispositions were ready made by history. The IRA did choose objectives that were more attractive than those of the Official branch, but these aims could be tailored to fit the prior beliefs of the population. Other factors of the situation – the existence of a free press to report IRA exploits, self-imposed limitations on the British response, an international climate that favoured national liberation (a mold into which the IRA sought to fit itself), and the establishment of terrorist groups in other countries and supportive states from which the IRA could obtain weapons and training – also benefited the IRA. The timing was right.

Furthermore, the British made a number of policy mistakes. The introduction of internment is probably the key among them. Others have criticized the British for not implementing direct rule earlier, since lukewarm efforts to uphold Stormont led Protestants to doubt Britain's goodwill and fed Catholic suspicions. Acting only after violence became uncontrollable created an appearance of desperation and of bending only to pressure.[43] Inconsistency in dealing with the IRA (especially allowing the IRA to become a rival authority in Catholic neighbourhoods), mistreatment, even if minor, of civilians by the army, failure to control Protestant extremism, and bragging about defeating the IRA were also errors. In defence of British policy, however, it must be noted that in general the British seem to be aware of the necessity of combining efficiency and legitimacy in the response to terrorism, and that given the structural constraints on their actions, little flexibility is possible. Destroying a terrorist organization that has a hardcore, if minimal, degree of popular support is enormously difficult.

Thus the British will stay in Northern Ireland until the British population tires of violence or until Protestants agree to a united Ireland. Neither change of opinion seems likely. Terrorism has in the end been self-defeating for the IRA, at least since 1972, because it has only hardened Protestant and British determination. The war over the Falkland Islands makes it even less probable that the British would abandon the Protestants of Ulster. Legitimacy in the eyes of a Catholic constituency does the IRA little good when faced with a million Protestants whose wishes will not be over-ridden by a democratic central government, which possesses superior force.

Yet the IRA persists. Terrorism has had the effect of increasing the likelihood of future violence. The lesson that violence pays has been widely learned among extremists of all stamps. The presence of the British army, something the IRA guarantees, provides a perpetual motive of vengeance. Protestant paramilitaries and the rhetoric of leaders such as Ian Paisley continue to alarm Catholics. The IRA, further-more, has a vested interest in conflict. As an organization, it has no other purpose or raison d'etre.[44] Members of the IRA live in an unreal isolation from anyone who thinks differently than they do. It is difficult for a member to change his or her mind; to do so would be to become a "traitor", in not only physical but moral danger, as heresy is the worst sin. The leadership of the IRA appears totally committed to continuing the struggle, regardless of the immediate consequences. The paradox that counter- productiveness leads to deeper commitment is frequent in religious sects as well as political conspiracies. The failure of prophecies - as clearly the IRA prediction of a British withdrawal has been disproved - produces only greater isolation of the believers from reality. As isolation makes them more dependent on the group and its goals for identity and personal integration, their commitment to action becomes more desperate.[45] The psychological and political costs of giving up the belief that physical force will lead to a united Ireland, especially in view of the sacrifices already made for the cause, are too great.

Notes
1   An earlier version of this paper was presented to a colloquium on Irish terrorism at the U.S. Department of

State, September 14, 1979. The views expressed here represent only those of the author. This paper also benefited from earlier work supported by a Fellowship for Independent Study and Research from the National Endowment for the Humanities in 1977-78.

2   John Devoy, Recollections of an Irish Rebel (New York: Charles Young, 1929; reprint edn. Shannon: Irish University Press, 1969), pp.10-11.

3   The concept of relative deprivation is developed by Ted Robert Gurr in Why Men Rebel (Princeton: Princeton University Press, 1971) esp. ch.2-5.

4   Richard Rose, Governing Without Consensus: An Irish Perspective (Boston: Beacon Press, 1971).

5   See Thomas Sheehan, "Myth and Violence: The Fascism of Julius Evola and Alain de Benoist", Social Research 48 (Spring 1981), pp.45-73. Sheehan argues: "...whereas social, political, and psychological analyses of terrorism do contribute greatly to our understanding of the phenomenon, they also leave untouched an essential aspect of it: its mythic appeal to the terrorist and, in his eyes, its quasi-metaphysical justification" (p.47).

6   J.C. Beckett, The Making of Modern Ireland, 1603-1923 (London: Faber and Faber, 1969), p.359.

7   See K.R.M. Short The Dynamite War: Irish-American Bombers in Victorian Britain (London: Gill and Macmillan, 1979).

8   Beckett, p.441.

9   The IRA is an interesting example of an organization that would like to think of itself as practising "guerrilla warfare", that is, as attempting to defeat the enemy's military forces by unconventional tactics, but actually uses a combination of guerrilla warfare and terrorism, which aims at undermining the enemy's will to fight, primarily through influencing public opinion.

10   See Charles Townshend, The British Campaign in Ireland 1919-1921: The Development of Political and Military Policies (London: Oxford University Press, 1975). See also Tom Bowden, The Breakdown of Public Security: The Case of Ireland 1919-1921 and Palestine 1936-1939 (Beverly Hills: Sage Publications, 1977).

11   Christopher Dobson and Ronald Payne, The Terrorists: Their Weapons, Leaders and Tactics, rev. edn. (New York: Facts on File, 1982), esp. pp.107-08. The procurement of weapons from the United States has not been halted by public disavowals of the IRA from prominent Irish-American politicians such as Senator Edward Kennedy and Governor Hugh Carey. The New York Times of 22 June 1982 announced the FBI break-up of a $1 million arms deal. The IRA shopping list included surface-to-air missiles.

12   On the relationship between urbanization and terrorism, see P.N. Grabosky, "The Urban Context of Political

Terrorism", in The Politics of Terrorism, ed. Michael Stohl (New York: Marcel Dekker, 1979), pp.51-76.
13   Christopher Walker, "Bright future for the Terrorists", Spectator, July 14 1979, pp.12-14, and Dobson and Payne, p.199.
14   Dobson and Payne, p.201.
15   Walker, p.13.
16   See Ken Heskin, Northern Ireland: A Psychological Analysis (New York: Columbia University Press, 1980). He argues that authoritarianism is the only unifying trait, but that it is hardly a quality limited to terrorists. See p.84.
17   See Martha Crenshaw, "The Causes of Terrorism", Comparative Politics 13 (July 1975). See also the memoirs of Maria McGuire, To Take Arms: My Year with the IRA Provisionals (New York: Viking, 1973).
18   The People's Will, for example, split from Black Repartition over the issue of using terrorism against the Russian autocracy in the 1870s. The Irgun and LEHI were divided from the mainstream of the Zionist resistance to the British in Palestine because of their reliance on terrorism.
19   MacStiofain, pp.47 and 145-46.
20   On not appearing weak, see McGuire, pp.110, 116 and 145. On demonstrating a position of strength, see pp.111, 129, 140 and 161-62.
21   MacStiofain, p.208.
22   Ibid., pp.220-22, 242-44.
23   McGuire, p.34.
24   Ibid., pp.33-34. It is indicative of the IRA's perception of Protestant opinion as insignificant that McGuire refers to undermining British government in Northern Ireland even before the institution of direct rule. Note also her naive assumption that terror would lead the public to want peace. She believes "that by terrorizing the civilian population you increased their desire for peace and blackmailed the British government into negotiating" (p.162).
25   The Guardian, August 15 1975, p.24.
26   See I.R.A., Provisional Wing, Freedom Struggle (Dublin, 1973).
27   MacStiofain, pp.237-38 and 330. McGuire, however, left the IRA because she disapproved of MacStiofain's leadership and of bombing civilians.
28   In 1974, a faction of the Officials split off to form the Irish Republican Socialist Party (IRSP), in 1975, it spawned an armed wing, the Irish National Liberation Army (INLA). The INLA is as dedicated to throwing the British out as the IRA is, but it is much more ideologically sophisticated. The INLA is smaller than the IRA, remarkably efficient, and well-connected abroad. Whereas the IRA is an indigenous terrorist group, inspired by its own parochial traditions and particularist goals, the INLA resembles modern terrorist groups in Western Europe, groups who also profess a corrupt

form of Marxist milleniarism. The INLA and the IRA cooperated, for example, during the 1981 hunger strike.
29   See Martha Crenshaw, "Reflections on the Effects of Terrorism", in Terrorism, Legitimacy, and Power: the Consequences of Political Violence, ed. Martha Crenshaw (Middleton, Ct.: Wesleyan University Press, forthcoming 1983).
30   On the other hand, this analysis does not go so far as to depict the situation as colonial, which, for example, Alfred McClung Lee does in "The Dynamics of Terrorism in Northern Ireland, 1968-1980", Social Research 48 (Spring 1981), pp.100-34.
31   Governing Without Consensus; see also Paul Wilkinson, "The Orange and the Green: Extremism in Northern Ireland", in Terrorism, Legitimacy, and Power, for an analysis of British power-sharing efforts and of Protestant extremism.
32   Brian Faulkner, Memoirs of a Statesman (London: Weidenfeld and Nicolson, 1978), p.171.
33   Ibid., p.167.
34   The Guardian, 15 August 1979, p.24.
35   Peter Janke, Ulster: A Decade of Violence, Conflict Studies No.108, June 1979 (London: The Institute for the Study of Conflict, 1979), p.12.
36   For a summary of Irish and British legal changes, see Edward Moxon-Browne, "Terrorism in Northern Ireland: The Case of the Provisional IRA", in Terrorism: A Challenge to the State, ed. Juliet Lodge (New York: St Martin's, 1981), pp.54-56. See also Conor Cruise O'Brien, "Broadcasting and Terrorism", in his Herod: Reflections on Political Violence (London: Hutchinson, 1978), pp.110-27. The article is from his speech, as Minister for Posts and Telegraphs, introducing the Broadcasting Authority (Amendment) Bill to the Irish Senate, March 27 1975.
37   The problem of popular approval for ends but not means is discussed by Moxon-Browne and also by O'Brien in many of his works, including the collection of articles in Herod. See also Terrance G. Carroll, "Disobedience and Violence in Northern Ireland", Comparative Political Studies 14 (April 1981), pp.3-30. Carroll argues that it is not experiencing violence but justifying it that leads people to support political violence.
38   Dervla Murphy, A Place Apart (Harmondsworth: Penguin Books, 1979), p.57.
39   See Heskin, ch.3, "People Under Stress", pp.52-73, and ch.6, "Growing Up in Northern Ireland", pp.126-52. For a somewhat different view, see Morris Fraser, Children in Conflict: Growing Up in Northern Ireland (New York: Basic Books, 1973).
40   See J. Bowyer Bell, On Revolt: Strategies of National Liberation (Cambridge, Mass.: Harvard University Press, 1976) for an analysis of revolts against British rule.

41   Conor Cruise O'Brien, States of Ireland (New York:
Pantheon Books, 1972), p.205.
42   See Conor Cruise O'Brien, "Terrorism under Democratic
Conditions: The   Case   of   the   I.R.A.",   in   Terrorism,
Legitimacy, and Power.
43   Maurice   Tugwell,   "Politics   and   Propaganda   of   the
Provisional I.R.A.", Terrorism - An International Journal 5
(1981), p.29.
44   Heskin   also   cites   the   IRA's   formal   organizational
structure as a cause of its persistence: pp.92-93.
45   Leon Festinger et al., When Prophecy Fails: A Social and
Psychological Study of a Modern Group That Predicted the
Destruction of the World (New York: Harper & Row, 1964).

INDEX